THE LAW OF BAILMENT

THE LAW OF BAILMENT

Robert H Tanha

IRWIN LAW

Published in 2019 by
Irwin Law Inc
Suite 206, 14 Duncan Street
Toronto, ON M5H 3G8
www.irwinlaw.com

ISBN: 978-1-55221-515-9 e-book ISBN: 978-1-55221-516-6

Library and Archives Canada Cataloguing in Publication

Title: The law of bailment / Robert H. Tanha.
Names: Tanha, Robert H., author.
Description: Includes bibliographical references and index.
Identifiers: Canadiana (print) 20190213906 | Canadiana (ebook) 20190214171 |
ISBN 9781552215159 (softcover) | ISBN 9781552215166 (PDF)
Subjects: LCSH: Bailments—Canada—Textbooks. | LCGFT: Textbooks.
Classification: LCC KE779 .T36 2019 | LCC KF718 .T36 2019 kfmod | DDC 346.7102/5—dc23

Canada

Ontario
Ontario Media Development Corporation
Société de développement de l'industrie des médias de l'Ontario

Printed and bound by CPI Group (UK) Ltd, Croydon, CR0 4YY

1 2 3 4 5 23 22 21 20 19

Summary Table of Contents

Detailed Table of Contents

CHAPTER 3

CHAPTER 6

Bailee Defences and Limitations on Bailee Liability 322

CHAPTER 7

Sub-bailment *386*

Preface

This book has been written to promote the importance of the common law of bailment to transactions that people engage in every day, such as depositing their goods for storage with a business or lending a friend their vehicle to drive for the weekend while they go out of town. Certain duties and rights arise from all these bailment transactions, not least of which is the bailee's overarching duty of safekeeping goods for the duration of the bailment, which, if breached, gives plaintiffs the right to sue in damages for their losses.

This book explores all aspects of the bailment transaction, both from the perspective of the bailee and bailor. It attempts to simplify the rules of bailment and make them more intelligible for the law student, lawyer, judge, and members of the public who are seeking to understand, or better understand, a bailment law rule. This is done using numerous examples arising from the caselaw and through providing the reader with statements of law on all aspects of bailment that are clear and understandable — but at the same time, appropriately qualified, meaningful, and usable. Major discrepancies in the caselaw have been noted and solutions have been offered up to address them throughout the book.

In terms of organizational structure, the general concepts of the law of bailment — including the elements and nature of a bailment, as well as how bailment differs from other heads of legal obligation — are discussed in Chapter 1. An effort is made to distinguish bailment from other types of legal obligations that may arise in circumstances similar to those triggering a bailment, including trust, conversion, consignment, and licence, to demonstrate that bailments are singularly distinct in the manner in which the law treats them. That is to say, bailments often impose higher obligations on the party in the position of the bailee than do these other areas of law.

Chapters 2 and 3 focus on the bailor's onus of proof. Chapter 2 provides a more general discussion of the bailor's onus, which is then followed by a more narrow and extensive discussion of the onus in Chapter 3. Many contexts and circumstances are considered. A bailor's onus of proof is found to be decidedly different than the onus of proof required of a plaintiff in a negligence action, in that unlike in negligence, a bailor is not normally required to provide evidence of affirmative wrongdoing on the part of a defendant to succeed.

Chapters 4 and 5 consider the bailee's onus of proof. Again, as with the bailor's onus of proof discussed in chapters 2 and 3, a general discussion of the bailee's onus occurs in Chapter 4, followed by a more detailed discussion of the relevant considerations dealing with the onus in Chapter 5. A bailee's onus is found to be quite variable; dependent on a number of factors, including the value and nature of the bailment; and is observed to be more variable and malleable than the bailor's onus of proof, which normally (only) requires a plaintiff to prove that their goods were lost or damaged while in the exclusive possession of the bailee in order to trigger a reverse onus of proof on a bailee to disprove negligence.

Chapter 6 is devoted entirely to defences that a bailee may have in terms of the breach of its duty of safekeeping owed to the bailor, such as contributory negligence or accord and satisfaction. As with the law of negligence and other torts, partial and full defences are found to exist in bailment law and each category of defence is fully explored in the chapter in the context of the relevant caselaw. Bailee defences are found to exist both at common law and pursuant to statute law, increasing the number of escape routes that a bailee may have on any given set of facts.

Chapter 7 deals exclusively with sub-bailment, a species of bailment that essentially arises where a second bailment of goods is made after a first bailment of those goods has already been created between two parties. While sub-bailments present challenges not encountered in single bailment transactions, discernable rules are found and uncovered and an attempt to bring coherence to this subset of bailment law is also provided.

The rules identified and discussed in this book emanate from the common law of bailment as found in Canadian jurisprudence, save and except for Quebec, which was not considered in this book—principally because of the author's limited expertise in the civil law system of Quebec. Indeed, bailment law is regarded by some as the "last bastion of the common law." This reality has necessitated consideration of a substantial body of caselaw from the common law provinces of Canada. In that connection, the reader is provided with my own rendition of the facts of each judicial decision, with a view to explaining each case in a way that illustrates the operation of the rules and principles of bailment law.

Acknowledgements

I wish to express sincere gratitude for the magnificent editorial work done by the editorial team at Irwin Law Inc, without whom this undertaking could not have been completed. I would like to especially recognize Lesley Steeve, Editor-in-Chief of Irwin Law Inc, for her marvellous work and dedication in helping me bring this book to completion.

I would also like to extend thanks to my students, colleagues, and friends who provided positive encouragement throughout the research and writing process. Last, and foremost, I would like to thank my family for their unwavering support. In the absence of that support and encouragement, the final product could not have been achieved.

CHAPTER 1

Introduction to Bailment Law: The Nature and Elements of Bailment and Bailment Distinguished from Other Heads of Obligation

A. BAILMENT DEFINED

A bailment at law, simply defined, is the voluntary transfer of personal property from one party (the bailor) to another (the bailee) for safekeeping, with or without consideration, with the property typically to be returned to its owner[1] or their agent, in its original or an altered form, upon the fulfillment of this purpose.

In its decision in *Seaspan International Ltd v The "Kostis Prois,"* the Supreme Court of Canada defined "bailment" as follows:

> The relationship of bailor and bailee is created whenever one person accepts the delivery and takes temporary possession of another's goods on the understanding that they are to be returned to the owner or his nominee.[2]

A bailment is *sui generis*. It can exist independently of a contract and is said to impose trust-like duties on the bailee — although a bailment is not a trust — where the bailee voluntarily takes into its custody goods that are the property of another.[3] It is also one of the last bastions of

1 In order for a bailment to be found, legal ownership must be retained by the bailor, with only possession passing to the bailee: *Lichti v Landmark Transport Inc*, 2006 BCSC 344 [*Lichti*].

2 *Seaspan International Ltd v "Kostis Prois" (The)*, [1974] SCR 920 at para 10 [paragraph numbers from French version] [*Seaspan International*].

3 *Punch v Savoy's Jewellers Ltd* (1986), 54 OR (2d) 383 at para 17 (CA); *Lichti*, above note 1 at para 61.

the common law. If its elements are present, a bailment may exist even where a contract specifically excludes it.[4]

You leave your laundry at a dry cleaner to be cleaned; you ask your friend to look after your car over the weekend while you are away; you vacate your rental unit as a tenant in a residential complex, leaving some or all of your personal belongings behind. In all these situations, a bailment may be created, meaning that all the elements required to form this legal relationship are present. The chief legal consequence of the creation of a bailment is that a heavy duty of care is placed on the bailee to keep the bailor's goods safe and to return them to the bailor upon completion of the purpose or purposes for which they were transferred. Where the bailor's goods go missing or are damaged while in the possession of the bailee, whether, for example, by fire, theft, or vandalism, the general rule is that the bailee must meet the heavy burden of proving that its negligence, or lack of reasonable care, did not cause the injury.[5] Where there is uncertainty as to the precise circumstances of the loss or damage, this means that the bailee is liable to the bailor in the absence of a contractual exemption (as it will not be able to disprove negligence).[6]

In the context of a bailment, "personal property" refers to moveable property, such as cars and jewellery, and explicitly excludes all forms of real property, including land and objects affixed to land.

While the idea of a bailment appears to be easily stated and understood, its exact legal requirements have been the subject of much debate by Canadian courts and academic commentators alike. This is because the constituent elements that make up a bailment, and the rules governing how they are to be interpreted and proven, unlike the general concept itself, are not so easily explained, understood, or applied. We shall see this in particular when considering the bailor's and bailee's respective burdens of proof.

---

4 *Coueslan v Canadian Mini-Warehouse Properties Ltd (cob Public Storage Canadian)*, 2000 BCPC 137 [*Coueslan*].

5 Sir George Whitecross Paton, *Bailment in the Common Law* (London: Stevens & Sons, 1952) at 166–67.

6 *Webb v Tyldesley's Ltd*, [1998] BCJ No 2978 at para 26 (Prov Ct (Civ Div)) [*Webb*]; *DeGrace v Central Garage Sales & Service Ltd*, [1979] NBJ No 45 at paras 11 and 20 (NBCA) [*DeGrace*]. The justification for such a harsh burden being placed on the bailee is that the chattels were exclusively in its possession at the time of the loss or damage and, so, it was the party in the best position to explain what happened to them: *Webb*, above in this note at para 26.

These sorts of perplexing questions are important not just from an academic and conceptual point of view, but also from a pleading one. As we shall see throughout this book, when a court finds a legal relationship other than a bailment, the bailor is sometimes left without a remedy.[7] This is because the rules of bailment usually place a substantially higher burden of proof on a party in the position of bailee than do other areas of the law, such as the law of negligence: the bailee is put to a reverse onus — that is, it is left to the bailee to disprove negligence. This, of course, greatly favours the bailor, who would otherwise normally have to meet a substantially higher burden of proof.

B. BAILMENT DISTINGUISHED FROM LICENCE

A bailment is not a licence, although the distinction between the two will no doubt sometimes be difficult to draw, especially where the licence is accompanied by additional undertakings by the licensor.[8] A bailment should *not* be regarded as a licence with special rights and duties superimposed upon it. In law, it is an entirely different kind of relationship from that established by a licence[9] and must be treated as such.

Where a bailment, as opposed to a licensor-licensee relationship, is found, the bailee will have to discharge the common law duty of safekeeping;[10] where it is not found, the bailee will not have any responsibility for safeguarding the chattel accepted unless by some special term of

7 See, for example, *Laursen v Bemister*, [1999] BCJ No 2464 (SC) [*Laursen*].

8 *Mercury Launch & Tug Ltd v Texada Quarrying Ltd*, 2006 FC 464 at para 44. In *Palmer v Toronto Medical Arts Building Ltd*, [1960] OR 60 (CA) [*Palmer*], the distinction proved difficult indeed where the defendant parking lot retained the plaintiff's keys in order to park his vehicle for him, but as agent for the plaintiff, not as bailee for him, the acts being viewed as nothing more than strictly gratuitous ones for the benefit and convenience of the plaintiff. While the Court of Appeal for Ontario found a licence and not a bailment, gratuitous or otherwise, the case demonstrates the struggle courts sometimes face in distinguishing between these two kinds of legal relationships. It goes without saying that much will depend on the particular facts before the court.

9 *Robertson v Stang*, [1997] BCJ No 2022 at paras 73–75 (SC) [*Robertson*].

10 This duty cannot be delegated away to another: see *Morris v CW Martin & Sons, Ltd*, [1965] 2 All ER 725 at 730 (CA), affirmed by the Alberta Supreme Court in *Alberta U Drive Ltd v Jack Carter Ltd* (1972), 28 DLR (3d) 114 at para 4 (Alta SCTD) [*Alberta U Drive*]. Of course, the particular standard of care owed by a bailee to a bailor in any given circumstance will vary depending on several factors, including the nature and value of the bailment. See Chapter 4, sections A(3), A(4), B, and E, and Chapter 5, sections B(5), B(16), B(18), and B(19) for further discussion.

the contract[11] or under some other (statutory) head of law.[12] Instead, the licensor will be viewed as having done nothing more than grant permission to the user or owner of the chattel (the licensee), as the case may be, to leave it upon the licensor's land, preventing that which would otherwise be a trespass.[13]

The marked divergence in the legal responsibilities assumed by bailees and licensors is well explained by Ziff, as follows:

> A licensor who allows a chattel to be left on his or her premises assumes no obligation in relation to it other than those imposed by the general law. Such a person would be liable for stealing or converting the goods, for trespass or detinue, or when his or her positive acts of negligence cause damage. At the same time, there is no need for the licensor to be vigilant against such things as the prospect of theft or damage.
>
> A bailee, on the other hand, must be more conscientious, and is governed by the general law (for example, the bailee may not convert the property) as well as principles that relate specifically to the bailment relationship.[14]

To similar effect, the Court of Appeal for Ontario in *Bata v City Parking Canada Ltd* states:

> There is a very wide divergence between the relationship of bailor and bailee and that of licensor and licensee in that the latter, in the absence of some special contractual provision, carries no obligation on the part

11 *Spooner v Starkman*, [1937] OR 542 (CA). A contractual term imposing a duty of safekeeping on the party in the position of bailee need not be express; it may be implied into a contract in the appropriate circumstances: see *Laursen*, above note 7 at para 12.

12 For example, provincial occupier liability laws can sometimes impose a duty of safekeeping on an occupier who is not found to be a bailee: see, for example, *Laursen*, *ibid*. In this situation, however, the defendant *will not* be put to a reverse burden of proof as bailee to disprove negligence; instead the plaintiff will have to prove negligence against the defendant in accordance with the statute.

13 At law, the formation of a licensor-licensee relationship by way of contract will sometimes require the offeree to perform a certain affirmative act (e.g., pay a fee) in order to convey its acceptance of the offer. The failure to perform the act in its entirety will result in a trespass, as no contract of licence will have been formed: see *Curlett v Murray*, [1992] NJ No 41 (SCTD). In the absence of evidence of actual damage to the landowner's or operator's premises or interests, proof of a trespass may not permit a landowner or operator the right of distress or the right to recover damages through the doctrine of distress damage feasant: *Controlled Parking Systems Ltd v Sedgewick*, [1980] SJ No 836 (Dist Ct).

14 Bruce Ziff, *Principles of Property Law*, 4th ed (Toronto: Thomson Carswell, 2006) at 299.

of the licensor towards the licensee with respect to the chattel subject to the licence.[15]

Unlike a bailee, a licensor at law assumes no responsibility whatsoever for loss or damage caused to the licensee's goods by fire, theft, or otherwise.[16] There is no duty on a licensor to hire employees of good character, to avoid misdelivery amounting to conversion, or to avoid such losses or damages.[17] In fact, if there is a licensor-licensee relationship, there is no duty on a licensor to explain any loss or damage that may arise with respect to the licensee's property[18] or to report losses or damages to the authorities.

Thus, there are significant legal consequences that flow from a court's decision as to whether a given legal relationship amounts to a bailment. While a finding of no bailment will not necessarily absolve the bailee of all liability, since it may still owe duties of care pursuant to other laws,[19] such as under Ontario's *Occupiers' Liability Act*,[20] these duties will usually be less onerous. Further, the bailee will not be faced with the reverse onus; instead, the bailor will have to prove liability in the ordinary way.[21]

In order to have a bailment, there must be a transfer of possession of the chattel in question from bailor to bailee.[22] A mere physical handing over of property to another, without more, is not enough.[23] The principle is well

---

15 See *Bata v City Parking Canada Ltd* (1973), 2 OR (2d) 446 at para 7 (CA) [*Bata*].

16 In the parking context, this must be viewed as extending to damage to or loss of a vehicle's contents, however caused. Admittedly, in this situation, the licensor will retain unfettered control over and access to its property, being at liberty to deal with it how he or she sees fit: see *Dixon v City Parking Canada Ltd*, [1981] AJ No 731 at para 17 (QB) [*Dixon*].

17 *Alberta U Drive*, above note 10 at para 49.

18 *Heffron v Imperial Parking Co* (1974), 3 OR (2d) 722 at paras 8 and 9 (CA) [*Heffron*]. In these circumstances, a defendant is not required to lead evidence to explain the disappearance of or damage to the plaintiff's goods or property: *ibid*; *McLennan v Charlottetown Flying Services*, [1979] PEIJ No 58 at para 30 (SC) [*McLennan*].

19 *Boire v Eagle Lake Enterprises Ltd*, 2009 SKPC 84 at para 43 [*Boire*].

20 RSO 1990, c O.2.

21 Very often, this will mean proving negligence against the defendant (bailee) in order to fix liability against it.

22 *Heffron*, above note 18 at para 12.

23 See the comments of Roach JA in *Palmer*, above note 8. See further the remarks of Evershed MR addressing the subject, with reference to *Ashby v Tolhurst*, [1937] 2 KB 242 [*Ashby*], in *Tinsley v Dudley*, [1951] 2 KB 18 at 26–27 ("one who leaves his motor car in a car park cannot assume or assert against the car park proprietor any obligation to use reasonable care to look after the car"). In *Vladimir v Dupont Auto Collision Ltd*, [1997] OJ No 4140 (Gen Div), the plaintiff's leaving his tools and tool box on the

enunciated by Romer LJ in the classic English decision of *Ashby v Tolhurst* as follows: "[I]n order that there shall be a bailment there must be a delivery by the bailor, that is to say, he must part with his possession of the chattel in question."[24] In other words, a transfer of possession in the property from bailor to bailee is the *sine qua non* of a bailment. It may be constructive or actual, and may be by access or control.[25] Courts have developed several factors to determine whether possession has been passed, giving rise to a bailment and to the duty of safekeeping arising thereunder.[26]

1) Bailments Generally

While this should not be considered an exhaustive list, consideration should be given to the following elements when distinguishing between licence and bailment generally:

1) the effect of the terms of any contract that the parties may have entered into;
2) whether the bailee exercised access or control over the bailor's property, and the purpose of such acts, whether for licence or bailment;
3) whether there was any particular purpose, or ancillary function, that required that the bailee should have possession of the bailor's property;
4) the relevant representations made by the parties as to the safekeeping of the goods;
5) the extent to which the bailee provided security and safekeeping with respect to the chattels, and the reliance by the bailor on such services;

---

defendant's shop floor, with the permission and knowledge of the defendant, without more, did not give rise to a bailment, but only created a licence. In the result, the defendant had no duty to safeguard the plaintiff's tools from the theft that occurred because of a break and enter into the defendant's premises.

24 See *Ashby*, above note 23, as cited and endorsed by the Court of Appeal for Ontario in *Heffron*, above note 18 at para 12.

25 *Laursen*, above note 7 at para 14; *Gropler v Bednesti Lake Resort Ltd*, 2001 BCPC 272 [*Gropler*] at para 25.

26 The distinction between bailment and licence is highly fact-dependent and nuanced. So much so, in fact, that the question of whether a given relationship amounts to a bailment rather than a licence *may not* be amenable to the summary judgment procedure: see, for example, *Complex Elements Corp v Atlantic Container Line AB (PUBL) 820302 Ontario Inc (cob Lynx Trucking Transportation & Leasing)*, 2008 CanLII 21223 (Ont SC) [*Complex Elements*]; *2934752 Canada Inc v 2789949 Canada Inc*, [2003] OJ No 3514 (SCJ); *JPM Express Inc v 2092889 Ontario Inc*, 2010 ONSC 4412 [*JPM Express*].

6) whether the bailee's service was provided gratuitously;
7) the bailee's provision of insurance against loss; and
8) the history of relations between the parties, as may be relevant.

a) The Terms of the Bailment Contract

i) Relative Importance of a Contract

In *Ashby*,[27] the court stated that the most important element in determining whether a transfer of possession has occurred between two parties, leading to the finding of a bailment, is to consider the terms of any agreement between them. In that case, the agreement consisted of a serialized "car park ticket" that had been received by the plaintiff upon his entry into the defendant's parking lot in return for payment of the parking fee. The plaintiff had parked his own vehicle, locked it, and retained the keys to the car in his own possession, having not been required to surrender them as a condition of parking. Later, when the plaintiff returned to the lot to have a rest in his car, he found that it was missing, the parking garage having released his vehicle to an individual masquerading as his friend, without the production of a car park ticket and or any proof that he had the plaintiff's authority to remove his vehicle from the grounds. The bandit obtained access to the vehicle through its windscreen, and the car was never recovered.[28] The car park ticket that had been given to the plaintiff contained the following disclaimer, upon which the defendant placed great reliance: "The proprietors do not take any responsibility for

---

27 Above note 23.

28 The court refused to incorporate an implied term into the contract that the car park would not release the vehicle without production of the ticket, finding that such an interpretation would import a duty of safekeeping that would be inconsistent with the express terms of the contract, which clearly negatived a bailment. According to the court, it would also be inconsistent with the phrase on the ticket stating that "owners are requested to show ticket when required," the ticket being no more than a means by which owners could demonstrate that they were entitled to park in the car park and were not trespassing. It is not clear on the facts of the case why the ticket, in the way it was constructed, could not also be used as a means by which car owners could identify themselves as such when they sought to reclaim their property, other than that such an interpretation would also seem to import an obligation with regard to safe custody, which would run counter to some of the other terms contained in the car-park ticket that pointed toward a licence. Such terms, however, have not proven to be a bar to Canadian courts' finding a bailment where control of the subject property has been surrendered to the parking operator: see, for example, *Dixon*, above note 16 at para 17. For an informative discussion of implied terms of a contract, see *London Drugs Ltd v Kuehne & Nagel International Ltd*, [1992] 3 SCR 299.

the safe custody of any cars or articles there nor for any damage to the cars or articles however caused, nor for any injuries to any persons, all cars being left in all respects entirely at owners' risk. Owners are requested to show ticket when required."[29]

The court took a narrow view on the question of whether possession of the vehicle had been transferred from the plaintiff to the defendant, holding that the relatively minimal security features present in the parking garage, namely a parking attendant and a ticketing system, were of no import. In the final analysis, the "document itself" was all that needed to be considered; nothing else was material. According to the court, this document indicated quite clearly that the relationship between the parties was that of licensor and licensee as opposed to bailor and bailee. The wording of the document was dispositive as to the "true" nature of the relationship, in particular its reference to a "car park" as the place in which the car was to be kept, and its title as a "car park ticket," both of which indicated a "mere license to park" and no more.

The following words of Sir Wilfred Greene MR, speaking for the court, are apposite:

> "Car park ticket": you take a ticket in order to park your car, and parking your car means, I should have thought, leaving your car in a place. If you park your car in the street, you are liable to get into trouble with the police. On the other hand, you are entitled to park your car in places indicated by the police or appropriate authorities for the purpose. Parking a car is leaving a car and, I should have thought, nothing else. The right, therefore, which this document starts off by giving on its face is a right to park the car.[30]

The court also placed some moment on the exemption clause, which it held excluded the notion of any contract of bailment. It is true that nowhere in the car park ticket in *Ashby* had the car park agreed to accept the bailee's duty of safekeeping with respect to the plaintiff's vehicle. In fact, the terms of the ticket made it clear that the car park had explicitly rejected such a duty and exempted itself from all liability regarding the vehicle and its contents.

---

29 *Ashby*, above note 23, as cited in *Bata*, above note 15 at para 8.

30 *Ashby*, above note 23, as cited in *Bata*, above note 15 at para 10.

It is trite law that a bailment is a voluntary relationship and cannot be foisted onto a bailee.[31] It follows that, in the presence of such explicit and counter-bailment terms within a contract, proving an act of delivery by a bailor will undoubtedly be a more difficult task, especially where it can be shown that such terms were sufficiently drawn to the bailor's attention, accepted by the bailor, and followed by the parties in practice.

Nonetheless, the court's approach in *Ashby*, in particular its undue and narrow focus on the terms of the contract to the virtual exclusion of all else, is highly problematic and misplaced, for it ignores many well-established indicators of a bailment relationship, including what has come to be regarded as the most important factor—that is, the degree to which the bailee exercised "control" over the bailor's property during the period of the bailment.[32] The court also neglected to consider (or, in any event, place enough emphasis on) several indicators that have since been developed by courts to apply to the distinct circumstances present in parking lot cases, including the presence of a ticketing system and whether vehicle owners were required to surrender their keys to the car park proprietor as a condition of the parking. Not surprisingly, such an approach to possession has not prevailed in Canada,[33] where courts have opted for a broader and more holistic and contextual approach.

This should not be taken, however, as suggesting that the terms of the contract can never be dispositive in the final analysis; sometimes they are, and properly so. And to the extent that *Ashby* stands for the proposition that the terms of the agreement between the parties are an important consideration in distinguishing between a licence and a bailment that can sometimes be determinative, it is good law and should be followed. But it is worth repeating that a more holistic and generous approach that considers all the circumstances, including whether control of the subject property was surrendered by the bailor, must be undertaken by a court before reaching that result.

---

31 *Visscher v Triple Broek Holdings Ltd*, [2006] AJ No 626 at para 31 (QB) [*Visscher*]; *Lichti*, above note 1 at para 60.

32 *Robertson*, above note 9 at para 64; *Dodd v Johnson*, [2010] OJ No 6195 at para 18 (SCJ) [*Dodd*]; *Webb*, above note 6 at para 22.

33 See *Trivett Estate v City Parking Canada Ltd*, [1976] OJ No 1378 at para 10 (CA) [*Trivett Estate*].

ii) The Contextual and Holistic Approach

Campbell (cob Soup's Welding) v 0698900 BC Ltd[34] is instructive of the contextual approach that should be taken by courts in distinguishing between licences and bailments. There, the plaintiff entered into a storage rental contract with the defendant to store both his travel and horse trailers at the defendant's storage lot (which was enclosed by a gated chain-link fence and accessible only by key) for a fee of $35 per month. The plaintiff's travel trailer and its contents were taken from the lot in circumstances that made it clear that there had not been forced entry: a key had been used by some unknown party to access the lot and remove the plaintiff's trailer, which could be moved without a key.[35]

The standard form contract signed by the parties stated that the defendant was neither a bailee nor a warehouser. (The court observed that the plaintiff had signed very similar contracts with a previous company for storage on the same lot in the years prior. He was, therefore, found to have sufficient notice and awareness of its terms, including the exclusion clause.) Specifically, the standard form contract stated, at clause 1:

> 1. Lessor owns premises at 8150 Old Waneta Road, Trail, B.C. (the "premises") for rental only and not as bailee or warehouseman [clause 1].[36]

In addition to this clause, the contract also contained a clause exempting the defendant from liability for theft or damage to the plaintiff's property. While Mrozinski Prov J placed much emphasis on these two clauses as demonstrating that no bailment existed on the facts, his analysis was not devoid of other considerations. In fact, he considered the extent to which the defendant controlled the plaintiff's access to his property, finding that it was insufficient to displace the contractual language indicating that the relationship was one of bailment, not licence. So long as he paid his rental fees, the plaintiff could, and did, exercise completely unfettered access to his trailers. Furthermore, the defendant did not have access to or control over the trailer that was unlawfully removed from the lot by some unknown third party.[37]

---

34 [2010] BCJ No 1366 (Prov Ct) [*Campbell*].

35 *Ibid* at paras 1–3 and 19.

36 *Ibid* at para 13.

37 *Ibid* at paras 16–28. To be specific, the defendant did not have authority to enter this trailer, nor was it provided with a key to the trailer's door: *ibid* at para 19.

Citing the facts in *Ashby* as being analogous to those before him, Mrozinski Prov J further stated that the "semblance of security" provided by the defendant was hardly sufficient to constitute a bailment or to evince an intention that the defendant was assuming a duty of safekeeping. Instead, the defendant was merely providing the plaintiff with a place to park his trailers, which happened to be enclosed by a fenced yard and locked gate, accessible only by those who, like the plaintiff (bailor), were provided with a key.[38]

While there were express contractual terms that on their face appeared to favour the finding of a bailment, Mrozinski Prov J paid them no heed because they were not observed by the parties in practice. While the plaintiff argued that access to his trailers was circumscribed by the terms of the contract, in that, if he fell behind in his rents, the defendant could deny him access to his trailers, Mrozinski Prov J underscored that, in practice, the defendant never exercised this right. The same applied to the clause that stated that the plaintiff could access his chattels only after making an appointment with the defendant. Thus, these provisions could not constitute evidence of possession sufficient to establish a bailment relationship.[39]

This view, however, neglects the reality that the defendant in *Campbell* had the legal power, certainly at the outset of the agreement, if not throughout, to deny access in the event of non-payment of rent or to require the plaintiff to make an appointment to inspect or remove his property from the lot. The fact that it never exercised these powers does not change this basic fact. That said, the view of Mrozinski Prov J on this point is still defensible if one accepts that evidence of "actual" control, access, or supervision by a bailee is required to help establish a bailment relationship; a mere contractual right to do so, upon the happening of certain events, not being sufficient.[40] If this be the state of law, however, it

---

38 *Ibid* at para 27. Interestingly, the trial judge (but not the appeal court) in *Ashby* found that the relatively minimal security features present in that case, in the form of a parking attendant and a ticketing system, were sufficient to create a bailment between the parties.

39 *Campbell*, above note 34 at paras 21–22 and 33. The defendant, however, was found to be an occupier within the meaning of the *Occupiers Liability Act*, RSBC 1996, c 337: *Campbell*, above in this note at paras 30–31, although it was found not to be liable for breaching its applicable standard of care, as such, either, by reason of the exclusion clause contained in the parties' storage contract: *ibid* at para 52.

40 See *Kieller v Sentinel Self-Storage Corp*, 2008 ABQB 783 at para 47 [*Kieller*]. As the defendant "had not exercised its contingent power to assert control of the Kieller's [sic] goods," it could not take possession of the goods for the purposes of establishing a bailment.

would seem to matter very little if such powers, contingent or otherwise, are provided for in the contract, for there is ample caselaw in support of the proposition that, where a bailee has exercised access to or control over a bailor's chattels, that same will be supportive of a bailment regardless of whether such acts have a contractual underpinning.[41] It is submitted, therefore, that the better view is to treat such powers, contingent or otherwise, within a contract as being supportive of a bailment relationship, to be given greater or lesser significance depending on whether they are actually exercised in the circumstances.

The Court of Appeal for Ontario followed and applied the *Ashby* judgment in *Palmer*.[42] It found that the plaintiff's car had not been delivered to the defendants for safe custody, as the terms of the agreement between the parties clearly negatived a bailment (and exempted the defendant from liability with respect to the safekeeping of the car).[43] As the plaintiff had notice of these terms, this indicated that the plaintiff's car was being left at a car park and nothing more.

While the decision is questionable for other reasons, the court's analysis in *Palmer* was not confined to the parties' agreement. In fact, several factors that were not addressed, or, in any event, inadequately addressed, by the court in *Ashby* were considered by the court in finding a licence rather than a bailment, including the absence of a ticketing system, the lack of strict surveillance over vehicles parked in the lot, and the fact that the plaintiff *had not been required* to surrender his keys to the car park as a normal condition of his parking.[44]

In *Kieller v Sentinel Self-Storage Corp*,[45] the Court of Queen's Bench of Alberta applied an *Ashby*-type analysis to the question of whether the relationship between the parties in that case amounted to a bailment, focusing almost exclusively on the storage agreement entered into between the parties. While the court noted several security features (far more extensive than those present in *Ashby* and *Campbell*) and procedures that

41 See *Laursen*, above note 7.

42 Above note 8.

43 The sign posted on the pillar at the entrance to the parking lot contained the words "parking, medical arts building only," indicating that the vehicle was being left merely for parking, rather than safekeeping: *Ibid* at para 4.

44 *Ibid* at para 6.

45 Above note 40.

should have pushed it toward a bailment,[46] Moen J, unlike the trial judge, paid them no heed, finding that the agreement expressly stated that the defendant was not a "bailee or warehouseman,"[47] but a mere licensor, only providing space to the plaintiff renter to park his equipment and not accepting a duty of safekeeping over the property. In the result, the defendant was not found liable for failing after hours to properly secure a gate leading into the compound where the plaintiff's trailer and all-terrain vehicle were stored, leading to a theft of those goods.

According to Moen J, the following clause in the storage agreement, together with the fact that the defendant *had not* exercised its contingent power to take control of the plaintiff's goods for non-payment of storage fees, was dispositive of the matter, as it clearly demonstrated that the defendant was not prepared to act as bailee:

> 5.1 Renter acknowledges that Sentinel is only providing space to Renter for the storage of unidentified goods at Renter's OWN RISK and that Sentinel is not a bailee or warehouseman, and does not have custody of and has no obligation to care for or preserve Renter's goods.[48]

Justice Moen's analysis fails to recognize that the presence of certain precautions and safeguards may evidence that a bailee has exercised the requisite level of control over the subject property by virtue of its control over the land on which the goods are located to make it bailee and to show that it has accepted a duty of safekeeping even in the absence of a transfer of keys, which transfer had not occurred in the case.[49] Such procedures cannot be summarily listed and ignored in favour of a written

---

46 The safeguards and precautions included an invisible beam surrounding the yard in which the bailor's goods were stored, the locking of the gate after business hours, extensive check-in procedures, and the defendant's contingent power to assert control of the plaintiff's goods for nonpayment of rent: *ibid* at paras 11 and 47.

47 *Ibid* at paras 46–50.

48 *Ibid* at para 47.

49 See *Visscher*, above note 31 at para 31; *McLennan*, above note 18 at para 22. See also *Stone v Sentinel Self-Storage Corp*, [1995] AJ No 1003 (Prov Ct (Civ Div)) [*Stone*], wherein the same provincial court judge (Skitsko Prov Ct J) who was overruled in *Kieller*, above note 40, demonstrates, as he did in that case, an appreciation that such safeguards may evidence a bailment rather than a licence, even in the presence of express terms to the contrary in the parties' agreement. The learned judge in *Stone* found a bailment on very similar facts and circumstances as those presenting in *Kieller*, noting several safeguards that demonstrated an acceptance of the duty of safekeeping by the bailee, including an eight-foot-high chain-link fence and video surveillance of the premises: *Stone*, above in this note at paras 17–18.

agreement; they must be analyzed in light of the relevant caselaw and the totality of the evidence, and then be given the appropriate weight, if any, in determining whether a bailment is present. As opined by Bruce J in *Coueslan v Canadian Mini-Warehouse Properties Ltd (cob Public Storage Canadian)*,[50] where the elements of a bailment are present, the terms of a parties' agreement may not exclude it.[51]

Hence, in *Coueslan*, Bruce J went beyond the parties' lease in considering whether a transfer of possession of the goods from the plaintiff tenant to the defendant landlord had occurred, even though it clearly negatived a bailment and all potential liability arising from the landlord's storage of the tenant's property.[52] "The key to distinguishing between bailments and other relationships is *control* over the subject property" (my emphasis).[53]

The serious deficiencies in the defendant's security system, as well as the plaintiff's completely unrestricted access to her storage locker (within which her goods were stored), led Bruce J to conclude that the plaintiff *had not* relinquished possession of her goods to the defendant. In no way could it be said that the tenant's control over or access to her chattels was dependent on the co-operation of the owner of the premises where they were stored. Hence, the landlord was not liable as bailee (or warehouser) for the theft of the plaintiff's goods.[54]

iii) Explicit Contractual Terms Supporting the Finding of a Licence

The Court of Appeal for Ontario's ruling in *Heffron v Imperial Parking Co et al*[55] indicates that a licence is less likely to be found where the terms of the parties' contract *only* oust liability in a general way (as relates to the subject property), as opposed to one that also expressly and specifically negatives a bailment relationship. In that case, the parking ticket stated

---

50 Above note 4.

51 *Ibid* at para 16. This, however, does not mean that a bailee may not protect itself from liability arising upon a bailment by way of an exclusion clause.

52 *Ibid* at paras 4–5.

53 *Ibid* at para 16. See also *Robertson*, above note 9 at para 64.

54 *Coueslan*, above note 4 at paras 14–20. As in *Campbell*, above note 34, however, the defendant was found to be liable as occupier. However, unlike in that case, Bruce Prov Ct J applied a higher standard to the exclusion clause, finding that the clause was inadequate to protect the defendant from liability under the *Occupiers Liability Act*, as there was no specific reference to the liability established under that Act: see *Coueslan*, at paras 28–32.

55 Above note 18.

merely that the defendant was not "responsible for theft or damage of car or contents, however caused,"[56] without expressly excluding a bailment.

The court noted that this distinguished the case from its earlier ruling in *Bata v City Parking Canada Ltd*,[57] where the terms of the contract—both of which were reinforced by signage on the premises—further provided that "charges are for use of parking space only," which it stated clearly excluded a bailment.[58]

It is submitted that, even where a contract or parking ticket contains these two explicit terms pointing toward a licence relationship, the other factors indicative of a bailment must still be considered in deciding whether possession has passed from bailor to bailee. It is probably for this reason that the Court of Appeal in *Heffron* proceeded to consider several other factors prior to making its ruling on this issue, including the bailee's use of a serially numbered parking ticket, its hours of operation, and standard operating procedures (it was normal practice for the bailee at closing time to take patrons' keys from the lot where their vehicles were parked to another lot it operated across the street for safekeeping, leaving a notice on the windshields of all cars advising of same).[59] Placing significant weight on the fact that the plaintiff had been required upon his entry into the lot to leave his keys in his vehicle for the "convenience and presumably the greater profit of the [parking lot] operator,"[60] the court ruled that possession had passed to the parking garage and that a bailment had been created.

---

56 *Ibid* at para 2.

57 *Bata*, above note 15. The case was also distinguishable from the court's earlier ruling in *Palmer*, above note 8, where the court found that the words describing the place in which the car was to be left as a "car park" and the limiting words excluding all liability "however caused" indicated a licence relationship, the retention of the keys by the parking attendant for the parking of the plaintiff's car being nothing more than a gratuitous act on the part of the garage as agent (and not bailee) of the plaintiff.

58 *Bata*, above note 15 at para 16. Of course, such a finding presumes that such terms are part of the "bargain" between the parties in the first place. In *Buccilli v Provincial Parking Inc*, [1988] OJ No 2672 (Prov Ct (Civ Div Sm Cl Ct)), the court refused to incorporate such terms into the parties' agreement (to exclude a bailment), despite their presence on signage and on the parking ticket that had been received by the plaintiff, because, in its view, the bailee had not taken reasonable steps to bring those terms to the attention of the bailor: see para 2.

59 *Heffron*, above note 18 at para 14.

60 *Ibid* at para 21.

iv) No Presumption of Licence in Presence of Certain Contractual Terms

Heffron demonstrates that there is no presumption in law in favour of a licence in the presence of certain contractual terms that define or "label" the relationship between the parties as one of licence as opposed to bailment.[61] This seems to have been the *modus operandi* of the Court of Appeal for Ontario in its earlier decision in *Bata*, where the presence of two terms in the contract led the court to conclude that the relationship between the parties was one of licence rather than bailment. Justice Schroeder of the Court of Appeal, in that case, addressed the matter as follows:

> The words on the two signs and the words which appear on the parking ticket given to the customer indicate in a very real sense the nature of the rights which the proprietor of a car may expect to enjoy under the arrangement into which he is entering. The words "charges are for use of parking space only," exclude at once any notion that the arrangement entered into is one of bailment, and if there is any doubt on that score the words "This company assumes no responsibility whatever for loss or damage due to fire, theft, collision or otherwise to vehicle or its contents, however caused" should effectively remove any doubt in the matter.
>
> With deference, I disagree with the conclusion of the learned trial Judge that the relationship between the plaintiff and defendant was that of bailor and bailee. Applying the test that was applied by this Court in Palmer v. Toronto Med. Arts Bldg. Ltd., ... which followed and applied the test laid down in Ashby v. Tolhurst, I am impelled to the conclusion that the relationship between the plaintiff and the defendant company was rather than of licensee and licensor. It follows that in the absence of proof of any stipulation placing an obligation on the defendant company as licensor towards the plaintiff as licensee, the defendant is not liable for the damage caused to the plaintiff's motor-car after it had been stolen.[62]

---

61 In *Samuel Smith & Sons Ltd v Silverman*, [1961] OR 648 (CA) [*Smith*], the presence of both limiting terms did not prevent the parties in the case from conceding a bailment where the evidence showed that, on the way into the lot, the bailor had been requested by the parking attendant to leave his keys and car with the parking attendant so that his car could be parked in a suitable place on the lot for the greater benefit, profit, and convenience of the parking garage. See further *Pickin v Hesk*, [1954] OJ 557 at paras 24-26 (CA) [*Pickin*]; *Appleton v Ritchie Taxi*, [1942] OJ No 456 at paras 4-9 (CA) [*Appleton*].

62 *Bata*, above note 15 at para 16.

The court appears to have put no weight on (and devoted no discussion in its reasons to) the fact that the bailor had been required to surrender possession of his keys to the parking lot attendant so that his vehicle could be parked.[63] Such a narrow analysis is to be avoided. As stated earlier, a more holistic approach in these circumstances is called for, one that goes beyond the terms of the parties' agreement as defined in a parking ticket and/or by parking signage and that closely considers whether the bailee exercised "sufficient control" over the bailor's goods by considering all the relevant circumstances.

This sentiment is well captured by Blair JA in the Court of Appeal for Ontario's later decision in *Trivett Estate*, as follows:

> Here, as in all the leading cases, the main question is whether the proprietor of the parking lot merely granted the owner of the automobile a license to park or assumed responsibility for its safe custody as a bailee. Whether a bailment is created depends, in turn, on all the circumstances surrounding the transaction and is not precluded by the parking lot operator's definition of the transaction as being only a license to park. In particular, the circumstances under which keys are transferred to a parking lot attendant are crucial to the decision whether a mere license was granted or a bailment was created by the parking lot operator assuming custody and control of the automobile itself.[64]

True to his words, Blair JA in his reasons for judgment considered all relevant circumstances in determining that the legal relationship between the parties was that of bailment, not licence, rather than basing his determination on the label that the parties had chosen to put on their document: "Charges are for use of parking space only."[65] In that case,

---

63 Some courts (see, for example, *JPM Express*, above note 26 at para 21 and *Trivett Estate*, above note 33 at para 11) have interpreted this to mean that the Court of Appeal for Ontario in *Bata* preferred the terms of the parking ticket in finding a licence over the fact that the driver had been required to surrender his keys to the parking attendant in order to park his car. While this might be true, it would have been preferable for the appeal court to have explicitly stated this in its reasons and to have engaged in a fulsome discussion of the legal effect, if any, of the patron having surrendered his keys to the parking attendant at his request, as a condition of the parking, as opposed to having just identified this fact and then applied an approach that appears to have placed sole importance on the terms of the parking ticket and signage to the exclusion of all other relevant factors.

64 *Trivett Estate*, above note 33 at para 6.

65 *Ibid* at para 3.

the parking attendant had mistakenly requested that the plaintiff (bailor) leave his keys in his vehicle's ignition (after he had obtained a ticket and safely parked his car). In making this request, he had assumed that the plaintiff had parked in the second row of cars in the lot, which cars sometimes needed to be relocated to permit the optimum utilization of the space in accordance with the lot's ordinary practices.[66]

Justice Blair of the Court of Appeal found that this request had violated the garage's rules for the safe custody of automobiles parked therein. This fact, combined with the periodic inspections of the premises undertaken by the garage to ensure no vehicles went missing from the lot, together with the policies in place for the safekeeping of keys for the vehicles left behind for relocation for the maximum utilization of the lot, led the court to find a bailment.[67]

The case demonstrates that certain circumstances can overcome and prevail over the label of "licence" that a parking ticket/agreement or signage, or both, may ascribe to a given relationship, leading to the finding of a bailment. It is submitted that parties should not be allowed by the mere insertion of certain words or phrases into a contract to defeat the true effect of the transaction as it appears from the whole of the relationship. Whether a relationship is one of bailment or licence must be determined by reference to the law and not by the label that the parties choose to put on it.

In *Dixon*,[68] the court undertook a contextual analysis with an eye toward all relevant circumstances. There, the plaintiff had parked his vehicle in the defendant's lot subject to terms indicating that the relationship was one of licence rather than bailment. But the court was quick to note that the plaintiff had been required by the parking attendant to leave his keys in the car if he double-parked, which he did of necessity, given the congestion on the lot.[69]

The court found that this single "act" had transformed the initial terms of the contract, as set out in the parking ticket and reinforced in the signage on the lot's premises (which clearly provided for a licence and nothing more), resulting in the creation of a bailment. This is because the plaintiff had relinquished control of his vehicle, and the contents thereof, to the parking garage. According to the court, the "sole essence" of the

---

66 *Ibid* at para 4.
67 *Ibid* at para 11.
68 Above note 16.
69 *Ibid* at paras 1–7.

parties' agreement was not adequately captured by the exclusion clause in the contract, which stated "Charges are for use of parking space only," or by the other written terms indicating a licence relationship.[70]

The holding in *Dixon* illustrates the malleability in the distinction between licence and bailment; a contractual relationship may at one moment be a licence but quite easily become a bailment at another when the emergence of new circumstances indicate that a bailor has parted with possession of his or her property in favour of the bailee. That is to say, even a slight factual change to a legal relationship can sometimes transform a licence into a bailment.

v) *Explicit Contractual Terms Supporting the Finding of a Bailment*

Where the contractual terms themselves indicate that a bailee has undertaken a duty of safekeeping, this favours the finding of a bailment, at least where such a duty is actually discharged by the bailee in practice. In *Gray v Canwest Parking Ltd*,[71] the ticket normally given to customers of the lot (one had not been given to the plaintiff on this particular occasion) read as follows: "The Company endeavours to protect property of its patrons but will Not be responsible for loss or damage to vehicles or contents. Lock valuables in your car trunk."[72]

The court went on to find a bailment on the basis that the plaintiff had left his vehicle keys with the parking garage at the request of the parking attendant in the usual course of defendant's business; the court appears to have not turned its mind to the ticket's terms for the purpose of distinguishing between a bailment and a licence.[73] Those terms, however, indicated quite clearly that the defendant bailee had accepted a duty of safekeeping by "endeavouring to protect property of its patrons."[74] At the same time, they also indicated that the defendant was attempting to exempt itself from responsibility for losses due to its own negligence or misconduct, as confirmed on signage in the parking lot stating that the vehicles and contents were left at the owner's own risk. A clause such

---

70 *Ibid* at paras 17–19.

71 [1965] BCJ No 41 (Co Ct) [*Gray*].

72 *Ibid* at para 4.

73 *Ibid* at para 8.

74 It is to be noted that there is no requirement that a bailee *expressly* accept liability for damages in the event of the breach of this duty. This is because "liability" (and the extent thereof) is a question of law: *British Motor Corp of Canada Ltd v Ross E Judge Auto Transport Ltd*, [1966] NSJ No 11 at paras 14–15 (SC) [*British Motor*].

as the above is probably best read as imposing bailee obligations subject to the limiting words, which may exclude liability for negligence by the bailee. Yet, as previously stated, a finding of either a bailment or licence should be informed and should be made only after all the relevant circumstances have been considered.[75]

In *Minichiello v Devonshire Hotel (1967) Ltd*,[76] the term "Reasonable care by our employees constitutes full discharge of our liability" contributed to a finding that the defendant bailee had accepted a duty of safekeeping in spite of the two terms in the parties' agreement that attempted to limit the car park's liability in the event of loss or damage to the bailor's car and to exclude a bailment.[77] Thus, the defendant was responsible for the theft of the plaintiff's jewellery left in the vehicle, by reason of its failure to securely keep the keys to the automobile, including the trunk keys, while leaving the vehicle unlocked and the vehicle and its contents susceptible to theft, as the vehicle was not under the constant supervision of a parking attendant.[78]

In *British Motor*,[79] the court found that a contractual understanding to the effect that the defendant would store the plaintiff's cars, and watch over them to the best of its ability (which included a watchmen service) for reward, was sufficient to create a bailment in the absence of any limiting terms.[80] The relation was clearly distinct from a mere licensor-licensee relationship. The mere fact that the plaintiff had the right to withdraw its cars from time to time was not enough to defeat the bailment in light of the defendant's undertaking, which required the defendant to have possession of the plaintiff's goods.

---

75 In any case, the terms of the exclusion clause, contained in the ticket normally given to customers and confirmed on signage on the lot, were found not to be sufficient to protect the defendant from liability for negligence ultimately imposed against it: *Gray*, above note 71 at paras 13–18.

76 (1976), 66 DLR (3d) 619 (BCSC) [*Minichiello*], aff'd (1978), 87 DLR (3d) 439 (BCCA).

77 *Minichiello*, above note 76 at para 10. For the text of the limiting terms, see para 8.

78 *Ibid* at para 14.

79 Above note 74.

80 *Ibid* at paras 38–40. Where such a bailment is for consideration, and the bailor stops paying, the bailment should be viewed as terminated. In the absence of proper authorization from the bailee, the bailor's continued storage of its property on the bailee's property must be viewed as a trespass: *Fong v Tinkess (cob Imperial Taxi)*, [1941] OJ No 198 (CA) [*Fong*].

Similarly, in *Dodd v Johnson*,[81] an agreement between the parties that required that the defendant (bailee) provide the plaintiff with safe storage of his expensive bicycle during the times when he provided piano lessons to the defendant's children at the defendant's residence contributed to a finding that the defendant had accepted a duty of safekeeping as bailee. In the result, the defendant was found to be legally responsible for the theft of the plaintiff's bicycle from the defendant's garage by reason of the defendant's failure to secure the door of the garage once the bicycle was placed in there or, alternatively, to be outside and monitor the area in which the bicycle had been placed.[82]

Where an agreement states (or emphasizes) that a bailee accepts property for storage (as opposed to, for example, parking or docking) for a fee, this may well be supportive of a bailment relationship as well.[83] Where the bailee has a right to a lien as storer under the *Repair and Storage Liens Act*, the finding of a bailment is unavoidable, since such a legal conclusion would mean that the bailor has parted with possession[84] of the article for storage purposes. Similarly, where a bailee receives and stores goods for profit, by agreement as a warehouser, it may be deemed a bailee by statute.[85]

In *Woodcock v Services Maritimes de Bas-Caraquet Ltée*,[86] the court appears to indicate that a written contract that merely binds a defendant to "monitor access" to an area in which a plaintiff's goods are stored is not sufficient, without more, to create a bailment, where such clause is not followed in practice and where the plaintiff has acquiesced to the minimal security measures actually implemented by the defendant.[87] The defendant

81 Above note 32 at para 17.

82 *Ibid* at para 22.

83 See *JPM Express*, above note 26; *Jaskiewicz v GSB Properties Ltd*, [2009] OJ No 2610 (SCJ); *Munro v Bluffer's Park Marina Ltd*, [2006] OJ No 825 (CA) [*Munro*].

84 Since "possession" is not defined in the *Repair and Storage Liens Act*, RSO 1990, c R.25, its meaning must be derived from the common law.

85 See *Martin v Stephens*, 2002 BCPC 196 at paras 36–47.

86 2006 NBQB 178 [*Woodcock*], aff'd 2007 NBCA 21.

87 *Woodcock*, above note 86 at paras 28–34. In the case, the plaintiff had been advised at the outset of the relationship, and on several occasions thereafter, about the lack of security to the defendant's premises, and was told by the defendant that he was solely responsible for theft or damage to his boat. In fact, before the incident in question, which caused considerable damage to the plaintiff's property, his boat had been broken into by vandals on numerous occasions. On each of these occasions, the plaintiff had been advised by the defendant that it was not responsible for the damage occasioned and that it would not be enhancing its security measures in response to such occurrences or otherwise.

in the case operated a boatyard under contract from the New Brunswick government. The pertinent clause in that contract read as follows: "Access to the Centre shall be monitored during business hours. Access doors shall be closed and access limited during off business hours."[88] This clause was not observed by the defendant in practice. Instead, only very minimal safeguards were implemented by the defendant with respect to the plaintiff's property. The gate to the premises was not closed at night, and it was possible for members of the public to gain access to the site by going around a chain-link fence. In the words of Guérette J, "Access to the site, despite gate closings (if any), night lights, chain link fence, and usually two employees operating the boat lift, is still '*wide open*.'"[89]

Thus, despite a clause that might be read as imposing same, the defendant had not accepted possession of the plaintiff's boat for the purposes of safekeeping and was not a bailee. Instead, it had merely accepted the property as licensor and was not responsible for the substantial damage occasioned to the boat by the unknown vandals.[90] This case, however, should be distinguished from those cases discussed earlier, where the bailee had expressly and clearly accepted a duty of safekeeping and, thus, assumed the risk of caring for the bailor's property.

vi) Exclusion Clauses

The presence or absence of exclusion provisions or limiting terms in agreements between parties can influence the distinction between licence and bailment, but they should not be treated as being dispositive. Quite paradoxically, the presence of an exclusion clause might be supportive of a bailment, on the one hand, and a licence, on the other. This is because there is no need to immunize a party from liability arising upon a bailment if the contract establishes a licensor-licensee relationship and nothing more. As discussed previously, a licensor owes no special duty to the licensee to safeguard its property in the absence of a contractual undertaking to that effect. In other words, a clause excluding a bailment is sufficient so long as the factual circumstances are consistent with a licence. All the above said, the presence of limiting terms is certainly a factor that will often weigh against the finding of a bailment, though it is only one factor to be considered in the equation, and not the most

88 *Ibid* at para 17.
89 *Ibid* at para 31 [emphasis in original].
90 *Ibid* at paras 38–39.

important one. As we have learned, the key is to ascertain the true nature of the parties' relationship, based on an analysis of all the circumstances, with a particular focus on whether control of the subject property was surrendered to the purported bailee for safekeeping.

In *Brown v Toronto Auto Parks Ltd*,[91] the Court of Appeal for Ontario refused to exclude a bailment on the basis of the words "car and contents at owner's risk" contained in the exclusion clause in the parties' agreement because those words did not sufficiently indicate that the bailee would be relieved of liability arising through the negligence of its employee.[92] Conversely, in *Robertson*,[93] the court stated in *obiter* that a bailment could be excluded by contract even where that legal relationship is not specifically adverted to in the exempting provision.[94] This sets a lower standard than some courts have been willing to set for the exclusion of occupier liability under provincial occupiers' liability Acts[95] and should not be followed. (That said, the court in *Robertson* refused to apply the clause for other reasons.[96]) In any event, as *Brown* is higher and better authority, it must be preferred. It is submitted that exclusion clauses should be interpreted narrowly; broad clauses that make no reference to a bailment either directly or by clear implication should not be viewed as being sufficient, without more, to oust the relationship.

Certainly a distinction must be drawn between those exempting provisions within a contract that may be read as merely excluding the liability arising upon a bailment without signifying a licence relationship and those that seek to exclude the obligations arising upon a bailment altogether, as well as any liability arising therefrom. The former should be interpreted as being supportive of a bailment; the latter supportive of a licence. Even where a court finds that a bailment has not been ousted by an exemption clause, the clause may still exclude all liability arising from a bailment.[97] The end result is the same: the plaintiff is denied redress for losses, the only difference being that the defendant is a bailee in the first case, but not in the second.

---

91 [1955] 2 DLR 525 (Ont CA) [*Brown*].
92 *Ibid* at para 4.
93 *Robertson*, above note 9.
94 *Ibid* at para 75. For the text of the exempting clause, see para 4 of the decision.
95 *Coueslan*, above note 4 at paras 14–20. But see *Campbell*, above note 34 at paras 49–51.
96 *Robertson*, above note 9 at para 74.
97 See *Gray*, above note 71.

In *Ashby*,[98] the court stated, albeit in *obiter*, that, even if a bailment had been created, something it did not find on the facts, the defendant parking attendant's mistake of fact, in not correctly identifying the true owner of the vehicle and mistakenly handing the car over to a thief, was protected by the terms of the car park ticket.

b) Access or Control

i) Transfer of Possession by Access or Control

In *Laursen*,[99] the court correctly notes that possession of goods may be transferred from bailor to bailee by means of access or control. Where neither is present, this will point away from a bailment relationship. In *Laursen*, the court found that the plaintiffs had not surrendered either access or control over their vehicles that were being stored in the defendant's barn, together with the defendant's own vehicles and horses during the winter months.[100]

There was no transfer of keys from the vehicle owners to the defendant, which can often signify a bailment of a vehicle by access and control. The defendant could not move or unlock the chattels, or operate them, and never attempted (or had any reason to attempt) to exercise any control or possession over them. The vehicles were parked in a fixed position in the defendant's barn for the duration of the winter, to be retrieved by the plaintiffs once spring arrived (with only the plaintiffs possessing the means of access and control to the chattels during the subject period). In sum, the defendant's ability to exercise any physical dominion over the chattels was completely dependent on co-operation from the plaintiffs, which he did not request or receive.[101]

The defendant also did not control the use of the barn made by the plaintiffs, another consideration in it not qualifying as bailee of the plaintiffs' goods. Neither parking nor removal required the defendant's co-operation; the plaintiffs could enter and exit the barn as they pleased with their property, with the defendant possessing no power to exclude

98 Above note 23.

99 *Laursen*, above note 7 at para 14.

100 *Ibid* at paras 14–15.

101 *Ibid*. Even if he had made such a request and received this assistance, this would still not have triggered a bailment, since the request and assistance would have indicated that the plaintiffs had not parted with possession of their chattels in favour of the defendant.

them.[102] In short, the premises were open, accessible, and insecure. In the result, a bailment was not found, and the defendant was not put to the reverse onus with respect to the collapsing of his barn's roof, which caused damage to the plaintiffs' property stored in that building.[103]

Similarly, in *Coueslan*,[104] the defendant landlord could not access the tenant's locker where her chattels were stored. The landlord had no key to the locker, and the chattels stored in the locker were not subject to any restrictions, save and except the limited circumstances arising from the landlord-tenant relationship. In other words, the tenant had exclusive control and access over the chattels. In the result, a bailment could not be found.

This is unlike the situation in *Dodd*.[105] There, the plaintiff required the defendants' co-operation (i.e., they needed to open the garage door) in order for him to access his expensive bicycle, which they had agreed to safeguard in their garage during the time he provided piano lessons to their children. Thus, there had been a transfer of possession from bailor to bailee by means of access and control. And the defendants, as bailees, were responsible for the loss of the bicycle due to a failure to safeguard the property of the plaintiff stored in the garage for the duration of the lessons by failing to close the garage or monitor the area in which the bicycle was stored.[106]

In *Quigley v Rands*,[107] an absence of a system for the monitoring of the chattels taken on or off the premises and an absence of documentation to record the exit or entry of the chattels stored thereon indicated a lack of control of the premises to qualify the defendant yard as bailee. Where

---

102 See *Lessor v Jones* (1920), 52 DLR 523 (NBSCAD) [*Lessor*]. There, the plaintiff rented space in a garage to store his vehicle and was provided a key to the garage, giving him an unfettered ability to park and remove his car at any time from it, as he saw fit. The court found a licence, in spite of representations by the defendant "that it would be in good condition and that nothing would happen to it while it was in the garage."

103 *Laursen*, above note 7 at paras 14–17. The barn was situated close to a country road, completely out of sight of the defendant's home, was completely open at one end, and half open at the other, and included two twenty-four-foot openings. There was no surveillance of the barn or the chattels whatsoever by way of security attendants or security equipment located in or around the barn: at para 16. *Contra*, see *Gobeil v Elliot*, 1996 CanLII 6802 (Sask QB).

104 Above note 4.

105 Above note 32.

106 *Ibid* at para 22.

107 [1982] BCJ No 367 at para 18 (Co Ct) [*Quigley*].

rents are based on a particular area used (which is not monitored), rather than based on the number of chattels in the given area (which is monitored), this will also indicate a lack of control over the subject premises to qualify a yard as bailee.

ii) Access or Control Must Be for the Purpose of Bailment, Not Licence

In *McLennan v Charlottetown Flying Services*,[108] the defendant's moving of the airplanes it was storing in a hangar by physically pushing them from one place to another, for the sole purpose of creating more space for the "parking" of other planes, did not amount to either access or control of the airplane to qualify the defendant as bailee.

This case indicates that the access or control effected by the bailee must be for the purpose of exercising exclusive possession over the chattel for safekeeping as a prudent owner would, as opposed to merely moving chattels around for parking purposes, parking being indicative of a licence and not a bailment. (The hanger door on the premises was left open at all times, and the plaintiff's property was not handed over at the request of the defendant, and so there was no reasonable expectation of safekeeping.)[109] The fact that a key is not used to relocate the property may not be dispositive where the purpose of the act constituting the access or control, or the exercise of physical dominion over the chattel, is to safeguard the bailor's property, or to assert control over its movements,[110] as only a bailee would.

In *JPM Express*,[111] the main question to be decided under the summary motion judgment procedure was whether the legal relationship between the parties was one of bailment or licence, based on an analysis of control over and access to the plaintiff's vehicles by the defendant. Justice Brown held that this was a serious issue that required a trial, and he refused to provide an answer to the question, dismissing the motion before him accordingly.[112] That said, a review of his comments on the

108 Above note 18.

109 *Ibid* at paras 8–15 and 25.

110 *Quigley*, above note 107 at para 18.

111 Above note 26.

112 *Ibid* at paras 40–47. This was of great consequence in the case, for if the defendant were a bailee (meaning it had received exclusive possession of the property), that would automatically make it a "storer" under the *Repair and Storage Liens Act*, above note 84, entitling it to assert possessory lien rights against the plaintiff's vehicles for what it alleged were arrears in the parking or storage fees.

issue based on the evidence that was before him suggests that, because the defendant parking lot operator in the case did not possess the keys to the plaintiff's vehicles during the course of the storage and therefore could not move them around the lot (that is, exercise control over them), it could not qualify itself as bailee.[113] With respect, Brown J's reasoning is questionable for at least two reasons. First, the defendant may have been made bailee by virtue of its exercise of its right to withhold access to the plaintiff's vehicles for non-payment of parking fees pursuant to the *Repair and Storage Liens Act*.[114] This point was not considered by Brown J in his reasons. Instead, he appears to have equated "control" with the parking operator's ability to move the plaintiff's vehicles around the lot through the use of keys belonging to the vehicles, which the defendant did not possess or have access to. However, by withholding access (i.e., blocking the vehicles in) for non-payment of its fees, the defendant was exercising control over the chattels.[115] That is to say, the plaintiff could not remove (or access) his vehicles without the defendant's co-operation. Second, Brown J's view does not account for exercises of control over chattels that may be operable by key but may be moveable in other ways, as was the case in *McLennan*.[116]

In *Munro*,[117] the appellant's docking of his vessel at the respondent's marina for a fee was not enough to create a bailment (but only a licence), because the appellant was occupying the vessel as a "home" throughout the relevant period, which indicated that he had not relinquished possession of the boat to the respondent. In *Melburn Truck Line Inc v Plastmo Ltd*,[118] the defendant's agreement to allow the plaintiff to park its trailers on its property in front of a loading dock, while they were unloaded with goods for the defendant, to free up the independent drivers of the plaintiff—who could then leave and attend to other things, as they were not being paid under the plaintiff's contract with them for wait-time—was not enough, without more, to create anything more than a licence between the parties. The licence was subject to the express condition between the

---

113 *JPM Express*, above note 26 at paras 18–26.

114 RSO 1990, c R.25.

115 This view of the law was endorsed by Mrozinski Prov J in *Campbell*, above note 34.

116 For a further example, see *Kieller*, above note 40 at para 46 (the plaintiff's trailer, alleged to be subject of the bailment, could be and was apparently moved by the defendant without the benefit of keys).

117 Above note 83.

118 [1992] OJ No 209 (Gen Div).

parties that, if access to the loading docks for outgoing shipments were needed by the defendant, then any plaintiff trailer parked in front of a loading dock would be relocated to the public street, where it would remain for pickup by the plaintiff. The practice developed between the parties that the trailers relocated to the public street would not be picked up by plaintiff drivers until they made another trip to the defendant's premises, which sometimes would not be for several days.[119]

As it happened, a certain trailer went missing and could not be found by plaintiff drivers who attended at the defendant's location to look for it. The plaintiff sued in bailment for the lost trailer.[120] Justice Thomas of the Ontario Court of Justice—General Division found that the terms of the parties' agreement indicated no more than a licence; the agreed-upon practice of moving the trailers to the street indicated that the defendant *was not* assuming a duty of safekeeping over the trailers and was only allowing them to be parked on their premises for a time, as a courtesy.[121] As apparent, the defendant's mere physical control exercised over the trailers in moving them to the street did not mean that the leaving of the trailers on the defendant's property reflected anything more than a mere permission to park, which was in accordance with the parties' intentions.

As these cases indicate, the purpose of the access or control exercised by the bailee must always be assessed. Is the act of control or access for the purpose of bailment or licence? Is a duty of safekeeping being assumed by the bailee?

In *Alberta U Drive Ltd v Jack Carter Ltd*,[122] the defendant car dealer granted the plaintiff a right to park its cars on the defendant's lot surrounding the garage building (no particular place was designated for the plaintiff's vehicles) for the purpose of renting them out to the defendant's customers while the customers' cars were serviced by the defendant. The plaintiff was also provided with some office space to run its rental business, within which the plaintiff stored the keys to its vehicles. No fee was charged by the defendant for the use of the parking or office space, as there was a close and friendly working relationship between the two companies.[123]

---

119 *Ibid* at paras 18–24 [paragraph numbers assigned by author].
120 *Ibid* at paras 12–15.
121 *Ibid* at paras 18–24.
122 Above note 10.
123 *Ibid* at para 1.

The parties agreed that the plaintiff would ensure the security of its own vehicles, which it did through the use of its own attendant, who would ordinarily park the cars and lock them up upon their return off rental. As a courtesy, when the plaintiff's attendant was off duty, the defendant provided the plaintiff with the gratuitous benefit of certain protective measures, which it had in effect generally at its business, including having a car jockey (i.e., a defendant employee) accept delivery of the plaintiff's rental cars once returned by the defendant's customers off rental, and securing the keys to those cars on behalf of the plaintiff. As it happened, one of the plaintiff's cars was stolen by a dishonest employee of the defendant after he had received keys to the car while the plaintiff's parking attendant was off duty (the exception rather than the rule). The employee had surreptitiously had these keys copied in order to steal the car. The car was later recovered by the plaintiff but in a damaged condition.[124]

The plaintiff sued in bailment for the damage that had been done to the car, but the court refused to find one. The court emphasized that the keys to the plaintiff's cars were in the possession and control of the plaintiff at all material times (as it maintained the counter of the office of the defendant within which such keys were stored). While access and control over the stolen vehicle, and its keys, had been exercised by the rogue employee, these acts were not connected in any way to a general duty of safekeeping that had been assumed by the defendant. Nor were they connected to some ancillary purpose that would require the defendant to have possession over the vehicle to ensure its safekeeping, such as would be the case with a pledge, sale, or where the plaintiff's vehicle would need be driven to some other location for an authorized repair to be made. As such, there was no bailment and no duty on the part of the defendant company to hire an honest and trustworthy servant. In the absence of a special contract obligating the defendant to assume a wider responsibility than that of licensee, the defendant was not *vicariously liable* for employing the dishonest servant who had caused damage to the plaintiff (bailor's) vehicle.[125]

The obvious question arises as to whether such gratuitous and precautionary acts taken by a defendant (bailee) could ever lead to a bailment, notwithstanding an existing contractual understanding to the contrary.

---

124 *Ibid* at paras 1, 2, 44, and 50.
125 *Ibid* at paras 48–54.

As noted earlier, a slight change in a parties' legal relationship can sometimes transform a licence into a bailment (and vice versa), regardless of what a contract might say, provided that it can be shown that a transfer of possession for the purpose of safekeeping has occurred. What if the defendant in *Alberta U Drive* had accepted delivery of the plaintiff's cars on a more than highly sporadic and irregular basis, leading to reliance and an expectation of security on the part of the plaintiff? Would a bailment, then, have been created?

Where more robust security and safekeeping measures are in place to protect a bailor's property, and are actually exercised, it is asking too much to require a bailor to point to a "special contract" obligating the bailee to assume a duty of safekeeping for the bailor's property where it may not have assumed such a duty at the outset of the legal relationship. If the elements of a bailment materialize based on the conduct of the parties, this must prevail over any contract or understanding indicating a contrary intention. It is trite law that a bailment can exist independently of a contract; it does not require a "special" contract (or any contract, for that matter) to come into existence. Where all the elements of a bailment are present, that is the legal relationship that a court must find.

iii) Inability to Determine Contents of a Bailor's Property

Where, because of a lack of access or control to the goods themselves, a bailee lacks the ability to determine the exact contents (or nature) of the property it is storing, this may indicate that an alleged bailee has not accepted a duty of safekeeping and is a mere licensee.[126] This issue will always be a question of degree of control, with "questions of control" having to extend beyond the goods themselves to a consideration of the premises on which the goods are being housed or stored.

---

126 See *Complex Elements*, above note 26. In this case, the defendant lot brought a summary judgment motion to have the plaintiff's case against it dismissed, on the basis that it had no access to the carriages, the container, or the goods that the co-defendant had parked on its lot on behalf of the plaintiff. It could not determine the character of the goods, or even whether individual carriages had cargo or were empty, which it argued was contraindicative of a bailment: see paras 16–17. Even though the motion was dismissed because of the material factual issues and matters of credibility in dispute (see paras 31–32), there is no question that an inability to access the bailor's goods, or to know their character, strains against the finding of a bailment and may well undermine the bailee's ability to safeguard the goods: see *Seaspan International*, above note 2.

iv) *Constructive Possession*

a. Transfers by Constructive Possession May Occur Without Physical Delivery of a Bailor's Goods into a Bailee's Immediate Physical Control

A transfer of possession by access or control may occur without physical delivery of the subject property to the bailee—that is, constructively. In *Letourneau v Otto Mobiles Edmonton (1984) Ltd*,[127] the plaintiffs left their trailer for repair in a designated spot in an adjacent lot of the defendant repair facility after business hours and secreted the key to the padlock of the hitch in the water compartment of the trailer (which was then locked). This was done in accordance with the defendant's specific directions, which had been received by the plaintiffs earlier the same day or previous day as a consequence of their not being able to drop off the trailer during the defendant's weekday working hours or on Saturday due to other commitments. The vehicle was to be picked up for repair from this lot the following morning by the defendant in accordance with its customary practice. (The defendant did not own the lot, but it was customarily used by its customers to park their vehicles for pickup after hours.) The day immediately following the drop off, the plaintiffs called the defendant to instruct it to look into a further problem they were having with the trailer. The plaintiffs made no mention of the drop-off the night before. The next day, the defendant contacted the plaintiffs to advise that the trailer could not be located. It was concluded that it must have been stolen.[128]

The court found a bailment, despite the fact that the trailer had not been physically delivered to the defendant's premises, on the basis that the plaintiffs had precisely done everything required to permit the defendant to assume control of the chattel in a physical sense. The plaintiffs had parked their trailer in the designated spot, secreted the keys to the padlock of the hitch as instructed by the defendant, and advised the defendant of the trailer's intended delivery. Hence, the court found that a constructive transfer of possession had occurred and that a physical assumption of the property was not a bar to finding a bailment.[129]

---

127 [2002] AJ No 825 (QB) [*Letourneau*].

128 *Ibid* at paras 3–15.

129 *Ibid* at paras 23–41. While it escapes mention in the court's reasons, the plaintiffs (technically) had not done everything required to permit the defendant to assume *immediate* control of the trailer. That is, they *did not* notify the defendant that the trailer had been dropped off and was ready for pickup, either on the day it was dropped off or on the next day when the plaintiffs contacted the defendant to ask it

While requiring only *notice* by a bailor of an act of intended delivery in order for bailee obligations to arise creates logistical and practical difficulties for bailees in carrying out their duty of safekeeping, it is supported by the weight of authority on the subject. That is to say, a bailor is not required to do *everything* to enable a bailee to acquire immediate physical control of its chattels so long as it notifies the bailee of its intended delivery. In order to protect themselves in these situations, bailees should secure their premises, pick up in a timely manner from designated drop-off points bailor property that has not been left in their immediate physical control, and probably put systems into place to monitor bailor property to ensure its safekeeping as soon as it is constructively delivered to them.

b. A Casual View of Goods Received by a Bailee Is Enough for a Transfer by Constructive Possession to Be Found

In *Kinsella v Club "7" Ltd*,[130] the plaintiff left some of his own chattels fixed in place, in two storage/garage areas in a commercial building he was subleasing to the defendants, with the defendants' consent. The plaintiff, in his evidence, stated that it was verbally agreed between the parties that he could leave his chattels on the premises (indefinitely) unless and until the defendant advised him that they needed them removed. The agreement was without consideration.[131] The defendants did not use any of these parts of the premises for storage and so only infrequently visited them, although, apparently, they allowed unrestricted use by other new, subtenants who were paying subrent to them. On the plaintiff's visits to the premises, he observed this usage but did not object to it or raise the issue with the defendants.[132] While the plaintiff surrendered all keys to the premises to the defendants, entry to the garage areas could be made from the interior of the premises by tenants without difficulty (they were not secured), and the keys provided were only with respect to exterior access points into the premises.[133] The plaintiff claimed that, during its previous possession of the premises, its then subtenants could also access these storage areas internally (as they were not securely locked as a matter

---

to look into a further problem they were having with the trailer. While the defendant anticipated delivery, it did not know (exactly) when it was coming.

130 [1993] NJ No 365 (SCTD) [*Kinsella*].

131 *Ibid* at paras 2–3.

132 *Ibid* at paras 59–61.

133 *Ibid* at paras 46–48.

of standard practice), but that none of his equipment or items ever went missing because the premises (in terms of exterior access) were secured by these tenants when they went in and out.[134]

According to the plaintiff, the defendant never demanded that the plaintiff remove his items from the premises. The plaintiff maintained that the goods went missing because of the defendant's negligence in failing to properly secure the goods (even after three additional tenants were added to the premises by the defendants with access to the storage areas in which the plaintiff's goods were housed, without the plaintiff's consent and in breach of the sublease)[135] and in circumstances that demonstrated that the defendants themselves may have disposed of the plaintiff's property as "junk" during a cleanup of the part of the premises housing the plaintiff's chattels.[136] While the defendants had knowledge of the location of the chattels upon the commencement of their lease, they argued that they did not know the precise character and nature of most of the items left on the premises. Indeed, no listing was provided by the plaintiff to the defendants, and the plaintiff had not expressly identified to the defendants the items he was leaving. The defendants also had made no inspection of the areas where the goods were stored to see what was there. The only witness for the defendants to testify did not deny having seen certain items in the storage areas, such as some scaffolding and tarpaulins, but his recollection was vague and he had no specific recollection of many of the items identified by the plaintiff in his pleading. The witness described many of the items left as "junk." But he conceded that, given that he had no categorical recollection of all the items left, he could not refute the plaintiff's assertion as to the chattels that were present at the time the premises were turned over to the defendants.[137]

The defendants argued that no "delivery of possession" had occurred with respect to items that it did not have specific awareness of, and that had not been physically delivered, or manually passed over, to them.[138] They further submitted that the plaintiff had agreed to remove the items left on the premises within thirty days, in accordance with the lease signed between the plaintiff and the corporate defendant, and did not

134 *Ibid* at paras 49 and 51–52.
135 *Ibid* at paras 3 and 61.
136 *Ibid* at para 71.
137 *Ibid* at paras 21–24, 41, and 90–92.
138 *Ibid* at para 90.

do so. They further argued that the items were stored in exactly the same manner as the plaintiff had done during its prior occupation of the premises. Finally, they stated that they did not remove the items from the storage areas and should not be held liable for their disappearance.[139]

The plaintiff had made one particular visit of importance to the premises after the defendants had taken possession, when he happened to be in the area and fortuitously observed a truck loading material from the garage areas where his items were stored, before the items in question went missing. The plaintiff testified that he observed an agent for the defendants attempting to remove one of his chattels for delivery to the dump, namely a table saw, and interfered to stop such removal. The plaintiff also noticed that some of his other items appeared to be missing. The plaintiff demanded to see a defendant. The plaintiff was assured by the defendant he spoke with that his items in the area would be relocated within the premises to another storage area because the area in which the items were located need to be cleaned up for the purposes of a health inspection—which was being conducted in connection with the additional tenants' use of that area of the premises—and would be secured there. The other area, the plaintiff was told, would not be the subject of a cleanup.[140] The plaintiff made no further visits to the premises to check on the whereabouts of his missing items, nor did he do anything further to ensure that his remaining items would in fact be moved to the other storage area and be secured.[141] None of the plaintiff's items were present on the premises when he attempted to retake possession of them following the end of the defendants' sublease.[142] The plaintiff, however, acknowledged that he had made no formal demand for return of the items, or an accounting of them, either when he fortuitously attended at the premises and saw the defendants' representatives removing one of his chattels from the premises for delivery to the dump without his consent or knowledge, at the termination of the lease, or when he reported them missing to the police.[143]

---

139 *Ibid* at paras 5 and 34.
140 *Ibid* at paras 26, 62–65, and 75.
141 *Ibid* at para 80.
142 *Ibid* at paras 82–84.
143 *Ibid* at paras 27 and 81.

The plaintiff sued in bailment for the missing goods and, alternatively, on the basis of conversion or detinue.[144] Justice Puddester of the Newfoundland Supreme Court Trial Division Judicial Centre of St John's found in favour of the plaintiff, finding that the "casual view" of the goods taken by the defendants at the beginning of the sublease was enough to bring the nature of those goods home to the defendants for the purposes of creating a gratuitous bailment by constructive possession. The fact that the defendants did not itemize the items, upon their delivery, was not fatal to the plaintiff's bailment claim, as the items were ones that could be observed and registered by a "casual look." This was evidenced by the fact that at least one individual defendant had specific recollection of certain items left by the plaintiff.[145]

The storage was also not found to be time limited, as argued by the defendants, since, even if originally it had been so limited as a result of statements made by the plaintiff, the defendants, by their conduct, had acquiesced in the plaintiff's leaving his chattels on the premises beyond this originally contemplated time until such time as the defendants demanded their removal.[146] Justice Puddester drew a negative inference against the defendants with respect to their state of knowledge as to the identity of the goods left on the premises, since only one of the six individual defendants had chosen to testify as to their state of knowledge, even though the witness who testified claimed that, at the point of takeover of the premises, several of the other defendants were also present and may have been in a position to identify the items left by the plaintiff.[147]

The decision in *Kinsella* to find a bailment based on constructive possession is eminently defensible. The defendants had received the requisite knowledge to enable them to act as bailee and to protect the plaintiff's chattels from loss or damage, which it failed to do in circumstances. They were also the party in the best position to explain what had happened to the goods.[148] The fact that they might have been in a better

144 *Ibid* at para 4.

145 *Ibid* at paras 90–92.

146 *Ibid* at paras 39–40.

147 *Ibid* at paras 25 and 41.

148 Admittedly the defendants were not "the only party" with knowledge of what may have happened to the goods at all times, as the plaintiff on a visit to the rented premises had discovered the defendants trying to dispose of one of his chattels from a storage area during a cleanup of that part of the premises and had made the further observation, at that point, that some of his goods might be missing as a result of

position to safeguard the plaintiff's goods had he made a formal demand for the return of his goods when he suspected that some might be missing should not shield them as bailees from liability in these circumstances.[149] Further, requiring either manual delivery of the goods (as argued by the defendants in *Kinsella*) or a resegregating of the goods into new locations within the premises, in these or similar circumstances, would be asking too much from a bailor and should not be required in order to effect a transfer by constructive possession.[150] It would also be asking too much to require the bailor in these circumstances to show that an inventory of the items had been provided to the bailee, or made by it, upon receipt of the goods. As pointed out by Puddester J, there is no requirement on bailors in these circumstances to individually identify the goods being delivered to the bailee in order for a transfer by constructive possession to be found to have occurred.[151]

c. Hard Limits on Transfers of Possession by Constructive Possession

In *Luider v Nguyen (cob Nanton Packers)*,[152] the court quite rightly places hard limits on transfers of bailor property by constructive possession, stating that bailors must act reasonably when leaving their property for pickup by a bailee. That is to say, for bailee obligations to arise, bailors

---

this cleanup. That said, it is submitted that *only* the defendants were in a position to explain what happened to the goods at the critical time—that is, when the plaintiff had "categorically" determined that the goods were missing, upon retaking possession of the premises from the defendants at the end of their lease—since, up until that point in time, they had had exclusive possession of the plaintiff's goods. The plaintiff's antecedent knowledge as to what may have happened to the goods should not be enough to disqualify a bailment by constructive possession in these circumstances, as it came too early, and is too uncertain, to be of any real value.

149 Indeed, in order to fix liability against a bailee in these circumstances, a bailor need not prove that such a formal demand was made, unless the duty to redeliver by the bailee is dependent on such demand. The agreement between the parties in *Kinsella* appears to have contained no such requirement. In any case, the defendants (bailees) in the case failed to properly plead this defence against the plaintiff, which was fatal to sustaining it: *ibid* at para 93. Once goods are placed and remain in the exclusive possession of a bailee, it is the bailee who is solely responsible for their safekeeping and who, to avoid liability, must offer up a satisfactory explanation where they are lost or damaged.

150 See *Hynes v Hynes*, [1995] NJ No 8 (Prov Ct (Sm Cl Div)), where a bailment was found to have been created when the defendant (bailee) ordered the plaintiff out of the matrimonial home, leaving the defendant in sole possession of the plaintiff's clothing remaining in the home.

151 *Kinsella*, above note 130 at para 92.

152 [1994] AJ No 494 (Prov Ct (Civ Div)).

must properly secure their property at the drop-off point. In this case, the plaintiff had dropped off a large hog at the defendant's premises for slaughter late into the night but, due to trouble with lighting inside the barn, was found to have improperly secured the various gates leading out of the pen in which the hog was left. The hog went missing (probably having escaped and then been stolen by third persons unknown), and the plaintiff sued in bailment.[153] Because of the plaintiff's negligence, no act of delivery was found to have occurred. The court rejected the argument that it was regular practice to deliver livestock at night without the purported bailee's prior agreement and without giving it any notice of the intended delivery. The court held that, even if such a practice existed, obviating the need for such notice and agreement, the act of negligence by the plaintiff had disqualified the bailment in any event.[154]

This is a very sensible position for the court to have taken. Where the bailee has not been advised directly of the delivery or intended delivery by the bailor, and has no knowledge of the character of the goods delivered, it would make a mockery of bailment as a voluntary relationship to allow a bailment to be found where the bailor has been negligent in its delivery of the goods.[155] It makes no sense to impose a duty of safekeeping on a bailee, regardless of whether it has received notice of an act of intended delivery, where their ability to discharge the duty has already been frustrated by a negligent act of a bailor in the manner of its delivery of its property to the bailee.[156]

---

153 *Ibid* at paras 1–8 and 13.

154 *Ibid* at paras 14–21.

155 Where the bailee has been negligent in receiving the goods, this will not disqualify the act of delivery. In *Macdonell v Woods* (1914), 20 DLR 366 (Ont SCAD), the plaintiff engaged a room in the defendant hotel, arranging for the delivery of a trunk full of clothes to the hotel at a time that had been agreed upon by the parties. When the trunk arrived, the plaintiff's delivery agent was instructed by the hotel to leave it inside the door, which he did. The trunk went missing, and the hotel was found liable as bailee for the loss, having left the trunk unprotected in the passageway.

156 Where the bailor has not been negligent, and a transfer of possession has occurred, a bailee's obligations to take the necessary precautions to prevent damage to the goods, and to prevent them from causing damage to other property, arises *immediately*, with all the attendant risks that this engenders. In *Costello Equipment Co v Shaw GMC Trucks Ltd*, [1975] AJ No 85 (SCTD), the defendant, Shaw GMC Trucks Ltd, was found liable as bailee for damage done to the plaintiff's building after the co-defendant Milchem Canada Ltd's truck rolled down an incline where it had been customarily parked while awaiting repair. Because the plaintiff was found to have taken the necessary steps to prevent it from moving (leaving his truck in the lowest gear and leaving the trailer's air brakes on), and the exact cause of damage was

The case also raises the larger question of whether delivery of property could ever trigger bailee obligations, depending on industry practice, where the bailor has not been negligent in delivering the goods to the bailee but has not given it any notification of a delivery or intended delivery. It is submitted that this would set the bar too low. No notification of a delivery or intended delivery severely limits a bailee's ability to take immediate control of the bailor's property to protect it from loss. In these circumstances, the bailee will sometimes be in no better position than the bailor to protect the goods from loss. As well, a bailee will be in no position to refuse the bailment, undermining the notion of a bailment as a voluntary relationship. It is accordingly submitted that the bailee must be made aware of a delivery or intended delivery, and must agree to it, before bailee obligations can be said to arise, regardless of what the industry practice might or might not be. In the alternative, the bailment should not be viewed as commencing until knowledge of an act of delivery is obtained by the purported bailee, which may occur either through the bailor's direct notification or through the bailee's own discovery and acceptance of bailor property it finds on its premises.

v) Delivery of Possession to a Bailee Requires the Bailee's Knowledge That an Act of Delivery Has Occurred to Enable It to Act as Bailee of a Bailor's Goods

The argument that there can be no delivery of possession without knowledge by the purported bailee of an act of delivery finds support in *Withers, Evans Ltd (Receiver-Manager and Trustee of) v Sterling Circuits Inc.*[157] There, a lessee who was leasing premises from the defendant lessor was winding up its business, and its trustee in bankruptcy (the plaintiff) negotiated a surrender of its lease and the assignment of its subleases to the defendant lessor. The lessee had a quantity of chattels of significant value on the premises, which it was in the process of selling (but had not yet sold). It was agreed by the parties that these could be left on the defendant lessor's premises and that the lessee would be given a reasonable time to remove them, allowing the plaintiff's trustee the needed time to put all the necessary agreements into place. A representative of the prospective third-party purchaser of the lessee's goods attended at

---

unclear, negligence was inferred against the defendant (bailee) Shaw, pursuant to the doctrine of *res ipsa loquitur*: see paras 3–5.

157 [1988] BCJ No 57 (SC).

the defendant lessor's premises and moved all the lessee's chattels to the main stockroom in the premises even though a sale of the goods to them had not been completed. The agent also purchased a padlock and hasp, which he installed on one of the three doors leading into the stockroom to secure it (the other two rooms were barricaded in by boxes and did not require the same treatment). The lessee was later advised of the steps taken by the third-party agent and approved of them. The defendant lessor *was not advised or aware* that the lessee's items had been relocated to a locked room (i.e., the main stockroom) on its premises by the prospective purchaser of the goods. A new lessee (defendant no. 2) later entered the premises of the defendant lessor to assess their appropriateness, and to take certain measurements for modification drawings, and forced open the door to the locked room where the lessee's property was located. The door to the stockroom was not resecured by defendant no. 2. Instead, it was left unlocked, with the hasp and lock ripped out and hanging on the door frame. As a result of further negotiations regarding the sale of the chattels, the prospective purchaser's agent re-attended the lessor's premises to check on the goods and discovered that the lock and hasp to the storage room had been torn out and that the lessee's chattels that he had relocated there the previous month were missing.[158]

There was some suggestion in the evidence heard at trial that defendant no. 2 had advised the defendant lessor of its discovery of the lessee's property on the day it attended the defendant lessor's property, and that the defendant lessor had advised defendant no. 2 that the chattels would be removed within a week. This evidence was rejected out of hand by Trainor J of the British Columbia Supreme Court. Indeed, Trainor J found that the defendant lessor *did not* become aware of the lessee's chattels having been placed in a locked room on its premises, of the steps that had been taken to segregate them, or of their specific location until after they went missing.[159]

This lack of knowledge on the part of the defendant lessor proved dispositive since *no act of delivery* could be found in its absence, and no bailment between the lessee and the defendant lessor could be found either. The defendant lessor was not in the accustomed position of bailee and could not explain what had happened to the lessee's goods in the absence of this

158 *Ibid* at paras 1–8 [paragraph numbers assigned by author].
159 *Ibid* at paras 12–13.

information. Thus, Trainor J found that the defendant lessor had merely granted the lessee a licence for its goods to remain on the premises for a reasonable time, permitting the plaintiff trustee to enter into the necessary agreements involving the surrender and assignments of the lessee's leases and the sale of its chattels. In the result, the plaintiff trustee was unable to fix liability against the defendant lessor pursuant to the law of bailment.[160]

As this case demonstrates, a bailor will not be able to show a transfer of possession to a bailee by constructive possession where the bailee has no knowledge of the act of delivery and is not in a position to ensure the safekeeping of the bailor's goods. While a physical, manual delivery of the goods to the bailee is not required, a bailee must have sufficient knowledge of the steps that have been taken to segregate the goods within its premises, as well as their location within its premises, in order for a bailment to be found.

vi) Transfer of Exclusive Possession Required

In order for a bailee to exercise access to or control over the bailor's goods in the required way for a bailment to be formed, there must be a transfer of *exclusive* possession of the goods to the bailee, for a certain finite period of time. A lack of exclusive possession by the bailee will point away from a bailment toward a licence relationship.

In *Gropler v Bednesti Lake Resort Ltd*,[161] the plaintiff operated her video rental business out of the defendant's store, under the defendant's goods and services tax number and business licence. The defendant provided space for the videos to be displayed and for the plaintiff's related equipment to be stored, in exchange for a fee (a percentage of the rentals). The defendant's employees were responsible for renting videos and collecting the rent payments. The plaintiff was an employee of the defendant company and assisted directly in conducting the video rental operation.[162] As

160 *Ibid* at paras 12–17. The defendant lessor *had not* been negligent in permitting defendant number 2 to enter and inspect its premises, notwithstanding its general awareness of the lessee's goods on its premises. Defendant number 2, however, was guilty of negligence for leaving the door to the storage room containing the lessee's goods insecure, with the lock and hasp torn off the door, which Trainor J found to be causally connected to the theft of the plaintiff's chattels that later occurred. In these circumstances, the defence of *novus actus interveniens* was unavailable to defendant number 2: see paras 16–21.

161 Above note 25.

162 *Ibid* at paras 2–9.

a result of such participation, the court surmised that the plaintiff had not relinquished exclusive possession of her property to the defendant, and it refused to find a bailment. In the court's view, the joint business relationship, combined with its manner of operation, prevented the formation of a bailment and was more akin to a licensee-licensor situation. In the result, there was no duty on the defendant to safeguard the plaintiff's property.[163]

In *Badgley v Country Storage*,[164] the parties signed a lease giving the plaintiffs exclusive use of a storage unit within which many of the plaintiffs' personal belongings and items were stored. In the lease, it was stated that the defendant did not have any responsibility to keep the goods stored in its rental units safe, and it was recommended that the tenants obtain insurance, which they did not do. While the defendant retained some ability to access the unit for repair or inspection, this was not enough to give it exclusive possession of the property for the purposes of creating a bailment, since it did not give it control of the tenants' rental units. Thus, the defendant was not liable in bailment for the damage caused to the plaintiff's property by rodents due to the poor conditions of the storage unit and facility.[165] Nor was the defendant liable as landlord, since the premises were commercial ones (to which the *Residential Tenancies Act* did not apply),[166] and the defendant had not assumed a duty of safekeeping over the goods pursuant to the lease. The court in this case was correct in finding that there is no "general overriding obligation" on a defendant landlord in such circumstances to keep a tenant's belongings reasonably safe. Such a duty must either be traced to a bailment or the tenancy agreement between the parties, or to some other head of law (such as that applicable to storers and warehousers), and will not arise upon the mere granting of a lease.

The mere fact that the bailor retains some ability to gain control over the subject property during the bailment may not defeat the bailment based on the need for exclusive possession, although it will always be a question of degree and all the circumstances will need to be considered.

---

163 *Ibid* at paras 25–27. A joint business venture or relationship is not always antithetical to the formation of a bailment, however. See, for example, *Lifestyles Kitchens & Bath, a division of GVBS Inc v Danbury Sales Inc*, [1999] OJ No 3097 (SCJ) [*Lifestyles*], discussed in Chapter 2, Section E(2).

164 [2008] NBJ No 221 (QB).

165 *Ibid* at paras 1–14.

166 *Ibid* at para 22.

In *Letourneau*,[167] the plaintiffs' (bailors) retention of a key with which they could retake possession of their trailer at any time after it was dropped off did not defeat the bailment, even though the plaintiffs never truly gave up exclusive control to the defendant. It is important to note that the plaintiffs in that case never exercised any control over their property constructively delivered to the defendant and had secreted a key to the padlock of the hitch of their trailer for the defendant's use, as they had been instructed to do by the defendant before they made the delivery. Possession and safekeeping of the trailer needed to be transferred to the defendant in order for the ancillary purpose of the bailment—namely, some repairs to be made to the trailer. In other words, the retention of the key by the plaintiffs did not prove to be fatal to their bailment claim. However, in *Lessor*,[168] a completely unfettered ability by the plaintiff to access his vehicle from the parking garage it was stored in, without the knowledge or consent of the defendant, prevented the creation of a bailment, despite a single representation by the defendant that the vehicle would be safe there. The plaintiff was thus left without a remedy for the damage caused to his vehicle while in the defendant's storage.

vii) Retention of Keys by an Alleged Bailee

Much ink has been spilled by courts, especially in the parking garage context, in assessing whether the retention of keys to a chattel by an alleged bailee should result in the creation of a bailment by access and control. This is a reflection of the fact that, where a defendant is given keys to property by an owner, it is clearly given the means of access and control over the property surrendered. With this obviously comes the risk that the property deposited may be lost, damaged, or stolen during the course of the storage, whether through negligence or inadvertence, or as a result of the party with custody of the property believing it is a licensor and exercising no duty of safekeeping in relation to the property. At the same time, the owner is very often denied access or control to its own property that it has deposited with the defendant. It relies on the bailee to regain possession of its property; indeed, a bailee is duty-bound to redeliver goods to the bailor in their original or an altered form, as the case may be. Undeniably, the owner of the property in these circumstances reposes

167 Above note 127 at paras 21–42.
168 Above note 102.

much trust in the storer of the property, and (often) expects that its property, and the keys belonging thereto, will be safeguarded and protected in a manner that prevents their theft or damage, irrespective of what a parking ticket or contract might or might not say, or what the circumstances might or might not be.

a. Canadian and American Positions

The law, as it has developed in Canada, has not been as hospitable as the law in the United States to plaintiffs who find themselves in the unfortunate position of having their vehicle stolen after depositing keys with a parking garage operator. Unlike American law, Canadian law does not embrace the presumptive rule that retention of keys over the subject property by a party in the position of bailee automatically makes that party a bailee of that property.[169] Instead, the law urges courts to look at all the circumstances before coming to such an effectual legal conclusion. That said, there is no question that retention of keys (or an absence thereof) by an alleged bailee is an important consideration that should never be ignored. Very often, where keys are surrendered to a parking garage operator *at its request*, a bailment will be found.[170] Such a legal conclusion would seem unavoidable where the keys delivered to the parking attendant are used by it to exercise control over the subject property, which is connected to an aspect of the duty of safekeeping that is assumed by the bailee upon the commencement of a bailment. While delivery of keys to a parking attendant at the attendant's request is the strongest evidence of possession in parking lot cases, it is not indispensable.

b. *Palmer*: Does a Parking Attendant's Gratuitous Offer to Park a Bailor's Vehicle for Him, as Agent, Create Nothing More than a Licence?

In *Palmer*,[171] the Court of Appeal for Ontario refused to find a bailment in circumstances where the plaintiff had surrendered his automobile's keys to the defendant parking garage so that his vehicle could be parked for him. The court pointed out that the parking lot attendant had received the keys in exceptional circumstances and merely as agent of the plaintiff, for his

169 *Kieller*, above note 40 at para 46; *JPM Express*, above note 26 at para 21; *Palmer*, above note 8 at para 6.

170 See, for example, *Heffron*, above note 18; *Brown*, above note 91; *Smith*, above note 61; *Appleton*, above note 61. But *contra*: see *Bata*, above note 15; *Palmer*, above note 8.

171 Above note 8.

greater convenience. In rejecting a bailment, the court considered the history of the legal relationship between the parties. In the past, the plaintiff had always parked his own car on the parking lot without charge or any direction from the attendants on the lot, but on the day in question the lot had been hit by a heavy snowstorm shortly before his arrival. The snow had not yet been removed, and the lot was heavily congested as a result. In fact, there were several vehicles in line ahead of the plaintiff's car, and there was no parking spot immediately available to him. As a consequence, the plaintiff was approached by a parking attendant, who explained the difficulty and instructed him that, if he would agree to leave his car with the attendant, the attendant would park it for him. The plaintiff accepted the attendant's gratuitous offer without qualification, receiving no ticket or voucher in return for the depositing of his automobile. There was no discussion about the keys at that time, although the plaintiff admitted that it was implied that, if he accepted the offer, he would have to leave the keys in his vehicle so that the parking attendant could park it for him (which is what he did). No charge was made for the additional service provided by the defendant on this occasion or for the parking spot (consistent with the ordinary practices of the parking garage).[172]

The parking lot in the case was maintained by the defendant landlord in conjunction with an office building, as a convenience to clients of the tenants of the building. Upon surrendering his vehicle, the plaintiff proceeded to accompany his wife to an appointment she had made with a doctor who occupied a suite in the office building. Prior to this occasion, the plaintiff had never had difficulty parking his own vehicle in a vacant parking spot, and locking his own doors, as there had always been ample parking spaces available to him on the lot. Indeed, he had never had any previous dealings with the parking attendants of the lot and had never surrendered his keys (or any control or access over his vehicle) to the parking garage operator. In short, all previous visits had resulted in the creation of licenses and nothing more.[173]

Unfortunately, on this occasion, when the plaintiff returned to retrieve his car from the garage, expecting to find his keys in the vehicle (in a concealed position), he discovered that his vehicle was missing. Justice Schroeder of the Court of Appeal for Ontario refused to find that

172 *Ibid* at para 6.
173 *Ibid* at paras 6 and 9.

a transfer of possession had occurred, concluding that a bailment had not been created in the circumstances. Justice Schroeder, in his reasons, stated that the attendant's act of parking the plaintiff's vehicle for him was a wholly gratuitous act for the benefit of the plaintiff, and that the attendant had performed this service as agent of the plaintiff in exceptional circumstances. Thus, the parking garage was nothing more than licensor and bore no legal responsibility for the loss of the plaintiff's automobile since it owed no duty of safekeeping whatsoever to the plaintiff under a bailment.[174]

If one focuses on access and control, there is no question that the plaintiff surrendered these, at least in a physical and factual sense, to the defendant parking garage. It is true that the plaintiff did not have to surrender his vehicle, along with its keys, to the attendant. He could have waited and parked the car himself after the congestion in the parking lot had cleared, and then taken the keys away as he always had. Or he could have parked his car at another lot that would not have required him to leave his keys as a condition of the parking. Had the plaintiff chosen either of these two options, legal and factual possession would have remained in him throughout, and the question of a bailment would never have arisen. However, he chose neither, because neither were practical or convenient. Instead, he accepted the gratuitous offer of the attendant to park his car for him so that he could accompany his wife to her medical appointment without any further delay.

Aspects of the court's decision in *Palmer*, analytically, are hard to square with some of bailment law's starting principles. Gratuitous acts can still make one a bailee. And while a "gratuitous agency" does not create a contract,[175] a bailment can exist independent of a contract.

Indeed, many circumstances in *Palmer* favoured the finding of a bailment (yet none was found):[176]

---

174 *Ibid.* The court also underscored the lack of a system for giving a car or a parking ticket to the patrons using the parking lot, which it states should have conveyed to the plaintiff an absence of a system for the supervision of the cars parked on the lot, because no person was required to surrender a ticket or produce any form of identification when removing a car therefrom: *ibid* at para 6. There were also the terms of the parties' agreement, confirmed in signage in the parking garage, indicating that the relationship between them was that of a licence not a bailment: *ibid.* at para 4.

175 *Davis v 850015 Alberta Ltd*, [2003] AJ No 428 at para 16 (Prov Ct).

176 See Spence J's summary of facts, as adopted by the appeal court in its reasons for judgment: *Palmer*, above note 8.

1) the parking garage's provision of parking attendants;
2) the attendant's exercises of access and control over the plaintiff's property, in parking the plaintiff's vehicle for him;
3) the parking attendant's requirement, and presumably practice, that the plaintiff leave his keys inside his automobile as a condition of immediate parking due to the congestion in the lot caused by the heavy snowfall, which made no parking spot immediately available to him (and a later parking of his vehicle necessary);
4) the parking attendants' practice of requiring automobile owners to leave their keys inside their vehicles if they parked in an area in which there were three lines of cars, so that their cars could be moved as necessary to allow other blocked cars to leave the lot (which accounted for 20 percent of the users of the lot);
5) the parking attendants' practice of relocating cars parked in inside lines to avoid congestion on the lot, to permit for the greater convenience and profit of the defendant;
6) the parking attendants' practice of parking vehicles for disabled persons; and
7) the parking attendants' practice, before going off duty, of placing keys found in the ignition in automobiles, or in exposed positions, into concealed positions, to prevent theft.

c. Points of Distinction

All the above said, the case is still distinguishable from many other cases where retention of keys by a parking garage supported the finding of a bailment on several possible bases.[177] First, the parking garage in *Palmer* did not ordinarily *require* the plaintiff to give over his keys to park his car in the lot, unless he parked in an area in which there were three lines of cars (which, evidently, he never did). The plaintiff was asked to do so on this occasion only because of the congestion in the lot due to the heavy snowfall on that particular occasion. Second, based on the history of the relationship between the parties, and the practices of the parking garage, the plaintiff had never in the past received anything more than a licence to park from the defendant, and therefore could not have reasonably expected the defendant garage to have accepted such an onerous duty on this particular occasion. Third, there was no ticketing system to safeguard

177 *Ibid.*

against theft of vehicles. The significance of this fact was brought home by Schroeder JA in the appeal court's reasons for judgment, as follows:

> The fact that there was no system of giving a card or parking ticket to the persons using this parking lot has vital significance and should have suggested to the plaintiff the absence of any arrangement for the supervision or control over the cars left on the lot, since no person was required to surrender a ticket or produce any other form of identification when removing his car.[178]

Fourth, there was no charge for parking the plaintiff's vehicle by the defendant in the course of a parking business. It was a gratuitous service provided to the plaintiff for his greater convenience by an agent of the plaintiff, rather than by an employee of the defendant.[179] Fifth, no systems were in place to keep the plaintiff's vehicle under strict surveillance while he was away from it (although, as noted, the attendants did engage in the practice of finding and repositioning keys found in exposed positions within parked vehicles, as a protection against theft). Sixth, the vehicle *had not* been parked for the greater convenience of the defendant, but instead for the plaintiff's own convenience.[180]

Whether these features, or some combination thereof, should be enough to prevent the formation of a bailment will be explored below in the context of other relevant cases that touch upon the same issues as were before the Court of Appeal for Ontario in *Palmer*.

d. Treatment of Parking Attendants' Request for Keys from Patrons as a Condition of Parking and Other Relevant Considerations: A Consideration of the Other Caselaw

In *Heffron*, the Court of Appeal for Ontario enumerates a host of factors to be considered in distinguishing between a licence and a bailment in the parking lot context,[181] including whether "the owner of the car delivered the keys and therefore the control over the movement of his automobile to the attendant at the attendant's request."[182] In *Heffron*, the

178 *Palmer*, above note 8 at para 6.
179 See *contra*, *Gray*, above note 71 at para 8.
180 See *contra*, *Appleton*, above note 61.
181 *Heffron*, above note 18 at para 13.
182 Whether this can be extended to a situation where a demand for keys by a parking attendant is made as a result of congestion that may build up in a parking lot, or in other unusual circumstances, and not as a matter of ordinary practice, is a contentious

plaintiff, in order to park his car, had been required to leave the keys in his automobile at the specific behest of the parking garage's attendant, in accordance with the ordinary practices of the lot. Under the policy of the defendant garage, if the vehicle was still on the lot at midnight (at closing time when the parking attendants left the lot), the keys were to be removed from the vehicle and placed in the custody of an attendant at the parking garage across the street, also operated by the defendant. A message was to be placed on the windshield of the vehicle left behind advising the patron of same. Based on the evidence at trial, it was unclear whether these practices were actually followed on this particular occasion with respect to the plaintiff's vehicle. Upon returning to the lot after it had closed, the plaintiff could not locate his vehicle or his keys.[183] The vehicle was later discovered abandoned in a damaged condition. The court found a bailment, albeit in more compelling circumstances than those presented in *Palmer*.[184]

That case is distinguishable from *Heffron* on no less than three grounds. First, the plaintiff in *Heffron* was *required* to surrender his keys in order to park his car on the lot, so that it could be moved around to permit for the optimum utilization of the lot, for the greater profit and convenience of the parking operator. This was an ordinary practice of the parking garage, unlike in *Palmer*, where such requirement was necessitated by an exceptional circumstance, namely the congestion present in the lot due to the heavy snowfall on the day in question. Second, there were posted closing hours for the parking garage in *Heffron*: the lot closed at midnight.[185] Patrons could not come and go as they pleased, parking and removing their vehicles at their leisure twenty-four hours a day, as would be the case in many licence relationships, since the parking garage would be locked down between certain hours. Third, there was a ticket system in place to protect against theft in *Heffron*, supporting the fact that the garage had accepted a duty of safekeeping over the plaintiff's vehicle; no such system existed in *Palmer*.[186]

---

issue, given the Court of Appeal for Ontario's decision in *Palmer*, above note 8, and discussed throughout this section.

183 *Heffron*, above note 18 at paras 1–6. The keys were also not found by the plaintiff at the lot across the street: see para 5.

184 *Ibid* at para 14.

185 *Ibid* at para 23.

186 The cases are also probably distinguishable in terms of each parking garage's policy on the disposition to be made of the keys received from an automobile owner. In

Curiously, in *Bata*,[187] the Court of Appeal for Ontario refused to find a bailment even though the plaintiff had been *required*, as a matter of the parking garage's ordinary practice, to surrender his keys to his automobile to the parking attendant in order to park his vehicle on the lot. As stated previously, the court's focus on the parking contract to the virtual exclusion of all else was misplaced, and appears to have caused it to ignore this fact, which was highly suggestive of a bailment.[188] It is submitted that the parking contract, and the label that it may attribute to any given relationship, must not be allowed to overtake the analysis of whether the defendant had control of the subject property at the material times to constitute it as a bailee rather than as a licensee. This analysis must, of necessity, include consideration of whether the vehicle owner was required to surrender the keys to the defendant parking lot as a condition of the parking.[189]

e. Bailors Sometimes Surrendering Keys to Bailees for Parking, Sometimes Not

In *Pickin*,[190] the plaintiff vehicle owners sometimes parked their own vehicles; at other times a defendant parking attendant parked them. One of the plaintiffs in the case would always give his ignition key to the attendant upon parking; each of the other plaintiffs, save for one who never surrendered his keys and always locked his own car, left their keys in the ignition switch of their respective vehicles to allow their vehicles to be relocated as necessary.[191] A bailment, applicable to all plaintiffs, was found by the Ontario Court of Appeal for Ontario in this pre-*Palmer* and *Heffron* case with little difficulty,[192] even though the surrender of keys

---

Palmer, before parking attendants went off duty, they would place the keys they found in ignition locks, or in exposed positions within automobiles, into concealed positions to protect against theft. In *Heffron*, the procedures to protect against theft were more extensive and protective: upon the parking lot closing, the parking attendants would retrieve the keys from the automobiles that remained in the lot and would place them for safekeeping in the custody of a parking attendant at a lot across the street, which was also operated by the defendant parking garage.

187 Above note 15.

188 There were other facts in the case that were also suggestive of a bailment, such as the presence of a ticketing system, but they also appear to have been ignored by the court in favour of the parking contract.

189 *Trivett*, above note 33 at para 6.

190 Above note 61.

191 *Ibid* at para 13.

192 *Ibid* at para 24.

to the parking garage was not a *strict* requirement of the garage, given the conduct of the single plaintiff who never surrendered his keys to the parking operator and always parked his own vehicle. However, given the degree of control exercised by the parking attendants over most of the plaintiffs' vehicles and the other factors suggestive of the assumption of a duty of safekeeping by the parking operator, including established closing hours for the lot, the court's finding of a bailment was the correct one to be made in the circumstances.

f. Parking as a Gratuitous Act, Not Arising in the Usual Course of Things: Further Consideration of *Palmer*

In *Alberta U Drive*,[193] while no mention is made of *Palmer* by the court, there is a useful parallel to be drawn between the two cases. In *Alberta U Drive*, the defendant would accept and park cars on behalf of the plaintiff in exceptional circumstances—namely, only when the plaintiff's parking attendant was off duty. A vehicle of the plaintiff's was stolen by an employee of the defendant after the defendant had received the vehicle, and the keys belonging thereto, on the plaintiff's behalf. The court, per Riley J, refused to find a bailment, despite the rogue employee's exercises of control and access over the vehicle. The benefits of the parking and any other ancillary services, as in *Palmer*, were provided gratuitously, and the acts of access and control did not arise out of the usual course of things. The defendant accepted delivery of keys and vehicles only when the plaintiff's parking attendant was off duty, and had not assumed a general duty of safekeeping with respect to the plaintiff's vehicles.

In *Gray*,[194] the court strained to distinguish *Palmer* on facts that in many respects resemble those of that case. The owner of the vehicle had arrived at the parking garage to a situation of congestion and accepted the parking attendant's offer to later park his vehicle for him, which the attendant later did. The attendant moved the vehicle once more, later, to enable another vehicle to leave the lot, reparking the vehicle thereafter. On this occasion, the owner did not receive a ticket from the parking operator and did not pay for the parking (though in the past he always had and was aware that the parking operator used a ticketing system). The court stated that a bailment for consideration existed, given the history

---

193 Above note 10.

194 Above note 71.

of the relationship between the parties, which always had created a bailment on previous occasions.[195] The parking garage had not been provided "for the convenience of customers of, and incidental to, another business," distinguishing the case from *Palmer*. The defendant was operating a parking lot as a business for profit as a general matter, and used a ticketing system for the release of vehicles from the lot, to the knowledge of the plaintiff. The court accordingly surmised that the act of the attendant in parking the plaintiff's vehicle was not gratuitous. It was a product of the business, and the attendant could not be considered to be an agent of the patron.[196] In the result, the defendant was found responsible for the damage to the plaintiff's car by the theft of the vehicle from the lot by a third party occasioned by the defendant's leaving of the automobile keys in the ignition switch of the vehicle with the doors unlocked, facing the rear entrance to the parking lot, and in the absence of an enforceable exemption clause.

The court's stated reasons for distinguishing the case from *Palmer* are somewhat artificial and hard to accept. The plaintiff had never received this particular service — a parking attendant taking custody of his car upon entry to the lot and parking his vehicle for him after congestion on the lot cleared — before from the so-called business, and he did not pay for it. The reason he did not receive a ticket and pay for the parking, as he usually did, was because he was not in the usual circumstance. So why could it not be treated as a circumstance analogous to that arising in *Palmer*, meriting the finding of a licence? Further, without a ticket indicating the date and time of entry of his car onto the lot, the plaintiff's charge could not be determined by the cashier for the purpose of check out. That is why he could not, and did not, pay. If no contract to pay was formed, then the acts of the attendant were truly gratuitous and *Gray* is distinguishable from *Palmer* only on the basis that the defendant operator ordinarily used a ticketing system for the parking of cars (though

---

195 While the courts in both *Palmer* and *Gray* appear to place much importance on the past legal relationships entered into between the parties in determining whether a given relationship amounts to a bailment or licence, this factor should not be over-emphasized. Past relationships, or intentions, while certainly relevant, are not always determinative of future arrangements entered into between the same parties. Instead, the degree of control of the subject property by the alleged bailee and the circumstances of the relationship between the parties, at the time of the loss of the bailor's property, must always be the focus of the analysis.

196 *Gray*, above note 71 at paras 1–8.

not on the occasion in question) as a precaution against theft, whereas in *Palmer* the operator did not.[197]

g. Cases Distinguishing *Palmer* by Focusing on *Sine Qua Non* of a Bailment: Control of the Subject Property

In *Dixon*,[198] the court avoids the difficulties plaguing the courts in *Palmer* and *Gray* by focusing on the *sine qua non* of bailment—that is, control of the subject property by the alleged bailee (which the court assumes carries with it a duty of safekeeping). In that case, a car owner was instructed by a parking attendant to leave his keys in the ignition of his vehicle if he wished to double-park, which is what he did (as no single parking space was available to him because the lot was full), to allow the parking operator to relocate his car for the greater profit and convenience of the parking lot operator. The plaintiff's vehicle was stolen.[199]

The court viewed the usual parking contract (which had provided for a licence) as having been transformed into a bailment contract by the plaintiff's act of surrendering possession of his keys to the attendant, at the attendant's request. The vehicle owner had relinquished control over his vehicle to the parking operator; he was no longer free to lock his vehicle or "even chain it to a post if he saw fit," as he would be if he had received a licence to park. The defendant was therefore liable, as bailee, for the theft of the vehicle.[200]

In *Schnelle v City Parking Canada Ltd*,[201] the plaintiff drove into the defendant's lot but was unable to park his own vehicle, lock it up, and take his keys to his vehicle away with himself, as he usually did under his monthly parking contract with the defendant. The language in the contract described the relationship between the parties as one of licence, rather than bailment. On the day in question, the plaintiff arrived to a situation of congestion, with no parking space immediately available to

---

197 *Ibid* at para 8. That said, the parking operator in the case had exercised control and access over the vehicle at least twice, and certainly that was a more substantial basis to find a bailment than was trying to make hair-splitting distinctions from the *Palmer* case.

198 Above note 16.

199 *Ibid* at paras 1–8.

200 *Ibid* at paras 17–19. Based on this analysis of control, the parking garage in *Palmer* would have been a gratuitous bailee rather than a licensee and likely liable for the loss of the plaintiff's vehicle in that case.

201 [1971] AJ No 100 (Dist Ct).

him, so the parking operator asked him to leave his car in the driveway of its facilities with its keys inside, so that it could later be parked for him. (This was in accordance with the parking operator's ordinary practice.) The plaintiff acceded to the request. After the car was parked in due course, the defendant employee left the key in the ignition lock and the car was stolen.[202]

Justice Haddad of the Alberta District Court, as the court did in *Dixon*, focused on the issue of control of the vehicle in deciding whether the parties' relationship gave rise to a bailment or licence, which control he found had been surrendered by the plaintiff to the defendant: "[I]t is my view that the defendant, by taking the plaintiff's vehicle into its possession and custody and by giving an undertaking to park the same, constituted itself a bailee of the vehicle."[203]

While no reference is made to the *Palmer* decision in this lower court Alberta decision, the fact that the exercises of access and control over the plaintiff's vehicle were not a usual occurrence and that the plaintiff accepted the parking operator's gratuitous offer to park his vehicle for him when a space became available (as there was only "lock-up" space available) were not bars to the finding of a bailment in this case. Nor, for that matter, was the contract, which labelled the parties' relationship one of licence rather than bailment. The transfer of a set of ignition keys to the parking operator upon leaving the vehicle was dispositive of the matter and indicated that possession had been passed and that a bailment had been created.

h. Conclusion: Distinguishing Bailments from Licences in the Parking Context Based on Treatment of the Bailor's Vehicle Keys

The foregoing discussion demonstrates the difficulty courts have encountered in distinguishing between licences and bailments in the parking context. It is submitted that situations of congestion, or the like, or other exceptional circumstances, which result in a vehicle owner being *required* by a parking garage to surrender the vehicle's keys (so that the car can later be parked or relocated for the optimum utilization of the lot) still result in control over the subject property being surrendered to the parking

202 *Ibid* at para 10.
203 *Ibid* at para 16.

garage. A surrender of control by the vehicle owner will usually mean that a bailment has arisen and that a duty of safekeeping has been assumed by the parking operator, although such an effectual legal conclusion can be made only after all relevant circumstances have been considered.

If *Palmer* is distinguishable from the other parking cases discussed, where a bailment was found, it should not be because the vehicle owner in that case was not *ordinarily required* to surrender his keys as a condition of his parking or because he had a choice to wait and park his own vehicle or to go elsewhere if he did not wish to surrender his keys to the parking attendant. These reasons are quite artificial and do not withstand scrutiny. Vehicle owners always have a choice to go elsewhere, or to wait for a situation of congestion to clear, if they do not wish to accept an offer being advanced by a parking lot operator requiring them to surrender their keys. The past intentions of the parties, while certainly relevant, should not be allowed to overtake or obscure the analysis of the present circumstances and whether they indicate that the bailor has transferred possession of its goods to the bailee. Distinguishing the case based on convenience or consideration is equally problematic, for bailments have been established in spite of convenience or consideration. Given the clear exercises of access and control by the parking attendant in *Palmer* over the plaintiff's vehicle, it is submitted that, despite the case having some distinguishing features from other parking cases in similar circumstances where a bailment was found, a bailment should have been found in the case and that the case was wrongly decided. The agency arguments, while a creative way to take away the exercises of control from the defendant (bailee) in the case and retain them in the plaintiff, are quite weak and artificial. The supposed agent was an employee of a landlord of the office building at all material times. He was ultimately assisting to park a vehicle so that an occupant of that vehicle — namely, the wife of the plaintiff — could attend a doctor's appointment in the office building operated by the landlord. While the parking garage was operated as a convenience for visitors of the tenants of the office building at no cost to them, it was presumably run for those tenants' greater profit and convenience, whose rents surely included charges for the running and operating of the lot. In these circumstances, it seems disingenuous to say that the attendant was an agent of the plaintiff. In the result, the defendant in *Palmer* should have been found a bailee and should have been required to negative negligence in order to exonerate itself from liability.

c) Particular Purpose of Bailment Requires Possession to Be Transferred

In *Ashby*,[204] Romer LJ stated the following with respect to the car that had been left by the plaintiff with the car park in that case:

> It is true that, if the car had been left there for any particular purpose that required that the defendant should have possession of the car, a delivery would rightly be inferred, and, if the car had been left at the car park for the purpose of being sold or by way of pledge or for the purposes of being driven away to some other place or indeed for the purposes of safe custody, delivery of the car, although not actually made, would readily be inferred.

In other words, if the car in *Ashby* had been left in the lot for a purpose other than "parking" that required the bailee to have possession, then a bailment would readily have been inferred because control would have to be obtained to carry out this other purpose. These ancillary purposes can be various and include consignments, sales, repairs, deliveries to third parties, and storage arrangements. In *Letourneau*,[205] possession was necessarily incidental to the service contract, because the defendant repair shop had to take possession of the trailer in order to perform the needed repairs. It was not a contract for the mere parking of a vehicle; the work to be done required possession to be passed from the plaintiffs (bailors) to defendant (though, in that case, the repairs never transpired because the trailer was appropriated by some unknown third party before the bailee commenced its work, but notably after possession had been passed, constructively, from bailor to bailee, making the bailee responsible for the loss).

d) Relevant Representations Made by Bailees and Bailors as to the Duty of Safekeeping of the Goods

Verbal representations as to safekeeping made by a bailee are supportive of a bailment, but only where they are unambiguous, are made by the bailee or an authorized agent thereof, and become a term of the contract between bailor and bailee. The bailee must unequivocally accept the undertaking of safekeeping in order for the representation to contribute to the finding of a bailment. Where the undertaking is accompanied

---

204 Above note 23, as cited in *British Motor*, above note 74 at para 25.
205 Above note 127.

by security and precautionary measures that serve to give effect to the undertaking, then the imposition of a duty of safekeeping on the bailee, and the finding of a bailment, is unavoidable.[206] In certain circumstances where a bailor retains unfettered access to its property, bailee representations as to safekeeping may be ineffectual to overcome circumstances that clearly indicate the creation of a licence between the parties and nothing more. Consideration must also be given to bailor statements or representations to a bailee, which can indicate that a duty of safekeeping no longer applies to the goods, if it ever did.

i) Bailee Representations as to Safekeeping Can Contribute to Finding of a Bailment

In *Robertson*,[207] a defendant manager of the defendant co-operative's false representations to the plaintiff (bailor) hoarder, that her personal items being moved from her apartment to its two storage rooms[208] would be safe and secure there and that she need not obtain additional insurance, and that only two people had keys to access the storage room where most of her goods were being housed—namely, the defendant manager who had made the representations to the plaintiff, and the hydro man—contributed to showing that the defendant managers and defendant co-operative were assuming a duty of safekeeping over the plaintiff's goods such that a bailment between the parties was found. The representations took on greater significance than they might otherwise have in the case because of the trial judge's finding that the plaintiff was unaware of the break-ins into the storage area from which her goods ultimately vanished, which had occurred during the time period when her goods were being relocated there. Indeed, the plaintiff did not learn of the break-ins until several months later, when she received correspondence from the co-operative asking her to remove all her personal items from the storage areas as part of the conversion of the premises from a co-operative to a strata corporation, otherwise they would be removed immediately and sold to cover the co-operative's removal costs. She then communicated with a defendant manager who told her that there had been a break-in and flood. At that

206 See, for example, *British Motor*, above note 74.
207 Above note 9.
208 The items were required to be moved to allow for her apartment to be measured for a conversion of the apartment building into a strata corporation that was then occurring, and to address the clear fire hazard that they presented: *ibid* at paras 9–10.

time, the plaintiff first discovered that some of her goods were missing from the storage areas.[209]

A bailment, rather than a licence, was found to apply to the plaintiff items in the storage areas, even though the plaintiff maintained the ability at all times to retake possession of her goods from these areas by coming and asking the defendant landlord for a key. Indeed, the plaintiff took such action when she discovered that some of her goods were missing when one of the defendant managers advised her that there had been a break-in and flood in the storage area housing most of her goods. That said, given the clear control over the goods exercised by the defendant bailee in moving the plaintiff tenant's goods (despite her reluctance and emotional state) from her apartment into the co-operative's two storage areas, and the plaintiff's inability to access her goods at any time without the defendant's co-operation, the finding of a bailment in the case is not at all surprising. In the result, the defendants were left to disprove negligence, which they could not do since the door leading into the storage area where the plaintiff's goods disappeared from could easily be breached; several master keys providing access into the area were missing; and the defendants had failed to notify the plaintiff of the two previous break-ins into the area that occurred while the defendants were still in the process of moving the plaintiff's chattels into the building's two storage areas and to suggest that perhaps she should obtain additional insurance coverage to protect her goods from loss.[210]

ii) Representations by Employees or Agents of a Bailee Must Be Made with Express or Implied Authorization of the Bailee to Be Supportive of a Bailment

In *Palmer*,[211] the plaintiff stated that a receptionist, who was an employee of certain doctors who occupied space in the office building that was adjunct to the parking lot, had communicated to him, following his parking, that his vehicle and keys would be taken into safe custody by the defendant company after the lot closed.[212] While the trial judge rejected

209 *Ibid* at paras 4–21.

210 *Ibid* at paras 57–71.

211 Above note 8.

212 Certainly, these duties would have arisen if the parking operator were found to be a bailee. That is to say, a bailee's duty of safekeeping with respect to a vehicle must extend to its keys, where possession of them is also surrendered to a parking lot operator.

this evidence, Spence J held that, even if the receptionist had made such representations — and the judge did not believe that she had — "she did so without authority." The receptionist *was not* an employee of the defendant and had not been instructed to make such representations. Her representations, therefore, could not have the effect of imposing a duty of safekeeping on the parking operator for the purposes of finding a bailment.[213] These holdings were quite properly left undisturbed on appeal.[214]

iii) A Single Verbal Representation of Safekeeping Made by a Bailee May Not Be Enough to Create a Bailment Where a Bailor Enjoys Unfettered Access to Goods

In *Lessor*,[215] one verbal representation by the defendant that the plaintiff's motor vehicle would be "safe" in his garage during the period of storage was not enough to overcome the plaintiff's unfettered access[216] to his vehicle during the course of its storage, which established a licence rather than a bailment. The plaintiff was accordingly denied damages for the injury that had been occasioned to his vehicle during the storage. As this case demonstrates, where a party has unfettered access to their property, the finding of a bailment may not be possible based on one bald representation as to safekeeping. This is because the necessary transfer of exclusive possession from bailor to bailee will not have occurred.[217]

iv) Unequivocal Bailor Instruction to a Bailee to Cease Its Duty of Safekeeping

In *DeGrace*,[218] the plaintiff's express and unequivocal instruction to the defendant repair shop that it not "touch his car" after his damaged vehicle had been delivered to it by another repair shop for repair, and a part from it delivered to the manufacturer for inspection without his knowledge or consent, was enough to terminate the existing gratuitous bailment between the parties that was in place at that point in time. The

---

213 Above note 8.

214 *Ibid.*

215 *Lessor*, above note 102.

216 In the case, the plaintiff was given a key to the garage and could enter at any time he saw fit and remove and return his car as he wished, without the knowledge or consent of the defendant: *ibid* at para 4.

217 But see, *contra*, *DJ Lowe Ltd v Roach (cob Vern's Auto Repairs)*, [1994] NSJ No 208 (SC); aff'd [1995] NSJ No 62 (CA), discussed in Chapter 3, Section D(1).

218 Above note 6.

plaintiff thereafter left his vehicle on the premises of the defendant with its express consent (having the unfettered ability to remove his vehicle at all times, and the vehicle sustained further injury and damage, becoming a total loss. Because the defendant had become a licensor following the plaintiff's communication, it bore no responsibility for the loss.[219]

v) *A Bailee's Detailed Instructions to a Bailor to Leave Property for It in a Designated Manner Can Lead to an Assumption of Duty of Safekeeping by the Bailee*

In *Letourneau*,[220] the plaintiffs were advised by the defendant (bailee) to leave their trailer locked in a designated spot in an adjacent parking of the defendant's repair facility after hours, from which the vehicle could then be picked up and repaired the following morning. The plaintiffs meticulously followed the defendant's instructions. While the defendant's representation was unaccompanied by any explicit assurance of safekeeping, it was meant to facilitate the defendant's taking of the trailer so that the needed repairs to it could be made. In these circumstances, the representation was supportive of a bailment by constructive possession, for the repairs could not be undertaken without the defendant taking possession of the trailer and ensuring its safekeeping until this purpose was fulfilled.

e) Security Services

The provision of extensive security services to safeguard bailor property is indicative of a bailment, rather than a licence, although not required in all circumstances for a bailment to come into existence.[221] That said, "some semblance of security,"[222] or the gratuitous providing of such services on occasion without more, might not be enough to establish a bailment.[223] The mere presence of security guards, where they play no role in restricting access to the subject premises on which the goods or property are stored, may also fall short, given the lack of control over the subject property that this will signify.[224] In *Ashby*, a semblance of security consisting of a ticketing system and a parking attendant was not enough for a

---

219 *Ibid* at paras 16–20.
220 Above note 127.
221 See, for example, *MacGillivray v Frizzel*, [1977] AJ No 666 (SCTD) [*MacGillivray*].
222 See *Campbell*, above note 34.
223 See *Alberta U Drive*, above note 10.
224 *Ledcor Construction Ltd v Polo Security Services Ltd*, [2002] BCJ No 294 (SC).

bailment to be found in that case. Certainly, more robust security measures such as an invisible beam around the premises where bailed goods are being stored, a barbed wire fence, security cameras, and rigorous check-in procedures will be supportive of a bailment rather than a licence. A bailee's use of watchmen to regularly monitor and secure bailor property will also be supportive of a bailment,[225] at least where the measures are observed in practice. Where extensive safeguards are part of the contract entered into between the parties, but not observed in practice, this may not be enough to create a bailment.[226] This is because a lack of such protective measures will indicate a lack of control of the owner's goods by the alleged bailee, which can be fatal to a bailment claim. It follows that the presence of such protective measures should be viewed as being supportive of a bailment even in the absence of a contractual underpinning.

Minor or temporary lapses of security are not enough to defeat a bailment. This is based on the theory that temporary lapses of duty might occur with anyone caring for their own property, no more being expected of a bailee than what an ordinary prudent owner would do.[227] Finally, the bailor need not show that the premises where the goods were stored was impenetrable at all material times in order for a bailment to be found. In *Clark and Pattison Painting Contractors Ltd v Osborne Contracting Ltd*,[228] the fact that the fence securing the bailed goods was scaleable did not prevent the court from finding a bailment.

f) Gratuitous Services

Where services by bailees are provided gratuitously, it would appear that the finding of a bailment is slightly less likely, in spite of consideration not being a strict requirement of a bailment. Certainly, the holdings in *Palmer*,[229] *Alberta U Drive*,[230] *and Fong*[231] can probably be read as being

225 See *British Motor*, above note 74.

226 See *Woodcock*, above note 86.

227 See *Pilot Insurance Co v Davis*, [1996] OJ No 2232 at para 11 (Gen Div); *Gavin v Douglas Securities Ltd*, [1958] BCJ No 12 at paras 10–12 (SC). According to the Supreme Court in the latter case, minor lapses in security are also not enough, without more, to make a bailee liable to a bailor, since a bailee is not expected to do anything more than "anyone safeguarding his own property might quite reasonably and conceivably be guilty of": see para 12.

228 [1980] BCJ No 704 at para 17 (SC).

229 Above note 8.

230 Above note 10.

231 Above note 80.

supportive of this proposition. However, as demonstrated in *Kinsella*,[232] a lack of consideration is not a bar to the finding of a bailment. Relatively speaking, little, if any, importance should be placed on this factor, since bailments can, and do, exist irrespective of consideration.

g) Bailee Provision of Insurance Against Loss

Where a bailee takes out insurance to protect against loss or damage to a bailor's goods, this will be supportive of a bailment, as it indicates that the bailee has accepted a duty of safekeeping over the bailor's goods. The insurance need not cover losses in all eventualities, although this would be more supportive of a bailment rather than less. A bailor's removal of its own insurance from its property in reasonable reliance on the bailee's provision of insurance, or promise to provide same, will also be supportive of a bailment.[233]

Where a bailor has obtained insurance for the goods that make up the subject matter of the bailment prior to the creation of the bailment, and for a purpose *unrelated to the bailment*, this should not preclude the finding of a bailment. Nor should the bailee be able to rely on such a policy to protect itself from damages arising from its own negligence. In *Provident Bank v Wells Fargo Bank Northwest*,[234] the defendant repairer of an airplane was denied the benefit of the plaintiff bailor's all-risk insurance policy with respect to the defendant's negligent loss of parts for the plane amounting to $375,000. The defendant had sought to use this insurance policy to protect against a complete set-off to its lien for storage and repair that would result if the policy were found inapplicable. The policy had been taken out prior to the formation of the bailment to protect the investments of two banks and was not intended to relieve the defendant repairer from liability for loss or damage caused by its negligence. In the result, no insurance policy was found to apply to the bailment. That being said, as this case demonstrates, that is not a bar to the finding of a bailment.

h) History of Relations Between the Parties

The history of the relationship between the parties should be considered in deciding whether they intended a bailment or a licence, but it should never overtake or obscure the main focus of the analysis, which always

232 Above note 130.

233 See *MacGillivray*, above note 221.

234 2006 CanLII 8364 (Ont CA).

needs to be on the present circumstances and whether they indicate that the bailor has parted with possession of its property in favour of the bailee — that is, whether the bailor has surrendered control over its property, indicating the voluntary assumption of a duty of safekeeping by the bailee. As indicated previously, a slight change in the current relationship between two parties, regardless of any prior history, can transform a licence into a bailment, making the history of relations between them relatively unimportant, except insofar as providing context.

2) Bailments Arising in the Parking Garage Context: Additional Considerations

Where the bailee is a parking lot, consideration should also be given to the following things:

1) the presence of a ticket system or the requirement to produce a form of identification when removing the vehicle from the lot;
2) whether the parking lot parked the motorist's car;
3) the provision of an attendant to oversee the parking lot and the extent of their role in supervising the vehicles parked therein;
4) whether the parking lot closed at any point during the period of the bailment and whether patrons were on notice that they had to remove their vehicles prior to that time; and
5) the operating habits and practices of the parking lot owner (which may or may not be known by the car owner).

a) The Presence of a Ticketing System

In *Palmer*, the Court of Appeal for Ontario, per Schroeder J, aptly states:

> The fact that there was no system of giving a card or parking ticket to the persons using this parking lot has vital significance and should have suggested to the plaintiff the absence of any arrangement for the supervision or control over the cars left on the lot, since no person was required to surrender a ticket or produce any other form of identification when removing his car.[235]

The presence of a ticketing system in a parking garage or lot will strongly support the finding of a bailment, as it will indicate an acceptance

235 Above note 8 at para 6.

of a duty of safekeeping on the part of the parking operator. A ticketing system serves as a protection against theft, since a person must surrender a ticket in order to remove a particular vehicle from a parking lot. Certainly, the lack of such a system in *Palmer* is a much stronger basis to distinguish that judicial decision from many other parking lot cases where a bailment was found. It is also worth recalling that in *Ashby* the presence of a ticketing system did not impel the court to find a bailment, given the terms of the parties' agreement, which the court found clearly negatived a bailment. (Note that the cases are readily distinguishable on the further basis that, in *Palmer*, the patron surrendered his keys to his automobile to the parking operator as a condition of the parking, while in *Ashby* he did not.)

b) The Parking of a Motorist's Vehicle by a Parking Operator

Where the parking operator takes possession of a vehicle owner's keys and parks the motorist's car in a location of its own choosing for its own greater profit and convenience, this will also suggest a bailment. In a licence situation, the licensee is usually free to park anywhere it wants and does not surrender control of its own property to the parking proprietor. In *Appleton*,[236] the defendant took charge of the plaintiff's vehicle at the entrance of its parking garage, asked the patron to leave his keys in the car, and parked the plaintiff's vehicle for him. The Court of Appeal for Ontario had no difficulty in finding a bailment in this pre-*Palmer* case: "I think it is clear that the defendants became bailees of the car. Possession of the car was delivered to and accepted by the defendants for safe custody. The defendants' agent took charge of the car at the entrance, and apparently parked it where he desired in the lot, and later another attendant, for his own convenience, moved it to another place."[237]

In light of the Court of Appeal for Ontario's decision in *Palmer*, however, this factor alone may not be dispositive of a bailment. The analysis may need to go further and consider whether the parking was for the greater convenience and profit of the bailee. Consideration might also be given as to whether the parking was provided for in exceptional circumstances — that is, not as an ordinary condition of the parking — as a favour to the bailor on a *de gratia* basis not signifying the assumption of a duty of safekeeping but merely an agency relationship.

---

236 Above note 61.

237 *Ibid* at para 9.

c) Closing Hours

Closing hours, during which vehicles are no longer retrievable (or readily retrievable) by patrons from parking premises, will signify a bailment, as licensees are generally allowed to come and go as they please or retrieve their property without restriction. Where there are closing hours and vehicle owners are put on notice to remove their property prior to closing time, a bailment should be readily inferable.[238]

d) Provision of Parking Attendants

The mere provision of parking attendants by a parking operator will not create a bailment, although, in their absence, one will be hard pressed to find a bailment in the parking context. Certainly, where the attendants exercise control and supervision over the vehicles for the purposes of safekeeping (e.g., moving vehicles into spots where they can be better monitored as a protection against theft) and control access to the parking garage, the finding of a bailment is ineluctable. Similarly, where keys are handed over to parking attendants so that vehicles can be parked or relocated for the greater convenience and profitability of the parking operator, a bailment will almost always be created.

e) The Operating Habits and Practices of the Parking Lot Operator

Where the parking lot operator has robust practices to protect a patron's vehicle against theft or harm, this will support the finding of a bailment. In *Heffron*, this standard was clearly met: the parking operator would retrieve the keys from the automobiles that remained in the lot at closing time and would place them in the custody of a parking attendant at a lot across the street, which the defendant also operated, for safekeeping of bailor property. In *Palmer* and *Ashby*, the parking operators' practices were less robust. They are probably best described as giving the vehicle owners only a "semblance of security," which practices alone, without more, will not be enough for a bailment to be found.

C. BAILMENT DISTINGUISHED FROM NEGLIGENCE

Distinguishing between bailment and negligence may be difficult in certain circumstances. Certainly, stated at its highest, a bailment may be

238 See *Heffron*, above note 18.

found to apply any time personal property is transferred voluntarily from a bailor into the exclusive possession of a bailee and is damaged or lost during that possession, regardless of the cause of the damage. There is law, however, that states that, if the goods in the possession of the bailee are damaged as a result of negligent performance of a service on those goods by the bailee, rather than through some other cause wholly unrelated to the service, that the action against the defendant must proceed in negligence and cannot proceed in bailment. This view finds support in James, wherein the learned author states:

> Where goods are delivered to a person who contracts to perform a specific service on the goods themselves and the performance of the service is, or is alleged to be, the cause of the damage to the goods, the law of bailment has no application and the action must proceed in negligence.[239]

The case relied upon by James for this statement of law is *Independent Tool & Die Ltd v DAW Steel Products Ltd*,[240] a decision of the Manitoba County Court. There, the plaintiff, a tool and die manufacturer, delivered some forty-four steel die blocks to the defendant for heat treatment for the purpose of hardening. The plaintiff advised the defendant that the work needed to be done relatively quickly, in two days, so that the dies could be delivered to one of the plaintiff's customers. The defendant agreed. During the processing, some of the die blocks cracked and were rendered completely useless. The plaintiff sued in bailment. Not surprisingly, the parties' respective expert evidence diverged considerably. The plaintiff's expert concluded that the occurrence was due to an improper heat treatment procedure having been employed by the defendant, while the defendant's expert attributed the cracking to the faulty design of the plaintiff's die blocks.[241]

Justice Ferg refused to allow the plaintiff to proceed with its action in bailment, because possession of the goods had been delivered to the defendant for a specific service to be performed on them and the damage done was alleged to have been done as a result of such service. It was not an ordinary storage, deposit, carriage, or hiring of goods resulting in damage to the goods by fire or theft triggering the application of bailment law. However, on the facts pleaded and the evidence heard, the plaintiff's

239 Andrew James, *CED* (Ont 3d), Supplement vol 2, title 13, Bailment at 38.
240 [1982] MJ No 240 (Co Ct).
241 *Ibid* at paras 1–12.

action could succeed under the law of negligence. Indeed, the learned judge relaxed the plaintiff's onus of proof in negligence, allowing the plaintiff to rely on the doctrine of *res ipsa loquitur* in the circumstances. In any case, the trial judge found that the plaintiff in the case had proven negligence against the defendant, as the judge accepted the plaintiff expert's theory of the damage as being far more credible and supported by the evidence than the defendant's (which was very speculative in nature), that the dies were cracked by the improper heating procedure applied in the defendant's plant by the defendant.[242]

It is to be observed that the allowance made by Ferg Co Ct J in the case in allowing the plaintiff to rely on *res ipsa loquitur* had the same effect as allowing the plaintiff's bailment action to proceed would have had—that is, the defendant was left with the ultimate burden of proof, to provide a reasonable explanation of what went wrong in its process and thus demonstrate that its actions were inconsistent with negligence. That was not possible, as the learned judge found the only reasonable and credible explanation for the damage to be one consistent with affirmative negligence on the part of the defendant.[243] Even though the location of the onus of proof in the case was therefore academic, it is nonetheless submitted that a plaintiff in these circumstances should not be denied the ability to proceed with an action in bailment, with the benefit of the reverse onus. The rationale for imposing the reverse onus is still present where a bailee is performing services to goods. That is to say, the bailee will be in exclusive possession and control of the goods at the time of the loss and will be the only party, as a result of that possession, who will be in a position to explain what occurred to the goods to cause the loss. So why should a bailor be denied the benefit of the reverse onus?

For this reason, it is submitted that negligence actions are better confined to situations where an injury results to a person outside of circumstances involving a transfer of possession of goods, such as where a plaintiff is injured while lawfully aboard a ship due to the apparent negligence of the barge owner or operator,[244] or where a plaintiff's building is destroyed by fire as a result of the alleged negligence of the servants of a

242 *Ibid* at paras 16–18.

243 *Ibid* at para 17.

244 See, for example, *Ferguson v Arctic Transportation Ltd*, [1998] FCJ No 634 (TD).

defendant who is leasing space in the building.[245] The fact of the matter is that, anytime goods are transferred from a bailor to a bailee and services are performed to them, a bailment can be formed, and a duty of care over the goods is likely going to be owed by the service person. That is to say, the service person must take reasonable care to protect the goods from any number of harms that could befall them, such as weather conditions, fire, and theft, or an injury that might arise as a result of it carelessly performing the service on the goods for which it was hired. Certainly, the mere fact a service is performed, or is to be performed, on the plaintiff's goods has not disqualified bailments in other contexts.[246] Indeed, such service does not appear to be inconsistent with the definition of a bailment either, which contemplates redelivery of a bailor's chattels to the bailor in either an original or an altered form, depending on the terms of the bailment. Nor is it inconsistent with the law that states that a bailee acquires legal possession of goods any time it takes those goods for certain, specific purposes such as repair work, which purposes necessarily require the bailee to assume a duty of safekeeping over the goods.

D. BAILMENT DISTINGUISHED FROM A GUARANTEE

A bailee at law is not an insurer and *does not* owe the bailor a standard of perfection unless a contract provides otherwise. If the bailee can show that it took reasonable care or that none of its acts were sufficiently negligent to be said to have contributed to the loss, it can escape liability. A bailee does not need to be perfect or near perfect in its actions to be exonerated from liability. However, the bailee, if it wishes, may take on a heightened standard of care by contract and guarantee safe return of the bailed property in all circumstances, such that, where the property is returned in a damaged state, there is no question of onus of proof at all, and the bailee will face liability accordingly for the bailor's losses, even in the presence of evidence that shows that the bailee took reasonable care in the circumstances.[247]

245 See, for example, *Shell Oil Co of Canada Ltd v White Motor Co of Canada Ltd* (1957), 8 DLR (2d) 753 (Ont HCJ).

246 See, for example, *Lavigne v Boyle*, [1989] NBJ No 106 (QBTD), discussed in Chapter 3, Section J.

247 See *Trans Canadian Crane Ltd v Baseline Industries Ltd*, [1990] BCJ No 1446 (SC).

E. BAILMENT DISTINGUISHED FROM A MASTER AND SERVANT RELATIONSHIP

Employment relationships will rarely lead to the creation of bailments between employers and employees over employer property, whether the property is owned by the employer or hired out by the employer from a third party for its use. That is to say, where an employee who is exercising exclusive custody and control over an employer's goods damages or loses them during the course of employment, the relationship is that of master and servant, and not bailment. Accordingly, the employee is not responsible for the employer's losses as bailee, and the employer's action against the employee, if any, must lie elsewhere.[248]

F. BAILMENT DISTINGUISHED FROM A SALE

A sale differs from a bailment in that ownership, rather than possession, is transferred. In a bailment, the bailor usually retains ownership and a reversionary possessory interest in the goods bailed. An ordinary sale will not trigger a bailment, although bailment obligations may arise between the parties and are not affected by the *Sale of Goods Act*.[249]

The question of when ownership in goods passes from seller to buyer for the purposes of assessing who bears the risk of loss is to be determined with reference to the contract, the conduct of the parties, and the circumstances of the case. If the intention of the parties cannot be ascertained by the contract, then reference must be had to the applicable provincial *Sale of Goods Act*, which provides several rules for ascertaining intention based on who holds title to the goods at any given point in time.[250] Unlike a sale, bailment obligations and a duty of safekeeping may arise when a party is in possession of the goods in question but does not hold title to them.

A "conditional sale" (where the parties intend that the property in the goods will pass to the bailee on the payment of the purchase price or in the performance of a condition),[251] unlike an ordinary sale, may create a

248 See *Wiebe v Lepp*, [1974] MJ No 26 (CA) and other relevant discussion in Chapter 3, Section G.

249 See, for example, section 21(b) of *Sale of Goods Act*, RSO 1990, c S.1.

250 See *ibid*, s 19, rr 1–5. See also *Jerome v Clements Motor Sales Ltd*, [1958] OR 738 (CA).

251 There must be a "mutuality" of obligations. That is to say, the seller must agree to sell and the buyer must agree to buy. In the absence of this, all one has is a lease: see *Doug Dunlop Leasing Ltd v Seward*, 1977 CanLII 541 at paras 10–12 (Alta QB) [*Dunlop*],

bailment. This is because, strictly speaking, title is retained by the bailor and only possession is transferred to the bailee until the purchase option is exercised. Certainly, a duty of care is placed on the bailee in the interim period and, if this duty is breached, the bailor may have the right to repossess the property pursuant to the contract entered into between the parties or at common law.[252] The fact that a bailor cannot recall its goods from the bailee while payments are being made should not be viewed as a bar to the finding of a bailment. In any event, conditional sale agreements have created bailments in the past under statute.[253] Certainly if this is the case, once title passes upon the performance of the conditions, the bailment must be viewed as being at an end.

G. BAILMENT DISTINGUISHED FROM A CONSIGNMENT

In the case of a consignment, ownership is not transferred to the bailee, but only the mere right to sell the bailor's goods to a third party for a pre-determined consideration, which consideration must be transferred to the bailor/consignor upon the making of the sale. If no sale is made, the bailee/consignee must return the goods to the bailor in their original form and the bailment arising from the consignment would be at an end. If a sale is made, then the bailment arising from the consignment is also terminated and the consignee would owe no more duties of safekeeping in relation to the goods, the difference being that in the case of a sale, title in the goods would be transferred from the bailor to the buyer of the goods, vis-à-vis the consignee, and would not remain in the bailor as in the case of a failed consignment.

H. BAILMENT DISTINGUISHED FROM A PLEDGE (OR PAWN)

A pledge arises where goods are delivered to a creditor of the pledgor to secure the pledgor's debt (or anticipated debt). Possession is given for the

---

affirming the UK decision of *Helby v Matthews*, [1895] AC 471. There is, however, "no necessity of a sale but a bailment with an *intention* that the property in the goods will pass to the bailee on the payment of the purchase price or in the performance of a condition" [*Dunlop*, above in this note at para 13].

252 See, for example, *International Harvester Credit Corp v Dolphin*, [1978] AJ No 581 (SCTD) [*International Harvester*].

253 See, for example, section 19(1)(c) of the *Conditional Sales Act*, RSA 1970, c 61. See also *International Harvester*, above note 252 at para 44; *Dunlop*, above note 251 at para 13.

sole and express purpose of giving security to a creditor, and not for the purpose of safekeeping.[254] For example, in *Senft v Bank of Montreal*,[255] a trucking company entered into a lease arrangement with the plaintiff owner of a truck (which was subject to a chattel mortgage in favour of Bank of Montreal) for the services of the truck, under which the plaintiff would earn fees by transporting cargoes for the company. The truck's insurance coverage and licence registration was put in the name of the trucking company, but the plaintiff was responsible for all other operating costs, including repairs. Under the arrangement, the trucking company would also make cash advances to the plaintiff against earnings and would advance monies in order to help the plaintiff meet the expenses involved in operating the truck.[256]

Difficulties arose between the parties when the monies expended by the trucking company for repairs became greater than the monies earned by the plaintiff through his operation of the vehicle. With respect to one of the repairs, the plaintiff authorized the trucking company to take possession of the vehicle after the repairs had been made and it had paid for them. The truck was to serve as security for the debt arising from the repairs. The truck thereafter remained in the possession of the defendant. A court application later followed, in which the court had to decide who had priority with respect to the proceeds arising from sale of the vehicle occurring through a court enforcement process.[257]

While the court found that the facts did not lend themselves to creating posssesory lien rights, or garageman's lien rights in favour of the trucking company,[258] they did give rise to a pledge. The pledge, however, did not prevail at the end of the day because it was viewed as a "mortgage," within the meaning of the *Bills of Sale Act*, which was subordinate to the

---

254 Edward Beal, *The Law of Bailments* (London: Butterworths, 1900), at 132; James Crossley Vaines, *Personal Property*, 5th ed (London: Butterworths, 1976) at 137.

255 1986 CanLII 1844 (Alta QB).

256 *Ibid* at paras 3–4.

257 *Ibid* at paras 1–6.

258 A possessory lien was not possible in the case because the trucking company had not effected the repairs and was not in the position of "a workman, tradesman, artisan, or mechanic having bestowed labour, skill, or expense in respect of the chattel of another" who was retaining possession until the charges for his services had been paid: *ibid* at para 12. As for the garageman's lien, it was similarly lacking. The repair shop had been paid for its work by the trucking company before it claimed and filed a garageman's lien, making its lien and its subsequent assignment of the lien to the trucking company invalid and unenforceable: *ibid* at para 8.

mortgage against the truck that had been previously validly registered by Bank of Montreal, which had financed the original purchase of the vehicle. Thus, the trucking company did not receive any of the proceeds arising from the sale of the truck that was ordered by the court as part of the enforcement process, as the funds generated by the sale were completely exhausted by the creditor with a superior claim, which had also decided to realize on its security interest in the event of default.[259]

Even though a pledge is not made or given for the express purpose of safekeeping, it nonetheless results in the imposition of a duty of safekeeping on the creditor storing the property. This creates a bailment, albeit of limited scope. Certainly the bailment terminates when the debt that is the subject of the pledge is satisfied by the pledgor, or where a court repossesses the property for the purposes of sale through a court enforcement process, which results in the pledgee (bailee) being dispossessed of the property.

I. BAILMENT DISTINGUISHED FROM A GIFT

An essential condition for a bailment to exist is that ownership in the property not be transferred permanently to the bailee. A gift does just that, as ownership is not retained by the bailor but instead is transferred permanently to the recipient of the gift.[260] The bailor retains neither possession nor ownership, nor a reversionary interest in either.

J. BAILMENT DISTINGUISHED FROM A LEASE

A lease of personal property where the lessee does not have or acquire any right, title, or interest in or to the property being leased, and is required to return the leased property to the lessor at the end of the lease, is a bailment and does not amount to a sale, conditional or otherwise. An option to purchase at the end of the lease, where the lessee is not required to buy, is not enough, without more, to create a sale, conditional or otherwise, either.[261] The key to distinguishing between a sale and a bailment in this context is to look at the intention of the parties at the time the lease was made, to see if they intended for title in the goods to pass from bailor

259 *Ibid* at paras 7–20.

260 See *Boire*, above note 19.

261 *Crosstown U-Drive v MacLean*, 1979 CanLII 1069 at para 14 (Alta QB).

to bailee. Exchanges between the parties at the material times and any written contract between the parties will always need to be considered in deciding what the parties intended with respect to the eventual disposition of the property.

In *International Harvester*,[262] a leasing agreement was entered into between the parties. The defendant was named lessee and the plaintiff lessor. Even though the defendant paid rent to the plaintiff for the use of the vehicle, the lease resulted in the defendant purchasing the vehicle and becoming its sole owner and proprietor. However, the defendant had made it clear to the plaintiff that it was buying the vehicle for its third-party employee, and did not require it for its own personal use, and had insisted that the third party would be the ultimate purchaser. The defendant suggested that it would make more sense for the third party to become lessee, but this proposal was ultimately refused by the plaintiff, who suggested that the defendant could enter into a separate sublease agreement with the employee to ensure his interests were protected, which it subsequently did.[263]

Under the terms of the lease, the defendant was responsible for all necessary repairs and maintenance. It was also obligated to become owner of the vehicle, as the parties were found to have intended that the property in the vehicle should pass to the defendant, although the defendant was given various ways in which to effectuate this.[264]

For the first eight months, the vehicle was utilized by the employee of the defendant company, and the defendant would issue payments in the form of cheques to the plaintiff under the leasing agreement from monies earned by the employee, on the employee's behalf. Following this period of time, the third party left the defendant's employ and went to work for a new company, where he continued to operate and use the vehicle. The defendant and third party entered into a sublease agreement, making

262 Above note 252.

263 *Ibid* at paras 1–6.

264 First, the defendant could pay the purchase price, being the present value of rental instalments remaining outstanding for the lease term plus the residual amount prescribed in the lease. Second, the defendant could sell the vehicle as beneficial owner, and then pay the purchase price to the plaintiff, irrespective of the amount of the sale proceeds received on the sale. Third, the defendant could surrender the vehicle to the plaintiff lessor, who would then sell the vehicle and provide the defendant with any excess monies received on the sale, above and beyond the stipulated purchase price. Or alternatively, the plaintiff could demand further monies from the defendant should the sale proceeds fall short of covering the purchase price: *ibid* at para 5.

the third party an assignee who assumed all of the defendant's rights and obligations under the leasing agreement with the plaintiff. Under the sublease, if the third party fell into arrears by at least two months or more, the sublease agreement would become void and the leasing agreement would automatically revert to the defendant's company.[265]

The defendant later tried to have the plaintiff approve the assignment of the leasing agreement to the third party, but the plaintiff refused. Consequently, rental payments continued to be made on the vehicle to the plaintiff by cheque issued by the third party and delivered by him to the defendant for mailing to the plaintiff. As it happens, the third party became totally incapacitated due to a back injury suffered by him while working on the vehicle a relatively short time later, and he asked the defendant to purchase his equity under the sublease agreement and reassume possession and ownership of the vehicle. The defendant refused, advising that it had no use for the vehicle. (At this time, the defendant had financial problems and was unable to make the rental payments on the vehicle.) The third party accordingly voluntarily surrendered the keys to the vehicle to the plaintiff, as his incapacity was anticipated to last six months, and the plaintiff then repossessed the vehicle and stored it on its own property.[266]

Not surprisingly, the rental payment for the current month was in arrears, and the defendant received notice of the default from the plaintiff and was given a short period of time to remedy it, which it did not do. The plaintiff accordingly sold the vehicle by private sale. The court found the leasing agreement to be a "sale pursuant to a contract of bailment under which it is intended that the property in the goods will pass to the bailee on the payment of the purchase price in whole or in part." This was a finding of some consequence, for the defendant's indebtedness on the lease was accordingly entitled to be extinguished pursuant to the *Conditional Sales Act*.[267]

Because the lease had made a transfer of title between the parties obligatory rather than permissive, the court was right to have rejected the argument that the agreement between the parties was merely a leasing agreement with an option to transfer title that did not have to be exercised. It is to be noted how aspects of the transaction in the case can

265 *Ibid* at paras 7–8.
266 *Ibid* at paras 10–12.
267 *Ibid* at paras 52–55.

be viewed as having characteristics of a lease, bailment, and sale, sometimes occurring at one and the same time, and how a slight variation in an agreement or in the relationship of the parties can morph one type of relationship into another, whether inadvertently or not. Certainly, the relation between the defendant and the third party was one of bailment at all times, under a sublease, while the relationship between the plaintiff and defendant involved ultimately a sale, although a bailment would exist between the parties until all rental and other required payments, including payment of the residual value of the vehicle, were made by the defendant to the plaintiff, entitling the defendant to have legal title over the vehicle transferred to it.[268]

K. BAILMENT DISTINGUISHED FROM AGENCY

An agent may or may not be a bailee, depending on the relationship of the agent to the principal. Much will turn on whether or not the principal itself is a bailee. In *Seaboard Life Insurance Co v Bank of Montreal*,[269] a bank's transferring of legal title in shares it was charged with keeping safe, along with its duty of safekeeping, to a subcustodian who became the new registered shareholder of the shares created a bailment relationship between it and this other party. While the bank retained responsibility for the forwarding of certain information to the owner of the shares (the bailor) pursuant to a custodian agreement, the transfer of possession and ownership of the fungible goods to a new entity, together with a duty of safekeeping, was enough to make the agent a bailee of the goods, irrespective of its more limited duties as compared with the bank's.

Conversely, in *Palmer*, a driver's availing himself of a parking attendant's *de gratia* offer to park his car after he arrived at a parking garage to a situation of congestion (a parking garage where he normally parked his own car and took his own keys with him) was not enough to create a bailment, despite the apparent control exercised over the automobile by the parking operator. Instead, the court found that the parking attendant had merely acted as "agent" of the plaintiff and was performing a gratuitous service rather than assuming a general duty of safekeeping over the plaintiff's vehicle. Presumably, the parking attendant satisfied his duty

268 *Ibid* at para 52.
269 2002 BCCA 192 [*Seaboard*].

of care to the plaintiff by doing what was reasonably expected of him in all the circumstances upon performing the agreed upon undertaking. He parked the plaintiff's vehicle in a parking spot, based on his actual skill and experience as a parking attendant, and, presumably, was not negligent in doing so. Thus, the parking garage was not responsible for the loss of the plaintiff's car.

Where only an agency relationship exists, possession will not be transferred from the principal of the goods to the agent but, instead, will remain in the principal throughout. In *Palmer*, this meant that the owner of the car had not relinquished possession of the car, despite the apparent exercises of control engaged in by the parking attendant, since the parking attendant's mandate was limited to parking the car for the owner (on a gratuitous basis) and taking no further steps on his behalf.

While there will always be a duty on agents to keep their principal's goods separate and distinguishable from their own, as well as a duty to avoid conflicts between their personal interest and their duty to their principal,[270] agents will not assume a general duty of safekeeping over their principal's goods. Further, the principal will usually be under a legal duty to indemnify the agent (except where the law relieves the principal of such obligations).[271]

L. BAILMENT DISTINGUISHED FROM A TRUST

A bailment is not a trust, because, generally speaking, title to the chattel is not transferred to the bailee and remains in the bailor. Only possession is transferred, for a time-limited period and usually for a specific purpose, with possession to be restored to the bailor. In a trust, the trustee holds title, though not necessarily possession, in the property for the benefit of the beneficiary.[272] The passing of title shows the parties' intention to create a trust. In *Blue Resources Ltd v Sherriff*,[273] the court notes that a distinction between trust and bailment based merely on locus of title may be a faulty one. According to the court, where the transfer of title is solely to facilitate an agreement under a bailment relationship, the person taking title is a bailee not a trustee. Since the defendant lawyer in that case had

270 *Ibid* at para 69.

271 GHL Fridman, Law of Agency, 7th ed (Toronto: Butterworths, 1996) at 55.

272 DWM Waters, *Law of Trusts in Canada* (Toronto: Carswell, 1974) at 60.

273 [1994] OJ No 2988 (Gen Div).

accepted the duties and responsibilities of trustee for all investors in the plaintiff company (upon taking title to certain shares on behalf of certain investors who had been denied their interest in the plaintiff company, which had been obtained using their funds), he could not be a bailee. The court identified the defendant lawyer's duty to exercise reasonable care over the share certificates that he was storing on behalf of the beneficiaries by maintaining them or by selling and investing them, in his sole discretion in the best interests of the beneficiaries, as being indicative of a trust. The lawyer trustee could deal with the shares or the sale proceeds thereof freely, however he wished, so long as he acted in the best interests of the shareholders until they demanded the shares' return. These duties, which went far beyond mere safekeeping of the share certificates, were generally dutifully carried out, demonstrating that the nature of the holding was trust rather than bailment (although a demand by certain shareholders for the return of their individual shares went ignored by the lawyer, in breach of his duties as trustee).[274]

In *Seaboard*,[275] a life insurance company transferred title in certain shares to a bank. However, the bank's lack of discretionary power over the shares, with no power to invest them, sell them, or convert them in the best interests of the beneficiaries, meant that no trust could be created and only a bailment could be found. The defendant could not place the insurance company "in a position of vulnerability,"[276] since it had no such discretion or power to do so. In the words of Newbury JA, addressing the matter for a majority of the Court of Appeal for British Columbia: "The Bank had very little scope for the exercise of any discretion under the Custodian Agreement; it was not an advisor to Seaboard and did not make decisions for it; and it was bound to carry out its instructions with respect to buying and selling securities, without more."[277]

The bank's powers and obligations were limited to safeguarding Seaboard's preferred shares, providing it with certain information, and returning the shares to it on demand, subject to payment of its fees. It could also receive and automatically deposit all dividends and interest cheques received on the portfolio into Seaboard's account. Even though

274 *Ibid* at paras 1–20.
275 Above note 269.
276 *Ibid* at para 74.
277 *Ibid* at para 54.

the information to be provided to the plaintiff under the contract was vitally important (information relating to a public offer to purchase the shares, which offer expired shortly after notice was given), this did not alter the basic nature of the relationship. Thus, the defendant's failure to provide Seaboard with information either directly or through its duly authorized agent, who was subsequently contracted to act as subcustodian of the shares, preventing Seaboard from selling its shares and causing it substantial losses, was merely a breach of an (arguably) absolute duty in a contract and did not signify any failing in the exercise of discretionary powers under a trust.[278]

While not addressed by the court in its reasons for decision, it is submitted that any discretionary power that the bank may have had with respect to safeguarding the shares concerned a bailment and should not be muddled up with the discretion required for a trust to be found. This kind of discretion requires the custodian to be able, in its sole and unilateral discretion, to make decisions that go beyond the mere storage of the goods and effect the beneficiary's legal or practical interest, including the ability to sell, invest, or otherwise deal with the goods in the best interests of the beneficiaries.

The thorny question of where to draw the line between bailment and trust was before the Court of Appeal for Ontario in the earlier case of *Elgin Loan & Savings Co v National Trust Co.*[279] There, the plaintiffs had received title in certain shares from company A as collateral security for a loan (as well as a debenture from the company). Title to the shares was subsequently transferred into the name of the defendants, a trust company, for safekeeping. The defendants were also responsible for collecting dividends on the shares as registered shareholder. Later, the defendants were made liquidators of company A and refused to deliver the shares to the plaintiffs on demand, on the basis that A had an interest in them.[280] While this was found to have been improper, the majority of the court, in affirming the trial judge's decision, refused to find that a trust relationship had been created as between the defendants and plaintiffs on the basis that, while title had been delivered to the defendants, the defendants' obligations were limited to restoring the share certificates to the

278 *Ibid* at paras 54–55.
279 [1905] OJ No 182 (CA).
280 *Ibid* at paras 35–45.

plaintiffs on demand or request, and, in the interim, to keep them safe, which were the hallmarks of a bailment and not a trust.[281]

The Court of Appeal's decision is eminently defensible. It is consistent with the decisions and the criteria laid down in *Seaboard* and *Blue Resources Ltd*. The mere fact that title was transferred should not be treated as dispositive of the distinction between trust and bailment. Instead, the question to be asked in all cases is whether the transfer of title was accompanied by the granting of discretionary powers in favour of the trustee empowering the trustee to affect the legal or practical interest in the property being held. A custodian's ability to collect or deposit dividends on shares being held as a registered shareholder is not enough, without more, to create a trust and to take the relationship outside the realm of bailment. The majority of the court in *Elgin Loan* was accordingly right to have rejected the standard employed by the dissenting judge in finding a trust: "I think the defendants were trustees of all the shares. The property in the shares was in them [the defendants] by express arrangement in trust for safe keeping and the collection of the dividends."[282]

In *Lichti*,[283] the court notes that, in order for a trust to be found, the trustee must receive both legal and beneficial ownership of the subject property; legal title alone is not sufficient. In that case, a plaintiff long-distance truck driver sued in bailment and contract after the defendants failed to make a single payment on a truck that he had previously purchased on a lease-to-own basis, resulting in its seizure. This was based on an agreement between the plaintiff, the defendants, and the finance company, whereby the plaintiff became an owner-operator for the defendants, in an attempt to ameliorate the financial difficulties he was having with respect to the financing and maintenance of the truck. The defendants agreed to hire drivers for the truck and assign them jobs (in the hope of generating enough income to put the plaintiff in a positive credit position vis-à-vis the finance company and defendants). The defendants further agreed to clear all the plaintiff's arrears with the finance company, advancing wages to the plaintiff accordingly. The defendants further agreed to remit the plaintiff's monthly truck payment directly to

281 *Ibid* at paras 5–55.
282 *Ibid* at para 53.
283 *Lichti*, above note 1 at para 66.

the finance company on his behalf moving forward.[284] This left the plaintiff free to drive a smaller, and less expensive, truck. The plaintiff was responsible for the costs of operating the truck, including but not limited to fuel, insurance, maintenance, and drivers' salaries. The plaintiff was also required to sign a wage assignment in favour of the finance company. To facilitate the agreement, the plaintiff was required to transfer legal title in the truck to the defendants.[285]

After the arrangement was put into place, the defendant ended up advancing additional funds to the plaintiff to assist him in making repairs to the truck, again in the hope of making the arrangement a profitable one for all concerned. As it turns out, the plaintiff's financial situation did not sufficiently improve, for a myriad of reasons, and the defendants subsequently failed to make a single payment on the truck, given their assessment of the plaintiff's financial situation. This resulted in seizure of the truck and several additional charges connected thereto. The defendants were not aware of the consequences of a single non-payment, which was the result of the plaintiff's previous payment difficulties with the finance company.

Relying on the law of both bailment and contract, the plaintiff argued that the defendants had breached their absolute duties to make the payments on the truck and to inform the plaintiff if a payment was not made, among other duties owed to him. Justice Silverman refused to find that the truck had been held in trust by the defendants, since "beneficial ownership" for the truck remained in the plaintiff throughout, with only legal ownership passing to the defendants: "Although registration of the Truck was legally in the name of the Defendants, the Defendants never had beneficial ownership of the Truck. Consequently, they never held the Truck in trust for the benefit of the Plaintiff."[286]

The fact that legal title in the truck was transferred to the defendants meant that a bailment could not be found either. This holding is more questionable, however, for it is clear that the defendants had exclusive possession of the truck at all material times, that they had assumed a

---

284 In the case, the judge found that the agreement to remit did not create an absolute duty, and that the plaintiff was ultimately responsible for ensuring that all payments were made, at least when he was in a negative credit position vis-à-vis the defendants, which he was at all material times: *ibid* at para 56.

285 *Ibid* at paras 9–42.

286 *Ibid* at para 66.

duty of safekeeping over it,[287] and that they had exercised a substantial amount of control over the truck vis-à-vis its drivers. It also goes against the grain of the caselaw just discussed, wherein title is sometimes transferred to facilitate a bailment (mere custodianship), or to advance its purposes, rather than to create a trust. Certainly, this was the case in *Lichti*, where no sale or trust was contemplated by the parties; the arrangements, instead, were entered into solely for commercial and financial reasons. Joint business ventures can, and have, led to findings of bailment.[288]

In summary, where the transfer of title to the property is merely to allow for the custodian of the property to effect their duty of safekeeping more effectively, this will establish a bailment and nothing more. In order that there be a trust, there must be additional duties assumed by the trustee, as demonstrated by the manner in which the subject matter of the trust is dealt with. A mere declaration, without more, should not be enough to create a trust as distinguished from a bailment; it must be accompanied by certain duties and obligations that show the presence of a fiduciary relationship between the parties. Unlike a bailee, the trustee must be empowered to do more than merely maintain the property in its current or modified form, or to keep it safe; it must have "a discretionary power" that goes beyond mere custodianship. It must be able to sell, encumber, or convert the property on whatever terms it wishes, in its sole discretion, in the best interests of the beneficiaries. The legal relationship must place the property holders in a peculiar "position of vulnerability," beyond those ordinary risks associated with the holding of property for safekeeping.[289] The foregoing finds support in Waters, wherein the learned author, commenting on the distinction between trust and bailment in the context of the *Elgin Loan* decision, states the following: "The distinction is probably as the Chief Justice put it. If the intention is really to give another custody, and that other is given 'the indicia of property' in order to assist his custodianship, then bailment is created. But if title passes in order to allow a range of duties to be discharged by the other, then a trust is created."[290]

---

287 The fact that the plaintiff remained responsible for several aspects of the truck's maintenance, including repairs and insurance, should not be enough to defeat a bailment in these circumstances, although it should certainly inform the standard of care owed by the bailee.

288 *Lifestyles*, above note 163.

289 *Seaboard*, above note 269 at para 74.

290 Waters, above note 272 at 66.

A transfer of title that does no more than facilitate the ability of the holder of the property to keep the goods safe, or to maintain the goods in their current form, will create a bailment, even though more than possession has been given, since ownership, like possession, is transferred temporarily and solely to assist the bailee in carrying out its duty of safekeeping rather than for some other purpose. Finally, a trust may not be possible, in circumstances such as those found in *Lichti*, where only legal ownership (but not beneficial ownership) to the subject property is transferred.

M. BAILMENT DISTINGUISHED FROM WRONGFUL FINDING

An *innocent* finder who takes a lost chattel into his possession becomes a gratuitous bailee and is responsible for the safekeeping of the chattel. A wrongful taking will never make a finder a bailee, although it may still give the finder a superior claim relative to a further wrongful taker of the same chattel and give that finder the right to retake possession so long as the power of resuming effective control remains in them. In *Bird v Fort Frances (Town of)*,[291] the plaintiff (a twelve-year-old boy) found a large sum of money in a can placed on a sill forming part of the under-structure of a building. The money had been secreted in a way that demonstrated that it had not been lost in the true sense of the word; instead, it was deliberately hidden. As pointed out by McRuer CJHC of the Ontario High Court of Justice, "the money was not found in a public highway or public conveyance or in any place to which the public had access by leave or licence, nor was there anything to lead one to believe that it had been lost in the true sense."[292] In addition, the plaintiff did not have the landowner's permission to be on the property and was therefore a trespasser. The taking was therefore wrongful. Because of the plaintiff's extravagant spending, he was later questioned by a constable and gave a full account of the finding. Thereupon, the constable secured the monies from the plaintiff's mother, holding them in trust for the true owner.[293] Chief Justice McRuer found that this taking was not authorized by law and therefore was also wrongful. As it turned out, no demand or legal claim to the money was advanced by the landowner's estate on whose property the money had been found

291 [1949] OJ No 453 (HCJ).
292 *Ibid* at para 26.
293 *Ibid* at paras 1–2.

(who might have asserted a superior claim), and the plaintiff's claims were therefore superior to all others. The money wrongfully taken from him was accordingly ordered returned by the court, which viewed the transaction arising between the mother and police officer as a "bailment," which was now at an end, since the estate of the late landowner on which the monies were found did not wish to make a claim.[294] Interestingly, the bailment between the mother (as agent for the son) and the police officer was not disqualified by the police officer's lack of legal authority for taking possession of the money. This means that, unlike the case of a finder, a wrongful taking does not necessarily disqualify a bailment.

The duty to take reasonable care owed by a bailee as finder is to the true of owner of the chattel, who may or may not be identifiable or locatable. According to the Court for Appeal of Manitoba in *Kowal v Ellis*,[295] the finder as bailee has a duty "to make reasonable efforts to locate the owner." That said, bailees may retain possession until they have opportunity to satisfy themselves that a claimant has a genuine claim to the property. As a general rule, the bailee is entitled to keep the lost property as against all the world except the real owner, subject to "a prior right to keep the chattel which right was subsisting at the time when the finder took the chattel into his care and control."[296]

However, as illustrated in *Bird*, a finder may become a bailee only where the chattel in question is truly lost rather than deliberately left. This was confirmed in the more recent case of *Trachuk*.[297] There, the court states that, when the acquired chattels of an unknown person are left under land or attached to land in some way that demonstrates that they have been deliberately left or secreted rather than lost, a bailment by finding will *not* be possible. In that case, the large sum of money obtained by the four defendants had been found eighteen inches below the surface of the land by way of backhoe, in a plastic bag wrapped with duct tape, under a sublease held by their employer. Clearly the monies had been deliberately left and secreted. These defendants, therefore, could not become bailees based on merely finding the property, and the general rule that a finder is entitled to the found chattel against all but the real owner did not apply. However, the defendants were found by the court to

---

294 *Ibid* at paras 26–32.
295 [1977] MJ No 22 at para 8 (CA).
296 *Trachuk v Olinek*, [1995] AJ No 1177 at paras 30–31 (QB).
297 *Ibid*.

have the most superior claim to the monies, since the owner of the land on which the money was found chose not to make a claim, and the evidence showed that the defendants had a *de facto* possession of the lands on which the money was found by virtue of their exercises of control over the land pursuant to the surface lease. The plaintiff farmer who lived on and leased lands adjacent to the wellsite on which the monies were found was not an occupier of the said lands (despite purportedly having been granted the right to possession of those lands and having some affect on them), and the fence that he had erected around the well site premises was for the sole purpose of keeping his cows out. There was no evidence that the plaintiff intended to exclude workmen, including the four defendants or any other persons of the petroleum companies involved in the surface lease, the well, or the easements, from entering upon the subject premises and affecting the land therein by drilling, constructing pipelines, or the like. In short, the plaintiff could not demonstrate the needed control of the subject lands to prevent strangers from interfering with them in order to establish a lawful occupation by him that would have given him the right to possession of the lands and all chattels thereon. Thus, the defendants' licence to use the land in question prevailed, giving them the most superior claim and entitlement to the discovered monies, despite their lack of status as bailees.[298]

As this case demonstrates, an occupancy of land adjacent to the subject land on which the goods are found, some interferences with that land, and a grant to use and occupy the subject lands that is not sufficiently exercised in practice does *not* always give one a superior claim to that of another claimant arising later in time, even where the other claimant is not a bailee by finding and has a lesser claim to the property. It will, however, be different where the occupier can show that it was in exclusive control of the subject lands at the time the other claimants found the chattel and took it into their care and control, which, to be sure, will be difficult in the presence of easements, surface leases, and the like, having been granted by the owner of the land and having not been objected to by the occupier. For, in the presence of these circumstances, it will not be possible for the occupier to show an intention to exclude all others from the land.

---

298 *Ibid* at paras 26–63.

N. BAILMENT DISTINGUISHED FROM A CONVERSION

Conversion differs from bailment because it involves specific types of wrongful acts taken in relation to another's property, including wrongful taking, using, or destroying goods, or the exercise of control over them that is incompatible with the title of the owner.[299] Such acts would place the bailee in breach of the bailment contract, since a bailee is not empowered to do any more than possess the goods for the purposes that have been agreed upon between the parties upon the commencement of the bailment. However, conversion would not capture a simple refusal by the bailee to return the bailor's goods or damage that results to bailor's goods as a result of bailee negligence. That said, damages for conversion are available to a bailor within the framework of bailment where a bailee wrongfully uses the bailor's goods for its own purposes or destroys them.[300] This is because conversion by a bailee clearly constitutes a breach of its standard of care owed to a bailor.

O. BAILMENT DISTINGUISHED FROM DETINUE

Detinue differs from bailment because it simply refers to wrongful detention of goods by another, or improperly parting with possession of someone else's goods. Detinue would not provide recourse where a bailee restores property to a bailor in a damaged condition, nor where a bailee misuses the goods without loss or damage being occasioned. In these circumstances, one must sue in bailment for a remedy or, alternatively, in negligence. That said, damages for detinue are available to a bailor within the framework of bailment where a bailee fails to return goods to the bailor when it is requested and required to do so.[301]

P. BAILMENT DISTINGUISHED FROM SECURITY INTEREST

It is true that a bailee sometimes acquires a security interest in the property being bailed, but this is not a defining aspect of a bailment. Instead, this interest is usually created by virtue of the breach of the bailment contract, such as where the bailor does not pay the required fee to the

---

299 *Robertson*, above note 9 at paras 36–40.
300 *Kinsella*, above note 130 at para 120.
301 *Ibid* at paras 116–20.

bailee for the repair of the bailor's automobile, creating possessory lien rights in favour of the bailee mechanic.

Q. BAILMENT DISTINGUISHED FROM A JOINT BUSINESS VENTURE

A joint business venture or enterprise will create a bailment only where the bailee exercises exclusive possession of the goods for some discrete period of time during which it is responsible to safeguard the goods and explain what happens to them in the event of loss or damage. Bailment law will apply only during those times, but not as a general matter.[302]

R. CONCLUSION

Canadian courts have struggled to distinguish between bailments and other legal relationships, in particular, licences. The distinction is not without consequence. If a legal relationship other than bailment is involved, the party in position of bailor will need to prove liability in the ordinary way, very often negligence on a preponderance of probabilities. (Where there is uncertainty as to the circumstances surrounding the loss or damage, this may prove to be an impossible task.) The tension between not wanting to impose an intolerably high burden on parties in the position of bailees while wanting to provide a certain level of protection to bailor's goods is evident in the caselaw. In resolving this tension, a holistic and contextual approach with an eye toward all relevant considerations must be adopted. Where a court finds that control of the subject property for the purpose of safekeeping has been assumed by the bailee, whether for consideration or not, a bailment must be found, with all the attendant consequences that relationship entails.

---

302 *Lifestyles*, above note 163.

CHAPTER 2

A Bailor's Onus of Proof: General Considerations

A. INTRODUCTION

In order for a bailor to fix liability against a bailee, the bailor must demonstrate that possession (not ownership) of its goods were transferred to the bailee for safekeeping, either actually or constructively, and that its property was damaged or lost during the course of the bailment. Ziff aptly calls these the "triggering facts"—that is, the facts that engage the presumption of negligence against the defendant bailee—signifying the fact that, in a bailment action, a plaintiff does not need to prove all elements of liability on a balance of probabilities. Where the bailor alleges that the goods were damaged during the subsistence of the bailment relationship, it must also prove the good condition of the goods when bailed and the unsatisfactory condition of the goods when returned.[1] An unsatisfactory condition can include a total loss of goods or, alternatively, lesser damage to goods.[2] Where the bailor fails to overcome its burden, the burden

1 See, generally, Bruce Ziff, *Principles of Property Law*, 4th ed (Toronto: Thomson Carswell, 2006) at 303–4. As a practical matter, this means that a bailor must call evidence first, before a bailee is called upon to do so, to meet its burden of proof, since there are certain "elements" in a bailment case that must be proven by the plaintiff (bailor) before the reverse onus of proof will be thrown upon the bailee to disprove that its negligence caused the losses at issue: see *Hogarth v Archibald Moving and Storage Ltd*, [1991] BCJ No 609 (CA) for relevant discussion.

2 In *Commercial Bakeries Corp v Frasier Transport Corp*, [2000] OJ No 1119 (SCJ), the plaintiff (bailor) succeeded in meeting its burden even though the cookies redelivered to the plaintiff were not a total loss, since the plaintiff had provided no expert evidence to show that they had become inedible. However, given the several months

of disproving negligence is not placed on the bailee, and the bailor must establish negligence against the bailee in the ordinary way.[3]

The requirement that the bailor prove that the loss or damage of property occurred during the term of the bailment is inextricably tied to the absolute duty placed on the bailee, in an ordinary bailment arrangement, to redeliver the bailor's goods at the conclusion of the bailment in either their original or altered form.[4] Even though this requirement is usually easily met and not at all contentious,[5] it has been the subject of some contention and uncertainty in the harder cases.

Much of the uncertainty involves the relative importance, if any, to be given to the requirement that a bailor prove that its goods were lost or damaged during the course of the bailment in order for the bailor to discharge its onus of proof, thereby shifting the onus to the bailee to disprove that its negligence caused the loss of or damage to the goods in question. As a starting point, clearly a more stringent requirement means that a bailor will have a more difficult time fixing liability against the bailee; conversely, a looser interpretation of the words "during the course or term of the bailment" means that the presumption of negligence against the bailee will be more easily triggered and therefore the liability of the bailee more easily established by the bailor.

In cases where the question of whether the loss or damage occurred during the course of the bailment relationship is a live issue in assessing the bailor's burden of proof, which to be sure will be a small minority of bailment cases, the finding made in this regard by the trial judge will almost always be dispositive of liability as between the bailor and the bailee. As a

---

the cookies were stored without being delivered to the plaintiff's customer, the cookies were clearly in a deteriorated and undesirable condition, which made them unsaleable: at paras 18–29.

3 Andrew James, *CED* (Ont 3d), Supplement vol 2, title 13, Bailment at 39. Where there is an inexplicable injurious event, the doctrine of *res ipsa loquitur*, however, can ease a plaintiff's ordinary burden in negligence and require a defendant to put forth an innocent cause for the injury that, on the evidence, neutralizes the inference of negligence otherwise shown by the evidence: see, for example, *Cogar Estate v Central Mountain Air Services Ltd* (1992), 65 BCLR (2d) 345 (CA).

4 Admittedly, certain kinds of bailment do not place an absolute duty on the bailee to return the goods to the bailor. The bailment agreement, for instance, may provide that the bailee is to deliver the goods to a third party or that the goods may be left with a bailee for sale on consignment, requiring the bailee to return the goods only if they cannot be sold: Ziff, above note 1 at 297.

5 See, for example, *Van Geel v Warrington* (1928), 63 OLR 143 (SCAD); *627360 Saskatchewan Ltd v Bellrose*, 2007 SKQB 14.

practical matter, it could very well be a live issue in cases where both the bailor and the bailee have had possession of the goods in question during the course of the bailment relationship and damage or loss to those goods has occurred, in circumstances where it is impossible to conclude on a balance of probabilities that the bailee was negligent or guilty of breach of contract in its handling of the goods during the periods of time in which it was in possession of the goods. It could also be a live issue where there has been exclusive possession by the bailee, accompanied by a significant degree of uncertainty as to whether the loss or damage at issue occurred prior to the creation of the bailment relationship or after it came to an end, as opposed to during the course of the bailment relationship and, again, in circumstances where it is impossible to conclude on a balance of probabilities that the bailee was negligent or guilty of breach of contract in its handling of the goods during the periods of time in which it was in possession of the goods.

B. A BAILOR'S ONUS OF PROOF IN THE ORDINARY CASE

In your garden-variety bailment, the bailee has exclusive possession of the bailor's goods for a specific purpose, such as repair or storage. Upon redelivery of the goods, if loss or damage is discovered by the bailor, the bailor can sue for the injury done. In most cases, the question of whether the loss or damage occurred while the bailee was in possession of the goods is not a contentious matter, and this part of the bailor's onus of proof is easily met, without the need of the bailor having to prove the good condition of the goods when bailed and the unsatisfactory condition of the goods when returned. The contention usually involves whether the bailee has met its applicable standard of care. For example, in *Hutchings v Loveless*,[6] the plaintiff left his motorcycle with the defendant repair shop to have the safety switch on the kickstand repaired. The defendant was too busy and could not attend to the work immediately, so the plaintiff agreed to leave the vehicle on the defendant's premises so that the repair could be made later. The plaintiff parked his motorcycle near what was known as the small motor repair room, promising to return later to check on the status of the repair. The next day, a sudden fire began in the ceiling of the small motor repair room, and the plaintiff's motorbike was destroyed. There was

6 [1990] NJ No 411 (SCTD).

no question of the bailor's onus of proof having been met in the circumstances: "Here quite obviously the motorcycle was a chattel and the possession and custody of it passed to the defendant on a temporary basis for the purpose of effecting repairs for which the defendant would be paid."[7] The only real question for the court was whether the defendant (bailee) had met his standard of care, as it was clear that the vehicle had been damaged while in the care, custody, and control of the defendant. Justice Easton of the Newfoundland Supreme Court Trial Division found that the fire had originated in a fluorescent light in the ceiling of the small motor repair room, but that the defendant had taken reasonable care throughout. The light was new, and there had not been any previous problems with it; there was no evidence that the light had been negligently installed; a recent report of the fire department indicated that the defendant's shop was in perfect order and made no recommendations; and the fire code had been complied with. No area could be found where it could be said that the defendant was guilty of some degree of negligence. The plaintiff (bailor) was accordingly denied damages for the loss of his motorcycle.[8]

Even where the bailee has not had exclusive possession of the bailor's goods at all times, or where there is some question as to when (exactly) the loss of the goods occurred, the bailor's burden of proof need not be a contentious matter. For instance, in *Pilot Insurance Co v Davis*,[9] two sets of golf clubs and related equipment that had been left with a golf club for storage, cleaning, and handling, under a contract, by the two plaintiff bailors (members of the club) after their respective use, were lost. The loss was discovered by the plaintiffs when each, respectively, arrived to the club to play golf following their last respective visits. The clubs had been last seen and handled by the plaintiffs on their last respective attendances (which occurred in the week prior to the discovery of the loss).[10]

The arrangements between the plaintiffs and the defendant were found to have created recurring bailments between them. Each time the plaintiffs delivered their clubs to the storage area at the end of an attendance, a bailment was commenced and was terminated only when the plaintiffs retrieved their clubs on their next visit. Specifically, under their bailment contracts, the plaintiffs were required to leave their clubs

7 *Ibid* at para 8.
8 *Ibid* at paras 17–25.
9 [1996] OJ No 2232 (Gen Div) [*Pilot*].
10 *Ibid* at paras 1–5.

in their bags on the ground or on carts outside the storage room door (at which point custody was considered to have been transferred to the defendant), which is what they did on the days in question.[11]

While it was not clear when the clubs disappeared, and what the precise circumstances of the loss were, the court easily found a bailment for reward.[12] The defendant did not deny or dispute the bailment or the loss of the clubs while in its custody; instead, it focused on meeting its burden of proof by demonstrating that it had taken reasonable care to prevent the thefts that the court had found to be the most likely explanation for the loss of the clubs. While the defendant failed to meet its burden of proof, showing that one's actions met the standard of reasonable care is normally the path of least resistance for a bailee who is defending against a bailment action, or the only path available to a bailee to exonerate itself from liability. In most circumstances, it will not be possible for a bailee to show that the goods did not disappear or were not damaged while in its own exclusive possession.[13]

As stated by Southin JA of the Court of Appeal for British Columbia in *BCFP Coast Sawmills Ltd v Tritow Systems Ltd*, "[I]n a bailment case, a sensible defendant admits the bailment and, if the goods were damaged in his custody, admits the damage and pleads affirmatively that he took proper care of the goods. It thus becomes plain on the pleadings that the only real issue is one upon which the burden lies upon the defendant who thereupon has the right and duty to begin."[14]

C. FORM OF PLEADINGS

In order for a bailor to put the bailee to the reverse onus, the caselaw indicates that the bailor must plead that the goods were damaged or lost while in the possession of the bailee and must, if necessary, where the bailee does not admit to same, prove, in the presentation of its case, by a balance of probabilities, that the loss or damage occurred during the course of the bailment.[15] Where important evidence is available, or might be available,

---

11 *Ibid* at para 6.

12 *Ibid* at para 6.

13 *Ibid* at para 8ff.

14 [1989] BCJ No 1473 at para 30 (CA) [paragraph numbers assigned by author].

15 It is also sufficient "if the bailor proves the contract and a failure to deliver the goods on demand": *Pilot*, above note 9 at para 8. This is essentially the stating of a bailment

establishing whether bailor property was damaged or lost during the course of the bailment, as opposed to before or afterwards, the failure of a bailor to call such evidence may result in it being unable to meet its burden of proof. This is likely to be true at least where there is no other reliable evidence in the record establishing that the goods were damaged during the subsistence of the bailment, rather than before or afterwards.[16]

As we shall see in Section E below, the requirement that a bailor prove that loss of its goods occurred during the course of the bailment tends to arise only in the harder cases where the timing and circumstances of the loss are unknown and vigorously disputed by the parties. The term "bailment" does not need to be referred to explicitly in a pleading for a bailment claim to be sustained at trial, though this is obviously preferable, so long as the facts pleaded are consistent with a bailment relationship.[17] This allowance (in *not* requiring bailors to specifically plead a bailment in order to sustain a bailment action) obviously greatly benefits plaintiffs (bailors), who would otherwise have to meet a substantially higher onus of proof by adducing evidence of affirmative negligence on the part of the defendant (bailee) to succeed.[18] A bailment action is usually advanced as part of the main action of the plaintiff, although it may also be advanced by counterclaim, third-party claim, or cross-claim.[19]

D. SUMMARY JUDGMENT MOTIONS

Given the highly fact-dependent nature of most bailment cases, a bailor (or bailee, for that matter) may have an uphill battle meeting its burden

---

action in detinue: *Lifestyles Kitchens & Bath, a division of GVBS Inc v Danbury Sales Inc*, [1999] OJ No 3097 at paras 41–42 (SCJ) [*Lifestyles*].

16 See, for example, *Gooding's Garage Ltd v Keeling*, [1982] NSJ No 133, especially paras 6–8 (Co Ct).

17 See *Bear Mountain Logging Ltd v KAT Lowbed Service Ltd*, [1998] BCJ No 177 at paras 24–29 (SC), where only negligence and breach of contract were strictly adverted to in the plaintiff's pleading, but where a "bailment" was nevertheless recognized to have been pleaded based on the nature of the relationships asserted, namely, a contract of carriage with a public authority. See further, *King v McLennan*, 2001 SKQB 179 at paras 7–8 [*King*].

18 For a consequential example of a case where a bailment was found using this relaxed approach, see *King, ibid.*

19 For an example of a case where a bailment action was advanced by counterclaim, see *Northern Industrial Carriers Ltd v Jasper Millwork Ltd*, [1978] AJ No 720 (Dist Ct).

of proof on a summary judgment motion.[20] However, a bailor's general onus does not change on these motions. A bailor should not be required to meet an increased burden of showing negligence in these circumstances, which would effectively result in a reduced burden of proof for the bailee. Once a bailor demonstrates that it transferred possession of its goods to the bailee, and they were damaged while in the bailee's possession, the bailee must negative negligence in relation to those goods to escape liability — that is, to avoid liability, it must show that it took appropriate care of the goods, as a prudent owner would. For a bailee to meet its burden of proof in order to have a bailment action against it dismissed by way of summary judgment motion, it is not enough for the bailee to show that the bailor, or another party, has *not* shown negligence on the bailee's part.[21] Such a standard would transform bailment actions into negligence actions, and destroy that which makes them singularly distinct — namely, the ability of the bailor to fix liability against the bailee by showing something short of negligence in circumstances where the bailee, because of its exclusive possession, is in a favoured position to explain what happened to cause the loss of or damage to the bailed goods.

The question of whether the bailee has met its standard of care, and the distinction between bailment and licence, are particularly fact- and credibility-dependent questions that will often require the full body of evidence offered by a trial to resolve. They are not very amenable to the summary judgment procedure. That said, where the judge can come to a "full appreciation of the evidence" on the motion without the need for a trial, and where there are no material facts in dispute, then a summary judgment may be possible and appropriate. No case could be found where a bailor was able to succeed in fixing liability against a bailee using the summary judgment motion procedure, though the same cannot be said of

20 See, for example, *Complex Elements Corp v Atlantic Container Line AB (PUBL) 820302 Ontario Inc (cob Lynx Trucking Transportation & Leasing)*, 2008 CanLII 21223 (Ont SC). See, further, *Concrete Shoring Technologies Inc v Civil Tech Construction Ltd*, 2014 NSSC 459. While both these cases dealt with motions by bailees to try to have the bailment actions that were brought against them dismissed (they failed in both instances), they demonstrate the highly fact-dependent nature of bailment cases and the fact that the summary judgment motion procedure will not always give a motions judge the necessary full appreciation of the evidence required for bailment questions, whether they deal with onus or otherwise, to be resolved.

21 *Merex Inc v Stoney Island Fisheries Ltd*, 2014 NSSC 67 at para 9.

bailees who have been able to overcome their burden and have bailment actions against them dismissed using the procedure.[22]

E. A BAILOR'S ONUS OF PROOF IN THE HARDER CASES

1) Exclusive Possession by the Bailee, but Uncertainty as to Whether Damage Occurred Before Bailment Commenced or After It Was Terminated

This category of cases admits of three possibilities. First, the goods were damaged before the bailment relationship began, and, therefore, the bailee should bear no legal responsibility for the damage, even if such damage went unnoticed by the bailee during the subsistence of the bailment relationship. Second, the goods were damaged after the bailment relationship was terminated, and, therefore, the bailee should bear no legal responsibility for the damage. Third, the goods were damaged during the course of the bailment relationship, and, therefore, the bailee might bear legal responsibility for the damage.

In *Calgary Transport Services Ltd v Pyramid Management Ltd*,[23] the appellant left its trailer in the care and control of the respondent for washing. The arrangement agreed upon required the respondent to wash the trailer during a slack period and, following the cleaning, to place the trailer on an adjacent lot, from which the appellant would pick it up at its convenience. This lot was unfenced, unlighted, and unguarded, to the knowledge of the appellant and was also used by the respondent as a truckstop for the greater profit of the respondent's business as a service station, restaurant, and truck wash. Owners and operators of trucks and trailers were provided with licences to enjoy the foregoing amenities on this lot, but no security over their units was provided, nor was access to the area monitored or controlled by the respondent.[24]

The appellant dropped off its trailer to the respondent during the day. It was washed later that day and placed in the adjacent lot. The next day, the appellant arrived to pick up its trailer, which was not equipped with a locking device, and found that hooks, rollers, and a spare tire from

22 See, for example, *Chiaravalloti v Leading Edge Auto Collision*, 2012 ONSC 4554.
23 [1976] AJ No 551 (SCAD).
24 *Ibid* at paras 1–4.

its trailer were missing. The appellant sued in bailment for the loss.[25] As noted by Prowse JA, speaking for the Appellate Division of the Supreme Court of Alberta, "This left two time periods to be accounted for—the one when the trailer's contents were in the possession of the respondent waiting to undergo and while undergoing the cleaning process; the other, being that period when the trailer was, after washing, left unattended on the adjacent lot."[26]

Justice Prowse of the Court of Appeal admonished the trial judge for not clearly parsing out these two time periods in assessing the respondent's responsibility as bailee for the loss, in light of the appellant's clear knowledge and acceptance of the respondent's lax security arrangements in the adjacent lot by virtue of its course of conduct over the years it did business with the respondent. As the learned justice correctly notes, the respondent as bailee did bear responsibility for the first period, since it had possession of the appellant's property during this period of time, but not for the second, when the bailment had been terminated and only a licence existed.[27]

The difficulty was that there was no substantial evidence led by either party on the key issue of when and where the aforementioned items disappeared. The appellant had merely pleaded that the items it had left with the respondent were stolen but did not specify the time or place of the loss. Nevertheless, the trial judge concluded on the whole of the evidence that the items had likely disappeared while the trailer was parked in the adjacent lot after it had been washed, when only a licence existed, relieving the respondent of liability accordingly.[28]

The appeal court, relying on higher authorities, reached the same conclusion but for different reasons. Justice Prowse underlined that the heavy onus placed on the bailee to negative negligence is triggered *only* where the bailor has established that the loss occurred at a time when the bailee was in possession of the subject property. The appellant had failed to do so in a case where the respondent was vigorously disputing this fact.[29]

---

25 *Ibid* at para 5.
26 *Ibid.*
27 *Ibid* at para 8.
28 *Ibid.*
29 *Ibid* at paras 17–18.

Justice Prowse of the Court of Appeal explained the court's conclusion as follows, providing helpful guidance on how bailors (plaintiffs) can trigger the "reverse onus" against a bailee:[30]

> In reaching this conclusion I am not unmindful of the fact that the respondent chose not to call any of its employees as witnesses at the trial. However, this must be considered in the light of the general onus on the appellant to prove it's [sic] case by the balance of probabilities, it's [sic] failure to suggest on cross-examination that the loss had occurred while the trailer was in the respondent's possession, and further, in directing it's [sic] cross-examination to the alleged failure of the respondent to properly secure the unit while it was in the parking lot after it was washed. Such examination and the arguments addressed to the Court make it clear that the breach of duty alleged by the appellant was with respect to the security afforded the unit on the parking lot, and in that regard the trial judge found that the respondent was not negligent.

According to this decision, if a bailor wishes to put the bailee to the reverse onus in these circumstances, the bailor must argue, clearly and convincingly, in both its pleading and the formal presentation of its case, that the loss occurred during the course of the bailment, with the necessary level of particularity as to time and place.[31] The appellant's failure to do so in this case was fatal to its bailment action.

In *Rowsell v Fountain Tire (Fort St John) Ltd*,[32] there again was uncertainty with respect to when the damage to the plaintiff's property, in this case a car, had been occasioned, with nothing more than highly speculative evidence on the precise cause of the damage. Thus, as in *Calgary Transport*, the decision as to whether bailor had met its burden of proving that the damage occurred during the course of the bailment was determinative of liability between the parties.

The plaintiff had brought his car to the defendant's shop to get a wheel alignment done. He alleged that there was no damage whatsoever

30 *Ibid* at para 20.

31 In *Bexley v Salmon's Transfer Ltd*, 2004 BCPC 266 at para 16, Dhillon Prov Ct J seems to posit a lower standard, stating that once the bailor pleads "that the goods are damaged or lost, the onus of proof rests with the bailee to disprove negligence." The better view is that the bailor must also establish, in the formal presentation of its case, by a balance of probabilities, that the loss or damage of goods occurred while the bailee was in possession of the goods, unless the bailee admits to same.

32 2005 BCPC 42.

to the body of the car when it was brought in but that, upon receipt of the car following the completion of the repair, he found two noticeable dents located on the driver's side of the vehicle. There was nothing on his drive to the repair shop (no banging sounds or accident) that might explain the dents. The appearance and similarity of the two dents were consistent with them having been made by a two-pronged object. The plaintiff claimed that he had first noticed the dents shortly after he picked up his car from the repair shop, following a car wash. According to the plaintiff, he was not able to make such an observation immediately upon picking up his car from the defendant because another car was parked too close (on the driver's side) to his vehicle, preventing him from fully opening the driver's door upon getting into his car and possibly noticing the dents at that time. Immediately upon the discovery of the dents on the driver's door, the plaintiff returned to the defendant's shop to make a complaint.[33]

The defendant took the position that the car was already damaged when one of its employees, a Mr Boland, had commenced his inspection of it and that the damage had not occurred while the vehicle was on its premises.[34] Considering the whole of the evidence, including both the plaintiff's and defendant's evidence, which he found to be generally credible and trustworthy, the trial judge concluded that the origin of the damage was truly unknown and remained a mystery:[35]

> No obvious cause of the damage to the Claimant's car emerged from the evidence; its origin remains a mystery. Could the Claimant have overlooked the damage when he drove the car to get the alignment done? (This is possible, but seems unlikely, as the dents appear very noticeable in the photographs). Could the car have been vandalized by some third party while parked and awaiting repair? Could it have been accidentally damaged by one of the other employees in the Defendant's shop, unbeknownst to Mr. Boland [mechanic of the bailee] or Mr. Gervais [manager of the bailee]? Answers to these questions are only speculation.

Nonetheless, Skilnick Prov Ct J found that the plaintiff had met his burden of proof in showing that the damage had occurred while the car was in the care of the defendant repair shop, triggering the presumption against the defendant as bailee to disprove that its negligence had caused

33 *Ibid* at paras 3–9.
34 *Ibid* at paras 7 and 19.
35 *Ibid* at para 11.

the dents. In finding that the plaintiff's burden had been met, Skilnick Prov Ct J made a careful and thorough review of the evidence stating that the plaintiff had discovered the damage at his earliest opportunity and had reported it to the defendant promptly. The judge also emphasized that the dents would have been of lesser importance to the defendant than to the plaintiff, and that the defendant mechanic had made conflicting statements to the plaintiff regarding the existence of the dents. Finally, Skilnick Prov Ct J could not rule out the possibility that the dents might have occurred while the car was in the custody of the defendant but before the mechanic had begun his work on the car.[36]

Not surprisingly, the defendant was unable to successfully defend against the reverse onus. The defendant's mere denial that it had caused the damage was not enough for it to meet its onus of proof,[37] nor was the defendant's evidence in the record that showed that there was nothing in the repair shop of the defendant that would be consistent with being the cause of these dents.[38]

This case illustrates that, even where there is reasonable disagreement between the parties on when the damage to the goods occurred, and each party's version of events is fairly credible, a bailor can still meet its burden of proof. Justice Skilnick himself acknowledged that it was possible that the plaintiff had overlooked the damage prior to attending at the repair shop,[39] and yet he still found him to have met his burden of proof. Where there are two roughly equal and credible theories in the evidentiary record as to when the damage to the subject property occurred, one that supports the damage having occurred during the bailment and one that supports the damage having occurred outside the bailment, it is submitted that the former must be preferred over the latter, given the reality that bailees, because of their exclusive possession of bailor property and control of the premises on which it is located, are normally in a superior position over bailors when it comes to explaining damage or loss to bailor property.[40]

---

36 *Ibid* at para 16. As to the latter point, it is also true that Skilnick Prov Ct J could not rule out the damage having occurred before the plaintiff had arrived at the defendant's shop.

37 *Ibid* at para 19.

38 *Ibid* at para 5.

39 *Ibid* at para 11.

40 *Ibid* at para 20.

In *H & K Packers Ltd v Diamond Cold Storage Ltd*,[41] the plaintiff, a meat packer and processor, delivered a large quantity of meat products to the defendant for freezing, handling, and storage for a seven-day period. After retrieving some product from the defendant and delivering it to a customer who refused delivery on the basis of spoilage of some of the product, the plaintiff contacted a government inspector to inspect the defendant's premises. The inspector found that some of the plaintiff's remaining meat product had "an off-colour" and "a gaseous condition," and issued a detention order accordingly. Given the enormous cost of a salvage operation, which might very well exceed the value of the salvaged meat, and the risk that contamination from the spoiled product might well result in the destruction of the entire allotment, the plaintiff undertook no salvage operation. As a result, all the meat products spoiled and became worthless.[42]

The plaintiff sued the defendant in bailment, claiming that it had failed to properly freeze its meat products and was responsible for the loss.[43] The defendant argued that it had applied its usual freezing procedures in the handling of the plaintiff's meat products and that it had never experienced any freezing problem with the plaintiff's meat before, or with that of any other customers. The implication was that some of the plaintiff's meat products were in a spoiled condition when delivered to the defendant. It is to be noted that the product was received by the defendant in sealed cartons without opportunity for inspection.[44]

The plaintiff, in its evidence, stated that no bad meat was detected on the days during the processing period in question when the meat was in its plant, prior to its delivery of the meat products to the defendant, and that the meat products were processed in accordance with its standard practices. However, the plaintiff acknowledged that, when it receives a carcass for processing from a supplier, it does not know its age and relies on the reputation of the supplier and the fact that the supplier's meat has satisfied government inspection. Processing by the plaintiff entailed defatting and deboning the meat cuts; a process of freezing and cooling; and packaging the meat products into cardboard boxes and placing them onto pallets for delivery. The processing period varied from twelve to forty-eight hours, during which time the meat was stored in the plaintiff's plant. Spacers

41 [1980] MJ No 532 (Co Ct).

42 *Ibid* at paras 1–4.

43 *Ibid* at para 5.

44 *Ibid* at paras 14–15.

were occasionally used between boxes by the plaintiff to provide enhanced air circulation and acceleration of the freezing process at the storage plant, but none were available from the defendant on this particular occasion. The meat was also subject to the standard high temperatures during certain stages of processing and at the delivery times.[45]

The plaintiff also relied on a government inspection of the meat that had been done at the time of deboning and defatting and that confirmed the meat's good condition at that time, prior to the placement of the meat into cartons for delivery for freezing to the defendant's plant. The plaintiff, however, acknowledged that a period of forty-eight hours can elapse between the inspection and delivery.[46]

In deciding whether a bailment could be found, the bailor's onus of proof was the dispositive issue before the court. There was no question that some of the plaintiff's meat had been found to be spoiled after the defendant's handling of it; however, the question was whether the plaintiff could prove that the deterioration had occurred during the period of the bailment due to the improper storage of its goods. Without proving the good condition of the goods when bailed, there was no way for the plaintiff (bailor) to overcome its burden in that regard.

At the same time, there were several incontrovertible facts established in evidence, identified by Dureault CCJ of the Manitoba County Court of St Boniface, that weighed against the plaintiff (bailor). First, only a minority of the plaintiff's meat products had spoiled under the same supposed deficient freezing procedures. This meant, based on the testimony of a government meat inspector, that the spoiled meat must have been contaminated at the time of storage, prior to the bailment commencing. Second, no other complaints had been received by the defendant with respect to the very large quantities of meat it was holding under the same conditions as the plaintiff's meat products and had released during the relevant period of time.[47] In the words of Dureault CCJ, "The evidence negates any suggestion of breakdown or malfunction of defendant's refrigeration equipment."[48] Third, only the plaintiff's pork products had spoiled; its beef products went unharmed. Pork was more susceptible to deterioration than beef and had been exposed to high temperatures during the processing and

45 *Ibid* at paras 9–12.
46 *Ibid* at para 18.
47 *Ibid* at paras 15–18.
48 *Ibid* at para 18.

delivery periods, when the meat was still in the possession of the plaintiff. Fourth, there was no way to establish the age of the carcasses when delivered to the plaintiff. Fifth, the inspection of the plaintiff's meat products had not occurred at the point of delivery, and it was possible that some forty-eight hours had passed before delivery, when the meat was exposed to high temperatures (which would have a deteriorating effect on it) and was not subject to any inspection.[49]

In the result, the plaintiff (bailor) was found not to have met its burden of showing the good condition of the goods when bailed.[50] It is submitted that a bailor will not be able to meet its burden of proof in the presence of such evidence, in the absence of some reasonable inspection and verification process at the time of pickup confirming the good condition of the product when bailed. The mere fact that a bill of lading, or an equivalent document, was signed by the parties should not be treated as dispositive where the parties' signatures merely verify the fact of pickup, including the quantity of goods being picked up, but where there is no opportunity for inspection of the goods.

In *Atlantic Furs Ltd v Moffat Moving and Storage*,[51] Adams CJDC found that the plaintiff (bailor), a furrier, had not proven that the loss of its goods had occurred while the goods were in the defendant's (bailee's) custody—that is, after the defendant had collected the plaintiff's goods housed in unmarked and sealed cartons from the plaintiff's premises and stored them in its warehouse, but before it had completed its delivery of them to the plaintiff's new premises. Three relevant time periods were identified for consideration:[52]

1) the period of time during which the plaintiff packed the goods into cartons, readying them for delivery to its new premises, a period of five or six days, before the defendant took custody of the goods, during which period the goods were out of the sight of the plaintiff;
2) the period of time during which the goods were in the defendant's custody after pickup (that is, before the goods were delivered to the plaintiff's new premises), a period of approximately eight days; and

49 *Ibid* at paras 15–18.
50 *Ibid* at para 19.
51 [1985] NJ No 173 (Dist Ct) [*Atlantic Furs*].
52 *Ibid* at para 26.

3) the period of time between drop-off of the goods at the plaintiff's new premises and the plaintiff's discovery of the lost goods upon unpacking, a period of approximately four days, during which period the goods were out of the sight of the plaintiff.

Justice Adams held that, for the plaintiff to succeed, it had to establish by a balance of probabilities that the losses had occurred during the second period of time, when the defendant was in possession of the plaintiff's goods. Justice Adams found that the plaintiff had not done so, stating that "[n]o evidence was adduced to support an inference that the loss occurred while the goods were in the custody of the defendant."[53] This must be viewed as an overstatement. As in *Rowsell*,[54] there was circumstantial evidence in the record, presented by the plaintiff, supportive of the losses having occurred during the course of the bailment. For example, the trial judge found, based on the testimony of three plaintiff witnesses, unshaken on cross-examination, that some of the missing items had most certainly been packed by the plaintiff into cartons for pickup by the defendant. (While the judge raised the possibility that the items may not have been there when the defendant picked up the goods or may have disappeared after the date of delivery, it was probably equally possible that the disappearance occurred while the defendant was in possession of the goods.) The plaintiff also presented an inventory of the goods, albeit one that was created about two months before its goods were picked up and went missing, which was also supportive of the loss having occurred during the term of the bailment. The losses had also been complained of promptly, and a reasonable explanation had been given by the plaintiff to explain its inability to ascertain whether the cartons had been opened and resealed as a possible explanation for the loss, based on their visual inspection of them—namely, that the items had been placed in cartons provided by the defendant, which had bits of sealing tape stuck to them.[55]

Quite paradoxically, Adams CJDC nonetheless put the defendant to the reverse onus stating,[56] "Although the evidence is uncertain as to how or when the jackets and fur pieces were lost the defendant must establish that the loss of these items was not caused by its negligence."

53 *Ibid.*
54 Above note 32.
55 *Atlantic Furs*, above note 51 at paras 13–16.
56 *Ibid* at para 17.

Justice Adams found that the defendant had exercised reasonable care at all times in loading, transporting, storing, and securing the plaintiff's goods and had thereby discharged its burden, even though the cause of the loss could not be identified. The plaintiff's mere speculation that the losses might have occurred due to a "lapse of vigilance" when the defendant's staff, while in the process of delivery, received new instructions to take the goods to the defendant's warehouse, rather than to the plaintiff's new premises (the original destination agreed upon) was rejected out of hand by the court.[57] Certainly, requiring a bailee to show that it took reasonable care of the bailor's goods at the material times, rather than having it explain how the loss could have occurred without its negligence, reduces the severity of the reverse onus and makes it less determinative of liability between parties where the circumstances of the loss are unknown.[58]

It is submitted that the question of the bailor's onus of proof—that is, whether the bailor has established by a balance of probabilities that its goods had disappeared during the course of the bailment—must always be determined first, and independently of the question of whether the bailee has met its onus of proof. Justice Adams seems to have used his later finding that the defendant *had not been* negligent in its handling of the plaintiff's goods at any time to buttress his earlier finding that the bailor had not met its onus of proof. If this was in fact the case, which is questionable, there was no reason to go further. If a bailor's burden of proof is not met, then the bailment action is at an end, and there is no reason to consider the bailee's onus of proof.

2) Where the Bailee Has Not Had Exclusive Possession of the Missing Goods Throughout the Life of the Bailment Relationship (Recurring Bailments)

In *Lifestyles*,[59] the defendant, in exchange for a fee, was engaged as auctioneer to conduct an auction on the premises of the plaintiff. However, the defendant was not given keys to the premises and therefore did not have continuous and uninterrupted exclusive possession of the goods throughout the life of the bailment relationship (as would be the case in

57 *Ibid* at paras 18–25.

58 Whether this is an appropriate standard of care in these circumstances, or in any circumstance, is explored in Chapters 4 and 5.

59 Above note 15.

an ordinary bailment situation) under the parties' agreement, which commenced 6 November 1995 and terminated 10 November 1995. Instead, the plaintiff would let the defendant's employees onto the premises each morning and lock up after them[60] when they departed in the afternoon. In essence, the goods were redelivered from the defendant to the plaintiff at the conclusion of each day, in the sense that exclusive possession of certain portions of the premises, in which the goods were located, was transferred back from defendant to plaintiff.[61] As it happened, certain goods—namely a cash counter, kitchen doors, and drawer items—not intended by the plaintiff to be sold as part of the auction (and not covered by the plaintiff's insurance policy under the parties' agreement) mysteriously disappeared. Even though no evidence was before the court to establish the identity of the persons responsible for their disappearance,[62] the plaintiff argued that the defendant as bailee was liable for the loss, irrespective of the identity of such persons, since the goods were under its care and control at all material times.[63] The plaintiff stated that the defendant had breached its duty as bailee requiring it to return the missing items that were under its care and control to the plaintiff at the termination of the bailment.[64] The plaintiff took the position that the goods had gone missing either when the defendant's staff were on the premises on Thursday, 9 November, or in the intervening one hour between their departure (at 4:00 PM) and when the plaintiff's staff locked the front door of the building later that same day (at 5:00 PM).[65]

While the court had no problem concluding that the level of physical custody that the defendant had exerted over certain portions of the

60 The plaintiff's staff had the responsibility to see that the doors were locked after the defendant's staff had departed the premises for the day: *ibid* at para 4.

61 As in *Pilot*, above note 9, the arrangements between the parties gave rise to recurring bailments. But, unlike in that case, the question of whether the goods disappeared while in the possession of the bailee was vigorously disputed between the parties. The court's ultimate finding that the plaintiff had not met its burden of proof in that connection meant that the court did not have to assess whether the defendant had met its applicable standard of care.

62 As Cullity J pointed out, "The persons responsible could have been employees of either party, purchasers of other items or other individuals who entered the premises lawfully or unlawfully": *Lifestyles*, above note 15 at para 5.

63 *Ibid.*

64 In the alternative, the plaintiff argued that the defendant was in breach of the agreement and was liable for the damages that flowed from the breach: *ibid* at para 9.

65 *Ibid* at para 19.

plaintiff's premises[66] used for the purposes of the auction gave it "possession" of the missing items,[67] to constitute it "bailee" at law, the question of whether the missing items disappeared during the course of the bailment was not as easily answered. As the court noted, the precise circumstances in which the property disappeared were unknown. And so, the answer to the question of when the goods ultimately vanished turned on the factual findings made by the trial judge, findings based largely on the credibility he ascribed to the testimony given by the parties' respective employees. One of the defendant's employees, Mr Lee, testified that, when he left the premises at 4:00 PM on 9 November (what was agreed to be the defendant's last day on the premises),[68] the cash counter was still there, although he could not remember if he had told the plaintiff's staff that he was leaving or if he had locked the front door. An employee of the plaintiff who had official responsibility for allowing the defendant's employees into the building each morning and locking up after them when they departed in the late afternoon, Mr Sanchez, testified that he had locked the front doors of the premises as usual at 5:00 PM on that day but had not noticed whether the counter was in its accustomed position near the front door. He further testified that he last remembered seeing the cash counter the day before, on Wednesday, 8 November,[69] and did not discover that it was missing until the morning of Friday, 10 November, when he unlocked the front doors of the building. As for the other items, Mr Sanchez stated that he did not discover that they were missing until Monday, 13 November.[70]

---

66 Exclusive possession by the defendant was confined to the front part of the ground floor and the upper portion of the building. The plaintiff's staff were in other parts of the premises during the time in which the defendant's staff enjoyed exclusive possession of said areas, but most of the employees could be excluded by the defendant from the two areas over which it had exclusive possession: *ibid* at paras 14–15.

67 In making this determination, the court found no reasonable reason to distinguish between the items intended to be sold and the missing items (which were not intended to be sold), since the defendant's level of custody over the parts of the plaintiff's premises needed for the purposes of the auction (which included controlling access to areas in which both the missing and the non-missing items were displayed or stored) was exclusive, complete, and undeniable: *ibid* at para 15.

68 On that date, the parties had verbally agreed to alter the fixed term contained in the written bailment agreement to provide that the defendant would vacate the premises at the conclusion of that day's work, as their assistance was no longer required, instead of the next day, Friday, 10 November 1995, the date provided for in the written agreement between the parties: *ibid* at paras 3 and 20.

69 Another plaintiff employee, Mr Ricciardi, had testified that he had last seen the cash counter on Thursday morning, 9 November: *ibid* at para 8.

70 *Ibid* at para 25.

In the end, Cullity J favoured the testimony of the defendant's staff over that of the plaintiff's, concluding that the goods had not disappeared while in the custody of the defendant and that the plaintiff had failed to meet its onus of proof. Specifically, the judge accepted Mr Lee's evidence that the cash counter was in its usual spot when he left the property at 4:00 PM on the Thursday, and rejected Mr Sanchez's evidence that the cash counter was not in its accustomed position on Friday morning, when he alleges that the defendant's staff entered the building. Justice Cullity also rejected evidence that suggested that employees of the defendant may have come onto the property on the Friday, which might have extended the bailment relationship to that day, putting the defendant at greater risk of liability for the loss of the missing items, given the clear evidence in the record to the contrary. He further found that the cash counter had not disappeared between 4:00 PM and 5:00 PM on Thursday afternoon,[71] before the plaintiff claimed it had secured the front doors of the premises, during which period the trial judge accepts that the bailment relationship may have continued to subsist.[72] Finally, the trial judge found that the other items, which Mr Sanchez testified he had discovered were missing on Monday, 13 November, must have been taken at the same time as the

---

71 Based on the evidence before him, the trial judge reasoned that it would have been unlikely that the perpetrators would have had time during this small one-hour period to dismantle the cash counter and remove it in sections, as would be required, unless the people responsible were employees of the plaintiff or defendant with knowledge of the existence of the location of the doors and drawer fronts, which he did not find to be the case: *ibid* at para 25.

72 On a careful reading of Cullity J's reasons, it would seem that the bailment relationship in the case could be terminated in any one of three different ways, even though the judge made no explicit finding on the issue. The first would be by the defendant's locking of the front door of the plaintiff's property when it left, even though this was understood to be the responsibility of the plaintiff's employees. The second would be by the plaintiff's locking of the front door of the property immediately following the departure of the defendant's staff. The third would be by the staff of the defendant informing the plaintiff's staff that they were leaving, including presumably advising the plaintiff that they were leaving with or without having locked the front door. While Cullity J found that there was insufficient evidence that Mr Lee had either failed to lock the front door before leaving or failed to advise the plaintiff's staff that he was leaving, it is not clear exactly when and how the bailment relationship was terminated. That said, his reasons do indicate that the bailment relationship must have been terminated in one of the three aforementioned ways either at the point when Mr Lee left Lifestyles' premises at 4:00 PM on the Thursday or at 5:00 PM later that same day after the plaintiff's personnel had secured the door to the premises: *ibid* at paras 19–25 and 35–45.

cash counter[73]—that is, at some point when the goods were no longer in the possession of the defendant. In sum, there was insufficient evidence of negligence or breach of contract on the part of the defendant while it was in possession of the goods to make it liable in bailment.[74]

In circumstances such as those presenting in *Lifestyles*, a bailor will be hard-pressed to meet its burden of proof without a clear and strong evidentiary foundation establishing that the goods went missing while in the possession of the bailee. Merely pleading or arguing that the loss occurred while the bailee was in exclusive possession will not be enough where the evidence does not show that the bailee committed negligence or breach of contract during its possession of the goods. Given the determinativeness of the location of the onus of proof in these kinds of cases, a thorough and probing assessment of the evidence will need to be conducted by the trial judge. The bailor will need to demonstrate, by a balance of probabilities, that its burden of proof has been met. Notable inconsistencies in the bailor's evidence, such as those found in *Lifestyles*, will often undermine the bailor's credibility and evidence, such that it will be unable to meet its burden, with the attendant result that the bailee will not be put to the reverse onus to disprove negligence. Justice Cullity correctly recognized the determinative nature of the location of the onus of proof, given the lack of evidence on the precise circumstances of the loss[75]—the bailee would not be able to disprove that its negligence had caused the loss to exonerate itself from liability in the absence of an exemption clause—and, quite rightly, conducted a probing assessment of the evidence concerning the bailor's onus of proof, finding that it had not been met.

---

73 *Ibid* at para 25.

74 *Ibid* at para 38. The plaintiff's evidence was significantly weakened by the fact that Mr Sanchez's testimony, which had been corroborated by another plaintiff employee, Mr Riccardi, with respect to the discovery of the missing items, was at odds with answers that had been furnished by a Mr Plastina, another plaintiff employee at the defendant's examination for discovery. The plaintiff's position was also undermined by Mr Sanchez's questionable testimony that he had not noticed whether the cash counter, a large item that had been placed near the front door, was in its accustomed position when he proceeded to lock the front door on Thursday: *ibid* at para 23.

75 There was insufficient evidence that Mr Lee had left the premises without securing the front door or without informing employees of Lifestyles that he was leaving: *ibid* at paras 38 and 44. In the presence of such evidence, Cullity J stated that it may well be appropriate to place the reverse onus on the bailee, regardless of whether the bailor can demonstrate that the loss or damage in question occurred during the course of the bailment.

3) *Wong* Exception: Dead Bailee and No Bailed Goods?

In *Taylor Estate v Wong Aviation Ltd*,[76] an aircraft and the pilot who had rented it, Mr Douglas Taylor, went missing, never to be seen again. There was no affirmative evidence of negligence on the part of the pilot or any direct evidence as to what occurred. The appellant's estate was sued by two respondents, the owner of the aircraft and the company to whom the aircraft had been leased by the owner for rental to others. The corporate respondent sued the appellant's estate for the appellant's breach of the contract of bailment because the appellant had failed to return the plane he had rented, and, in the alternative, for negligence for loss of the plane. The individual respondent's action was limited to negligence, as he was not a party to the contract of bailment.[77]

The Supreme Court's treatment of the respondents' negligence and bailment actions in this case reveal much about the bailor's burden of proof. It concluded that the respondents had not met their respective burdens in negligence, based as they were on the doctrine of *res ipsa loquitur* ("the thing speaks for itself"), which allows for a finding of negligence against a defendant to be inferred from the nature of the event itself.[78] The Court reached that conclusion because there were explanations for the loss of the aircraft that did not support negligence by the deceased pilot, specifically those relating to inclement weather such as loss of vision, air turbulence, and carburetor icing, which were as convincing as explanations tied to negligence. (It is important to note that the doctrine of *res ipsa loquitur* does not need to be relied upon by a bailor to meet any part of its burden of proof in a bailment action and has no role to play in

76 [1969] SCR 481 [*Wong*].

77 *Ibid* at 483.

78 In *Marchuk (cob Gerry Marchuk Contracting) v Swede Creek Contracting Ltd* (1997), 43 BCLR (3d) 342 (SC) [*Marchuk*], the court stated that the doctrine operates "(1) when the thing which caused the injury complained of is under the management and control of the defendant and (2) the occurrence is such as would not happen in the ordinary course if the appropriate standard of care was exercised by the defendant": at para 10. (Where a plaintiff (bailor), or its counsel, admits that the injury complained of could have occurred in the absence of negligence, the doctrine of *res ipsa loquitur* is not invocable: *Tobin Tractor (1957) Ltd v Ideal Crane Rentals Ltd*, [1971] SJ No 311 at paras 13-14 (CA).) While Meiklem J in *Marchuk* held that exclusive possession of the subject property at the material time is a prerequisite to the application of the maxim, there is contrary authority from higher courts in Ontario: see *Kirk v McLaughlin Coal & Supplies Ltd*, [1968] 1 OR 311 (CA).

this area of the law. This is because a bailor need not show negligence by the bailee to put it to the reverse onus of disproving negligence. The doctrine is relevant to a negligence action only where the bailor is unable to meet its burden of proof and the event or circumstances lend themselves to an inference of negligence.[79])

In the bailment action, the Supreme Court transformed the law on burdens of proof for both bailors and bailees to apply in the anomalous factual circumstances arising in *Wong*, where the following circumstances apply:

1) there is a dead bailee
2) there are no bailed goods
3) nobody knows anything about the loss
4) there is no evidence of negligence or breach of contract by the bailee

First, the Court found it appropriate to transfer the burden of proof from the corporate respondent (bailor) to the appellant (bailee) in the case, albeit not in the usual way. This is not surprising; it was clear that the bailed goods disappeared while in possession of the appellant, remained missing, and had not been returned to the respondent as required. These were unassailable facts. Second, the Court decided to lower the appellant's (bailee's) onus of proof, deciding that, in the circumstances (no one could attest to what happened to the bailed airplane), the appellant should have to do no more than provide an explanation equally consistent with negligence and with no negligence to satisfy its burden of proof.[80] (This

79 *Wong*, above note 76 at 483. Justice Laskin of the Court of Appeal appears to have been attuned to this in the Court of Appeal below in *Wong*, when he aptly stated, "Since I do not agree that *res ipsa loquitur* has any place in our law of bailment I need not deal with the contention that it is inapplicable to the facts": [1966] 2 OR 182 at para 7 (CA). While the Supreme Court's decision in *Wong* calls this into question, it is now probably a moot point in light of the Court's later decision in *Fontaine v British Columbia (Official Administrator)*, [1997] SCJ No 100 [*Fontaine*], where the Court discards the doctrine from the law of negligence and, probably by extension, from the law of bailment.

80 Certainly, this means that the theory advanced by the bailee must be plausible and find support in the evidentiary record; mere conjectural possibilities are not enough for a bailee to meet its burden of proof here: *Marchuk*, above note 78 at para 11. In *Wong*, above note 76, for example, had the appellant's estate (bailee) advanced the theory, in response to the respondent's, that the plane's disappearance might be due to it being hit by another plane, this would have been mere conjecture without any support in the evidentiary record, such that the appellant would have been faced with liability and the respondent (bailors) would have been found to have met their respective burdens of proof.

burden of proof is obviously easier to meet than the ultimate burden of proof in ordinary bailment actions, which requires the bailee to disprove negligence or show that reasonable care over the goods was taken to avoid a judgment against them.) The appellant (bailee) was able to meet this reduced burden easily by showing that inclement weather causing loss of vision, or another like circumstance, could have caused the loss of the plane just as much as the deceased's negligence arising from inexperience or otherwise.[81] Having done so, the Supreme Court, thirdly, transferred the ultimate burden of proof back to the respondent (bailor) to establish that the deceased had been negligent in losing the aircraft. The respondent was essentially left with proving negligence in the ordinary way. With no evidence in the record showing fault by the deceased, this obviously proved to be an impossible task, forcing the respondent to rely on the doctrine of *res ipsa loquitur* to try to discharge the ultimate burden of proof that had been foisted upon it under the law of bailment.[82]

Justice Ritchie summarized the unenviable position in which the respondent (bailor) found itself:

> As the respondents in the present case have not adduced any evidence to "establish a fault or default in the defendant," the outcome of the bailment action must depend upon whether "the event is of such a nature as of itself to raise a prima facie case of fault or default . . . ." In other words, the bailor's action depends upon the application of the rule embodied in the maxim res ipsa loquitur.[83]

Justice Ritchie quickly disposed of the bailment action on the same basis as the respondents' negligence actions: the nature of the event was not one to which the doctrine of *res ipsa loquitur* should be invoked, given the reality that there were two equally credible theories supported by the evidentiary record as to what happened to cause the loss of the plane and that they were equally consistent with negligence and no negligence.[84]

It is submitted that, if the bailee succeeds in discharging its burden of proof under this formula by providing an explanation for the loss that

---

81 In the earlier case of *United Motors Service Inc v Hutson*, [1937] SCR 294, Duff CJC classified such an explanation by a defendant as falling within the category of "inevitable accident," which will allow a defendant to neutralize the inference of negligence otherwise arising from the evidence.

82 *Wong*, above note 76 at 491.

83 *Ibid* at 490.

84 *Ibid* at 490–91.

is consistent with no negligence and equally credible with those explanations pointing the other way, then the bailor will have no means of fixing liability against a bailee by meeting its further burden of showing negligence on the part of the bailee. If the evidence on both sides is roughly equal in support of negligence and no negligence, then how can a bailor possibly break the logjam in circumstances where there is no evidence of what actually happened? This makes the last stage of legal analysis established by the Supreme Court in *Wong* quite superfluous. As well, there is no question that the modifications made to the law of bailment by the Supreme Court in *Wong* strip bailment law of one of its essential characteristics — that is, the ability of the bailor to put the heavy and ultimate burden of proof on the bailee by showing something short of negligence by the bailee. That said, the *Wong* criteria are *not easily met*,[85] and the facts requiring its application rarely arise.

F. *RES IPSA LOQUITUR*

Clearly, the doctrine of *res ipsa loquitur* has no relevance to bailment actions outside the unique circumstances presenting in *Wong* because a bailor is not required to prove negligence against a bailee to succeed in a bailment action. All that has to be shown by the bailor is damage or loss to its goods while they were in the possession of the bailee.[86] Once this is done, the bailee, to avoid liability, is required to disprove that its negligence caused the loss. Even in the circumstances presenting in *Wong*, where

---

85 In *Amo Containers Ltd v Mobil Oil Canada Ltd*, 1989 CanLII 3947 (Nfld CA), the court found, Goodridge CJN, that the information about the cause of the sinking of the respondent (bailee's) ship housing containers with the appellant's goods in them in a severe storm, obtained by way of a royal commission, meant that the *Wong* exception could not be invoked, since "the threshold point" for the invocation of the exception — "nobody knows anything about it" — had not been met: paras 1–3 and 15. Similarly, in *Marchuk*, above note 78, Meiklem J also held, albeit in *obiter*, that the *Wong* criteria had not been met because the defendant (bailee) had not disappeared and because the bailed goods had not been destroyed completely but only severely damaged: paras 31–33.

86 For these reasons, decisions that attribute the justification for the reverse onus in bailment actions to the application of the doctrine of *res ipsa loquitur* are misplaced and should not be followed: see Bridges CJNB's discussion in *Northumberland County School Finance Board v Stewart* (1965), 54 DLR (2d) 657 at para 9 (NBSCAD). The reason for the reverse onus is that, because of the bailee's exclusive possession of the goods, it is usually the *only* party that can explain what has happened to the goods during its custody of them.

the bailee is relieved of such burden and the bailor is required to prove negligence in the ordinary way, it is unlikely that the doctrine will be of any assistance to the bailor. This is because the bailor, as happened in that case, will be at a loss to show that an inference of negligence against the bailee should be maintained in the presence of an evidentiary record that gives roughly equal credibility to theories in support of negligence and no negligence on the part of the bailee, and where there is no evidence as to what actually transpired to cause the loss of the bailed property. As stated by Meiklem J of the British Columbia Supreme Court in *Marchuk*, when the doctrine of *res ipsa loquitur* has been invoked by the presence of the necessary facts, "an inference of negligence may be made unless the defendant offers an explanation for the occurrence which at least neutralizes the persuasive effect of the inference of negligence."[87]

In any event, the point is probably moot in light of the Supreme Court's decision in *Fontaine*,[88] a negligence case involving the death of the plaintiff's husband who was travelling with a driver in bad weather with no evidence as to how the accident occurred, where the high court decided to discard the doctrine of *res ipsa loquitur* from negligence actions altogether:

> It would appear that the law would be better served if the maxim was treated as expired and no longer used as a separate component in negligence actions. After all, it was nothing more than an attempt to deal with circumstantial evidence. That evidence is more sensibly dealt with by the trier of fact, who should weigh the circumstantial evidence with the direct evidence, if any, to determine whether the plaintiff has established on a balance of probabilities a prima facie case of negligence against the defendant. Once the plaintiff has done so, the defendant must present evidence negating that of the plaintiff or necessarily the plaintiff will succeed.[89]

This holding is likely applicable to bailment actions as well. In *Marchuk (cob Gerry Marchuk Contracting) v Swede Creek Contracting Ltd*,[90] the Court of Appeal for British Columbia, while finding that the doctrine of *res ipsa loquitur* had been discarded from negligence actions by virtue of the Supreme Court's decision, confirmed that the principles governing

---

87 *Marchuk*, above note 78 at para 10.
88 Above note 79.
89 *Ibid* at para 27.
90 (1998), 116 BCAC 318 at paras 10–16 (CA).

the use of circumstantial evidence in determining liability for negligence had not changed, minimizing the impact of the decision. The appeal court, after considering "the whole of the direct and circumstantial evidence," agreed that the inference drawn by the trial judge of negligence against the defendant for the damage caused to the plaintiff's grapple skidder while it was in the defendant's care and control was reasonable in the circumstances. There was also insufficient evidence to negate the inference or to neutralize it. These findings obviated the need for the appeal court to rule on the plaintiff's alternative claim in bailment and any role the doctrine might have to play there. Nonetheless, it is submitted that, outside of the *Wong* circumstances, the doctrine of *res ipsa loquitur* has no applicability whatever to bailment actions, and even in circumstances similar to those in *Wong*, it may not, in light of the Supreme Court's holding in *Fontaine*. In any event, even if the doctrine had not been discarded by the Supreme Court in *Fontaine* from bailment actions, it will likely not be invocable for the reasons discussed earlier.

G. CONCLUSION

In the usual bailment case, the bailor's onus of proof will easily be met. The bailor will simply have to demonstrate that the goods disappeared, or were damaged, while in the possession of the bailee to trigger an onus on the bailee to disprove negligence. However, the bailor's onus of proof may present real difficulties where the evidence before a court is equivocal, or conflicting, on when the damage to the bailed goods occurred—that is, before a bailment began or after a bailment was terminated. Certainly, a bailor is required to show, by a balance of probabilities, that the goods were damaged while in the bailee's possession, which may require the bailor to show the satisfactory condition of the goods when bailed, and the unsatisfactory condition of the goods when returned. A bailor's mere allegation, statement, or plea that the goods were damaged during the course of the bailment is not enough, without more, for a bailor to meet its onus of proof where there is a real question as to whether the goods were damaged or lost during the term of the bailment. In the harder cases, a trial judge must undertake a very probing analysis of the evidence and credibility of the parties, for a decision on the bailor's onus of proof may well be determinative as a result of the uncertainty surrounding the loss of the goods. Finally, in the anomalous circumstances presenting in

Wong, while a bailor will have no trouble placing a burden of proof on a dead bailee's estate, it will not "pack the same punch." That is to say, the defendant will enjoy a relaxed onus: the bailee's estate *will not have to disprove negligence to be exonerated from liability*. Instead, to succeed, the estate will merely have to advance a theory of loss consistent with no negligence on the part of the dead bailee that is as convincing as any theory presented by the bailor going the other way.

CHAPTER 3

A Bailor's Onus of Proof: More Specific Considerations

A. INTRODUCTION

Besides the more general considerations that were canvassed in the preceding chapter, several specific considerations or factors might arise on any given set of facts, each of which requires specific treatment. While the discussion in the following sections should not be considered exhaustive, certainly these considerations should be looked at where a court is trying to ascertain whether a bailor's onus of proof has been met.

B. TO SUCCEED, A BAILOR MAY NEED TO SHOW THAT THE LOSS OCCURRED WHILE THE PURPOSE OF BAILMENT REMAINED TO BE COMPLETED

Where the purpose for which a bailment was created has been completed, in the absence of special arrangements being made between the parties with respect to the safekeeping of the subject property, or a reasonable expectation that the bailment continues, the relationship can quickly become one of licence, meaning that the bailee will have no duty whatsoever to safeguard the bailor's property. In these circumstances, the bailor, to succeed, will be required to show that the loss or damage to its property occurred during the former period, when a bailment existed. Alternatively, the bailor will be required to show that special arrangements were made to extend the bailment relationship between the parties—for example, to allow the bailor extra time to make the necessary arrangements to have its property picked up[1]—or that the bailee's act of redelivery was negligent such that the bailment should be viewed as continuing for a reasonable time following the act of negligence, or until the property is properly redelivered to the bailor.

Furbank v Andersen[2] is instructive. There, the plaintiff drove her vehicle into the defendant car wash's parking lot, leaving her vehicle in one of the defendant's marked parking spaces. She was about to depart the premises with her son when she was stopped by the defendant and asked if she wished to have her car washed. She indicated that she did and then left immediately without paying for the wash in advance, as was the defendant's standard practice. She did not state when she would return, or what was to be done with the vehicle after it was washed.[3]

The defendant completed the wash and placed the plaintiff's vehicle on his premises, awaiting collection by the plaintiff. The defendant left the keys in the ignition of the plaintiff's car, stating in his evidence that he had no facilities for storing such items, that it was not his practice to assume responsibility for ignition keys, and that he expected cars to be picked up immediately after the washing process and removed from his premises, as he has no space to store vehicles. Both the car wash and the parking lot were unenclosed areas. The plaintiff did not return that day to pick up her vehicle, and, during the night hours, her vehicle was stolen by a thief and subsequently damaged by this person.[4]

The plaintiff sued in bailment, but Tyrwhitt-Drake Co Ct J of the British Columbia County Court refused to find that a bailment applied to the parties at the time of the theft, as the purpose for which the car was bailed had been completed:

> There is no doubt, I think, that the defendant, as operator of a car-wash, is a bailee for hire of cars in his possession, while they are being washed, and perhaps for a reasonable time before and after the washing process. It is simply a question of possession, and the duration of the bailment would vary in each case. He is paid (though he was not in this instance) for washing, and his liability as a bailee would be limited to the duration of his possession for this purpose. Once a car is washed, he has no

1 See, for example, *Ritchie Bros Auctioneers Ltd v Chabot & Levesque Logging Ltd*, [1982] BCJ No 1415 at para 3 (Co Ct).

2 [1966] BCJ No 49 (Co Ct) [*Furbank*].

3 *Ibid* at paras 2–3.

4 *Ibid* at paras 4–5 and 8.

> further interest in it; unless special arrangements are made, he says, he expects a washed car to be removed from his premises at once. He has no room to store cars, and only does so by special arrangement. In my view, once a car is washed and ready to be taken away, there is an end to mandatum. There is not even simple depositum, for the purpose of the defendant's possession has been accomplished.[5]

In the result, only a licence was found to apply, and the plaintiff's bailment action failed accordingly.[6] In the colourful words of Tyrwhitt-Drake Co Ct J, "a person who loses an automobile (an article particularly attractive to the idiot as well as to the criminal) left by him on premises, as open to depredation as any public way[,] cannot attach blame for such negligence to the owner of the premises who is not a bailee of the automobile."[7]

In circumstances such as those presenting in *Furbank*, where there is no negligence in redelivery by the bailee, no special arrangements are made for disposition of the bailed property once the work agreed upon between the parties has been completed, no reasonable expectation exists that the bailment is to continue, and it is clear that the damage occurred during a period of time subsequent to the expiry of the bailment, a bailor will not be able to meet its burden of proof and will likely be left without a remedy for losses.

1) Gratuitous Bailments

A lesser standard *should not* be applied for gratuitous bailments. The court's holding in *Odian v Capalla Holdings Ltd (cob Capalla Car & Truck Sales)*[8] is therefore questionable. There, the plaintiff, Gordon Odian, relinquished possession of his truck to the defendant Jeffy Zachariuk, who was employed by a car sales dealer, the defendant Capalla Holdings Ltd, for sale by consignment. Odian had purchased the truck from an acquaintance whom he trusted and therefore did not take any steps to confirm whether or not the vehicle had sustained previous damage or whether there were any liens against it. After using it for a few years and having no more use for the vehicle, Odian decided to try to sell the vehicle and posted an advertisement in the local paper accordingly. At that time, the truck had

5 *Ibid* at para 8.
6 *Ibid* at para 10.
7 *Ibid* at para 11.
8 [2009] BCJ No 2040 (Prov Ct).

a brake problem, which was the only problem Odian was experiencing with it. Zachariuk expressed interest in buying the vehicle and did eventually purchase it for sale through Capalla, pursuant to a consignment agreement. Zachariuk was told about the brake problem and he agreed to repair it. The repair was made immediately upon Zachariak's picking up the vehicle from Odian, prior to him delivering the vehicle to the car sales lot, given the apparent seriousness of the problem, as determined by Zachariak upon driving the vehicle. The truck had to be returned to the repair shop a little while later for a more complete repair when the brake calliper started seizing up again. It was eventually agreed by the parties that the total costs of the repairs could be deducted from the net proceeds of the sale for the truck when the vehicle sold.[9]

The duration of the agreement was for thirty days, and the minimum selling price for the sale of the vehicle was set at $8,000. The vehicle was placed in a prominent location on Capalla's lot, with high visibility to passing highway traffic. As it happened, Zachariuk, in anticipation of making a sale to a potential purchaser, conducted a search of the vehicle's history and discovered two glass and two collision claims. Odian expressed surprise at the discoveries, and he claimed that, when he visited the lot, Zachariuk nevertheless reassured him that he remained willing to keep the vehicle on the lot and to attempt to make a sale, despite the impact that these disclosures might have on the vehicle's saleability. Zachariak, however, stated in his evidence that he told Odian that these disclosures would be concerning to any customer, and, after another potential purchaser had advised him that the truck was known to him and had had its odometer rolled back considerably, that he had moved the truck to the back of the lot, had firmly advised Odian he was no longer prepared to sell it, and had told Odian to come and pick up the truck from the lot. He stated that he had been misled by Odian as to the condition of the truck and that Odian needed to pay him for the repairs that Capalla had incurred on his behalf prior to taking the vehicle away. Zachariak also stated that Odian, at some point subsequent to this, had attended at the lot and had tried to persuade Zachariak to keep the truck and attempt to sell it for less, namely $7,000, but that Zachariak had declined his offer. Odian denied that these events had occurred. In their respective statements, each party claimed that the discussions and events had occurred at the end of the one-month

9 *Ibid* at paras 1–21.

agreement. Later, the vehicle was stolen from the lot by thieves and located near the local cemetery. It was damaged beyond repair.[10]

As apparent, the evidence was conflicting on what (exactly) the parties had agreed to following the expiry of the thirty-day period, with each party, as described above, claiming something disparately different than the other. Odian's evidence, if accepted, pointed to a "continuing bailment," while Zachariak's evidence, if accepted, pointed to the termination of the bailment following the thirty-day period and to the creation of a licence relationship thereafter. In addition, the defendants themselves in their submissions argued, alternatively, that, if there was a bailment in existence at the time of the loss, it was a gratuitous one.[11]

Justice Brecknell of the British Columbia Provincial Court favoured Zachariak's version of events — that, by the time of the theft, the defendant Capalla was no longer attempting to sell the truck. That is to say, the purpose for which the bailment was formed was at an end. But, strangely, the trial judge found that this was fatal only to the plaintiff's (bailor's) ability to prove a bailment for reward, *but not* to a gratuitous bailment. The judge proceeded to fix liability against the defendant Capalla, on the basis of a gratuitous bailment, for not leaving insurance on the vehicle when it was placed at the back of its lot, as a prudent owner of the vehicle would have done, or, alternatively, for having failed to redeliver the truck to Odian's residence, which was only a short drive away, when dealer plates were available for them to do so.[12]

However, it is submitted that there could be no continuing bailment of any nature if the learned judge accepted Zachariak's evidence in its entirety. The term of the bailment (i.e., thirty days) was over; the plaintiff (bailor) had been asked to pick up his vehicle and had presumably failed to do so within a reasonable time (having had the opportunity to do so on a previous visit to the defendant's premises); the defendant Capalla was no longer attempting to sell the vehicle; and an act of redelivery had occurred. The terms of the bailment contract did not require the defendants to return the plaintiff's truck to his residence, and this has not been required of bailees at law in similar circumstances in order to dispossess themselves of bailor

10 *Ibid* at paras 12–36.

11 *Ibid* at paras 43–44.

12 *Ibid* at paras 48–54.

property.[13] The placing of the vehicle at the back of Capalla's lot was sufficient to qualify as an act of redelivery and was probably in accordance with industry practice. As a result, there was no negligence in redelivery that may have extended the duration of the bailment beyond a reasonable time for the plaintiff (bailor) to pick up his property; and only a licence was in existence at the time of the loss. A licensor is not a gratuitous bailee and is not required to insure a vehicle and owes no duty of care to a licensee. In these circumstances, a bailor should not be able to meet its onus of proof.

C. BAILEE NEGLIGENCE AT THE TIME OF REDELIVERY EXTENDS THE DURATION OF A BAILMENT

If a bailee is negligent at the time of redelivery, it is submitted that a bailment should not be considered to have been terminated. Instead, it should be viewed as continuing until the property is properly redelivered to the bailor or a reasonable time has passed since the delivery was made, with the attendant result that a bailee is responsible for any damage or loss that befalls the goods during these further periods of time. If the time of the loss is uncertain, but bailee negligence can be shown to have occurred at the time of redelivery, then it seems prudent to put the bailee to the reverse onus.

This position is consistent with the view of the law propounded in Chapter 1, Section B(1)(b)(vii)(c) and the discussion of *Luider v Nguyen (cob Nanton Packers)*[14] in relation to acts of delivery by bailors, where an act of negligence by a bailor during its delivery of goods to a bailee was found capable of disqualifying a bailment. Accordingly, bailee negligence at the time of redelivery must similarly be considered by a court when deciding whether a bailor has met its burden of proof. Where an act of negligence has occurred, a bailor may have a greater window of time within which to meet its burden of showing that the loss or damage to its goods occurred at a time when the bailee was in possession of them.

There is support to be found in *Lifestyles Kitchens & Bath, a division of GVBS Inc v Danbury Sales Inc.*[15] There, Cullity J stated the following, albeit in *obiter*:

---

13 See *Furbank*, above note 2; *Calgary Transport Services Ltd v Pyramid Management Ltd*, [1976] AJ No 551 (SCAD) [*Calgary Transport*].

14 [1994] AJ No 494 (Prov Ct (Civ Div)).

15 [1999] OJ No 3097 (SCJ) [*Lifestyles*].

> It is not necessary for me to express an opinion whether the position would be different if the evidence was sufficient to establish that Lee departed the premises without securing the front door and without informing employees of Lifestyles. In that situation, the location of the onus of proving, or disproving, a want of reasonable care would be irrelevant but there would still be a question with respect to the onus of proving that the negligence caused the loss. Notwithstanding the general statements in the cases to which I have referred, a bailee who is shown not to have exercised reasonable care in attempting to redeliver possession to the bailor might well be fixed with the burden of proving that its default did not cause the loss in a case like this where the time of the disappearance of the items is uncertain.[16]

In other words, if the evidence had shown that Mr Lee of the defendant had been negligent in transferring the premises back to the plaintiff by not locking the front door of the plaintiff's premises and by not informing the plaintiff that he was leaving, then the defendant might well have been put to the reverse onus of proving that its negligence had not caused the loss (meaning that the plaintiff bailor would have been found to have met its applicable burden of proof). Given the uncertainty surrounding the loss, this would most certainly have resulted in liability being fixed against the defendant.

Whether there is negligence by the bailee in redelivery, extending the duration of the bailment and making it easier for the bailor to meet its burden of proof, will depend on the circumstances, of course. In *Calgary Transport*,[17] the appellant's trailer was placed in an adjoining lot of the respondent (bailee) for pickup by the appellant after it had been washed by the respondent. To the knowledge of the appellant, this lot was insecure, and the respondent took no responsibility for goods once deposited there. The respondent made no assurances of safekeeping; the lot was provided simply as an amenity to its customers at no additional cost. Certain items were found to be missing from the trailer when the appellant later picked it up from this lot. The appellant sued in bailment but did not properly plead or meet its burden of proof at trial of showing that the loss had occurred while the respondent was still in possession of the goods, which proved to be fatal to its bailment claim.

---

16 *Ibid* at para 44.

17 Above note 13.

At any rate, the court found that any bailment of the appellant's trailer would have terminated after it was washed and delivered to this adjoining lot awaiting pickup by the appellant, with only a licence relationship existing thereafter. The respondent was not found to have been negligent in its delivery of the trailer to this insecure lot. Thus, the appellant (bailor) was left to prove that its losses had occurred while the trailer was being washed, during the subsistence of the bailment, which it did not do, resulting in its bailment claim failing. The case demonstrates that whether an "act of redelivery" amounts to negligence, causing a bailment relationship to continue and creating a larger window of time for a bailor to meet its burden of proof, depends on the parties' agreement, the bailor's knowledge of the bailee's measures (or lack thereof) in place to protect its goods, and the bailee's representations as to safekeeping.

Whether a bailee's leaving of keys in the ignition switch and the doors of a bailor's vehicle unlocked on an unenclosed lot on its premises, following completion of the purpose for which a bailment was formed, amounts to negligence in redelivery, such that the bailment should continue, depends on context and the reasonable expectation of the parties.[18] No such finding was made in *Furbank*,[19] in the circumstances of that case. There is contrary authority, which, at its highest, states that, where a repair or service cannot be effected immediately and a bailor leaves a car behind, then the bailee, if it is going to park the car on its lot after the work is done, must secure the keys and lock the car's doors and cannot be relinquished of possession or the duty of safekeeping until the bailor collects the car or clearly relieves the bailee of its duties and responsibilities in some other acceptable manner.[20] There is another line of caselaw that appears to support a lower standard and states that bailee responsibilities in these circumstances can be met by the bailee's mere securing of the keys to the vehicle, such that the keys cannot be used to facilitate an easy removal of a bailor's car from a bailee's lot. This means that, if a vehicle is removed from the bailee's lot by a thief without the benefit of keys, the bailee will not be responsible in the absence of a contractual

18 As we saw in Chapter 1, a parking operator's leaving of a vehicle in such a state on its lot where only a licence exists between the parties is acceptable, as a licensor does not owe a licensee any duty of safekeeping over its property.

19 Above note 2.

20 *St-Isidore Asphalte Ltée v Luminex Signs Ltd*, [1996] NBJ No 62 (QBTD) [*St-Isidore Asphalte*], aff'd [1997] AN-B no 72 (CA).

duty to obtain insurance for the bailor's vehicle to protect against theft.[21] It is submitted that no absolute rule should apply here; instead, all relevant factors must be considered, including the reasonable expectation of the parties; any communications exchanged between the parties at the material times; and the bailee's capacities and abilities, as may be known by the bailor.

D. CONTINUING BAILMENTS IN OTHER CIRCUMSTANCES

Where a bailment is found to be a "continuing one," a bailor will have a larger time window within which to satisfy its burden of showing that the loss or damage to its goods occurred during the period of the bailment.

1) The Possibility of Further Work to Be Done to a Bailed Property

In *DJ Lowe (1980) Ltd v Roach (cob Vern's Auto Repairs)*,[22] the plaintiff left its truck, which had a boom crane mounted on the back, with the defendant for repair. The truck was to be converted into a water tanker truck. The parties discussed the defendant's remounting the plaintiff's crane onto another truck following its removal from the plaintiff's truck, but the first job was to take priority and be done quickly (which it was). The defendant agreed to do the second job if the plaintiff wished, but no agreement between the parties was ever reached. When the plaintiff arrived to pick up the newly converted truck, it found that its crane had been placed by the defendant outside of the defendant's building on the ground. A discussion over this ensued, in which the court found that the defendant represented to the plaintiff that its crane would be safe there and that he had never lost any equipment from its yard.[23]

When the plaintiff decided that it did not wish to have the defendant complete the second job, since it was not pleased with the quality of the work done by the defendant, it attended at the premises to pick up its crane. However, the plaintiff found the crane to be missing from the location in the yard in which it had been placed, and could not find it anywhere in the yard. The defendant stated that he thought that the crane had been picked up by employees of the plaintiff over two weeks earlier and had been taken

---

21 *Simon v MacDonald*, [2000] NBJ No 479 (QB).

22 [1994] NSJ No 208 (SC) [*Lowe*], aff'd [1995] NSJ No 62 (CA).

23 *Lowe*, above note 22 at paras 1–12.

away with them at that time. The area from which the crane was taken was insecure and easily accessible by customers of the defendant. The plaintiff sued in bailment. Justice Grant found that the defendant could have easily secured the plaintiff's property (by putting it inside its locked facilities or in a less conspicuous and more secure location), in circumstances where it decided not to use a watchperson to oversee the property, and had been negligent in not doing so.[24]

A key issue in the case was whether a bailment continued to apply to the crane after the plaintiff's pickup of its converted truck, to the time that it went missing. Justice Grant found it did and relied on three facts. First, the parties had agreed to leave the crane at the defendant's premises for a reasonable time for the plaintiff to consider the further job.[25] Second, the defendant had given the plaintiff assurances of safekeeping with respect to the crane. Third, the defendant misled the plaintiff about the level of security in the part of the yard in which its crane would be stored. Had the defendant not done so, the plaintiff would have likely opted for a safer alternative.[26]

The plaintiff (bailor) was easily able to meet its onus of proof in these circumstances. When an employee of the plaintiff attended at the defendant's premises, the crane was missing. But, unlike the subject property in *Calgary Transport*, the crane was still the subject of a bailment. According to Grant J, based on the parties' dealings with each other, the plaintiff was to be given a reasonable time to consider whether it wished to proceed

24 *Ibid* at paras 14–20 and 35–40.

25 It is submitted that the "mere possibility" that a second job may be done involving part of a bailor's property (originally delivered to a bailee for a separate purpose), even where parties agree that this remaining property is to remain on the bailee's property for a reasonable time for the bailor to consider a further job with respect to the property, is not enough, without more, to create or to continue a bailment. There must be a clear assumption of safekeeping by the bailee over the remaining property for a bailment to come into being.

26 Justice Grant's decision to find a bailment might be questioned on the basis of the unfettered access to the crane that the parties intended the plaintiff (bailor) to have, and that it did in fact have, while it remained on the defendant's premises: see *Lessor v Jones* (1920), 52 DLR 523 (NBSCAD). This intention was shown on the plaintiff's unscheduled visit to the defendant's yard with its own boom truck to pick up its crane when it decided it did not wish for the defendant to do any more work for it. The plaintiff searched the yard, expecting to find it and take it away itself without any assistance from the defendant. The crane was found to be missing, and the defendant was later contacted and so advised. The defendant was surprised to learn this, advising that he thought that the crane had been picked up by a plaintiff employee over two weeks prior, when it first noticed it was gone: *Lowe*, above note 22 at paras 15–17.

with the second job. The roughly two months that passed from the pickup of its converted truck from the defendant's premises (and the completion of the first job) and the disappearance of the crane was viewed as a reasonable amount of time for the plaintiff to consider the second job, and, so, a bailment of the crane was found to still exist.

This case demonstrates that the time at which a bailment is found to terminate (or not terminate) can be determinative of whether a bailor can meet its burden of showing that the loss occurred during the period of the bailment, resulting in the heavy onus to disprove negligence being placed on the bailee. This decision should not be made lightly and must consider whether possession has been transferred back to the bailor. Much will depend on the parties' agreement, states of knowledge, and communications at the material times. As illustrated in *Calgary Transport*, physical redelivery of the subject property may not be required for a bailee to dispossess itself of a bailor's property. A constructive transfer of possession is sometimes sufficient. In *Lowe*, however, the mere fact that the plaintiff reserved a right to repossess its crane at any time from the defendant's premises, within a reasonable time following completion of the first job, was not enough to defeat the bailment.

2) A Bailment to Continue for a Reasonable Time Following Its Completion

Whether a bailment of goods should continue for a reasonable time after its stated purpose is completed, to allow a bailor to retrieve the property, is a question of some difficulty. As we have seen, physical redelivery of property to a bailor is not necessary to end a bailment. And when the purpose for the bailment ends (e.g., the car is washed), a bailment can be at an end either immediately or perhaps after a reasonable time has elapsed to allow the bailor to pick up the property.[27] This result, it is submitted, must obtain unless there is a reasonable expectation that the bailee retain the property for safekeeping for a further period of time. Such an expectation can arise from industry practice or from the circumstances, including any relevant discussions that may have occurred between the parties. For example, where a bailor leaves a vehicle at a repair shop for a repair because the repair cannot be effected immediately, it may be reasonable

---

27 *Furbank*, above note 2.

to expect that the bailee will notify the bailor to pick up the car from its facilities once the repair has been made, and to allow the bailor a reasonable opportunity to do so before the bailment is at an end. During this period of time, the bailee would have a duty to safeguard the vehicle owner's keys and to protect the vehicle from harm or loss. Whether the bailee has the facilities or capability to safeguard the bailor's property once the purpose of the bailment has been completed, and the bailor's knowledge of this capability (or lack thereof), must always be considered by courts in deciding whether there was a reasonable expectation between the parties that a bailment should continue after the stated purpose of the bailment was completed; no absolute rule should apply here. Certainly, where the purpose for the bailment is over, and the bailor is put on express notice to pick up the property and fails to do so within a reasonable time, the risk of loss should be on the bailor.

3) An Absolute Duty of Safekeeping Until Clearly Relieved of Possession by the Bailor

Admittedly, there are judicial authorities that appear to place an "absolute duty" on bailees in all circumstances to safeguard a bailor's property even after the stated purpose of a bailment has been completed, and the bailor has been notified of same, until the point that the bailor has relieved the bailee of its duty in some affirmative manner, most commonly by removing its property from the bailee's premises. In *St-Isidore Asphalte*,[28] the plaintiff, a contractor, delivered its truck to the defendant to have its company name, logo, and telephone number painted on the doors. The said work could not be completed immediately, and the truck was placed inside the defendant's shop overnight. Two days after the vehicle had been dropped off by the plaintiff, the lettering was completed and the vehicle was driven out of the shop and parked outside on the defendant's parking lot. The keys were left in the vehicle's ignition and the doors left unlocked while the vehicle awaited pickup. The plaintiff was notified that the work was completed and that the truck was ready to be collected from the defendant's premises. The plaintiff claimed that, during this communication with the defendant, he notified the defendant to take the vehicle to Radio Shack and that the defendant had agreed to do so. The

28 Above note 20.

defendant denied this, stating that he had received a call from someone inquiring whether the vehicle was still on the lot, that he told the individual it was, and that he closed the shop and left for the day without making any further inquiries or receiving any further instructions from the plaintiff. The defendant stated that he knew that the door was unlocked and that the keys were in the ignition, but that he had anticipated that someone from the plaintiff company would come by and pick up the vehicle that day and that it therefore did not present a problem.[29]

As fate would have it, no one from the plaintiff company retrieved the vehicle that day, and, during the night hours, the vehicle was stolen from the defendant's lot and damaged beyond repair. The plaintiff was paid for its loss by its insurer (which happened to be the same insurer that the defendant had), but the insurer sought reimbursement from the defendant, and that reimbursement turned on the question of whether a bailment could be said to have been in place between the parties at the time of the loss. If so, the insurer's waiver of subrogation in the plaintiff's automobile policy did not apply; if not, the waiver did apply, meaning that the insurer would receive no reimbursement for its payments to the plaintiff. The defendant argued that the bailment had been completed when the work was done and the vehicle was parked on his lot and that he had no more responsibility for it and should not be responsible in damages to the plaintiff.[30]

Justice McIntyre of the New Brunswick Court of Queen's Bench disagreed and rejected this argument out of hand, stating the following:

> His [the defendant's] contention that the contract was completed and therefore his duties were terminated when he parked the truck on his lot is incorrect at law. Once he accepted the care and control of the plaintiff's truck for the purpose of doing the lettering on the doors for a fee he became a bailer for hire and his responsibility as such continued right up until the plaintiff had picked up his vehicle or otherwise clearly relieved the defendant bailee of his contractual obligation.[31]

Because a bailment was found to apply to the vehicle at the time of loss, compensation was ordered paid by the defendant to the insurer.

Justice McIntyre's desire to fashion an absolute rule here is problematic to say the least. It goes against *Furbank* and other caselaw examined

29 *Ibid* at paras 1–3.
30 *Ibid* at paras 3–10.
31 *Ibid* at para 6.

in this chapter stating that a bailment can be at an end immediately after the purpose for which it was formed is completed, with no further duty on the bailee to guard the subject chattel from harm. It would be asking too much from a bailee in all circumstances to continue to act as a bailee over a bailor's property once the stated purpose of the bailment has been completed. This would be the case, for example, in the following situations: in circumstances that indicate that the bailee has no ability to store the property for safekeeping following a repair or the completion of the assigned work, to the knowledge of the bailor; in circumstances that indicate that the parties intended a licence, and not a bailment, to apply to the property for the further period; or in circumstances that should have made clear to the bailor that it was to remove its property immediately once the assigned work by the bailee was completed. Equally, however, it would be wrong to state that bailee responsibilities always expire following completion of the purpose of a bailment. Instead, a contextual approach should always be used in deciding this question.

The decision in *St-Isidore Asphalte* was made on the basis of an absolute rule and does not appear to have considered, or adequately considered, industry practice, the parties' reasonable expectations based on the communications exchanged between them, or the defendant bailee's ability to safeguard the plaintiff's vehicle or vehicle keys for a reasonable time following the completion of the assigned work. Certainly, had McIntyre J found that the defendant had agreed to deliver the vehicle to Radio Shack following the placing of the vehicle on its lot, by virtue of agreeing to same in its alleged phone call with the plaintiff, then its failure to do so would have been a reasonable basis on which to fix it with liability as a bailee.

4) Where the Terms of Agreement Between the Parties Require the Bailee to Hold Goods for Pickup by the Bailor

Where the terms of the contract between the parties require that the "bailee hold the bailed goods until they are picked up by the bailor," then a direct transmission of the goods to the bailor will need to be made in order for the bailment to be put to an end; otherwise it continues. In *McKinnon v Acadian Lines Ltd*,[32] the plaintiff's father arranged with a bus company for the shipment by road of the plaintiff's two trunks containing her personal

32 [1977] NSJ No 586 (CA).

belongings from Kenora, Ontario, to Halifax, Nova Scotia, after the plaintiff had notified her parents that she had arrived in Halifax. The terms of the shipment, evidenced in the defendant shipper's receipt, included the term "hold for pick up" in relation to the delivery of the plaintiff's goods. Upon learning, through her parents, that the trunks had been forwarded to Halifax, the plaintiff contacted the defendant's Halifax bus terminal to check on the status of her trunks and was informed that they had arrived. The plaintiff later arranged for a delivery service to collect the trunks from the bus terminal and deliver them to her address. When the carrier arrived to pick up the trunks, they were missing, having been turned over to an unknown male third party who had stated that he had been travelling together with the plaintiff and would ensure that she would get her trunks. As it happened, the defendant bus company did not have a policy requiring evidence of ownership of the goods, or a ticket, or evidence of identification, before releasing customer property. Justice Cooper of the Nova Scotia Supreme Court Appeal Division found that the bus company was a common carrier while it transported the goods as well as for a reasonable time thereafter, bearing the liability of an insurer during these times and an obligation to protect the plaintiff's property against all risks of loss.[33]

The evidence before the court as to dates was unsatisfactory. What was clear, however, was that the plaintiff arrived in Halifax on 27 October; that the trunks were shipped on 17 November (according to the bus receipt); and that they were misdelivered to the unknown third-party rogue on 9 December. Despite the gaps in the evidence, Cooper JA found that the defendant's common carrier status had terminated by this last date, "a reasonable time" for the plaintiff to demand and receive delivery having passed. However, Cooper JA found that the defendant was still a bailee at the time of loss, fixing liability against it accordingly for turning over the trunks to the rogue third party in breach of its duties as bailee.[34] While Cooper JA did not provide reasons for finding a bailment to be in existence between the parties despite an extended period of time having passed since the goods became available to the plaintiff for pickup, it must be because the terms of contract between the parties made physical redelivery of the trunks to the Plaintiff, or her agent, a requirement for the storage to be brought to an end. In the absence of

33 *Ibid* at paras 1–8.
34 *Ibid* at paras 10–12.

the plaintiff's abandonment of her property, which could not be shown without a much longer period of time having elapsed,[35] the defendant, as a continuing storer of the goods, was a bailee and had an absolute and continuing duty of redelivery, which duty it failed to carry out. In these circumstances, a bailor will be able to meet its onus of proof and will be able to receive recompense for its losses.

5) Whether Control Has Been Retained by the Bailee Following Completion of the Purpose of the Bailment

Another factor that should be considered by courts in deciding whether a bailment should continue after its avowed purpose has been completed is whether control of the goods has been surrendered or retained by the bailee. The line between bailment and licence will sometimes be very difficult to draw here, especially where the act of redelivery of the goods does not remove the goods from the bailee's premises. In *Alcan Canada Products Ltd v Schenker Warehousing, a division of Schenker of Canada Ltd*,[36] the plaintiff Alcan Canada Products Ltd agreed to sell a quantity of aluminum to the plaintiff Stollco Industries Ltd. Alcan's place of business was in Ontario, while Stollco's place of business was in British Columbia. The aluminum arrived in British Columbia via train at the defendant Schenker Warehousing Ltd's warehouse, where the goods were unloaded by Schenker staff and stored on its premises awaiting pickup by the defendant Dolphin Delivery Ltd, a delivery service. Schenker covered the aluminum with a tarp during this period of time to protect it from the elements. When Dolphin arrived about a week later to pick up the goods, Schenker loaded the goods onto two flatbed trucks belonging to Dolphin for transport to Stollco. The goods were left uncovered once relocated by Schenker onto the flatbeds, the tarp covering them having been removed.[37]

Because it was the holiday season, the plaintiff Stollco was closed, and Dolphin could not effect delivery of the goods to its premises, even though they were ready for transport and it was Dolphin's intention to deliver them. So the goods were left on Dolphin's trucks in Schenker's yard for the balance of the holiday season, with the consent of Schenker and at no charge. When Schenker's employees resumed work in the new

35 See *Chiaravalloti v Leading Edge Auto Collision*, 2012 ONSC 4554 at para 15.
36 [1985] BCJ No 1256 (SC).
37 *Ibid* at paras 1–5.

year, they discovered that the aluminum had been damaged by the elements. An employee of Schenker testified that he did not know that the aluminum would be damaged by rain and snow over the holiday period, otherwise he would have left the tarp in place. Dolphin claimed it had not noticed that the aluminum had previously been covered with a tarp but that it had two tarps available to Schenker, which could have been used for this purpose but were not.[38]

The central question on which liability rested was whether possession of the goods could be considered to have been transferred from Schenker to Dolphin when the goods were loaded onto their flatbed trucks, even though those trucks remained on Schenker's premises due to Dolphin's inability to effect a delivery to Stollco due to its offices being closed. Had Schenker taken back, or retained, possession of the goods after they were loaded onto the flatbeds by merely allowing the goods to remain on its premises, or did this just amount to a licence? Not surprisingly, Dolphin and Schenker each laid the blame at the feet of the other; Schenker argued that its duties of safekeeping terminated when the goods were loaded onto Dolphin's trucks and that those trucks were allowed to stay on its premises only as a courtesy. Dolphin stated, conversely, that Schenker had voluntarily taken the goods back into its possession following their loading, such that Schenker never ceased to be a bailee and never became a licensee of the goods.[39] Justice Oppal accepted the latter's position, stating:

> While there may have been a form of delivery that took place on December 30th, the goods were always in the actual care, control and custody of the Defendants. Furthermore, it was out of the existing bailor/bailee relationship that Schenker allowed Dolphin to store the goods upon its premises. There was at least an indirect benefit to Schenker in allowing this storage.[40]

While Oppal J's decision in this case is defensible enough, the learned judge's reasons do not recognize that acts of redelivery can occur without the bailed goods leaving the bailee's premises, and that licences often do arise out of bailment relationships. If Schenker did retain or resume possession of the goods, it must be because of its control over the goods during the relevant period. On the evidence, Schenker's premises were

38 *Ibid* at para 5.
39 *Ibid* at paras 9–11.
40 *Ibid* at para 18.

presumably not accessible by Dolphin over the holiday period, which means that, during this period, Schenker had exclusive possession of the goods and could exclude all others from its premises where the goods were stored. Schenker's continued possession until after the new year was supported further by the bill of lading executed between the parties, which stated that delivery to Dolphin did not occur until after Schenker's premises had reopened in the new year, after the damage to the goods had been occasioned. The learned judge's finding that Schenker had admitted in its evidence that it had voluntarily accepted back possession of the goods was supportive of a bailment as well, but certainly was a less substantial basis on which to have found a bailment. Because a bailment was found to apply to Schenker during the relevant times, Dolphin's failing in not covering the aluminum with a tarp once on its flatbed trucks was immaterial. Certainly, had Dolphin taken away the goods, as it had planned to do, and assumed bailee responsibilities immediately upon loading, this failure could well have made it liable if the aluminum had been subsequently damaged during transport, due to its exposure to the elements. Schenker's removal of its own tarp from the aluminum for loading onto Dolphin's trucks was reasonable and would not have amounted to a negligent redelivery of the goods in these circumstances, meaning its bailee obligations would have been at an end and the plaintiff bailors' only recourse would have been against Dolphin.

E. SUSPENDED BAILMENTS

In *Valley Auto Wrecking and Demolition Ltd v Colonial Motors Ltd*,[41] the defendant Michael Allen was on a vacation when the vehicle in which he was transporting his family back to Kamloops, BC, from Vancouver broke down at a late hour outside of the business of the plaintiff Golden Ears Motor Ltd in Maple Ridge. The motor vehicle he was driving was owned by his employer at the time, the defendant Colonial Motors Ltd (hereinafter Colonial), which operated out of Kamloops and held a franchise from American Motors. Allen found no one at the plaintiff business's car lot but was able to reach one of the owners of Golden Ears by phone, a Mr Arthur Street, who got out of bed and travelled down to the hotel where Allen and his family were staying to offer assistance. It

41 [1976] BCJ No 1193 (SC).

was arranged that Allen would borrow a vehicle owned by Golden Ears to enable him and his family to make the trip back to Kamloops. Allen's vehicle would remain behind for repairs, and the parties agreed that each vehicle would be returned to the other as soon as possible. This arrangement was made possible by virtue of the fact that Golden Ears held a franchise from American Motors too. Allen claimed there was also some discussion between the parties about selling Street's vehicle in Kamloops. At this juncture, Street testified that he had advised Allen that he did not have collision insurance on his vehicle.[42]

Two days later, Allen was advised by Street that his vehicle had been repaired. Street also spoke with the principal of Colonial at this juncture, David Melnychuk, who advised him that someone would be coming down to pick up the car, and Street confirmed that this was acceptable. Melnychuk also enquired as to whether Street was interested in selling his car, and Street advised him to sell it if he could make a sale. A further two days later, Allen telephoned Street to inform him that someone would be driving Street's vehicle back to Maple Ridge for him the next day. Street cautioned Allen "not to let any punks drive the car because it was kind of swift." Allen stated that, as at this time, he was acting on the instructions of Colonial in both placing the phone call and arranging for the driver. On the return trip, the vehicle, driven by the defendant's employee Richard Osborne, went off the road and was heavily damaged. The wrecked vehicle was returned to Street, who sued both Allen and Colonial in bailment for the damage.[43]

Colonial advanced no defence to the action. Allen, for his part, argued that the defendant Colonial, and not him, was a bailee and in possession of the vehicle at the time of the loss and that he could therefore not be held liable as bailee for the loss. At most, any bailment applying to him terminated when he reached Kamloops, and Melnychuk, on behalf of Colonial, took over possession of the vehicle from him. Justice Hutcheon of the British Columbia Supreme Court rejected this line of argument and found that no discussion of a possible sale of the vehicle had occurred at the initial meeting between Allen and Street. Based on that meeting, Allen had assumed a clear duty of safekeeping over the car, which included redelivering the vehicle to Street in reasonably good condition. Those arrangements involved Street helping Allen out of his troubles and

42 *Ibid* at paras 1–2.
43 *Ibid* at paras 3–7.

had nothing to do with Melnychuk or Colonial. Indeed, Colonial and Melnychuk had had no previous dealings with Street. During the period of time that Melnychuk was trying to effect the sale of the vehicle for Street, the bailment between Allen and Street was simply "suspended" but not terminated. The sale not having occurred, the arrangement between Allen and Street was revived, and Allen had to ensure that he redelivered the car to Street in good working order to avoid liability, which duty he failed to discharge. Liability was accordingly fixed against Allen for the damage to the vehicle.[44]

A "suspended" bailment, as articulated by Hutcheon J within the context of this case, meant that, if the car had been lost while Melnychuk was trying to effect the sale of the car, the bailors would have had to look to Colonial as bailee for recompense, but that, once it was determined that a sale of the vehicle would *not* be occurring, then the plaintiff bailors would have had to look to Allen as bailee to succeed. Justice Hutcheon's view and application of the law here are questionable for at least three reasons. First, he neglects to consider that the touchstone of a bailment is exercise of control over the subject property, which indicates that the bailee has assumed a duty of safekeeping. At the latest, Colonial assumed safekeeping when it took control of the vehicle for the purposes of effecting a sale. In any vehicle sale, the seller ordinarily has to show the vehicle to potential buyers and sometimes let them test drive the vehicle, which clearly requires a bailee to have both access to and control over the subject property, creating a bailment in the process. It seems a stretch to suggest that Allen's communications to Street and subsequent actions broke this chain of possession, in light of the fact that he was acting on his employer Colonial's instructions at that specific time. Second, Hutcheon J's position seems to undermine the notion of a bailment as a voluntary relationship. Once Allen lost control of the vehicle, the bailment was at an end, and Allen was relieved of all duties as bailee, including the duty of redelivery. The only way another bailment could have been created was for Allen to resume possession and control over the vehicle and once again assume its safekeeping. Allen's statements to Street and actions were too equivocal to allow for this to occur. Moreover, as noted, they were not accompanied by any exercises of physical control over the vehicle by Allen in his personal capacity. The vehicle was driven back to Maple Ridge by Osborne,

---

44 *Ibid* at paras 8–19.

who was acting as an employee of Colonial, not as an agent of Allen's. Third, Allen was acting as an employee of Colonial, and not in his personal capacity, when making the arrangements with Street for the return of his vehicle after it was determined that the vehicle could not be sold. By that point in time, the vehicle had been turned over to his employer, and his employer had taken control of it (with the permission of Street) and had released it to one of its own employees (not Allen) for redelivery to Street. The fact that Allen facilitated the arrangement does not change the underlying reality here that possession had been transferred to, and remained in, Colonial, nor does the fact that Allen and Street may have subjectively believed in their own minds, based on their own agreement and dealings, that they owed each other bailment-like duties at the time of the loss, where the circumstances belied this.[45] It is accordingly submitted that the plaintiff's (bailor's) burden of proof in the case could only be met vis-à-vis the defendant Colonial and that it was wrong for Hutcheon J to have fixed liability against the defendant Allen for the plaintiff's losses.

F. NO EXCLUSIVE POSSESSION EXERCISED BY THE BAILEE OVER THE BAILOR'S GOODS AT THE TIME OF THE LOSS

Where a court finds that the defendant did not have any exclusive possession of the bailor's goods at the time of the loss to constitute it a bailee, a bailor will not *usually* be able to satisfy its burden of showing that the loss or damage to its goods occurred during the course of the bailment. In consequence, the bailee will not be put to the heavy onus of disproving negligence. This result will often obtain where the owner of a piece of equipment rents it out to another person or company along with an operator (who is an employee of the owner's) and where the operator remains in control of the machine and is the only party capable of ensuring its safekeeping.

45 Justice Hutcheon was correct to have refused to consider the parties' later after-the-fact conduct in determining the bailment questions — namely that Colonial had promised Street that it would "take care of everything," which prompted Street to write Colonial two separate letters seeking settlement. A bailment is to be determined principally with reference to the present circumstances, without undue regard for the past or future events occurring between the parties: *ibid* at para 17.

1) Where the Bailor Retains Control of Goods by Delivering to the Bailee a Machine with an Operator Who Remains Under the Bailor's Control

In *Coast Crane Co Ltd v Dominion Bridge Co Ltd; British Columbia Power Commission v EB Investments Ltd*,[46] the defendant hired a crane from the plaintiff for use at a large power project, specifically to replace its own crane, which needed to be moved to another operation elsewhere. The operator of the crane, Turner, was assigned by the plaintiff. He manually operated the crane at all times and ensured its safety and appropriate use. He also submitted daily reports to the plaintiff showing the day-to-day activities of the crane. Turner was paid by the defendant, in accordance with the terms of the hiring agreement. The defendant was also responsible for fuelling the crane and for ordinary maintenance costs. The crane was used only very minimally by the defendant at the material times and was, for the most part, used by a major, separate contractor on the site. (This contractor would instruct Turner on the uses to which the crane was to be put, which instructions were generally followed, and exercised control over the crane to this extent.) This was specifically contemplated by the parties' agreement; the crane was available for use by various contractors on the site, in accordance with industry practice. The third parties would pay the defendant for their individual uses of the crane, and the defendant would in turn pay hiring fees to the plaintiff, based on an hourly rate. The defendant directed the general use of the crane at all times, by telling Turner where he should go on the site to use it. The project site itself was under the control and direction of the British Columbia Power Commission.[47]

Following the crane's use at the end of a work week, the crane was parked by Turner on a portion of earthen dam then under construction about seventy feet from a lake's edge on the defendant's work site. Turner parked the crane as he saw fit, and after working hours, without direction from the defendant or any contractor under whom he was working. There were no obvious dangers in the area on which it was parked. Nonetheless, the crane ended up sliding, along with a portion of the earthen dam, into the lake, causing serious damage to the machine. The plaintiff sued the

46 *Coast Crane Co Ltd v Dominion Bridge Co Ltd; British Columbia Power Commission v EB Investments Ltd*, [1961] BCJ No 128 (SC) [*Coast Crane*].

47 *Ibid* at paras 2 and 4.

defendant in bailment, among other causes of action, arguing that the crane was in their "exclusive possession" when it was damaged.[48] Justice Verchere of the British Columbia Supreme Court disagreed. The learned judge placed tremendous emphasis on the following two facts:[49]

1) The crane was used almost exclusively by a party other than the defendant, namely, a major contractor on the site, and such use was specifically contemplated by the parties' agreement. (This was the party that put the crane to its last use prior to its damage.)
2) Turner, the plaintiff's agent, retained control over the crane after it was hired out by the defendant, in manually operating and parking it at all times, and reserving the right to refuse any job or action that might endanger the crane, even if this resulted in Turner and the crane's removal from the job on which they were working.

While the defendant did exercise some control over the plaintiff's crane, it did not have the power to ensure its "safekeeping," given the arrangements in place. This is the key point. The defendant, or its contractors at the site, could direct the crane to a new job, in terms of time and place of operation, but it did not operate it or park it and could not protect it from damage in the same way Turner could, nor could it provide directions with respect to parking and protection. In addition, it barely used the crane for its own work. Similarly, while the foreman of the contractor of the defendant for which Turner was last working before the accident had a measure of control over the crane, as he could direct the uses to which the crane was to be put, the contractor did not have substantial control over the crane, as this remained in the plaintiff vis-à-vis Turner. The defendant's paying of the rent and maintenance costs of the crane was not enough to give it control of the crane to put it in exclusive possession at the material times either, nor was the fact that the crane had been sent to the site to replace its own crane enough to find a bailment. The plaintiff was required to show that the defendant (bailee) was in exclusive possession of the crane at the time the damage occurred, such that it was the *only* party capable of explaining what happened to the goods. Clearly, this was not the case. Turner and the contractor who was directing the use of the crane were far better positioned to do this than the defendant.[50]

---

48 *Ibid.*
49 *Ibid* at paras 6–8.
50 *Ibid* at paras 6–20.

More to the point, since the defendant and its contractors could not, as temporary or special employers of Turner, dictate what Turner was to do and how he was to do it in absolute terms, given Turner's ability to countermand any directions or orders received from them to safeguard the crane, the defendant, as temporary employer, had no duty to explain Turner's conduct, or any legal responsibility over his actions, whether tortious or not, since it did not have possession of the crane. In any case, the injury to the crane had not occurred as a result of direction received from the contractor's foreman while the crane was working for it, which, the learned judge stated, might have changed the situation.[51] Turner's involvement, as it was, meant that the plaintiff could not relinquish exclusive possession of its crane to anyone, it would seem. Such a circumstance makes it impossible for a bailor to satisfy its onus of proof, since it is not possible to show damage or loss during the course of a bailment when no transfer of exclusive possession from the bailor to the bailee has occurred.[52]

In a later case involving similar facts, *Great Lakes Steel Products Ltd v ME Doyle Ltd et al*,[53] Verchere J's statements of law are vindicated. There, the respondent agreed to rent a crane to the appellant company for its use in the dismantling of dredges and certain machinery at a work site of the appellant. As part of the leasing agreement, an operator (Kroker) was provided to the appellant together with the crane. The operator was required to operate the crane at all times while it was in the physical possession of the appellant. However, unlike the crane, which would be leased, the operator would become an employee of the appellant company under this arrangement (with the understanding that the operator would be rehired later by the respondent company after he was no longer needed by the appellant). As a result, he was no longer on the respondent's payroll and no longer under the direction or control of the respondent. He had effectively become a full-fledged employee of the appellant and was so at the time that the crane was damaged while he was operating it to make a lift. That is to say, the appellant received more than just the benefit and use of the crane operator; it had an untrammeled control over him as an employee who was subject to its dictates, orders, and commands. The

51 *Ibid* at paras 23–30.

52 For an example in a different context, see *MacTague v Inland Lines Ltd*, [1915] OJ No 411 (SC HC Div).

53 *Great Lakes Steel Products Ltd v ME Doyle Ltd*, [1968] OJ No 1270 (CA) [*Great Lakes* (CA)], aff'g [1967] OJ No 1068 (HCJ) [*Great Lakes* (HCJ)].

respondent retained no ability to control or direct the use of its crane or the operator, and the operator no longer reported to them.[54]

Not surprisingly, the respondent (bailor) was able to meet its onus of showing exclusive possession by the appellant (bailee) of the crane in these circumstances. The crane operator was an employee of the appellant; he was subject to its senior management's direction; and the operation of the crane was being directed by the appellant at the material times, including at the time of the injury. The operator owed no allegiance whatever to the respondent, despite his long-standing previous employment relationship with them, and did not report back to them with respect to the use of the crane. In these circumstances, the respondent could not be considered to have retained the necessary incidents of possession over the crane vis-à-vis its operator, since he was no longer answerable to them with respect to the operation of the crane, such that a bailment could not be found. Instead, the appellant had received the necessary control of the crane from the respondent to create a bailment of the crane, requiring it as bailee to assume a duty of safekeeping over the crane and to negative negligence to escape liability.[55]

The mere fact that, under the parties' contract, the respondent's operator was required to operate the crane did not mean that possession could not be transferred to the appellant, as this did not reserve control over the operation of the crane in the respondent, since the respondent was no longer the operator's master. Justice Schroeder, speaking for the Ontario Court of Appeal, stated the following in this regard:

> The fact that Kroker, a skilled crane operator, was required by the respondent plaintiff to operate the crane while it was in use by the appellant is of no special significance and does not modify the transaction so as to derogate from its quality as a contract of bailment. It is clear from the evidence that Kroker's sole duty was to manipulate the controls of the crane's mechanism in co-operation with the employees of the Doyle Company, and more particularly under the orders and directions of its foreman and superintendent, Hardy, who gave Kroker the necessary signals in directing the movement of the load.[56]

---

54 *Great Lakes* (CA), above note 53 at paras 1–2. See further: *Great Lakes* (HCJ), above note 53 at paras 1–8.

55 *Great Lakes* (CA), above note 53 at paras 1–6; *Great Lakes* (HCJ), above note 53 at paras 8–10.

56 *Great Lakes* (CA), above note 53 at para 8.

In the result, the defendant had to negative negligence,[57] which it could not do in the absence of expert evidence explaining how the mishap could have happened without its negligence; in the absence of a company investigation into the cause of the accident; and without having adduced evidence of the defendant's riggers, who had placed stabilizers at the direction of the employee of the defendant superintending the operation prior to the crane's collapse.[58]

2) Where the Operator of Bailed Property Remains in the General Employment of the Bailor

The fact that the operator of the hired property may remain in the general employment of the bailor at the time of the loss or damage is not a bar to finding a bailment. In *Allison Concrete Ltd v Canadian Pacific Ltd*,[59] a machine was rented out by the plaintiff to the defendant, along with an operator, to assist in the recovery of overturned coal cars. The machine ended up falling through the ice on a lake during the working day and was severely damaged while being operated by the plaintiff's operator. The operator, although operating the machine at the relevant time, was following the direction of the defendant and its guide, who had directed the operator to the location on the ice where the machine fell through.[60] The current operator had not been told by the employee in charge of the recovery operation for the defendant not to take the machine onto the ice, though a previous operator had been so advised.[61]

The plaintiff's operators kept the key to the machine at all times and were responsible for maintenance and minor repairs; major repairs were the responsibility of the president of the plaintiff company. The machine

57 Interestingly, even though the trial judge in the court below had exonerated the appellant (bailee's) employees, namely Hardy (the employee supervising the operation) and Kroker (the employee operating the crane at all material times), of negligence with respect to the actions in negligence brought against them by the respondent, and this holding was not appealed from, this was not dispositive of the bailment question before the appeal court. This is because negligence requires affirmative proof of a lack of due care on the part of the defendant, while bailment puts the defendant to the reverse onus of disproving negligence where bailed goods are returned to the bailor in a damaged condition — a much higher standard indeed: *ibid* at paras 6–7.

58 *Ibid* at para 9.

59 [1973] BCJ No 579 (SC) [*Allison Concrete*], aff'd [1974] BCJ No 27 (CA).

60 *Allison Concrete*, above note 59 at paras 12–13.

61 *Ibid* at para 14.

was operated exclusively by the plaintiff's operators.[62] Nonetheless, the plaintiff sued in bailment for the damage, arguing that the defendant controlled and directed the use of the machine for the duration of the hire,[63] notwithstanding that the plaintiff's operators operated the machine at all times. Not surprisingly, the defendant argued that exclusive possession had not been transferred by the plaintiff and that no bailment could be found. The plaintiff operators, according to the defendant, were acting either as independent contractors or under the general employ of the plaintiff company.[64]

The British Columbia Supreme Court agreed with the plaintiff's position, finding that a bailment had been formed between the parties. It distinguished *Coast Crane* on the basis that the working day had not come to an end, and that the defendant had directed the machine to the location where it met its demise. The plaintiff's operators had nothing to do with it; they were just following the defendant's orders and directions, as required.[65] While the operators in the case had discretion and power over how the machine was to be used to perform the assigned work,[66] and were the machine's exclusive operators, this was *not* a bar to a transfer of possession occurring. Justice Aikins's statements on the issue are apposite:

> I have not overlooked the consideration that by the contract the payloader was to be operated exclusively by the plaintiff's operators. This does not, in my view, touch the issue of possession: the contract was one of hiring with a condition that the machine be run exclusively by operators sent with the machine and in the general employment of the plaintiff. The defendant had the right to dictate the tasks to be performed by the machine and when and where it would do assigned tasks. The plaintiff's operators were to run the machine. It was within their discretion, not the defendant's, to decide how the machine should be manipulated to perform assigned tasks. I do not think this right to control the machines in performing assigned tasks derogates from the defendant's right of possession.[67]

62 *Ibid* at para 17.
63 *Ibid* at para 4.
64 *Ibid* at paras 4–5.
65 *Ibid* at para 23.
66 Certainly any improper use of the crane by the operator, in the application of its own discretion, should absolve the bailee from liability for negligence, even where a bailment is found.
67 *Allison Concrete*, above note 59 at para 24.

A further point of departure between *Coast Crane* and the instant case, which may be a more substantial basis on which to distinguish the two cases, is that, in *Coast Crane*, the plaintiff's operator was duty-bound to safeguard the crane and could countermand any order received from the defendant or others at the site that he felt could endanger the crane during working hours, including presumably with respect to the assignment of tasks. It is not clear that the operators in *Allison Concrete* had this right; they were, instead, subject to the dictates of the defendant (bailee). This view finds support in the reasons of Aikins J in *Allison Concrete*, where the learned judge states that, during the period of hire, no one "could rightfully take the machine from the possession of the defendant because, the work not having been completed, the term of the hiring had not come to an end."[68] In *Coast Crane*, the operator of the crane, in the employ of the plaintiff, could, it appears, rightfully assert a claim for possession of the machine if the operator felt that same was necessary to preserve or protect it from damage or loss. (Where this is so, a bailor will not be able to meets its onus of proof and no bailment will be possible.)

While a bailment was found by Aikins J, the defendant argued that it was not liable as bailee, because the negligence causing the damage to the machine was wholly attributable to the plaintiff operator, who was operating the machine at the time it went through the ice. While the court agreed that this would be a complete defence if the operator were acting within his general employment, it never had to decide the question of whether the operator was in the employ of the defendant (as temporary employer) or the plaintiff (as general employer) at the material time, since it found that the operator had not been negligent. He was simply acting on the instructions he had received from the defendant's employer, who was in charge of the site, and that the defendant bore responsibility for ensuring that the ice was of sufficient thickness before sending the payloader onto the ice, which responsibility he had failed to discharge. According to Aikins J, if the plaintiff operator had taken the machine out onto the ice without any investigation or inquiry, this probably would have resulted in a finding of negligence against him. Yet, again, this would have inured to the benefit of the defendant only if it were shown not to be a temporary employer of the plaintiff operator at the time of the damage,

68 *Ibid* at para 23.

which seems unlikely given its power of control over the operator's activities and the operator's lack of ability to countermand its orders.[69]

3) General Legal Standard to Be Applied to Determine if a Machine Operator Has Become an Employee of the Defendant Hirer

In *Annapolis Valley Construction Ltd v Wisen*,[70] MacQuarrie J of the Nova Scotia Supreme Court posits a useful test for determining whether a machine operator has become an employee of a defendant hirer, such that exclusive possession of property should be considered to have passed from bailor to bailee: Who had the right to assume control of the subject property at the material times?[71] In that case, a crane was hired by a general contractor for work at a site involving the removal of part of an old wharf, including dredging out at the end of that wharf. The plaintiff knew what the crane was going to be used for and sent an operator along with the crane to the defendant's job site.[72]

The crane operator was instructed by the defendant on the work that needed to be done at the site using the crane. The defendant also placed a buoy in the water about forty feet from the end of the wharf in question to enable the plaintiff's operator to know how far out to throw the dragline and bucket. But beyond this, the crane operator had total control of the crane, including where it was to be parked at all times. The operator was also in charge of repositioning the crane to complete the job. On the day in question, following some dredging, the crane was repositioned backwards, resting on a rock. It was then used to remove four or five loads of silt directly in front of the machine. This caused a weakening of the foundation supporting the rock such that the rock on which the crane sat gave way, causing the machine to settle into the water. The plaintiff

---

69 *Ibid* at paras 25–32. For this reason, it also seems unlikely that the plaintiff operator was operating as an independent contractor, another argument that had been advanced by the defendant in its pleadings, but did not have to be addressed by Aikins J: *ibid* at para 35. Certainly, a finding that the operator was an independent contractor, and was negligent in that capacity, leading to the damage to the machine, would also have absolved the defendant of liability and allowed it to have met its reverse onus of proof.

70 [1965] NSJ No 21 (SC) [*Annapolis Valley Construction*].

71 *Ibid* at para 28.

72 *Ibid* at paras 1–6.

thereafter hired the defendant to assist it with salvaging the machine by raising it from the water, which efforts after some time were abandoned and the machine sold to the defendant. The plaintiff later sued the defendant in bailment with respect to the damage that had been occasioned to its crane.[73]

Not surprisingly, one of the defendant's principal arguments was that the crane operator was an agent of the plaintiff, and, as such, no bailment could be found, as he was operating the crane at the time the injury to it occurred.[74] Justice MacQuarrie accepted this argument, finding that the crane operator had indeed remained in the employ of the plaintiff. The judge highlighted the following: the crane operator was hired by the plaintiff; he was compensated by the plaintiff; he could be terminated only by the plaintiff; and the terms of his employment were set by the plaintiff.[75] The operator was also solely responsible for the crane's maintenance and operation while at the site.[76]

The greatest emphasis, however, was placed on the fact that the operator was responsible for the crane's safekeeping and answerable to the plaintiff in that regard. The operator could assume control at all times to ensure that the crane was being used in a safe manner, and indeed was in control at all times, including at the time of the accident, when the defendant was away from the site. The operator took his marching orders from the plaintiff, not the defendant. Indeed, the operator presumably could reject orders from the defendant, although in this case no such orders were given. Consistent with the previous caselaw examined, the fact that the defendant could direct the plaintiff's operator (in a general way) as to the tasks to be done with the crane was not enough, without more, to give the defendant exclusive possession of the crane.[77]

Justice MacQuarrie's observation that the focus of the analysis be placed on who has the right of control of the subject property is spot on; exercise of control over the bailed goods is key to finding a bailment. And here we see this rationale in action. If the hirer can dictate the manner in which the crane is to be used by the operator, and is in a position to place it in a situation of danger, then control rests with he hirer. With control

73 *Ibid* at paras 8–13.
74 *Ibid* at para 14.
75 *Ibid* at paras 19–20.
76 *Ibid* at para 25.
77 *Ibid* at paras 21–25 and 38–43.

comes the duty of safekeeping. But no such duty will exist where the hirer lacks such power, and a bailor will not be able to meet its onus in such circumstances. In the result, there was no need for MacQuarrie J to go any further and consider the bailee's onus of proof, or its advanced defences, since the bailment action was at an end.[78]

4) Other Relevant Considerations: Transfer of Machine Operators with Cranes to Bailees

In *Gemco Equipment Ltd v Westen*,[79] we are provided with yet more guidance. There, a crane operator was sent along with a crane owned by the plaintiff to the defendant. The crane was damaged when assisting the defendant with the elevation of a large and heavy concrete slab from a completely horizontal to almost completely vertical position.[80] The slab went past vertical and fell over against the plaintiff's crane, damaging it. At the time this occurred, the plaintiff's servant had failed to obey, or did not see, a signal that he had received from the signalman to stop. At the time of the loss, the plaintiff's crane was collaborating with another crane operating at the site.[81]

The plaintiff (bailor) took the position that, despite its operator being at the controls of the crane at the time of the damage, possession had passed to the defendant under the contract of hire for the crane, and that the defendant was liable as bailee for the damage, regardless of whether fault was attributable to the operator of the crane, the operator of the other crane at the site, or the defendant's signalman.[82] The plaintiff submitted that the operator was in the employ and control of the defendant

78 The mere discussions, established in evidence (*ibid* at paras 17–18), that may have occurred between the plaintiff's crane operator and the defendant as to precautions to be taken to safeguard the crane and prevent it from going into the water, while eliciting no direct comment from MacQuarrie J, should not be enough, without more, for a bailor to meet its burden of showing that a transfer of employment has occurred such that exclusive possession should be found to rest with the bailee at the material times. Where a bailee has no power to ensure safekeeping of the bailed property, such discussions are meaningless and will not be enough to permit a bailor to show that the bailee enjoyed an exclusive possession at the material times.

79 [1965] BCJ No 13 (Co Ct) [*Gemco*].

80 Admittedly, the crane had been used, together with another company's crane, previously and successfully, with respect to the erection of smaller slabs: *ibid* at para 15.

81 *Ibid*.

82 *Ibid* at paras 2 and 25.

at the material times and that the defendant had wrongly directed the use of the plaintiff's crane, resulting in the damage.[83]

The defendant argued that it had no control over the manner in which the work was done, and that possession remained in the plaintiff throughout, never passing to the defendant at any time. It further argued that the damage was due solely to the negligence of the plaintiff's operator, who was unqualified or incompetent.[84] The question of whether the bailor's onus was met was entirely dependent on whether control of the crane could be said to have passed with the operator to the defendant, in which case it would have been in possession of the crane at the time of the loss.

Justice Washington made a careful, and enviable, review of the English authorities on point. Much like in *Coast Crane*, the justice found that the plaintiff's operators had sole responsibility for the safekeeping of the crane, as part of their general employment with the plaintiff.[85] This went beyond the mere handling of the crane's controls, to include the ability to refuse directions or orders from the defendant that would endanger the crane or require it to be used in a way that went beyond its known capabilities. Justice Washington addressed the matter as follows: "I am satisfied that he [the plaintiff's crane operator] had the right and indeed the duty to his own employer, to insist upon the crane being moved to a proper position for the safe operation of the job to be done if he felt it was improperly positioned."[86]

The defendant also had no ability to displace the operator and to use one its own operators to manipulate the controls of the crane.[87] The plaintiff's operator's refusals to obey the defendant's signals, or failure to be on the lookout for them, on at least two occasions, including at the time of the damage, demonstrated the plaintiff's operator's ability to ignore, disregard, or not follow the defendant's instructions. The judge was unwilling to find that the mere verbal contract of hire, the mere assigning of work during the work day for the crane to do, the signalling, or the general direction "in respect of the time and place of movement of the crane" provided by the defendant was enough for the plaintiff (bailor) to show that control had passed to the defendant and that the injury to the

83 *Ibid* at para 18.
84 *Ibid* at paras 6–8.
85 *Ibid* at para 68.
86 *Ibid* at para 38.
87 *Ibid* at para 39.

crane had therefore occurred during the course of a bailment.[88] These are reasonable holdings in light of the judge's findings that the plaintiff operators, to safeguard the crane, could veto or counter instructions received from the defendant as they saw fit, which demonstrates that the plaintiff had retained a controlling influence over the manner in which the crane was to be used.[89] Where a controlling influence is maintained, a bailor will not be able to demonstrate that the necessary transfer of possession has occurred and will not be able to meet its burden of proving exclusive possession by the bailee at the material times.

Since the damage in *Gemco* was found to have been caused by the operator's negligence in failing to abide by a signal that had been given to him,[90] it is unlikely the defendant would have been liable even if a bailment had been found. This is because the plaintiff's controlling influence over the crane and its operator meant that the operator would likely have been viewed as having committed the negligent acts within his general employment, rather than his temporary employment by the defendant.

In *Gemco*, and the English cases cited therein,[91] we are given further indicators of a bailment in this context, which should guide decision making in this area, where a bailor will be able to meet its burden of showing that the bailee was in exclusive possession of the subject property at the relevant times. This may occur in the following circumstances:

1) where the bailor can show that the bailee had the right to dislodge the bailor's operator and assume control of the manner of operation of the machine for itself, without the bailor's further involvement
2) where the bailor can show that the bailee had the ability to place the crane in a situation of danger, against the wishes of the bailor's operator
3) where the bailor can show that the bailee had the ability to use the crane in an unusual way beyond its capabilities, against the wishes of the bailor's operator

---

88 *Ibid* at paras 68–71.

89 Where the bailor crane operator retains the ability to intervene only where something is "blatantly wrong," the needed controlling influence *will not* have been retained by the bailor, and a bailment of the subject property will be possible: see *JD Irving Ltd v Mojan Ltée*, [1983] NBJ No 386 at paras 14 and 32 (QBTD) [*JD Irving Ltd*].

90 *Gemco*, above note 79 at paras 70–73.

91 *Ibid* at paras 20–67.

While the crane in *Gemco* was used for an unusual purpose,[92] this use had been agreed upon by the plaintiff (bailor) and was not imposed on it by the defendant (bailee). This fact alone, therefore, was not enough to show that "control" had been assumed by the defendant and that a bailment should be found.

The bailee's ability to "place or spot" a crane from which position or location a lift is to be made is also supportive of a bailment relationship (at least where the bailor has no, or a very limited ability, to countermand the bailee's actions in this regard). The same is true for controlling the "slinging" of the subject property by the crane—that is, the speed and movement of the property being slung, including when to stop or go.[93] An agreement that places all responsibility and liability for a bailed crane, including in operating and controlling it and in indemnifying others for injuries caused by it, in the hands of the hirer, especially where the agreement is carried out in practice, is also supportive of a bailment.[94] Where an insurance policy requires that the crane be in the "care, custody, and control" of the bailor in order for the policy to apply to any damages or losses caused by its operation, a court's finding that a transfer of possession has occurred between the parties will be very consequential indeed, and will mean that the bailee will not receive the benefit of any such coverage. It is thus advisable for bailees to ensure that any such policy put in place by a bailor extends to any losses or damages that it may cause during its operation of the bailor's crane, or, alternatively, that the bailor retains a controlling influence over the crane, such that the finding of a bailment will not be possible.[95] Where no operator of the machine is provided by the bailor to the bailee under the terms of hire, meaning that the crane is operated exclusively by the bailee, a bailment will be unavoidable.[96] In these circumstances, a bailee will be under an obligation to take reasonable care of the crane during the course of the bailment to avoid liability for any injury that may befall the crane. As a general matter, bailee responsibilities with respect to the safekeeping of a crane

92 *Ibid* at para 28.

93 See *JD Irving Ltd*, above note 89 at paras 11–32.

94 See *Catalytic Construction of Canada Ltd v Austin Co*, [1957] OJ No 184 especially at paras 4, 12, and 15 (CA) [*Catalytic Construction*].

95 See generally, *ibid*.

96 See *Trident Construction Ltd v Capital Crane Ltd*, [1987] NJ No 94 (SCTD).

must be defined with reference to the contract of bailment, and should apply only to things within the control of the bailee.[97]

G. WHERE THE BAILOR AND THE BAILEE ARE IN A TRADITIONAL EMPLOYMENT RELATIONSHIP: EMPLOYER AS BAILOR

A bailor who is an employer will not likely be able to meet its burden of proof in a bailment action where its own property is damaged while in the possession of one of its own employees acting within the course of their employment, even where this property is in the employee's exclusive possession at the time of loss. This is because no transfer of possession, necessary for a bailment to be found, can usually occur between employer and employee over company property or third-party property being used by the employer. Control over the property rests in the employer (owner), even if an individual employee is operating it, using it, or handling it in that individual's exclusive possession. Thus, where property is damaged by an employee pursuant to an employment relationship and while in the employee's sole possession, an employer will generally need to pursue the employee in negligence in order to be successful.

1) Two Approaches Recognized in the Caselaw

In *Robins v Rainbow Dairies Ltd*,[98] the defendant (employer) countersued one of its employees in bailment for damage done to one of its trucks while it was in the possession of the plaintiff within the course of his employment. Essentially, the employee had collided with an underpass that was too low to permit the vehicle to pass beneath it. (The main action was for unpaid wages and does not concern us here.) The trial of the counterclaim proceeded based on certain important admissions—namely, that the employee was the driver of the motor vehicle and in exclusive possession of it at the time it had sustained the damage. The employee moved for non-suit, which was granted by the trial judge. The employer had taken the position on the motion that a relationship of bailment existed between the parties at the material times.

97 See *JD Irving Ltd*, above note 89 at paras 35–37.

98 [1962] OJ No 93 at paras 1–3 (CA).

On appeal, the employer maintained its position in bailment, but the Ontario Court of Appeal, per Mackay JA, held that it was unnecessary for the court to determine whether the parties' relationship amounted to a bailment in order to dispose of the appeal, because of the failure of the employee's motion for the non-suit:[99]

> I think it is unnecessary for me to determine in this case whether the relationship of bailor or bailee existed because I am of the opinion that on the admissions agreed to by counsel the proper inference is that the defendant by counterclaim, the driver of the truck, had exclusive possession of the truck at the time the damage occurred and on this admission, and on the admission that there was damage to the truck as alleged in the counterclaim, the onus in my view was upon the defendant by counterclaim to show that the damage did not arise through any fault on his part. He chose to rely on his motion for non-suit and did not adduce any evidence. I think in these circumstances judgment must go against him.

Clearly, the court's disposal of the counterclaim was based on the premise that the employee had failed to show in his motion for non-suit that the employer *had failed* to make out a *prima facie* legal case against him. And now, as a result, the employee was precluded from defending against the counterclaim by calling evidence to show how the loss to the subject property could have occurred in the absence of his negligence. Interestingly, though the appeal court refused to find a bailment by name, their ruling in requiring the employee to adduce evidence negativing negligence to stave off liability on the counterclaim, in effect, resulted in the employee facing the same onus as a bailee in a bailment action, which seems to have been predicated on the same rationale that exists to justify the onus in those actions — namely, that the employee had "exclusive possession" of the vehicle at the material times and was answerable to explain how it could be damaged while in his sole custody. With respect, a bailment between the parties could not be created in these circumstances, and the motion for non-suit should have been granted by the appeal court if the employer's action was founded in bailment, which appears to have been the case. The defendant (employer) could not transfer legal possession of its truck to the plaintiff (employee) in order that a bailment be created between the parties; possession in law remained with the

99 *Ibid* at para 3.

defendant, as employer, throughout, and it remained vicariously liable[100] for the plaintiff's actions done within the course of his employment. Generally speaking, an employment relationship is inconsistent with a bailment relationship. In these types of circumstances, a bailor *should not* be able to meet its onus of proof. It is not enough for a bailor (employer) in these circumstances to show exclusive possession by the employee of its property at the time of injury to prove a bailment; it must also establish the absence of an employment relationship or, alternatively, perhaps that bailment obligations were assumed by the employee pursuant to the employment contract. Otherwise it can not overcome its onus and must proceed in negligence against the employee.

There is support to be found in the Manitoba Court of Appeal's decision in *Wiebe v Lepp*.[101] There, the plaintiff farmer hired the defendant truck driver to transport grain from certain farmers' fields to elevators. On the day in question, the defendant driver picked up a load from the plaintiff for delivery to a town, where the grain would be loaded into an elevator. Prior to attending at the field for the pickup, the defendant had carried out his standard, usual check on the truck (he checked the gas, oil, battery, and water) and had found no problems.[102]

While en route to his destination, the defendant observed that the motor was operating warmer than usual. When the defendant reached the town, he unloaded the grain. When he was done and was on his way out of town, he noticed that the plaintiff's truck was at a repair shop and decided to drive over to report the problem he had experienced with the vehicle to his boss. The plaintiff and defendant discussed the problem while the engine was permitted to run. They also looked under the hood, but since the engine was running too hot and steam was coming from it, it was not possible to unscrew the radiator cap and put water into it.[103]

Not surprisingly, the parties' respective evidence on what happened next differed considerably. The plaintiff claimed that he had instructed the defendant to wait for the engine to cool, pour some water into the radiator, and then take the vehicle into a service station to determine

---

100 That said, an employer can seek indemnity from an employee where the employer has been found vicariously liable for the employee's tortious conduct, or alternatively, damages for negligence: see *DH Overmyer Co of Canada Ltd v Wallace Transfer Ltd*, [1975] BCJ No 1171 (CA).

101 [1974] MJ No 26 (CA) [*Wiebe*].

102 *Ibid* at paras 2–5.

103 *Ibid* at paras 6–7.

what the problem was. The defendant testified that, upon telling the plaintiff that the engine was running a little hotter than usual, the plaintiff told him that he had never experienced that problem before and that there was some urgency for the defendant to return to the field with the truck as the machines were being held up; and that he proceeded as instructed, to drive out to the field. About two miles from the field, the defendant stated that he heard a "ticking" sound coming from under the hood and shut off the engine. The defendant was able to get a ride the rest of the way and, once at the field, advised the plaintiff what had occurred and returned to the vehicle with the plaintiff. The truck's engine was not operating properly; indeed, it was so noisy it had to be turned off. The next day, the truck was towed to a service station, where it was found that the engine had sustained heavy damage.[104]

The plaintiff sued the defendant in negligence as employee for permitting the engine to run dry and argued that the defendant owed duties analogous to those of a bailee; but the facts, such as they were, caused the trial judge to view and decide the matter as one of bailment. The learned judge, while making some specific findings in favour of the defendant against the plaintiff (stating that the plaintiff had instructed the defendant to go back to the field), ultimately held that it was not the intention of the plaintiff for the defendant to return to the field without first allowing the engine to cool and checking and adding water as required.[105]

Justice Matas, speaking for the Manitoba Court of Appeal, quite rightly overruled the trial judge, distinguishing between the relationship of master and servant, on the one hand, and bailor and bailee on the other. The defendant in the case was an employee with "merely the custody of his master's goods," and had not been entrusted with possession of a chattel by its owner, required for a bailment to come into fruition. There were no "special circumstances" justifying the imposition of a bailment in the case. As a consequence, the employee could only be sued for his negligence with respect to the damage, and the plaintiff could not be accorded the benefit of the reverse onus as bailor.[106]

Justice Matas of the Court of Appeal quashed the trial judge's holding that the defendant had breached his applicable standard of care, finding that the plaintiff in his evidence had not qualified his instruction for the

---

104 *Ibid* at paras 8–11.

105 *Ibid* at paras 15–18 and 22.

106 *Ibid* at paras 16–17.

defendant "to go back to the field" and had not advised the defendant to do anything more with respect to the overheating engine. He also noted that the trial judge's ruling was baffling in light of the earlier specific findings of credibility the judge had made against the plaintiff.[107]

As this case demonstrates, there is a clear distinction to be drawn between employment relationships and bailment relationships. The mere fact that employer property in possession of an employee is damaged does not make the employee liable or require the employee to disprove negligence to exonerate himself from liability. The applicable law here is well summarized by Batt, in *Law of Master and Servant*, wherein the learned author states:

> The servant may also be sued by his master if by his negligence, fraud, or other wrongful act damage is caused to his master's business or property, but the mere fact that property entrusted to a servant is damaged or lost does not make him liable; he does not warrant absolutely to keep safely his master's property entrusted to his care, but merely to exercise care and skill: in short, he is liable therefor only if he has been guilty of negligence.[108]

2) Strength of Justification for an Employer Not Enjoying the Benefit of Reverse Onus: A More Contextual Approach

In *Canada Packers Inc v Kennedy*,[109] the justification for an employer not enjoying the advantages of the bailor's burden of proof in situations where an employee loses the employer's property within the course of employment was raised by the Saskatchewan Court of Queen's Bench Judicial Centre of Saskatoon and was found wanting. There, the defendant truck driver collected certain sums of money from a plaintiff customer but failed to provide them to the plaintiff (employer), or to account for their whereabouts, following the collection. The defendant claimed that he had attempted to deposit the monies on the Friday at a designated bank in Moose Jaw, Saskatchewan, after he had received them, in accordance with the company's collection practices, but that he found the bank

---

107 *Ibid* at paras 23–24.

108 Francis Raleigh Batt, *The Law of Master and Servant*, 4th ed (London: Sir Isaac Pitman & Sons, 1950).

109 [1983] SJ No 643 (QB) .

to be closed so decided to place the monies in a bundle in the truck door's pocket and make the trip back to Saskatoon, where he parked his truck in the plaintiff's garage, leaving the money in the truck's door pocket. The truck was left in the garage with the keys in the truck and the doors unlocked. On the following Wednesday, the defendant saw the money in the pocket and told the plaintiff's office manager, who had contacted him by phone that day to discuss the money collected but not deposited (after she had been made aware of the situation), that he was going to Regina the next day and would make the deposit at that time. But the defendant failed to do so, and the defendant again parked the truck in the plaintiff's garage, which was accessible to all the plaintiff's drivers, the night shipper, and in all likelihood other employees of the plaintiff. The truck was loaded for the defendant Wednesday night, and Thursday night he discovered that the money was missing from his truck. He reported the disappearance to the plaintiff's office the following Monday (some ten days after he had received it from the customer).[110]

The plaintiff sued the defendant and argued that the defendant was strictly liable for the loss of the monies, for his failure to deposit them to the plaintiff's account. Clearly, the plaintiff was relying on the law of bailment in advancing its position. The defendant argued that he was not liable, and that the loss was wholly attributable to third parties unknown who had wrongfully converted the monies in question by stealing them. Chief Justice Batten considered the various judicial and academic authorities on point, including *Wiebe*, in deciding whether the defendant employee was answerable as bailee for failing to deliver up the monies to the plaintiff (employer). Chief Justice Batten found the authorities to be conflicting, and did not choose to unequivocally endorse the approach from *Wiebe* (holding that, absent "special circumstances," a bailment relationship between employee and employer involving company property is not possible) or the approach advocated for in other cases that state that employees who lose or damage their employer's property within their possession are answerable as bailee and must negative negligence to escape liability.[111] Instead, Batten CJ laid down a contextual approach[112] that puts the onus on the employer to prove the following elements to the satisfaction of the court:

---

110 *Ibid* at paras 1–6.
111 *Ibid* at paras 7–15.
112 *Ibid* at para 15.

1) the terms of the contract of employment entered into between the parties, including both explicit and implied terms, including whether an employee owed its employer bailee-like obligations for company property used during the course of employment;
2) whether those terms were breached by the employee; and
3) whether the damages or losses are attributable to that breach.

Chief Justice Batten found that the plaintiff had discharged its burden of proof and that the defendant was liable in damages for the value of the money not turned over to the plaintiff, as the evidence made clear that the defendant had acted in contravention of the collection procedures contained in his employment agreement and had contravened the direct orders of his employer. Such actions were the direct cause of the loss.[113]

While Batten CJ found in favour of the plaintiff, it is not clear the judge did so pursuant to the law of bailment. Chief Justice Batten simply disposed of the question of liability by stating, "The evidence, in my opinion can only lead to the conclusion that the employee/defendant acted in contravention of the established practice and the direct orders of his employer. This breach of contract was the direct cause of the loss for which he is liable to his employer."[114] In any event, it is clear that the defendant employee's actions amounted to breach of his contract of employment, and probably negligence, and that the plaintiff could have succeeded against him on either of these bases, making the bailment question a non-issue in the case. This is because the defendant under the company policy was suppose to deliver the money to the plaintiff's office if a deposit at a designated bank could not be made. Alternatively, if the plaintiff's office was closed, the defendant was supposed to contact personnel from that office and arrangements were to be made for the money to be picked up by that office.[115] The defendant took neither of these steps and proceeded in a rather haphazard and careless manner with the monies, not depositing them in Regina, as he had promised the plaintiff's office that he would do the day following his phone conversation with them.

However, assume that the defendant driver had acted more reasonably and prudently throughout, finding the bank to be closed on the Friday, parking his truck in the plaintiff's parking garage thereafter (after

113 *Ibid* at paras 8 and 15.
114 *Ibid* at para 8.
115 *Ibid* at para 2.

hours), secreting the moneys in his locked truck, and notifying the plaintiff's office of the situation at his earliest opportunity thereafter, and then discovering that the monies had disappeared the next day at the beginning of his shift, with no obvious cause for the loss (i.e., no signs of theft). In these circumstances, the location of the onus of proof could well have been dispositive of liability between the parties. Based on Batten CJ's legal framework, it is not clear whether a bailment would have been found, although the learned judge's approach leaves more room for such a finding than the approach endorsed by the Manitoba Court of Appeal in *Wiebe* (which, to succeed, will almost always result in the employer having to prove affirmative acts of negligence by the employee with respect to the lost or damaged property within its care).

3) Conclusion

Based on the various conflicting authorities,[116] including appellate authorities, the law cannot be said to be fully settled on the question of whether an employee owes bailee obligations to its employer where the employer's goods are lost or damaged when in the employee's sole possession.[117] However, when one considers that an employer can direct an employee's use of its property, or property under its control, at all times (and is virtually, if not completely, inseparable from the employee when it comes to safeguarding and using its own property, or third-party property under its control),[118]

116 For judicial authority in support of an employer enjoying the benefits of the reverse onus in a bailment action where an employer's property was damaged while in the sole custody of its own employees, see *LaFlamme v Howard*, [1996] AJ No 444 (Prov Ct).

117 In *Tremear v Park Town Motor Hotels Ltd*, [1982] SJ No 436 (QB), a bailment relationship was created between the plaintiff (employee) and defendant (employer hotel) because it was an implied term of the employee's contract of employment that the plaintiff required a secure place to hang her winter coat while she worked. The plaintiff was left to leave her coat in a public coat-check area in the central lobby of the hotel without any protection, since there was no secure location available for her to store her coat, to the knowledge of the defendant, which resulted in its theft, together with the car keys in one of its pockets. The defendant was held liable in damages to the plaintiff (bailor) despite its master/servant relationship with the plaintiff, since the plaintiff had not agreed to run the risk of theft without compensation and could not be considered to have been contributorily negligent in leaving her coat in the most secure area that was available for it: see paras 17–20.

118 In *Ware Chemical of Canada Ltd v Cosmos Chemical Ltd*, [1973] OJ No 2013 (HCJ), Fraser J found that, even though the plaintiff's action named three individual employees of the defendant in their individual capacities, all of whom were the defendant's employees at the relevant times, none of them was *individually* a bailee

and that the employer may have some knowledge of the circumstances surrounding the loss of or damage to its goods, the justification for the reverse onus breaks down, since, in a garden-variety bailment, this will not be the case. An employee cannot, for example, exclude its employer from using the subject property, or ignore the employer's dictates regarding its use and safekeeping. These limitations are antithetical to a bailment, where a bailee will generally be able to exclude all others from possession and where it will be able to exercise exclusive possession of the subject property, independent of other parties or legal actors. Based on this analysis, it would seem that the *Wiebe* approach should always be preferred. The fact that this may sometimes impose an impossibly high onus on the plaintiff (employer), or make it harder to fix liability against employees where they lose or damage property in their possession in certain circumstances, is no reason to advocate otherwise.[119]

H. THE BAILOR NEEDS TO SHOW THE BAILEE EXERCISED A HIGH DEGREE OF PHYSICAL CONTROL OVER THE GOODS TO THE EXCLUSION OF THE BAILOR FOR AN EXCLUSIVE POSSESSION TO BE FOUND

As was seen in Chapter 1, Section B(1)(b), the bailor will need to show that the necessary incidents of possession were transferred to the bailee and that the bailee exercised the necessary degree of control over the goods at the time of the loss or damage, to the exclusion of the bailor, in order to meet its onus of proof. In *Clark and Pattison Painting Contractors Ltd v Osborne Contracting Ltd*,[120] the defendant's (sub-bailee's) ability to rent out pieces of scaffolding without the plaintiff's (bailee's) prior approval, along with its responsibility for storing and recovery of the owner's goods from renters, signified that exclusive possession had been transferred from the

---

of the plaintiff's goods, despite any control they may have exercised over the goods. Control of the premises where the plaintiff's materials had been stored and processed, and control of the plaintiff's materials, rested with the defendant (employer/bailee) alone, and not with any of the defendant's individual employees. In the result, the defendant (alone) was answerable for the loss of the plaintiff's materials destroyed in the fire at its premises: at para 29.

119 For an example of a case applying the *Wiebe* approach, see *Pelzer's Garage Ltd v Rathgeber*, [1976] SJ No 91 (Dist Ct).

120 [1980] BCJ No 704 (SC).

plaintiff to the defendant and that the bailor's onus had been met.[121] The fact that the quantity of the defendant's inventory went up and down and that the plaintiff, from time to time, picked up surplus stock from the defendant's yard on request (as well as supplied additional stock as required) did not prevent exclusive possession from passing and a bailment from applying to the goods that were in possession of the defendant at any given time. Nor did the fact that the defendant had been careless in recording the coming and goings of the scaffolding on these visits by the plaintiff, and similarly in its rentals to its own customers, make any difference in the final analysis.[122] In the result, the defendant in *Clark* was not in a position, at trial, to explain the shortage of the scaffolding found by the plaintiff based on the defendant's own records when the plaintiff, after about a four-year period, terminated its bailment (at will) relationship with the defendant and demanded return of the goods.[123] The defendant was accordingly found liable as bailee. It is submitted that the bailor's onus of proof was correctly found to be met in this case. A bailee's carelessness in not keeping track of bailed goods in its possession at all times (in breach of its obligations as bailee), or the fact that the inventory of the bailed goods may fluctuate, should *not* prevent a bailor from satisfying its onus in these circumstances where it can show that the goods were lost at a time when the bailee was in sole possession of the goods.

In *Mercury Launch & Tug Ltd v Texada Quarrying Ltd*,[124] the plaintiff sued the defendant in bailment after its unmanned barge was heavily damaged after breaking its moorings, which had secured it to the defendant's loading berth, and drifting onto nearby rocks, where it was severely damaged. The plaintiff had brought its barge to the defendant's loading facility earlier in the day, using its own tug pursuant to a contract with its customer Chemical Line Company of Canada Inc (CLC), despite repeated forecasts calling for a severe storm to hit the area. The defendant was not privy to this contract. The contract of carriage between the plaintiff and CLC involved the plaintiff picking up limestone from the defendant's loading facility for the plaintiff, who had purchased the limestone

121 *Ibid* at para 19.
122 *Ibid* at paras 10–13.
123 *Ibid* at paras 14–16 and 25. In point of fact, the plaintiff was terminating its bailment (at will) relationship with the owner of the goods, which meant that it had to terminate its relationship with the defendant and demand the return of all its goods, so that it could account to the owner for all the bailed goods: *ibid* at paras 10 and 23.
124 2006 FC 464 [*Mercury Launch*].

pursuant to a separate contract with the defendant (and its predecessor), for transport to CLC's facility. Under the terms of carriage between the plaintiff and CLC, "custody and control of the barge" was to be with the plaintiff while the barge was at the defendant's facility. The defendant had taken over quarrying on the island and was the operating company in charge of the loading berth on the fateful day. Pursuant to CLC's separate purchase contract with the defendant, the defendant had "responsibility" for loading and dispatching the barges and had "responsibility" for barges until the point that loading was complete and the parties or their agents had executed bills of lading. Risk of loss, liability, and title to the limestone remained with the defendant and its predecessor during this period of time.[125] Despite this, CLC never asked the plaintiff to name the defendant as an additional assured under the marine insurance policy covering the barge.[126]

The plaintiff's tug crew initially secured the plaintiff's barge alongside the defendant's loading facility for the purpose of loading, using lines supplied by the defendant. (The defendant's agents thereafter adjusted the lines and added lines, as required, for the loading of the limestone to be carried out safely.) The plaintiff's tug crew thereafter made the decision to leave the berth, even though they could have remained, to anchor the tug, with a three-person crew, at a can buoy located about three-quarters of a mile away, and the master and the mate of the ship went to bed, leaving the deckhand on watch.[127] This was done mainly for safety and security reasons, to avoid collisions between the tug and the barge, and the tug and the loading dock when the sea was choppy, and to avoid damage that could possibly be done to the tug from pieces of limestone and other debris that would sometimes fall into the water during the loading process.[128] From the location of the plaintiff's tug, the tug's crew could not see the barge in the defendant's loading berth.[129] The defendant possessed no tug at any time and lacked the ability to remove the barge from the berth. In any case, this responsibility lay with the tug crew, who had to approve any such removal before it could occur.[130]

125 *Ibid* at paras 1–11.
126 *Ibid* at para 20.
127 *Ibid* at paras 21 and 23.
128 *Ibid* at para 62.
129 *Ibid* at para 64.
130 *Ibid* at paras 56–57.

After approximately six hours of loading, which had begun about an hour or an hour and a half after the ship had been moored at the defendant's facility by the plaintiff, the conveyor system on the defendant's barge loader had to be stopped by the defendant's personnel due to a problem with a bearing. The plaintiff's tug was contacted by the defendant, who advised that there would be a couple hours of "downtime" due to the repairs that had to be made to the conveyor belt and that there was still a further two hours of loading of limestone into the barge to do after this. At this juncture, defendant personnel attached two further lines to the barge. The plaintiff's tug crew did not remove the ship from the berth at this time.[131]

A few hours later, after the barge's bow line broke and the barge was damaged on its portside, the tug was again contacted by the defendant, but crew members of the tug could not get on board the barge to address the matter because of the high sea and winds. As a result, the mate and deckhand were dropped further down on shore and then proceeded to the loading facility, where they assisted defendant in putting additional lines belonging to defendant on the barge. The crew then stayed at the facility while two defendant employees went searching for more additional lines at the defendant warehouse. But all these efforts were to no avail: a little while later, all lines securing the barge to the berth (but one) broke, causing the barge to drift into some nearby rocks, where it sustained heavy damage.[132]

The plaintiff argued that a bailment of the barge was created when it transported its barge to the defendant's loading birth using its tug, and that a bailment was in existence at the time that the barge sustained the damage. The plaintiff also argued that the damage was as a result of the defendant's failing to discharge its duty of safekeeping in ensuring that the berth was "safe" and that the barge would not sustain damage while docked there for loading. In the alternative, the plaintiff accused the defendant of negligence in its handling of the barge and operation of its berth. The defendant, for its part, denied the bailment and denied that it had any duty to warn the plaintiff as to the deleterious effects the severe weather could have on its barge docked in its berth. Indeed, it argued that the occurrence was due solely to the negligence of the crew

131 *Ibid* at paras 26–27.
132 *Ibid* at paras 28–29.

of the plaintiff's tug and that it was not responsible for the damage to the barge.[133]

Justice Gauthier of the Federal Court accurately identified the key issue before the court as being whether the defendant had "sufficient possession of the Barge to become its bailee," which the learned judge stated is a question of fact, the burden of proof of which rests on the bailor, who, in the case, was the plaintiff carrier.[134] Justice Gauthier stated that a sufficient possession requires a bailor to show that it delivered "a high degree of physical control over the chattel in question to the exclusion of the bailor,"[135] which, in the case, the judge refused to find had been conveyed by the plaintiff to the defendant. The following facts,[136] relied on by the plaintiff (bailor), were not enough to demonstrate the "high degree of control" on the part of the defendant needed to create a bailment and to place the reverse onus on the defendant to disprove negligence:

1) The defendant had supplied the mooring lines with which the barge was tied up upon its arrival at the berth.
2) The defendant had adjusted the mooring lines throughout the loading of the barge, and after loading had stopped, so that the repairs to the conveyor system could be made.
3) The defendant had agreed to trim the vessel in accordance with directions received from the plaintiff.
4) The defendant had approved the location of the barge alongside its facility.
5) The defendant had ascertained, after the plaintiff's tug crew had left the berth and before they returned, the number of lines that would be used to secure the barge as well as the slack to be left on those lines.
6) The defendant had kept the barge loader at the berth to watch over the barge after the loading process had stopped.
7) The plaintiff had left no representative on board the barge, and it was agreed and understood between the parties that the tug would wait at the can buoy until the loading was completed.

These facts were not enough to create a bailment because the plaintiff's tug crew was on duty and on standby at all times nearby and had

133 *Ibid* at para 31–35.
134 *Ibid* at para 43.
135 *Ibid* at para 46.
136 *Ibid* at paras 47–50.

not relinquished a substantial control of the barge to the defendant.[137] Most notably, only the plaintiff had the ability to remove the barge from the berth to ensure its safekeeping. To the knowledge of the plaintiff, the defendant had no tug available to it for this purpose. In any event, it was clear that the defendant could not remove the barge from the berth without the approval of the plaintiff's tug, or its master. It was also clear that the plaintiff had the responsibility to determine whether or not the barge should get in or out of the berth because of the weather conditions and to monitor conditions accordingly.[138] In short, the "keys to the barge" were not delivered to the defendant.[139]

Even though the terms under the contracts between CLC and the plaintiff and CLC and the defendant pointed in different directions when it came to "custody and control of the barge" at the material times,[140] it is submitted that "who had physical control over the barge, for the purposes of safekeeping" was the central issue when it came to assessing whether a bailment had been created between the plaintiff and the defendant. The defendant's mere loading of the goods on to the barge and the tying and adjusting of lines to the barge, while requiring it to exercise some control over the barge, and to assume some safekeeping over it, were not "plenary

137 The learned judge contrasted this to the situation when the plaintiff (bailor) was at CLC's facility, where during the eighteen to twenty-four hours required for the unloading of the goods from the barge, the barge was left in the care, custody, and control of CLC, and the plaintiff's tug was off duty or working elsewhere during the subject period: *ibid* at para 54. In those circumstances, clearly, a bailment was created between the parties.

138 *Ibid* at paras 56–66.

139 *Ibid* at para 66. Justice Gauthier refused to disqualify the plaintiff's possession based on the fact that the plaintiff's tug was 0.75 miles away from the berth. This is because it could have remained at the berth, but chose not to do so. Even though this limited the plaintiff's ability to remove the barge from harm's way with immediacy, this was the plaintiff's failing and did not thereby give the defendant the requisite control to render it bailee, since its powers were far more limited than the plaintiff's when it came to the barge's safekeeping: *ibid* at para 65. This proved to be very consequential indeed, when the inclement weather required the barge's immediate removal from the berth. The defendant had no way to protect the barge from harm when the high sea and the high winds might cause the barge to break loose, as it did, or to hit the loading facility, by removing it from the berth.

140 Under CLC's terms with the plaintiff, the barge was in the care and control of the plaintiff while docked at the defendant's facility, while, under CLC's terms with the defendant, the barge was in the defendant's control, since the loading of the limestone had not yet been completed by the time the storm befell the barge: *ibid* at paras 49 and 51. Justice Gauthier decided that the defendant could not benefit from the terms of CLC's contract with the plaintiff, since it was not party to it: *ibid* at paras 51–55.

or substantial enough" to create a full bailment of the barge—at least not in the circumstances, where the plaintiff tug's crew was on standby in the immediate area and possessed the *only ability and right* to exercise a far greater control over the barge than did the defendant, in being able to remove the barge physically from the berth at any time when the inclement weather might require same to protect the barge from harm and ensure its safekeeping in all circumstances.[141]

I. WHERE THE BAILOR RETAINS UNFETTERED ACCESS TO THE GOODS

A bailor will not be able to show the needed substantial control over the goods for a bailment to be found where they possess an unfettered access to the goods, having the ability to remove them from the bailee's premises at will, but where they choose not to exercise such a right fully before the point of loss. In *Bonnell v Bonnell*,[142] a matrimonial proceeding, the defendant husband argued that he should be entitled to a set-off from monies that his plaintiff wife argued he owed on a tax bill of hers pursuant to their separation agreement, on the basis that during the four-year period before the agreement was signed, certain goods stored in a shed behind

141 In the alternative, Gauthier J concluded that, even if the necessary possession had been transferred to the defendant (bailee), the plaintiff's actions, when the loading operation had stopped, but before the barge had broken loose and crashed onto the rocks, in assisting the defendant's personnel in trying to secure the barge to the dock, had created a joint possession between the parties, severing any bailment that may have existed before that time. In accordance with President Thorson's reasons in *R v Halifax Shipyards Ltd* (1956), 4 DLR 566 (Ex Ct) [*Halifax Shipyards*] the defendant *was not* the only party in the position to explain what happened to cause the damage to the bailed goods, given the plaintiff employees' presence at the material times, and the finding of a bailment between the parties thus was not justified. The plaintiff's bailment action was dismissed accordingly: *Mercury Launch*, above note 124 at paras 74–75. In the result, the plaintiff had to try to fix liability against the defendant in negligence. This claim failed, on the basis that the plaintiff's own carelessness in failing to ascertain the exact weather conditions in the berth, which might require the barge's removal, in circumstances where a prudent mariner would have done so, was the reason for its losses. The defendant's failure to give the plaintiff formal notice to remove its barge due to the weather conditions, or to advise the plaintiff as to the berth's limitations, was not required in the circumstances, since the forecasted extreme weather conditions should have alerted the plaintiff's tug crew, as reasonable mariners, to the need to monitor the barge closely and remove it from the berth when it was clear that the berth's "comfort zone" had been exceeded: *ibid* at paras 87–94.

142 [2002] NJ No 137 (SCTD).

the former matrimonial home were lost or severely damaged as a result of the wife's failure to care for them as a prudent owner would have. The wife had exclusive possession of the matrimonial home during this period of time and had signed a bill of sale as part of the division of matrimonial assets, recognizing that the husband was the "absolute owner" of certain recreational assets stored in the shed. In essence, the defendant (bailor) was relying on the law of bailment to establish a set-off defence in relation to the outstanding debt he owed to his wife by virtue of the injury done to certain items of his property that he claimed was caused by his wife's failure to ensure their safekeeping while they were in her care and control.[143]

Over the course of the four years between the separation and signing of the separation agreement, the defendant had visited the property and retrieved various goods from the storage shed, including a skidoo, without incident, but he argued he could not go to the property any time he wished and retrieve all of his property, because of the intimidation tactics he had experienced at the hands of the plaintiff, his former spouse, on a certain visit to the property in which the plaintiff had exhibited an aggressive disposition toward him. Justice Handrigan rejected the defendant's safety concerns out of hand and found them unreasonable on the basis of the husband's visits to the property over the four-year period leading to retrievals of certain items of his "recreational assets," which went completely unimpeded by his wife. Justice Handrigan further noted the existence of a letter that the defendant had written to the plaintiff after the incident in question, indicating his intention to attend the property to pick up all outstanding items at future points in time, with no indication that he (the defendant) had any fear of doing so because of the wife's intimidation tactics or otherwise. In short, the defendant had unfettered access to his property at all times, despite the one visit to the property during which the plaintiff had expressed some hostility toward him, and this access was fatal to his establishment of a bailment, which requires a bailor to show an exclusive possession by the bailee. In the result, the defendant was unable to meet his onus of proof as bailor and was not entitled to a set-off against the debt he owed to his wife pursuant to the separation agreement.[144] It is submitted, however, that, had such safety concerns been present on the facts, preventing the defendant

143 *Ibid* at paras 1–13.

144 *Ibid* at paras 15–22.

(bailor) from having unfettered access to his personal items on the former matrimonial property, such a circumstance could be enough to create a bailment and foist a duty of safekeeping on the plaintiff (bailee). Access to or control of goods that cannot be exercised by a bailor because of a reasonable fear of harm by a bailee who is in possession of the goods supports the finding of a bailment.

J. MINOR BAILOR INTERFERENCES AT THE POINT OF DELIVERY OR SUBSEQUENTLY DO NOT NECESSARILY DETRACT FROM THE BAILEE'S EXCLUSIVE POSSESSION

A bailor's own minor interferences with its goods at the point of delivery, or subsequently, do not necessarily detract from the bailee's exclusive possession of the goods and should not necessarily prevent a bailor from meeting its onus of proof. In *Columbia Steel Fabricating and Engineering Ltd (Trustee of) v Arrow Transfer Co*,[145] the plaintiff hired the defendant to transport two trusses along a hazardous roadway to a construction site. Two plaintiff (bailor) employees mounted the trusses to the defendant's tractor-trailer, connected them with X-frames, and helped the defendant lash them down. The defendant supervised and directed the manner in which the trusses were tied down by chains to the tractor and to the steering dolly, but took no part in the installation of the X-frame braces, which was done exclusively by the plaintiff's employees.[146] Subsequently, one of the plaintiff's employees followed behind the defendant's tractor-trailer driver in a motor vehicle; the other went on ahead in a vehicle to clear bridges and to ensure that the road ahead was clear, dropping back as necessary to warn the defendant driver. The latter employee also warned the defendant driver, on one occasion, when he came to a corner and hill that he thought might pose difficulty for the transport. This, however, did not prove to be the case. (These arrangements appear to have been spontaneous and not the subject of a formal bailment contract.)[147]

The trusses ended up falling to the road along the route and were severely damaged. At the time of the fall, the plaintiff's driver who was travelling ahead of the defendant transport was way ahead, and it was not

145 [1974] BCJ No 414 (SC).
146 *Ibid* at paras 9, 13, and 21.
147 *Ibid* at paras 15 and 20.

clear where the other driver following the transport was. Neither of the plaintiff's drivers observed the accident.[148]

Despite its involvement in the transport and the loading, the plaintiff took the position that the defendant was a bailee at the material times and had exclusive possession and control of the trusses at the time of the fall and was therefore responsible for the cost of the repairs. The defendant took the position that, because of the plaintiff's said actions, exclusive possession was not transferred to it. Without exclusive possession, there could be no bailment.[149] The court found that the actions of the plaintiff's (bailor's) employees were not enough to prevent a bailment from coming into fruition, and that the bailment began once the defendant's transport commenced.[150]

Justice Aikins, speaking for the British Columbia Supreme Court, made a useful analogy in coming to his conclusion:

> I am not of the opinion that Mr. Burwash [bailor employee] and Columbia's workmen having loaded the trusses and having helped in lashing them down, all under Mr. Beare's [bailee employee] direction, shows that Columbia, by its servants, had any continuing possession after the loading had been done and the haul had started, any more than a householder who helped movers carry things from his house and put them where directed in a moving van could be said to be still in possession after the van left. The consideration that Columbia's employees tied the two trusses together with cross braces after the trusses were loaded, and that Columbia may well have still been in possession up to the time that the loading was completed, does not in my view touch the issue of whether trusses were in the exclusive possession of Arrow once the haul started. I go back to my analogy of a householder moving his furniture. If the householder drove ahead of the van, it would be sensible if he saw some danger on the road to stop and warn the van driver; this would not detract from the carrier's exclusive possession of his furniture. Likewise if the householder followed the furniture van in his car, that would not detract from the exclusive possession of the carrier.[151]

148 *Ibid* at paras 16 and 22.
149 *Ibid* at paras 20–21.
150 *Ibid* at para 22.
151 *Ibid.*

In the result, the defendant (bailee) was put to the reverse onus to disprove negligence, which it could not do, despite calling expert evidence. Its theory in support of no negligence, that the cause of the trusses falling was the manner in which the X-frame bracing was installed to the trusses, which installation was completed by the plaintiff employees, was too conjectural, with a lack of reasonable support in the evidentiary record.[152] The plaintiff's theory in support of negligence, that the fifth wheel of the dolly was ill-suited to carry the trusses because of their height, was well explained by the plaintiff's rebuttal expert evidence, and was more probable and logical, and found support in the evidentiary record before the court.[153]

In *Lavigne v Boyle*,[154] a similar result obtained. There, the plaintiff brought his truck to a service station for an inspection, as he wanted to know what was causing a vibration in his vehicle so that a repair could be made if necessary. The defendants were the service station proprietor and his employee. The vehicle had to be placed on a hoist by the employee, who was still in training, not a mechanic, and had no experience in service stations, but had been trained on how to use the hoist safely and properly. The employee's use of the hoist was not always supervised. The employee advised the plaintiff that he was not a mechanic, but the plaintiff (bailor) nonetheless wished to proceed with the inspection and have his vehicle placed on the hoist. No other service station employees were present when the inspection was performed and the vehicle fell from the hoist to the ground and was damaged.[155]

The plaintiff took it upon himself to assist the employee beyond driving his vehicle onto the steel plates resting on the floor of the service station in accordance with the employee's direction after the employee had installed the bars of the X-model hoist and raised the vehicle off the ground. (The employee testified that he had followed the correct procedure in operating the hoist, including ensuring that the vehicle was securely positioned after raising the vehicle a few inches off the ground before raising it to the required height of 6 ½ feet). Specifically, the plaintiff (bailor)

152 *Ibid* at paras 28 and 50. According to Aikins J, such support could potentially have been found in one of the defendant driver's observations as to what occurred, as he was at the right vantage point, but he was not present at trial to give evidence. This led Aikins J to draw a negative inference against the defendant, namely, that the driver must not have had favourable evidence to give in support of the defendant's avowed theory: *ibid* at paras 43–44.

153 *Ibid* at paras 46 and 50.

154 [1989] NBJ No 106 (QBTD).

155 *Ibid* at paras 1–5.

joined the employee in inspecting the underside of the vehicle once it was hoisted, using a crowbar to nudge the transmission and other parts to determine if any were loose. The vehicle was then lowered. At some point, a shock absorber was found to be loose, though the evidence of the two men was conflicting on when (exactly) this finding was made and whether the car had been lowered completely to the ground or not before the fall occurred. The plaintiff (bailor) claimed that the vehicle was completely lowered to the ground and that he and the employee together had pressed on the bumper of the vehicle and thus determined that a shock was loose and decided to raise the car for a second time to address the issue. The employee claimed that the plaintiff had made the discovery while he was underneath the vehicle before it was lowered and that the vehicle was not lowered fully before it was raised for a second time.[156] In any case, the vehicle was raised a second time by the defendant employee so that the loose shock absorber could be tightened. While the (bailee) employee was under the vehicle and the plaintiff was in front of it, the employee heard a snap and the plaintiff scream, and the employee exited from underneath the vehicle before it fell to the ground.[157]

Despite the plaintiff's involvement in the inspection, Jean J found a bailment. The judge emphasized that the defendant employee had, alone, operated and controlled the hoist from which the truck had fallen, and that the use of the crowbar on the underside of the vehicle by the plaintiff (bailor) had not been shown to have caused the vehicle to move from its position on the paws of the hoist or to have interfered with the defendant's ability to safeguard the truck on the hoist. In sum, the plaintiff's work and presence did not interfere with the defendant's ability to discharge his duty of safekeeping:[158]

> The fact that the plaintiff was present and actually did some work on the vehicle has nothing to do with the defendants' contractual obligation to securely install the vehicle on the hoist, to raise the vehicle and to lower it without causing damage in the process. The defendant Roy had possession and control of the vehicle for those purposes.[159]

---

156 Justice Jean, of the New Brunswick Court of Queen's Bench Trial Division – Judicial District of Bathurst, preferred the plaintiff's recollection on this point to that of the employee's: *ibid* at para 13.

157 *Ibid* at paras 6–13.

158 *Ibid* at paras 15–19.

159 *Ibid* at para 19.

Justice Jean stated that the case might have been decided differently if the plaintiff's work had been in the nature of repairs, as this would have required the plaintiff to retain control over the vehicle for the purpose of effecting the repairs, preventing the defendant from assuming a duty of safekeeping.[160] In the result, to avoid liability, the defendant was left to disprove that his negligence had caused the fall. The defendant employee's evidence that the paws were installed, and that there was no inherent defect in the hoist mechanism, was not enough to overcome the heavy burden placed on the defendant as bailee. The defendant proprietor had to offer an explanation for how a half-ton truck could fall from a hoist without the negligence of his employee, which he could not do.[161]

With respect to the bailor's onus of proof, the obvious, and difficult, question raised by these cases is when bailor involvement does step over the line and prevent a bailment from being formed, or kills a bailment in its tracks. It would seem, to revert to a point made in the discussion in sections F(3), H, and I, above in this chapter, that it all comes down to the question of control and responsibility for safekeeping. If the defendant transport company in *Arrow* was truly in control of the goods in the case, this would mean that it could refuse to follow the directions received from the plaintiff employees when it felt that such directions were not appropriate or judicious, and that the decisions with respect to the transport of the goods and their safekeeping were made solely by the defendant (even if some were made after receiving advice from the plaintiff's employees). On this test, it would seem that a bailment was the appropriate finding to be made in that case. The defendant controlled the speed of the transport, the route, and the manner in which the trusses were to be secured to the tractor-trailer for delivery. Similarly, in *Lavigne*, the defendant controlled the hoist and was solely responsible for securing the hoist to the vehicle, and the plaintiff's actions were not shown to have played any part in preventing the defendant from ensuring the safekeeping of the vehicle while on the hoist. In addition, the plaintiff had not exercised control over the vehicle in a way that would have prevented the defendant from taking possession and ensuring the vehicle's safekeeping, such as would be the case if the plaintiff had performed repairs to the vehicle while in the defendant's shop. Certainly, if any of those things

160 *Ibid* at paras 20–21.
161 *Ibid* at paras 15–17.

were not true, the plaintiff would not have been able to meet his burden of proving that a transfer of possession had occurred in that case. Still, if the duty of safekeeping in a bailment is indivisible, there is no question that a bailor who goes too far in assisting a bailee in protecting its goods during the course of the bailment could very easily rupture the bailment relationship, or prevent one from forming, with all the adverse consequences that that would engender. In order for a transfer of possession to occur, the bailor must surrender the duty of safekeeping to the bailee. Without this, there can be no bailment.

In *Albert v Breau*,[162] one of the plaintiff's (bailor's) actions in relation to his own property did cross the "proverbial line" and thus prevented a bailment from forming. The plaintiff had brought his truck in to a service station to have its fuel pump changed. The defendant service station operator advised the plaintiff that he did not have time to do the job that evening. The plaintiff asked the defendant if he could use some of his tools and do the job himself. The defendant was not opposed to this. Indeed, one of his employees offered to assist the plaintiff to replace his fuel pump. While they were working, the defendant owner was welding the tailboard of a truck; several sparks were being emitted; and hot slags were dripping onto the cement floor. When the plaintiff and the defendant employee were wrapping up the job, a sudden and ferocious fire started on the insulation of the wall, spreading quickly, and requiring everyone to exit immediately. Everything in the garage was destroyed, including the plaintiff's truck. The cause of the fire was concluded to have come from the welding operation.[163]

Chief Justice Cormier, of the New Brunswick Supreme Court Queen's Bench Division, refused to find that a bailment had been formed with respect to the plaintiff's truck. The judge found that the plaintiff's own actions in effecting the repairs indicated that he had not parted with possession or control of his vehicle in favour of the defendant and that his onus of proof in bailment could not be met.[164] The defendant's own actions in leaving the highly flammable wall insulation uncovered were found not to have been negligent, or to have been the cause of the fire, because the third-party defendant distributor in the action had not properly warned the defendant of the need to cover such insulation and of its

162 [1977] NBJ No 255 (SC QB Div).
163 *Ibid* at paras 1–6.
164 *Ibid* at para 1.

highly flammable nature.[165] All of the actions of the other plaintiff bailors who had property stored in the defendant's shop at the material times were accordingly dismissed.[166]

K. TERMS OF ANY WRITTEN AGREEMENT BETWEEN THE PARTIES

Whether the bailor can meet its onus of proof will sometimes be affected by the terms of any written agreement entered into between the parties, at least where those terms are carried out by the parties in practice. In *Catalytic Construction*,[167] the defendant, in June and November of the same year, hired the plaintiff's crane pursuant to two written contracts to complete construction work on the premises of a corporation with which it had contracted. The crane was damaged during lifting operations occurring in November when it tilted forward and crashed to the ground during a lift; some of the surrounding property on which it was stationed was also damaged. While in both instances the crane was being operated by the plaintiff's operator, each of the two contracts between the parties contained different terms, which were followed by the parties in practice. The first contract required the plaintiff to "furnish crane supervision," while the latter contract was subjected to an addendum, which expressly removed the said condition; most other contractual terms between the parties stayed the same.

This change was addressed by Schroeder JA of the Ontario Court of Appeal speaking for the court, as follows:

> It will be observed that the essential difference between the June contract and the contract as altered in November, 1952, is that under the former the plaintiff was to furnish supervision and to be paid therefor at a stipulated rate. This term was expressly deleted from the later contract, with the result that the lifting operations to be carried out on the premises of Dow Chemical company in November, 1952, were to be under the sole supervision and control of the defendant company. There was a special reason for making this amendment to this agreement as initially

165 *Ibid* at paras 13–18. Notably, the court held that no such duty to warn the ultimate consumer exists with respect to the manufacturer of the product, where the manufacturer sells the product to a distributor for application: *ibid* at para 8.

166 *Ibid* at para 19.

167 Above note 94.

> framed. The task of lifting the "stiff leg" was a delicate one and an undertaking which was fraught with extreme difficulty; it was an operation that called for special skill and experience. This was recognized by the defendant from the beginning, and it arranged for the attendance of its rigger superintendant Henry Briggs, who resided in the State of Michigan, for the special purpose of superintending the execution of this difficult and hazardous work.[168]

The defendant's actions vis-à-vis its employees, pursuant to the amended later agreement, confirmed that it had indeed taken control of the crane. Unlike with the first contract and the previous contracts it had entered into with the plaintiff for use of its crane, the crane was transported to the worksite by the defendant's employees. The defendant thereafter closely directed the operation of the crane through its employee Briggs as it performed a difficult and risky lift of a steel tower onto a pre-arranged foundation. Another smaller crane was used to assist in the lift, to avoid the risk of over-loading. Numerous signalmen were also utilized to assist with the lift. The plaintiff's operator was at the controls of the plaintiff's crane when it crashed to the ground, apparently due to overloading.

Possession was found to have been passed to the defendant and a bailment was found to apply to the crane at the time it was damaged. This is because the plaintiff's operator was completely under the control of the defendant in terms of the manner in which the lift was to be carried out, and in terms of the placement of the crane on the foundation that had been prepared for it. The operator was subject to the orders of the defendant and could not, it appears, countermand orders received from the defendant. In the words of Schroeder JA, when it came to the operation of the crane, "nothing was left to his discretion."[169]

In attempting to negative negligence, the defendant advanced several theories, including that the plaintiff's operator had been negligent in working the controls of the crane, that he had caused either a sudden lifting of the load or too quick a descent of the load following its ascent, such that he had exerted extra weight on the boom of the crane that it could not withstand. The appeal court affirmed the trial judge's ruling that operator negligence was not the cause of the crane's fall but rather that the lack of almost "perfect co-ordination" needed to carry out the lifting

168 *Ibid* at para 4.
169 *Ibid* at para 13.

was the reason for the accident. The defendant was fixed with liability accordingly.[170]

The finding of a bailment was very consequential in this case when it came to the terms of the insurance policy that had been procured by the plaintiff, that was the same between the two contracts, and that protected only against damage caused by use of the crane while under the plaintiff's supervision and not against "all risks." Since the crane was not in the plaintiff's control at the time of loss, the policy was not applicable.[171]

This case illustrates that the terms of the bailment contract can be relevant to the question of whether the bailor's onus of proof has been met — that is, whether possession over the subject property has been passed from bailor to bailee. However, where the terms of the contract are not carried out by the parties in practice, and the bailor retains important indicia of control of the subject property, it is submitted that a bailment should not be found to apply. Had the operator in *Catalytic Construction*, for instance, retained the ability, on behalf of the plaintiff, to countermand orders received from the defendant with respect to the use of the crane where he believed the crane would be placed in a situation of danger, or to decide on the coordination of the movements between the plaintiff's crane and the other crane being used in the operation, a bailment would not have been possible, irrespective of the terms of the parties' agreement. In other words, terms of agreements should not be able to overcome a "clear lack of control on the part of the bailee," although, admittedly, they may be dispositive in cases where the circumstances are roughly equally in support and against the finding of a bailment.

L. LACK OF A FORMAL AGREEMENT TO ACCEPT EXCLUSIVE POSSESSION OF THE BAILOR'S GOODS

A bailor does not need to prove that a bailee has accepted exclusive possession of its goods pursuant to a formal agreement in order to meet its burden of proof. It is enough for the bailor to show that the bailee received such possession voluntarily with the permission of the bailor. In *Equirex Leasing Corp v 2028260 Ontario Ltd (cob Ocean Bay Restaurant and Night Club)*,[172] some equipment was rented by the plaintiff to the defendant

170 *Ibid* at paras 10–12 and 18.

171 *Ibid* at para 15.

172 [2010] OJ No 3646 (SCJ Sm Cl Ct).

nightclub for use in the club. The club ran into financial difficulties and significant arrears on the lease accrued. The plaintiff advised the club that, unless immediate arrangements were made to remedy the situation, the equipment would be seized. The principal of the club informed the plaintiff to contact the defendant's successor Pasceri, who was taking over the club and business, as he was leaving the country to start a new club elsewhere. A satisfactory agreement was reached with Pasceri, whereby he would make an immediate payment toward the arrears and would pay off the balance of the arrears and the remaining lease payments over time. Pasceri proceeded to make some cash payments to the plaintiff as well as provided the plaintiff with postdated cheques, which the plaintiff duly accepted. Based on this understanding, Pasceri was allowed to use the equipment at the nightclub's premises, which business and premises he had now taken over.[173] Much like his predecessor, Pasceri, after making a few payments, began to have trouble making the payments on the lease, and several of the cheques (and replacement cheques) he provided to the plaintiff's agent were returned for insufficient funds.[174] The arrangements continued despite the defendant's defaults, based on the defendant's assurances that he would bring himself back into good standing by providing replacement cheques, and based on the plaintiff's hope that a generous accommodation might allow the defendant's business to remain open so that he could generate the income to enable him to make the required payments to the plaintiff.[175]

The defendant Pasceri used the equipment at the club's premises until he closed the nightclub a few months later.[176] No attempt to contact the plaintiff was made at this time to have the equipment picked up.[177] The equipment then went missing and disappeared.[178] The defendant Pasceri could offer no explanation as to what happened to the plaintiff's equipment. It is to be noted that the plaintiff made no demand for the return of the equipment at any time prior to the loss.[179] The evidence was conflicting as to whether the equipment was removed from the club before it

173 *Ibid* at para 11.
174 *Ibid* at paras 18–19.
175 *Ibid* at para 81.
176 *Ibid* at para 12.
177 *Ibid* at para 80.
178 *Ibid* at para 14.
179 *Ibid* at para 58.

disappeared.[180] In any event, the defendant argued that he had not agreed to assume the defendant nightclub's lease agreement (i.e., there was no assumption of the lease agreement), to accept exclusive possession of the plaintiff's equipment, or to accept delivery of it. The defendant further submitted that, while he used the equipment in the club, the plaintiff was free at any time to come and pick up the equipment and that no bailment should be found.[181]

The plaintiff sued in bailment, among many other causes of action, for the loss of the equipment, and, while several other defendants were named in the lawsuit brought by the plaintiff, including the original nightclub with which the plaintiff had entered into the original leasing agreement, the trial on the merits proceeded solely against the defendant Pasceri.[182]

The Ontario Superior Court of Justice Small Claims Court quite rightly rejected the defendant's arguments in their entirety, finding that the plaintiff (bailor) had met its onus of proof and that a bailment had been created between the parties in the circumstances. Deputy Judge Prattas stated:

> From the evidence adduced the plaintiff allowed the defendant to use the equipment in exchange for the Lease payments and this was done for the mutual benefit of both parties. The defendant paid some cash and delivered several post-dated cheques, all in accordance with the existing Lease. He also delivered replacement cheques for some of the returned cheques. It is the court's conclusion that under these circumstances at a minimum the defendant thereby became a bailee.[183]

In the result, the defendant was put to the reverse onus. As the defendant could not demonstrate that his actions did not contribute to the loss, he was found to be liable as bailee.[184] As apparent, a bailor should not be required to point to a formal agreement, wherein a bailee has agreed to take a bailor's goods into its exclusive possession, in order for it to meet its burden of showing exclusive possession by the bailee at the material times. A bailment, and the assumption of exclusive possession by a bailee, is to be determined with reference to the circumstances and the conduct of parties, not by sole reference to the terms of an agreement

180 *Ibid* at paras 20 and 25.
181 *Ibid* at paras 23 and 60.
182 *Ibid* at para 3.
183 *Ibid* at para 61.
184 *Ibid* at para 63.

or to the execution of such an agreement. Where a bailee has assumed exclusive possession of a bailor's goods voluntarily with the permission of the bailor, and they are lost while in its custody, the bailee must account for their loss to avoid liability.[185]

M. EXCLUSIVE POSSESSION IN CASES OF JOINT POSSESSION BETWEEN BAILOR AND BAILEE

1) Where the Bailee Has Surrendered Control of the Bailed Goods Back to the Bailor

In *Halifax Shipyards*,[186] the court found that there was no exclusive possession of the subject matter of the bailment by the defendant (bailee) at the time of the loss, and so the plaintiff (bailor) was unable to satisfy its burden of proof. Specifically, the repairs to the plaintiff's ship had been completed by the defendant some fifteen hours prior to the commencement of the fire of unknown origin, which caused the damage to the ship when only members of the plaintiff's ship's crew were aboard.[187] The following statements relied on by President Thorson of the Exchequer Court of Canada, from Atkin LJ in *The "Ruapehu,"*[188] summarize the relevant law here (and remain good law):

> It seems to me impossible to throw upon a bailee the onus of accounting for injury happening while he and his servants are away and the bailor is there: and at the same time unreasonable to alter the rule if the injury happens while the bailee or his servants are there and in charge, even though some of the bailor's servants may be there as a term of the bailment.[189]

---

185 The court was also right to have not required the plaintiff (bailor) to prove that a demand for the return of the goods was made, since the defendant's return of the goods was not dependent on such demand. The parties had agreed that the equipment was to be used in the club; once the club closed, as Prattas Deputy J noted, the defendant should have notified the plaintiff and returned the equipment (and its failure to do so prevented the plaintiff from mitigating its damages arising on the breach of the bailment, if it had any such duty to do so in the circumstances): *ibid* at para 80. The mere fact that the bailment was at will was not a reason to disqualify it either, or to find that the bailor had not met its burden of proof. A bailor needs to demonstrate only that possession by the bailee was exclusive at the time when the goods are lost; there need not be an "interminable exclusive possession" for the bailor to succeed.

186 Above note 141.

187 *Ibid* at paras 18–19 and 21.

188 (1925), 21 Ll LR 310.

189 *Halifax Shipyards*, above note 141 at para 23.

During the repairs, bailee obligations were quite reasonably imposed on the defendant (bailee), despite the plaintiff's crew's presence on the ship, on the basis that the defendant was in charge (at least of the portions of the ship undergoing the repairs). As in *Lifestyles*, control and exclusive possession of a bailor's property by a bailee, for the purposes of creating a bailment, can still be found even where the bailee controls only certain portions of the bailor's premises where the bailor property is located (with the bailor controlling the remaining portions). President Thorson explained as follows:

> Where a ship has been delivered to a ship repairer for the making of repairs to her, and the ship repairer's possession of her is not exclusive by reason of the fact that the ship's crew remains on board during the course of the repairs as a matter of right and the ship is damaged while undergoing the repairs, the ordinary rule that the onus of proof that the damage was not due to negligence on the part of the ship repairer's employees lies on the ship repairer applies only in cases where the damage originated during the period of working hours when the ship repairer's employees were in charge and does not apply in cases where the damage originated during the period when the only persons on the ship were members of the ship's crew.[190]

President Thorson found no negligence by the defendant's employees when they left the ship, or while they were on board the ship, that might have been the cause of the fire. This is not surprising in light of the unknown origin of the fire and the mostly bare assertions that the plaintiff had to level against the defendant to try to fix liability against it. Admittedly, the defendant also presented a strong case in showing that that it had not been careless, negligent, or reckless in doing its work. (Certainly such negligence by a bailee should result in it having to bear the heavy onus of having to explain that the loss was not as a result of its negligence, at least where the loss occurs within a reasonable time of it giving up possession of a bailor's property.) In the result, the plaintiff (bailor) was unable to meet its burden of proof.[191]

---

190 *Ibid* at para 24. See also *Lifestyles*, above note 15.

191 *Ibid* at paras 26–28.

2) No Bailment Is Possible Where a Bailor Cannot Confirm the Good Condition of Goods upon Retaking Possession of the Subject Premises from a Bailee

As indicated, a "joint possession" between bailor and bailee, in accordance with President Thorson's dictum, is not necessarily fatal to a bailor's ability to show an exclusive possession on the part of the bailee at the time of the loss. In *Milosevic v Sterling Shipyards*,[192] the plaintiff transported his vessel to the defendant shipyard for engine and electrical repairs following a (second) sinking of his ship and made a bailment claim for the loss of certain items left aboard the ship while the defendant effected the repairs over several months while the plaintiff was not on board. After the electrical and engine work had been completed by the defendant, the plaintiff moved back into the ship, deciding to remove the old cabin and replace it with a new one. During this time, the defendant's employees remained on board to do some additional work arising from the cabin's removal.[193] Upon his return to the vessel, the plaintiff had attempted to locate his personal items aboard the vessel, but could not find them, and proceeded to make an inquiry with the defendant about their whereabouts, whereupon he was told by the defendant that they were in storage. The plaintiff demanded their return, but the defendant failed to deliver them up.[194]

At trial, the defendant, relying on President Thorson's dictum from *Halifax Shipyards*, took the position[195] that the plaintiff's conduct with respect to the changing of the cabin and his moving into the ship in connection therewith, caused possession of the vessel to be vested in him from that point forward, such that the defendant *should not* have to account for the missing items.[196]

This argument was rejected by Trainor J of the British Columbia Supreme Court, who found the defendant liable on the basis that it had

192 [1979] BCJ No 57 (SC).

193 *Ibid* at paras 4–5.

194 *Ibid* at para 8.

195 The defendant also argued that the items may have gone missing while the ship was en route to the defendant's shipyard, prior to the defendant's taking possession of the plaintiff's vessel. This evidence was rejected out of hand by the trial judge, who found that the items were in fact on board when possession of the ship was transferred to the defendant: *ibid* at para 7.

196 *Ibid* at para 8.

not delivered up the plaintiff's property when called upon to do so.[197] It is submitted that the rule from President Thorson's judgment in *Halifax Shipyards*, relieving the bailee from having to account for items previously in its possession in circumstances where possession of the subject premises in which the bailed property was located had become shared between the bailor and bailee, is applicable only where the bailor was able to bring the property into its own exclusive control and assess whether any injury had befallen the property while it was in the exclusive possession of the bailee before the bailor resumed control. This will not be possible where the bailee cannot locate or account for the bailor's goods upon commencement of the joint possession. In other words, not all "joint possessions" will qualify.[198]

The fact is, in *Milosevic*, the goods were likely lost prior to the plaintiff's arrival onboard the ship, which is why the defendant could not account for them or deliver them up upon the plaintiff's making the needed inquiries. Without the knowledge that the goods were in a satisfactory condition aboard the ship when the plaintiff reboarded the ship, such that the plaintiff could exercise control over them for his own purposes and resume possession of them, no act of redelivery of the items, constructive or otherwise, could be made by the defendant, and the plaintiff's presence was merely a "passive factor" on which the defendant could not succeed. In these circumstances, a bailor should still be able to meet its burden of proof.

N. EXCLUSIVE POSSESSION OF THE PREMISES ON WHICH THE BAILED GOODS ARE LOCATED

Where a bailor can show that a bailee had exclusive possession of the premises on which the bailed goods were located at the time of the loss, a bailment of those goods can be found. A bailor, in order to satisfy its onus of proof in these circumstances, will need to be able to show that the bailee had a high level of control of the portion of the property on which the bailor's goods were located, including the right to exclude the bailor from that property for certain periods of time during the bailment. This will generally indicate that the bailee has assumed a duty of safekeeping

---

197 *Ibid.*

198 For an example of a case where the said rule from *Halifax Shipyards* was properly engaged and applied, see *Annapolis Valley Construction*, above note 70 at para 35.

over the goods and justify the imposition of the reverse onus, since the bailee will be the only party in a position to explain what happened to cause the loss of or damage to the bailed goods at the material times.

In *Pickin v Hesk*,[199] most of the nine plaintiff drivers were assigned stalls, for rental on a monthly basis, to park their individual vehicles in the defendant parking garage. The plaintiffs removed their own cars from this large public garage daily as circumstances required. Sometimes the drivers parked their own cars on the lot; at other times an attendant did it for them. One of the drivers gave the ignition key to his vehicle over to the parking operator, while another retained it in his own possession. The remainder of the drivers left their keys in the ignition switch. The garage was locked between 2:00 and 7:00 AM, during which times none of the plaintiffs could access their vehicles or the inside of the parking garage.[200]

A fire erupted in the garage, starting in a repair area of the garage from work being done by the defendant employee, and the plaintiffs' vehicles were heavily damaged as a result. The plaintiffs sued in bailment. The defendant parking operator denied the alleged bailment, and pleaded "that he rented a specific stall in his garage building to each of the Plaintiffs at a rental of $10 per month and that each of the Plaintiffs used his stall to accommodate his motor vehicle and at all times had exclusive possession and control of his stall."[201]

This argument was quite properly rejected by the Ontario Court of Appeal. As found by Roach JA, the vehicles were in the control and custody of the parking operator, despite the fact that most of the plaintiffs had been assigned specific stalls within which to park their vehicles. In finding a bailment, Roach JA focused on the level of trust placed in the defendants by the plaintiffs, by virtue of the access and control reposed in the parking operator and its employees by most of the plaintiffs' leaving their keys in the ignition switches of their vehicles, and by the plaintiff's lack of access to their vehicles during certain prescribed hours.[202]

---

199 [1954] OJ No 557 (CA).

200 *Ibid* at paras 1–13. As discussed in Chapter 1, Section B, certainly the control exercised over most of the plaintiff's (bailors') vehicles by the defendant parking operator in the case, in parking the vehicles, in retaining the keys in their ignition switches, and in providing parking attendants to superintend the parking of the plaintiffs' vehicles were probably enough, without more, to show a bailment.

201 *Ibid* at para 7.

202 *Ibid* at para 24.

In the result, the defendant parking operator had to disprove negligence. It could not do so in the face of the totality of the evidence, which showed that his employee must have not taken the proper precautions before using a torch to remove nuts off the vehicle he was working on in the parking garage.[203]

The mere fact that most of the plaintiff drivers in *Pickin* were assigned specific stalls within which to park their vehicle was not a reason to preclude them from showing (as bailors) that "exclusive possession" had been passed to the parking garage operator at the time at which their property was damaged. Clearly, the defendant parking garage had the power to exclude all persons from accessing their vehicles parked on the premises between the hours of 2 and 7 AM, including the plaintiffs themselves. The presence of this circumstance alone, it would seem, precludes the finding of a licence (since the bailors had no access to their property and only the bailee would be in a position to ensure the property's safekeeping during these times), and once that circumstance is established by the bailors, it will make the finding of a bailment unavoidable.

1) No Bailment Is Possible Where Bailor Goods Are on Bailee Premises for Primary Use by Bailor, Who Retains Unfettered Access to Them

In *Reed v Econo Leasing Ltd*,[204] the plaintiff mechanic brought his own personal, and growing, collection of tools to the defendant's place of employment, a motor vehicle franchising establishment where, as a licensed mechanic, he repaired and serviced the defendant's vehicles (leased out to third-party customers for use) for his own employment. The "lesser-used" tools were stored in his own tool chest on the premises near his work bench, while the tools that were used more frequently were left out in the open on a "tool board" that he had constructed, which was located on the wall above his work bench. The tool chest was initially locked by the plaintiff, but the lock broke and was not repaired by the plaintiff thereafter. While the plaintiff's tools were used principally by

203 *Ibid* at paras 15–22. The defendants were also not protected by the exemption clause contained on signage inside the parking garage, since it was not placed in a location so as to come to the attention of the "reasonably observant person," which explained why the majority of plaintiff drivers did not see it: *ibid* at paras 25–31.

204 [1986] NBJ No 982 (QBTD).

him, the plaintiff from time to time lent his tools to other employees of the defendant and to neighbouring establishments when his tools were needed and not in the defendant's or these other establishments' inventories. The plaintiff would also lend out the defendant's tools, though he was cautioned against this by the defendant.[205] The plaintiff further testified that he felt free to, and did, take tools home after work hours when he required them for personal use.

As it happened, upon the plaintiff's arrival to work on the day in question, all his tools on his tool board were missing, and a substantial number of tools from his tool chest had disappeared, representing a theft of two-thirds of his tools by an unknown party. The plaintiff sued the defendant in bailment for his losses, which bailment was denied by the defendant.[206] Justice Jones of the New Brunswick Court of Queen's Bench refused to find a bailment, stating tersely and simply: "I cannot find that there was a delivery of the chattels in question to the defendant. They were on the defendant's premises for the purpose of their use by the plaintiff in his employment. They were not in my opinion turned over to the possession of the defendant."[207] The learned judge buttressed his legal conclusion by pointing out that the plaintiff had never requested a secure area from the defendant for storage of his tools and that he had chosen to leave his own tools insecure.[208]

There is no question that the plaintiff (employee) retained many (substantial) incidents of possession of the tools and had, at least for a time, restricted the defendant's access to certain tools in his tool chest, when it could be locked. Without the ability to access and exercise control over the subject property, there can be no bailment. While the defendant's premises were locked when they were shut down for the night, the premises were accessible by four employees of the defendant, including by the plaintiff. The plaintiff could, and presumably did, access the premises and remove his tools for personal use when the need arose. In other words, access to the tools on the premises was not restricted entirely for any period of time, showing that the defendant never exercised an exclusive possession over the plaintiff's tools. This is fatal to the finding of a bailment;

---

205 *Ibid* at paras 1–11.
206 *Ibid* at paras 8–12.
207 *Ibid* at para 12.
208 *Ibid* at paras 14–15.

indeed, it is indicative of a licence.[209] Had the defendant's premises *not been* accessible by the plaintiff at all times, the case for a bailment would have been stronger but not at all assured, since the plaintiff's actions in restricting access to some of his tools may have meant that the needed control and trust reposed in a bailee for a bailment to be found would have been missing, at least with respect to some of the tools. It follows that employees who bring their own property to the workplace for use in employment may face an uphill battle in showing a bailment, since the employer may not have the "substantial control and exclusive possession" of the subject property needed for a bailment to come into existence.

2) Where a Bailor's Access to Bailed Goods Requires Co-operation of a Bailee

In *Robertson v Stang*,[210] even though the plaintiff (bailor) retained some measure of control over the goods being stored by the defendant landlord in its storage areas, in that she could, at any time she pleased, ask the landlord for a key to access the areas where her goods were being stored, this was not an unfettered access, and the British Columbia Supreme Court was still willing to find a bailment in all the circumstances.[211] It is submitted that a bailor should not be precluded from meeting its onus of proof in these circumstances—that is, where the bailor may be able to gain access by itself to the areas where its goods are being stored on the bailee's premises, but only with the bailee's co-operation. As we have seen, where property is truly the subject of a licence, access to the property by the bailor will generally be unfettered and unrestricted and will not need to be facilitated by the bailee in any way.

---

209 See *Boire v Eagle Lake Enterprises Ltd*, 2009 SKPC 84 at paras 37–42. There, a bailment was rejected because the plaintiff (bailor) retained the only key to her storage unit with which to access her goods on the defendant's premises, which the court found to be fatal to the plaintiff's bailment action, even though the defendant's co-operation needed to be obtained in order for the plaintiff to gain access to the defendant's premises where the storage locker was housed.

210 [1997] BCJ No 2022 (SC).

211 These circumstances included misrepresentations as to the security of the facilities to be used, including the fact that more than just a couple of people had keys to access the storage areas in which the plaintiff's (bailor's) goods were stored. For more discussion of the effect of representations on the finding of a bailment, including consideration of this case, see Chapter 1, Section B(1)(d).

O. NO PRESUMPTION OF EXCLUSIVE POSSESSION OF CONTENTS OF LARGER BAILED PROPERTY UNDER CONTROL AND CUSTODY OF A BAILEE

Even where a bailor can prove that a piece of bailed property was in the exclusive possession of the bailee at the time of the loss, the bailor may also need to prove that the *contents* of that property were in the exclusive possession of the bailee before liability can be fixed against the bailee for the loss of the contents. For example, in *Neil's Trailer & Equipment Ltd v Butler, Maveety & Meldrum Ltd*,[212] a company delivered a trailer van to the plaintiff for repair of a damaged dolly located on the exterior and underside portion of the van. During the course of repairs, the trailer and its contents were damaged by a fire. As a result of a previous litigation, the plaintiff had to pay the customer for damages to the contents of the van and to the van itself. The question before the court was whether an exclusion clause in the defendant's insurance policy applied to exempt indemnity of the plaintiff with respect to the damages paid out for the contents of the trailer van. The policy contained an exemption as follows:[213]

> 6. to injury to or destruction of
> (a) property owned, used or occupied by or rented to the insured, or
> (b) except with respect to sidetrack elevator or escalator agreements insured hereunder, any other property in the care, custody or control of the insured.

While it was clear that the "exterior" of the trailer van was in the possession and control of the plaintiff, given the repairs that were being made to it, and that control had to be exercised over the exterior of the vehicle during the repairs, the plaintiff did not have the keys to the vehicle and had no access to the contents of the van. Justice Moore stated poignantly:

> One cannot have "care" of something that is locked away from that person. To care for something means simply to preserve or look after it. A person cannot care [for] or preserve something that he does not have access to. In my view one cannot care [for] or preserve something if he does not have physical possession or "custody" of it. The two words "care and custody" go together in that in order to have care or custody of

212 [1977] AJ No 545 (SCTD).
213 *Ibid* at paras 1–5.

> something one must have actual and physical possession of it. "Control" too, supposes physical possession of something. One cannot have care, custody or control without access — in this case, the key.[214]

While this case dealt with an insurance clause in a bailment context, it raises an important question: Must a bailor, as part of its onus of proof, prove control by the bailee of the contents of larger bailed property specifically, before a duty of safekeeping by the bailee will apply to those contents in these circumstances? Certainly knowledge of the contents, and the ability to safeguard them, would seem like prerequisites to the finding of a bailment. It is difficult, if not impossible, for a bailee to safeguard property that it cannot access without a key in all circumstances. That said, access should not be viewed as indispensable where the circumstances make clear that a duty of safekeeping has been assumed by the bailee, and where the ability to safeguard the goods has not been *substantially* frustrated by the lack of access. For example, where a bailor gives a bailee a jewellery box (let's say containing a single necklace) to store in its safe for safekeeping, showing the bailee the contents of the box before the beginning of the storage but restricting access thereafter, the bailee's ability to protect the box from loss or theft during the period of storage is not substantially frustrated. That said, a lack of access will not give a bailee every means at its disposal to protect the contents of the larger bailed property from harm. There will also be no way for the bailee to check on the condition of the contents of the larger bailed property to ensure their safekeeping. Even if these things do not preclude a bailment, they certainly must be accounted for when assessing whether the bailee has met its standard of care.

P. EXCLUSIVE POSSESSION OF A BAILOR'S GOODS REQUIRES A BAILOR TO SHOW THAT A BAILEE KNEW OF THEIR PRESENCE

In order for a bailor to meet its burden of proof, it needs to show that the bailee was "knowingly" in possession of its goods at the time of the loss or damage. In *Withers, Evans Ltd (Receiver-Manager and Trustee of) v Sterling Circuits Inc*,[215] the plaintiff lessee's bailment claim failed because, even though it left its chattels on the defendant lessor's premises with

---

214 *Ibid* at para 19.
215 [1988] BCJ No 57 (SC).

its consent, the lessor had no knowledge of where they had been placed and what steps the lessee had taken to segregate them within the defendant's premises. This meant that the defendant bailee could not protect the goods or ensure their safekeeping, and that an act of delivery had not been made by the plaintiff (bailor) lessee. In the result, the defendant lessor was not found to be responsible as bailee for the disappearance of the plaintiff lessee's goods after it departed the premises and a new lessee broke open the door of the room containing its goods without resecuring it thereafter. In *Kinsella v Club "7" Ltd*,[216] however, it was demonstrated that the bailor need not show any more than that the bailee had taken a "casual look" at the goods left by the bailor with its consent on its premises. Then the required knowledge on the part of the bailee may be inferred, and it may face liability for their loss even where it does not inspect the goods or receive an inventory of them. As occurred in *Kinsella*, the mere fact that, after the bailment has begun, the plaintiff (bailor) attends the bailee's premises where the goods are located and notices that some of his goods may be missing or in danger of being destroyed, without making a demand for their return or collecting them at that point in time, is not necessarily fatal to the plaintiff's ability to prove his case, at least not where the plaintiff is given assurances, following such discoveries, by the defendant (bailee) that the goods will be secured and safeguarded immediately. This is because the duty of safekeeping on a bailee is generally indefeasible and is not easily transferred during a bailment.

Q. A BAILEE'S LACK OF RECORDS WILL NOT NECESSARILY PREVENT A BAILOR FROM MEETING ITS ONUS OF PROOF

A bailee's failure to keep track of goods in its possession during a bailment, or to record the goods specifically that it has received from the bailor at the beginning of a bailment, is not necessarily fatal to a bailor's ability to meet its onus of proof. The bailor can meet its onus of proof in terms of the identity of the goods delivered to the bailee, based on its own knowledge, recollection, and records. The bailee only has to be shown to have had knowledge of the general nature of the goods delivered to it, and in its possession at the material times, in order for liability to be fixed against it. A bailee's lack of records, or recollection, as to the specific items in its

216 [1993] NJ No 365 (SCTD).

possession at the material times should not prevent a bailor from meeting its onus of proof. A bailee's standard of care must be understood to include keeping track of the goods in its possession at any given time to prevent their loss — that is, their comings and goings. In both *Withers, Evans Ltd* and *Kinsella*, the bailors' records and recollections as to the identity of goods in the bailees' possession at the material times were accepted, and their respective onuses of proof were found to have been met based on them, despite the courts' acceptance in both cases that the bailees did not have records, or independent recollections, establishing the identity of all the bailed goods in their possession at the relevant times. It is clear that bailees should keep accurate records of the identity of bailed goods in their possession at all material times, in terms of what remains in their possession at any given time and what has been redelivered back to the bailor; otherwise they may not be able to refute evidence from a bailor that the missing items were lost while in their possession, and they may face liability accordingly.

R. A BAILOR MUST SHOW A "PRESENT" EXCLUSIVE POSSESSION AT THE TIME OF THE LOSS, NOT A "FUTURE" EXCLUSIVE POSSESSION

A bailor must show a "present" exclusive possession by the bailee at the time of the loss; a "future" exclusive possession is not enough for it to meet its burden of proof. In *Seaspan International Ltd v The "Kostis Prois,"*[217] a barge owned by the appellant, Seaspan International Ltd, carrying a load of lumber then belonging to the appellant Seaboard Lumber Sales Ltd, broke loose from the portside of the respondents' ship the *Kostis Prois*, to which it had been "tethered alongside" at a berth in Vancouver Harbour for over a day while the barge's cargo awaited unloading onto the *Kostis Prois*. The barge later drifted away and collided with a bridge. The collision resulted in damage to the barge and the loss overboard of some of the cargo from the barge. The breaking of two of the three strands of the spring line that held the *Kostis Prois* to its wharf and of the lines securing the barge to the ship had been caused by a sudden and significant swell of water arising from the departure of a vessel from a neighbouring berth. The appellants sued the respondents in bailment for the damage

217 [1974] SCR 920 [*Seaspan International*].

done to the barge as well as the loss overboard of certain cargo. The key question before the Supreme Court of Canada was whether the appellant bailors had met their onus of proving a transfer of exclusive possession of the barge, and its contents, to the respondent ship *Kostis Prois* and its respondent owners.[218] The specific circumstances and relationships between the various parties in this case giving rise to the loss are complicated but need to be reviewed thoroughly as they are relevant to the question of the bailor's onus of proof.

The transaction began with the purchase by Seaboard Lumber of a quantity of lumber from its related company, Wellword of Canada Ltd. The latter company hired a barge and tug from Seaspan to transport the cargo belonging to Seaboard Lumber to a stevedore facility in North Vancouver where the respondent *Kostis Prois* was tethered and awaiting the cargo. This ship was owned by the respondents but under a time charter to Seaboard Shipping Company Ltd at the material times. Seaboard Shipping, the charterer of the *Kostis Prois*, was a company associated with Seaboard Lumber, which was tasked with removing the cargo from the barge and loading it onto the *Kostis Prois* after the barge had been tied alongside it and when there were stevedores available to do so. An agent of the appellant Seaspan who was in charge of the tug, indeed the captain of that vessel, supervised the tying up of the barge to the *Kostis Prois*. Because it was dark, the captain could not personally verify that the tying of the lines to the ship had been done correctly by the watchman of the respondent ship, whose crew had provided lines to him, but indicated in his evidence that it appeared to be so. The captain had intervened to prevent the use of a "light line" by *Kostis*'s crew, which he thought was of insufficient strength for the job, resulting in "manilla lines" and a wire cable being used instead. After the tying up was completed, the tug left the barge and its cargo alongside the *Kostis* and departed the area.[219]

The tying up of the barge "free alongside"[220] the *Kostis Prois* for the period of time that it was awaiting unloading had been done at the behest of Wellword and with the knowledge of Seaboard Lumber. The barge had not been unloaded immediately upon arrival in North Vancouver Harbour because it was dark and no stevedores were available to unload the

218 *Ibid* at paras 1–5 [paragraph numbers from French version].

219 *Ibid.*

220 "Free alongside" is a trade term requiring the seller of goods to deliver them to a named port alongside a vessel designated by the buyer.

lumber from the barge to the ship. For the period of time that the barge remained alongside the ship, prior to the loss, no representative of either Seaspan (the owner of the barge) or Seaboard Shipping (the charterer of the *Kostis*), who was responsible for moving the cargo from barge to ship, seems to have done anything to check on the condition of the goods.[221]

There was a seaman on the respondent *Kostis Prois* on night watch doing the rounds of the ship the night before, and the morning of, the loss, who could evidently see the lines and the barge, based on certain evidence adduced at trial, although no member of the crew of the ship saw the barge break away. Later, however, on the morning of the loss, the watchman did observe that the barge was missing and that the lines had broken, and he blew his whistle to try to gain the attention of a passing tug for assistance, but to no avail; and it appears that he did nothing more.[222] There was no contract between either of the appellants — that is, Seaspan or Seaboard Lumber — and the respondent *Kostis Prois* or the respondent owners of this vessel at the material times. The only contracts in place were between Seaspan and Wellwood for the transportation of Seaboard Lumber's wood to a harbour in North Vancouver by barge delivered by tug, and between Seaboard Lumber and the charterer of the *Kostis*, Seaboard Shipping, with respect to the further transportation of the lumber in the *Kostis* to Seaboard Lumber.[223]

Nonetheless, the appellants took the position that a bailment for reward should be found to apply to the barge and the cargo at the time of the loss, as possession of the property had already passed into the care, custody, and control of the respondents upon the barge being tied up alongside the *Kostis*. Justice Ritchie, speaking for the majority of the Supreme Court of Canada, aptly summarized the appellants' position:

---

221 *Seaspan International*, above note 217 at para 5.

222 *Ibid* at para 23. Justices Hall and Laskin, in dissent, stated that the duties of the watchman on the *Kostis* included checking the lines of the barges and tugs moored to the *Kostis*, including the appellants' barge and cargo until the cargo was moved onto the *Kostis*. Notably, the majority of the Supreme Court, per Ritchie J, in their reasons made no similar comment in their recital of the facts of the case. It is submitted that, even if the watchman had assumed such duties over the barge, they were merely gratuitous ones that were too sporadic and irregular and too incomplete to signify a transfer of possession for a bailment to be found. The respondents still lacked the ability to access or control the goods to safeguard them, since they were still aboard the barge, such that a bailment should have been found.

223 *Ibid* at paras 7 and 11.

> [I]t was . . . strongly contended by counsel for the appellants before this Court that when the laden barge was tied up alongside the ship the respondents became fixed with responsibility for it as bailees for reward on the ground that the ship was to carry the lumber to its ultimate destination at the behest of the time charterer and that the leaving of this cargo "free alongside" the ship set in motion a chain of events for which the ship owners were to be rewarded under the terms of the charter. It was contended on this basis that in permitting the barge and cargo to tie up to the ship the respondents were acting in their capacity of "carriers of the said cargo by water" and in part discharge of an obligation which they had undertaken for reward.[224]

The position of the appellants essentially was that the happening of these events caused possession of the cargo to be transferred to the respondents, such that a bailment should be found to apply to them at the time of the loss. This position was rejected by the Supreme Court, which found that possession could not be transferred until the goods were loaded onto the *Kostis* by Seaspan. This never occurred. The goods were merely being prepared to be transferred to the respondents' ship for consideration,[225] and had not been so transferred. Seaspan—not the respondents—was responsible for loading the goods and for approving the manner in which the barge had been tied to the *Kostis* by the ship's crew. So, during the loading process, a bailment could not be formed between the appellants and the respondents, since the respondents had not assumed a duty of safekeeping. In all these circumstances, a bailment for reward, a gratuitous bailment, or a sub-bailment was not possible. In short, the tying up of the barge containing the cargo "free alongside" the *Kostis* created (only) a licence between the parties, nothing more.[226]

---

224 *Ibid* at para 9.

225 While the respondents did not receive a consideration directly from the appellants, clearly the charterer was paying the respondent owners for use of their ship to sustain a profit and a business, which would presumably help it pay remuneration to the respondent ship owners for the use of their vessel.

226 In the result, the appellant (bailors) were left to prove negligence in the ordinary way against the respondents, which proved to be an impossible task. Justice Ritchie refused to find that the ship's crew had been negligent in the manner in which they had tied the barge to the ship, or that the lines that had been used by them to tether the barge to the ship were too weak for their intended task. Indeed, Ritchie J underlined that the lines and their attachment had been approved as satisfactory by an employee of Seaspan and that the ship had broken loose because of the "unusual" swell caused by the departure of the ship from the neighbouring berth. Furthermore, Ritchie J refused

As this case demonstrates, it is not sufficient for the bailor to demonstrate that it was in the process of transferring the goods to the bailee for safekeeping, where the bailee has still not assumed possession. The situation must have moved beyond "mere preparation" for a transfer of possession from bailor to bailee, to an actual transfer, for a bailor's onus of proof to be met and for a bailment to be found.[227] In *Seaspan*, this meant that the lumber needed to be moved from the barge to the ship; until this happened, no more than a licence between the parties arose. No access or control could be exercised over the goods for the purpose of safekeeping until this happened, and therefore a bailment could not be found. The minor, equivocal, and irregular interferences with the barge (containing the bailed goods) exercised by the respondent ship's crew, established in evidence, before the appellants' goods were aboard, did not exhibit the necessary degree of control over the goods for a bailment to be found. The respondent crew could not even check on the condition of the goods aboard the barge, let alone exercise reasonable care over them to ensure their safekeeping in all the circumstances. While Ritchie J in his reasons somewhat muddled through whether certain acts by the *Kostis*'s crew constituted negligence, such that the appellants could still succeed, the fact is that, because only a "licence" existed between the parties at the material times, the respondents did not owe the appellants a duty of care. That is why any failings by the *Kostis*'s crew to monitor the lines, or to discover promptly that the barge had broken loose, were of no consequence in the final analysis. Justice Ritchie seems to have been attuned to this toward the end of his reasons, where he states that the aforementioned

---

to find the needed fault in the watchman's actions in failing to notice that the lines had broken for quite some time after the barge broke loose, as the crew was under no legal duty to check the lines after they had been secured: *Seaspan International*, above note 217 at para 17.

227 In *Northland Navigation Co v Finning Tractor & Equipment Co*, [1976] FCJ No 407 (TD), no bailment between the plaintiff and the defendant shipyard was found to apply to the plaintiff's tugboat while it was tied to the defendant's dock, since it had not yet been removed from the water and parked on the shipyard's marine railway by the defendant for the purposes of the maintenance and inspection work to be carried out on it. The fact that it was tied to the defendant's dock while it underwent other repairs by a separate company was a matter of convenience only. Exclusive possession was being prepared to be transferred and had not yet been so transferred to the defendant's shipyard, since the defendant had advised the plaintiff that its ship could not be accommodated until sometime later, as the marine railway was not available for use. In the result, the plaintiff (bailor) received no recompense for its losses.

omissions by the ship's crew were "purely passive factors" on which the appellant bailors could not succeed.[228]

S. A BAILOR DOES NOT HAVE TO SHOW THE PRESENCE OF CONSIDERATION TO MEET ITS ONUS OF PROOF

A bailor need not show the presence of consideration at the time of the loss in order to meet its onus of proof, since bailments can and do exist independent of consideration and contract. In *Vlastakis (cob All Season Upholstery & Storage) v National Frontier Insurance Co*,[229] the plaintiff (bailee), who was storing items for two specific individuals in his upholstery store, among others, was found to be a bailee of those particular goods by the court, despite the fact that, at the point of loss, one of the two individuals for whom property was being stored could not be located, and the other had not paid rent for the storage in three years. Justice Shaughnessy of the Ontario Superior Court of Justice found that the plaintiff, by the date of a fire that caused extensive damage to the business, was no longer a bailee for reward and had effectively become a "gratuitous bailee" of the goods, since payment by the bailors for the storage of their goods to the plaintiff had ceased. Still, the plaintiff was found to be entitled to coverage for the losses from the defendant insurer (who had refused to pay out the plaintiff's claim for the loss of the bailors' property) under his policy with them since he was found to be "legally liable" to the owners of the goods for the damage to their property occasioned on his premises by the electrical fire, in violation of his duties of safekeeping as a gratuitous bailee.[230] In other words, a lack of consideration was not a bar to the court

228 *Seaspan International*, above note 217 at para 17. The dissent of Hall and Laskin JJ (at paras 19–25), in which they hold that the respondents had an implied duty to safeguard the barge and its cargo, given the temporary mooring it was providing, by making sure that the barge remained tethered to the ship, was not concurred in by the majority of the Supreme Court. This view would allow a bailor to succeed through the back door and effectively make the distinction between bailment and licence otiose. The respondents' lack of control over the appellants' lumber meant that possession had not, and could not, be passed from bailor to bailee. That meant that only a licence existed; and licensors, unlike bailees, *do not* owe bailors duties of "continuing surveillance," or any other duties of care for that matter. For this reason, the dissenting judges' finding of liability against the *Kostis*'s crew for negligence, for failing to keep a proper watch with respect to the breaking loose of the barge, which they state could have averted the accident, was misplaced.

229 [2002] OJ No 4684 (SCJ).

230 *Ibid* at paras 1 and 65–72.

finding that a bailment was in existence between the plaintiff and the two bailors at the point of loss, for the purpose of requiring the defendant to pay out the required insurance proceeds to the plaintiff for the losses that had been occasioned to the bailor's goods while on the plaintiff's premises.

T. BAILOR NEGLIGENCE AT THE TIME OF DELIVERY OF THE GOODS DOES NOT NECESSARILY PRECLUDE IT FROM MEETING ITS ONUS OF PROOF

Where a bailor has been negligent in delivering goods to the bailee, this does not preclude a court from finding that a bailor has met its onus of proof, meaning that the bailee, to escape liability, will need to show that reasonable care was taken of the goods at the material times. That said, such negligence may inure to the benefit of the bailee in terms of whether it has met its applicable standard of care at the material times, and may be dispositive of that question. In *Canadian National Railway Co v Alweather Windows and Doors Ltd*,[231] the plaintiff's (bailor's) agent delivered a closed trailer housing a load of wooden frames and windowsills to the defendant's premises for unloading. He arrived late, when the defendant's business was closing, because he got lost on the way, and the goods could not be unloaded that day by the defendant's staff. The plaintiff's agent had some concerns about the location where he had been told to place the trailer by the defendant, in the unloading area, eventually detaching it from the tractor he was driving and placing some planks provided by the defendant's employees under the dolly wheels of the trailer to secure it. The plaintiff's agent conducted a visual inspection before departing the defendant's premises five minutes later. The defendant's employees played no role in "blocking" the trailer with the planks and the plaintiff's agent had exercised his own independent judgment in securing the trailer, receiving no guidance or instruction from the defendant. (Because of the late arrival, it was not possible to do what was the ordinary custom of leaving the trailer attached to the tractor to ensure the stability of the trailer during the unloading process, with the trailer being removed from the defendant's premises immediately after all the defendant's purchased

231 [1993] NSJ No 155 (SC) [*Canadian National*].

goods had been removed, avoiding the defendant's acting as a temporary storage depot for the plaintiff's trailer).[232]

The next day—before the defendant's employees had fully completed the unloading of the trailer and after they had returned from their lunch break to do so—they found the trailer damaged, lying on its side, with some of the planking that had been securing the trailer broken. The plaintiff sued the defendant in bailment for the injury done to its trailer, claiming that a bailment had been formed between the parties, and denying any negligence on its part at the point of delivery.[233]

Justice Goodfellow of the Nova Scotia Supreme Court found that the plaintiff agent's negligent actions in failing to properly secure the trailer, through the use of grossly insufficient blocking, even though he had been alive to concerns about the placement of the trailer, were solely responsible for the plaintiff's losses and that the defendant employee's unloading of the trailer the next day had not disturbed that negligence. This was confirmed by the defendant's expert evidence in the record. Notwithstanding this finding, the trial judge found that, when the defendant employees had begun unloading the trailer, a bailment, albeit one that was limited to the period of unloading, was commenced[234] between the parties, given the control exercised by the defendant's staff over the property during that time.[235] However, since the trial judge found the plaintiff agent's negligence to have been the sole cause of the damage, the defendant (bailee) was found to have met its standard of care. The defendant *could not* be liable for the plaintiff's losses where it played no role in causing them.

It was correct for the court to find that the bailor's onus of proof was met on these facts, despite the negligence committed by the plaintiff's agent, since control of and access to the trailer was surrendered to the defendant for the purpose of unloading, and was exercised by it on the day following delivery by the plaintiff, and since the losses were found to have occurred during that possession. The plaintiff's negligence in

---

232 *Ibid* at paras 1–6, 17–24, and 30 [paragraph numbers assigned by author].

233 *Ibid* at paras 6–8.

234 Because the leaving of the trailer was found to be a matter of the plaintiff's convenience (the plaintiff did not want to have to take the trailer away and have to come back for it) rather than the defendant's, convenience could not be used to justify the creation of a bailment at an earlier point in time: *ibid* at paras 24–25.

235 In the interim period, it stands to reason that only a licence existed between the parties, which licence permitted the plaintiff (bailor) to park its trailer on the defendant's property until the unloading could be completed.

delivering the goods was not enough to disqualify the bailment, since it did not prevent the defendant from taking possession of the trailer and exercising control over the trailer for the limited purpose for which it had been retained.[236] That said, any obligations of safekeeping assumed under the limited bailment clearly did not extend to repositioning the trailer, or to having to inspect the blocking that had been done by the plaintiff's agent to ensure that the trailer was properly secured, and were limited to unloading the trailer in a safe and proper manner. This, of course, proved to be dispositive of liability between the parties in the final analysis, as the defendant (bailee) was found to have met its standard of care in the manner in which it had unloaded the trailer.[237] Even though in circumstances such as those presenting in *Canadian National* the bailor's onus of proof will be met, it will be meaningless, because the bailee will easily be able to escape liability by pointing to the bailor's negligence at the time of delivery as the *sole cause* of the bailor's losses that occur thereafter.

U. WHERE THE CAUSE OF DAMAGE TO THE BAILED GOODS NEGATES THE DAMAGE HAVING OCCURRED OUTSIDE OF THE TERM OF THE BAILMENT

Where a court finds on the evidence that the cause of damage to bailed property has occurred in such a manner as to negate the damage having occurred outside the course of the bailment, then this will mean that the bailor will have met its burden of showing that the damage occurred at a time when the bailee was in exclusive possession of its goods. In *Vestergaard (cob JP Excavating) v All-Trac Transport Ltd*,[238] the plaintiff contracted with the defendant (bailee) carrier to transport an excavator from

236 *Luider v Nguyen (cob Nanton Packers)*, above note 14, and discussed in Chapter 1, Section B(1)(b)(vii)(c), is distinguishable. There, the plaintiff (bailor) was found to have left a heifer on the defendant's premises in a negligent manner, in having failed to properly secure various gates leading in to the pen in which the heifer was left. The plaintiff's negligent delivery of the subject property of the bailment was sufficient to disqualify the bailment, since it prevented the defendant (bailee) from taking possession of the property for the purpose of safekeeping.

237 Had the defendant (bailee) played a substantial role in the securing of the trailer upon the plaintiff's arrival at the defendant's premises, or in directing how it was to be secured, and had been found to have assumed control of the trailer and goods at that point in time, the defendant may well have faced liability, as bailee, for the plaintiff's losses.

238 [1984] BCJ No 884 (Co Ct).

one job site to another in the same city. Damage was discovered the next morning by the plaintiff after the delivery had been made and the bailment had been concluded. The plaintiff, when it started up its machine, noticed "an unusual rocking motion." Upon further immediate examination, the plaintiff found that bolts were missing from the gear system of the machine. The plaintiff immediately advised the defendant of its discovery and requested that it move the machine to a repair shop for repair, which it did. The plaintiff proceeded to sue the defendant in bailment for damages for the cost of the repairs.[239]

At trial, the defendant driver responsible for loading and unloading the excavator testified that he had followed an acceptable procedure for the moving of heavy-duty machinery and that nothing out of the ordinary occurred with respect to the unloading of the excavator.[240] In any event, the theory advanced by the defendant was that the damage was the result of either latent defects in the equipment itself or from strenuous operational use ("operational wear and tear"), and had not been caused by the defendant during the period of the bailment.[241] The plaintiff's theory, buttressed by expert evidence, was that the bolts failed and that the damage had been caused by an "instantaneous and catastrophic event"—namely, the careless and abrupt dropping of the machine by the defendant while it was driven off the trailer deck by the defendant's driver. Based on the totality of the evidence before him, including the fact that there was a gash mark located on the road surface where the machine had been unloaded, Wong Co Ct J rejected the defendant's theory out of hand and ruled that the cause of the damage was as indicated by the plaintiff's expert witness.[242]

Justice Wong's conclusion as to the specific cause of the damage meant that the bailor had met its onus of proof of showing that the damage had occurred during the course of the bailment. Interestingly, the judge's conclusion as to the cause of the damage, which was consistent not only with the damage having occurred during the period of the bailment, but also

---

239 *Ibid* at paras 1–9.

240 *Ibid* at para 15. Justice Wong expressed some serious reservations about this employee's testimony, given his limited experience and the cavalier attitude with which he presented his evidence on his knowledge and responsibilities in moving the machine, questioning whether the operator had in fact followed the required procedure meticulously, as claimed.

241 *Ibid* at paras 19–20.

242 *Ibid* at paras 17–20.

with the defendant (bailee) having committed negligence in dropping the machine from the trailer deck, meant that there was no way for the defendant to exonerate itself from liability by negativing negligence, or by showing that it had exercised reasonable care at the material times.[243]

V. LOSS OR DAMAGE TO A BAILOR'S GOODS OCCURRING AFTER BAILMENT IS CONCLUDED, BUT THE CAUSE OF INJURY INTRODUCED THROUGH BAILEE NEGLIGENCE DURING THE TERM OF BAILMENT

Sometimes a bailee, by its negligence, introduces the cause of the loss or damage of the bailor's goods prior to a bailment relationship concluding, but the injury may not crystallize until a point in time after the bailment has been concluded and the goods have been returned to the bailor. In these cases, at least where the loss or damage occurs within a reasonable time of the bailment concluding, the bailor should be required to do no more than show that the cause of the loss or damage was introduced by the bailee while the bailment still subsisted, to throw the reverse onus on it. This must be viewed as an exception to the usual rule that requires that the bailor show that the loss or damage to its goods occurred during the course of the bailment when the bailee was in exclusive possession of the goods. This departure, however, is justified only where there is a clear causal connection between the loss or damage to the bailor's goods and the bailee's handling of the goods during the period of the bailment.

There is support for the foregoing to be found in the British Columbia Supreme Court's decision in *Marchuk (cob Gerry Marchuk Contracting) v Swede Creek Contracting Ltd.*[244] There, the plaintiff lent its grapple skidder to the defendant's employees to remove the defendant's service truck, permission having been conveyed through the plaintiff's contractor for whom the defendant was doing work. During the defendant employees' initial use of the skidder in the early morning hours to remove the truck, damage was caused to the left cab door. It was removed by the defendant and taken to a repair shop, where it was repaired and then reinstalled by

243 *Ibid* at paras 21–23.

244 (1997), 43 BCLR (3d) 342 (SC) [*Marchuk*], aff'd 116 BCAC 318 (CA). Only the trial judge's findings in negligence were affirmed by the appeal court. The alternative submission, in bailment, was not considered: see paras 11–13 of the British Columbia Court of Appeal's reasons for decision.

the defendant employees later in the evening hours of the same day. Following this, the defendant's employees proceeded to drive a short distance of 100 meters, and then walked a further 400 meters to an excavator they had been repairing. On a second stroll back to their vehicle, approximately 1.5 hours after reinstallation of the skidder door, they saw smoke rising from the skidder. The employees attempted to put the fire out, but were unsuccessful and the equipment was damaged.[245] The plaintiff sued the defendant in bailment for the damage and, alternatively, for negligence.[246]

The defendant employees were found to have been in exclusive possession of the skidder from the time they borrowed it in the early hours of the morning until they completed the reattachment of the door in the evening later that same day at 6:30 PM (at which point it could be said that the employees had restored the bailed property as near as possible to its condition at the start of the bailment), for the purposes of both the negligence and bailment actions.[247] This was found even though there were large gaps in time when the defendant employees were away from the skidder (when they took the door to town to be repaired) and not using it, before the reinstallation of the door.[248] The area in which the skidder was located was remote, and Meiklem J found it very improbable that any other agent or force would have intervened with the employee's exclusive possession.[249]

There was no direct evidence of negligence on the part of the defendant employees.[250] However, the plaintiff's expert testified that the fire had been caused by sparks generated by the defendant employees during the reinstallation of the door, which provided a reasonable inference of negligence. This evidence went unchallenged. The employees denied using a torch or welding equipment at the location of the skidder, or smoking during the reinstallation of the door (which could have been the cause of a spark). The defendant put forward other possible causes for the fire to counter the plaintiff's theory—namely, exhaust system leaks, hot carbon sparks, electrical short circuit, and dragging brakes—and stated that, to engage one of these causes, someone must have started the

245 *Marchuk*, above note 244 at paras 1–2.
246 *Ibid* at paras 5–6.
247 *Ibid* at paras 18 and 30.
248 *Ibid* at para 18.
249 *Ibid* at paras 18–26.
250 *Ibid* at para 6.

machine before or after the thirty-minute period between 6:00 and 6:30 when the employees completed the reinstall. This possibility, and these causes, were rejected out of hand by Meiklem J as being very improbable, based on the plaintiff expert's unchallenged evidence, inconsistencies in the defendant employees' evidence, the circumstantial evidence indicating that a torch had been used on the machine, and the low probability that anyone else had operated or had taken possession of the machine at the material times from the defendant. Some of the causes were also inconsistent with common sense, based on the expert evidence heard. For example, a fire caused by a short circuit resulting from one of the defendant employees' leaving the battery disconnect "on" after operating the skidder in the morning would not have taken twelve hours to ignite a fire. Thus, Meiklem J concluded that the defendant had not offered an explanation sufficient to neutralize the reasonable inference of negligence to be drawn from the plaintiff's theory and evidence.[251]

Even though the case was resolved on the basis of the negligence action, and the application of the maxim of *res ipsa loquitur*,[252] Meiklem J's conclusions regarding the bailor's onus of proof are worthy of review and comment. The plaintiff could not show, as in the ordinary case, that the loss or damage to the skidder occurred during the course of the bailment, since the borrowing was found to have ended at 6:30 PM, when the reinstallation of the door was completed, a full 1.5 hours before the fire damaging the skidder started. However, Meiklem J stated that, based on his findings of fact in the negligence action, the "introduction of the cause of the fire probably occurred during the half hour period when the defendant's employees were unquestionably in sole exclusive possession, and the defendant must bear the burden of disproving negligence during that time frame, which I hold is a second period of bailment, incidental to the borrowing for the defendant's benefit in the morning."[253] The defendant could not meet this burden in the circumstances; mere "conjectural possibilities" inconsistent with negligence were not enough for the defendant to show that its standard of care was met in the circumstances.

It was right for Meiklem J to have concluded that the heavy onus of disproving negligence remained with the defendant in these circumstances. Where damage occurs within a reasonable time following the

251 *Ibid* at paras 16–26.
252 *Ibid* at paras 8–26.
253 *Ibid* at para 30.

conclusion of a bailment, a bailor who can demonstrate, by a preponderance of probabilities, that the introduction of the cause of the damage occurred while the bailment was still alive, and the bailee was in exclusive possession of the goods, will have met its burden of proof such that the bailee will need to disprove negligence in order to avoid liability for the loss. A bailor, in these circumstances, should *not* be precluded from meeting its burden of proof merely because the usual requirement that it show that the loss occurred during the term of the bailment is missing.

W. A BAILOR TO PROVE VOLUNTARY ACCEPTANCE OF THE GOODS BY THE BAILEE

To succeed, a bailor must show that the bailee accepted the bailor's goods voluntarily. Otherwise, the bailor must proceed under some other head of law, such as conversion or negligence. In *Maritime Coastal Containers Ltd v Shelburne Marine Ltd*,[254] the plaintiff, due to a downturn in its container shipping business, decided it no longer needed cell guides in both of its container ships, and so had the approximately forty tons of steel constituting the cell guides in one of its two ships, the *Hansa Bay*, cut and removed from the ship. Thereafter, the steel was stored for a time in a shipyard in Liverpool, Nova Scotia, for a fee. The steel was then cut into shorter pieces and transported to Halifax, where the steel was loaded into the hold of the plaintiff's other container ship, the *Berglind*. Later, the plaintiff contacted the defendant and arranged for the removal of the disassembled cell guides from the *Berglind* and for some work to be done to the ventilator of the *Berglind* at the defendant's shipyard, instructing the defendant that the work had to be done quickly. The plaintiff further claimed that it had arranged for the cell guides to be stored by the defendant "indefinitely" following the repair until the plaintiff came to retrieve them. This was vehemently denied by the defendant in its evidence, which stated that its role was limited to the mere removal of the steel from the ship and that there was no discussion of storage of the cell guides to be made thereafter, evidenced by the fact that the plaintiff was not billed for storage. The plaintiff employee who communicated with the defendant to make the arrangements testified that there had been no discussion of a fee for the storage, as he was hoping that the defendant

254 [1982] NSJ No 401 (SCTD) [*Maritime Coastal Containers*].

would provide the storage as a courtesy in the hope of future work from the plaintiff.[255]

The defendant received the plaintiff's ship at its shipyard in Shelburne, Nova Scotia, and removed the steel from the hold of the *Berglind*, as it had been contracted to do, using a crane. The defendant deposited the steel on a common wharf utilized by both the defendant and fisherman working at a fish plant adjacent to the defendant's premises. It was then moved the same day by mobile crane to an open area of land nearby, which was not owned or leased by the defendant, where it was piled in a haphazard manner in an area that the defendant used for piling scrap, steel, and iron. This area, as well as other areas being used by the defendant, was located in an industrial park operated by the Nova Scotia Department of Public Works. No representative of the plaintiff ever visited the defendant's yard to view the steel or inquired about the disposition that was made of the steel once it was unloaded. Indeed, the main two employees representing the plaintiff *had not* seen the cell guides since before they were removed at Liverpool and did not communicate with the defendant about their status until more than two years later. As noted, a plaintiff employee claimed that this was because he did not want to be billed for the storage. There was no evidence that the captain of the *Berglind* had complained or taken issue with how the steel was dealt with by the defendant, ultimately being piled up or positioned by the defendant's employees on the open area of land, or had had any conversations with the defendant about it at all, prior to him departing the area after the repairs to the ventilator of the *Berglind* had been completed.[256]

After winding down its business and selling the *Berglind*, the plaintiff called the defendant, as it had found a possible buyer for the *Hansa Bay* cell guides and needed to take some measurements to respond to a query that it had received from the buyer. The plaintiff proceeded to attend at Shelburne to view the steel, whereupon it discovered the steel to be missing. The plaintiff, in an effort to strengthen its position, upon discovering the loss, sent a telex message to the former captain of the *Berglind*, now in other employment, asking him to confirm that he had directed the representative of Shelburne who had accepted the ship to store the steel until the vessel returned to pick it up. But as indicated

255 *Ibid* at paras 1–11.
256 *Ibid* at para 12.

earlier, the evidence adduced at trial showed that the captain had had no such exchange with the defendant's representative and that this was just a self-serving attempt by the plaintiff to bolster its own position and that it did not accurately reflect the communications that had occurred between the captain of the *Berglind* and the defendant at the material times. The evidence also indicated that the Department of Public Works had previously asked the defendant to move the steel from the Department's land as it was "unsightly," but that the defendant had refused to do so, and that much of the steel may have been subsequently plowed under the department's land by the department when it was extending the shoreline in the area. The evidence further indicated that some of the steel had been appropriated by the defendant and used to construct a makeshift gantry and for other purposes without the knowledge or assent of the plaintiff.[257]

The plaintiff sued in bailment for damages for the loss of its steel. Justice Hallett of the Nova Scotia Supreme Court Trial Division posited the main issue before the court as follows:

> The question to be asked in this case is whether under the circumstances did the unloading of the steel by the defendant and the movement of that steel from the wharf to the land constitute voluntary taking of possession of the steel by the defendant in circumstances that would impose on the defendant the obligations of a bailee to take reasonable care of the steel?[258]

Justice Hallett found that the defendant had *not* agreed to accept the steel for storage and that it had never received instructions from the plaintiff, or the captain of the *Berglind*, to accept the steel on that basis. The mere fact that the plaintiff's property was unloaded by the defendant from the *Berglind* under a contract between the plaintiff and defendant and was located onto land by the defendant did not make the defendant a bailee, or create a bailment between the parties.[259]

The learned judge pointed out that the steel was ultimately left on open land in an industrial park, where it was accessible to both the plaintiff and the defendant and by others using the area, "with access to all by water or road."[260] The judge further noted that this had not been objected to by the captain of the *Berglind*. While the captain may not have known

257 *Ibid* at paras 14–15.
258 *Ibid* at para 20.
259 *Ibid* at paras 23, 29, and 36.
260 *Ibid* at para 25.

that the land that the steel had been placed on was not owned or leased by the defendant, he must have observed, concluded Hallett J, that the steel had been piled in a haphazard manner and had been dealt with by the defendant in a casual manner, which did not indicate that the defendant was undertaking to protect the steel from harm. Prior to this, the steel had been unloaded onto a common wharf used by the defendant and other plants in the area. At no point had the material been placed in an enclosed, secure area on the defendant's premises. All of these circumstances were inconsistent with the creation of a bailment.[261]

Nonetheless, the plaintiff argued that the defendant had evinced an intention to accept a "degree of responsibility" over the cell guides by moving the steel from the wharf to the land, such that an exclusive possession should be viewed as having been transferred from plaintiff to defendant. Justice Hallett rejected this argument, stating, "It could be equally inferred that in moving the cell guides off the wharf to the scrap pile, the defendant was simply getting the cell guides off the wharf and out of the way."[262] Justice Hallett noted further the lack of consideration for the supposed storage; the lack of ancillary function to be performed on the steel; the lack of a procedure for the recovery of the steel as between the parties; the lack of any long-standing relationship between the parties that would support the finding of a bailment; the total lack of interest showed by the plaintiff company's principals over a two-year period with respect to the status of the cell guides; the rushed manner in which the steel had been removed from the *Hansa Bay* by the plaintiff; and no clear indication to the defendant, based on the appearance of the steel, that the steel was of any appreciable value. All of these were contraindicative of a bailment.[263]

As apparent, the exercise of some control over a bailor's chattels by a bailee does not necessarily create a bailment or indicate that the bailee

---

261 *Ibid* at paras 15, 26, 31, and 34.

262 *Ibid* at para 41.

263 *Ibid* at paras 36–40. Despite the aforementioned indices pointing away from a bailment, Hallett J found that, if there were a bailment, it was a gratuitous one that would have ended within a reasonable time of the steel being unloaded, being six months, which deadline date had long passed by the point of the loss. He noted as well that the degree of care the defendant owed the plaintiff was exceedingly low, given the defendant's lack of ability to care for forty tons of steel (i.e., it was not a storage facility, but a shipyard), and given the plaintiff's apparent insouciance toward its own property. The defendant, however, was found liable for conversion and was ordered to pay damages for using some of the plaintiff's steel to construct a makeshift gantry and for other purposes without the plaintiff's consent or knowledge: *ibid* at paras 41–47.

has accepted a duty of safekeeping over the property. Certainly the acts of the defendant were too equivocal here; they did not clearly demonstrate that it was assuming a duty of safekeeping over the plaintiff's steel. That said, drawing the lines will sometimes be difficult in such circumstances, for, as we learned in the parking lot cases, the mere movement of a bailor's car for the greater convenience and profit of a parking lot operator (e.g., to accommodate more cars) can be sufficient to illustrate that the needed degree of responsibility has been assumed by the bailee for a bailment to be found. This can be the case even though, strictly speaking, the control being exercised by the bailee in relocating the vehicle does not necessarily indicate that the bailee has assumed a duty of safekeeping over the vehicle for all purposes. But a finding of bailment seems justifiable particularly where a vehicle may be moved again and again, given the amount of control being exercised over the vehicle and the need for the safekeeping of the vehicle to be ensured during these times. Certainly, in *Maritime Coastal Containers*, while the defendant was moving the steel from the ship to the land pursuant to its contract with the plaintiff, there was a bailment in existence between the parties, despite no explicit finding being made in this regard by Hallett J, requiring the defendant to remove the steel with care and place it on the land with care. Once this was done, however, the defendant did not owe any further bailee obligations to the plaintiff, as the bailment was at an end.[264]

X. WHERE A BAILOR CAN SHOW THAT BAILEE RESPONSIBILITIES WERE ASSUMED INCIDENT TO ANOTHER LEGAL STATUS HELD BY THE BAILEE AT THE MATERIAL TIMES

A bailor can sometimes meet its onus of proof indirectly by showing that bailee responsibilities were assumed by the bailee incident to another legal status held by it in relation to the bailor at the time of the loss. For example, in *Chief Construction Co v McDonald*,[265] the defendant trucking

---

264 While it is true that the defendant (bailee) was in a better position to explain the loss of the steel than was the plaintiff, and likewise was in a more favourable position to exercise control over the steel (which was evidenced by the Department of Public Works' request for the defendant to relocate the steel that had been piled haphazardly on the department's land: *ibid* at para 15), the lack of control being exercised by the defendant for the purpose of safekeeping at the material times should be enough to defeat a bailment in these circumstances.

265 1987 CanLII 3337 (Alta QB) [*Chief Construction*].

company agreed to haul the plaintiff's trailers loaded with molten sulphur (and specially designed for that purpose) by tractor from a gas plant to a town approximately eighty miles away for further shipment. The parties agreed that the defendant would supply drivers and tractors and the plaintiff would supply the trailers filled with sulphur. The defendant's role was solely with respect to transportation; the defendant, it appears, played no role in loading or unloading the plaintiff's trailers.[266]

En route to the destination on the day in question, the defendant tractor overturned into a ditch when the defendant employee driving the tractor swerved to the right when going around a curve in the road to avoid another vehicle that was coming toward him over the centre line, partly on his side of the road. The trailers sustained heavy damage, and the cargo being hauled was lost. This was the first such accident by the defendant employee, who, prior to the incident, had successfully completed fifty-five similar round trips involving the plaintiff's cargo for the defendant company without incident.[267]

The plaintiff argued that the defendant trucking company was acting as a "private carrier" at the time of the loss, with the applicable duties incident to that status — namely, those of a bailee for reward. The finding by the judge in this case as to whether the defendant company was a common carrier[268] or private carrier, was of great consequence, since a private carrier is a bailee for reward and must negative negligence, while a common carrier is not and does not face a bailee's onus of proof.[269] Justice Stratton of the Alberta Court of Queen's Bench Judicial District of Edmonton posited the applicable legal test in question form, with an affirmative answer resulting in the imposition of the common carrier status to the defendant: "Did the Defendant while inviting all and sundry to employ him, reserve to himself the right of accepting or rejecting their offers of goods for carriage whether his lorries were full or empty, being guided in his decision by the attractiveness or otherwise of the particular

266 *Ibid* at paras 1, 5, and 9.

267 *Ibid* at paras 11–13.

268 Indeed, where the bailee is found to be a "common carrier," it will bear a substantially higher burden of proof than a bailee for reward. That is, it will be strictly liable as an insurer for any losses occasioned. A bill of lading may lower the standard of care on the bailee by exempting acts of God and inherent defects in the goods: see *Tri-City Drilling Co Ltd v Velie* (1959), 22 DLR (2d) 341 at paras 4 and 22 (Alta SC) [*Tri-City Drilling*], aff'd [1960] AJ No 61 (CA).

269 *Chief Construction*, above note 265 at paras 25–28.

offer and not by his ability or inability to carry having regard to his other engagements?"[270]

The evidence showed that the defendant company was not involved in any other carriage contracts or trucking operations, and was not carrying on business as a public employment carrying goods for persons generally. Instead, as with the plaintiff, private contracts on particular terms were negotiated with customers for specific jobs. These facts established that the defendant company was a private carrier, despite the evidence in the record being conflicting as to whether the defendant had turned down any hauling jobs from the plaintiff in the past.[271] In the result, the defendant *was required* to disprove that its negligence had caused the losses at issue occurring during the accident. Justice Stratton concluded that the accident had been caused by the actions of the unknown driver and that the actions of the defendant driver in swerving his vehicle quickly and sharply causing the tractor to overturn was reasonable in the circumstances to avoid a collision with the oncoming vehicle — indeed, it very likely avoided much greater damage to the plaintiff's property and possibly loss of life. There was no evidence of excessive speed by the defendant driver or that he was driving too close to the centre line of the road, which may well have resulted in a finding of negligence against the defendant. Moreover, the defendant driver was entitled to assume that oncoming traffic would be travelling on the proper side of the roadway, especially given the winding and uneven surface of the road in the area of the accident site.[272]

As this case illustrates, where a plaintiff (bailor) can demonstrate that the defendant was a "private carrier" at common law, that will make the defendant a bailee for reward and will require it to meet the heavy onus of a bailee — namely, it will have to disprove that its negligence caused the loss at issue. The same result will obtain with certain other legal designations and classes created by statute, where bailee responsibilities are incident to that status, such as "warehousemen" who, under certain provincial statutes, are also considered bailees for reward.

---

270 *Ibid* at para 26.
271 *Ibid* at paras 29–31.
272 *Ibid* at paras 35–38.

Y. A BAILOR TO PROVE CONDITION PRECEDENTS ARE MET FOR A BAILEE'S DUTY OF SAFEKEEPING TO COMMENCE

If the undertaking of a bailment has been made the subject of certain special preconditions, pursuant to the parties' contract, such as the obtainment of insurance cover by the bailor for the goods for the duration of the bailment, the bailor must prove that these have been met in order for it to meet its onus of proof, unless the bailee concedes same. Where the bailee has frustrated the bailor's ability to fulfil the condition precedent by reason of its own misrepresentations, a bailment may still be created and a bailee may still be found liable for breaching the standard of care set by the terms of the contract, irrespective of the non-performance of the condition.[273]

Z. WRITTEN NOTICE OF THE ALLEGED LOSS IS SOMETIMES REQUIRED FOR A BAILOR TO SATISFY ITS ONUS OF PROOF

Satisfaction of a bailor's onus of proof will sometimes depend on whether the bailor has given the bailee sufficient notice as to the particulars of any goods missing or damaged during the course of the bailment, within the period of time specified in the parties' agreement. In *Atlantic Furs Ltd v Moffatt Moving and Storage*,[274] the bailment contract contained a clause that read:

> The owner agrees to notify the company in writing within seven (7) days of delivery of the goods to the owner or anyone appointed by the owner, with full particulars of any goods missing or damaged and in the event of the owner not so notifying, the owner hereby waives and agrees to waive all claims for missing or damaged goods.[275]

Certainly, such a clause, if enforceable, must be satisfied by a bailor in accordance with its terms in order for a bailor to meet its burden of proof and put the bailee to its heavy onus of disproving that its negligence caused the loss or damage of the goods. That said, in *Atlantic Furs*, the defendant frustrated the plaintiff's ability to do so by failing to provide it with the claim form promptly after receiving verbal notification of the loss despite having a branch manager visit the plaintiff's premises and promise to send

273 See *Bell v Tinmouth*, 1988 CanLII 3220 (BCCA), discussed in Chapter 5, Section B(7)(a).
274 [1985] NJ No 173 (Dist Ct) [*Atlantic Furs*].
275 *Ibid* at para 6.

a claim form. Certainly, such actions by a bailee cannot be countenanced, and Adams CJDC was right to reject the defendant's argument that the plaintiff's claim should be denied as a result of the delay in receiving its written notification, which delay the defendant had substantially, if not solely, caused.[276] In any event, the delivery of the written notice would have been quite superfluous in these circumstances, since the defendant (bailee) was well aware of the losses.

Perhaps more important, Adams CJDC ruled that the limitations clause was unenforceable in any event, as the defendant had not taken reasonable steps to draw the clause to the attention of the plaintiff. In the case, the mere fact that the plaintiff had signed and been presented with a moving order on the delivery of the goods confirming that the plaintiff was the legal owner of the goods, and subjecting it to the conditions appearing on the front and back of the form, was not enough to meet this requirement.[277]

All the above said, the plaintiff's bailment claim still failed, because the plaintiff failed to prove by a balance of probabilities that the loss of its goods had occurred during the period of the bailment, rather than in the period of time when the goods were being packed (before the bailment started) or after the goods were delivered (after the bailment concluded) before they were unpacked. While Adams CJDC's conclusion that "no evidence was adduced to support an inference that the loss occurred while the goods were in the custody of the defendant" is questionable for reasons already stated, the bailor's mere giving of notice of a loss to a bailee does not obviate the need for it to prove further, by a preponderance of probabilities, that the loss occurred during a period of time when the bailee was in exclusive possession of its goods. A mere declaration to this effect, or merely pleading this, is not enough for a bailor to meet its onus of proof in these circumstances, or in any circumstance.

---

276 *Ibid* at paras 6–8. The notice requirement should be viewed as being met where the bailor has made the bailee aware of the losses but was not able to give it a formal notice because the bailee failed to provide it with the appropriate documentation. Otherwise a bailee would essentially be able to set up its own default, or frustrating act, to defeat a bailor's otherwise *bona fide* claims. See further *Tri-City Drilling*, above note 268 at paras 23–26 and 29–31.

277 *Atlantic Furs*, above note 274 at para 8.

AA. A BAILOR TO PROVE THAT DEMAND WAS MADE FOR RETURN OF ITS GOODS

Under some bailment contracts, there will be no agreed upon date for delivery of a bailor's goods. Instead, delivery will be conditional upon a request or demand being made by the bailor. In such circumstances, the bailor must prove in its action for breach of the bailment contract that such a demand was made and refused, to fix liability against the bailee, unless the bailor can show waiver of the condition precedent. Certainly, such a requirement will apply to bailments at will, where the bailor has the right at any time to recall its goods from the bailee, such as where a bailor lends a neighbour (bailee) a shovel for its subsequent use with the specific understanding that the bailee must return same when called upon to do so.

In *Priceville Fox Co v Jordan*,[278] the parties came to an agreement whereby the defendant would sell the plaintiff company twenty pairs of foxes for $24,000, but would retain care and control of five pairs of the twenty, and would deliver same with their increase to the company "on demand" before a named day. Claiming that the defendant had delivered only three of the five other pairs of foxes to it, the plaintiff sued in bailment for the value of the other two pairs.[279]

The Ontario Supreme Court—Appellate Division refused to find a breach of the bailment contract, due to the fact that the plaintiff (bailor) did not establish in evidence that a demand for the return of the pairs of foxes had been made, or that there had been a waiver of said condition, overruling the trial judge's earlier decision to hold the defendant liable as bailee. As a result, the defendant's duties as bailee never went beyond safekeeping with respect to the pairs of foxes in his custody to include redelivering them to the plaintiff. The mere fact that the plaintiff had a right to recall the foxes before a specified date was not enough to trigger a duty of redelivery on the defendant; the right actually had to be exercised. In the result, the defendant was never put to his reverse onus of disproving negligence.[280]

As this case demonstrates, a bailor is required to prove its case strictly. This means that it must plead and prove by a preponderance of

278 [1929] OJ No 32 (SCAD) [*Priceville*].
279 *Ibid* at paras 1–4.
280 *Ibid* at paras 14–22.

probabilities that a demand for a return of its goods was made to the bailee where the bailee's promise to redeliver is conditional on such demand.[281] A failure to do so will mean that the bailor has not overcome its burden of proof and that the bailee will not have to offer up any explanation for its non-return of the bailor's goods.

BB. A BAILOR'S SIGNING OF A DELIVERY RECEIPT

A bailor's mere signing of a delivery receipt acknowledging "receipt of all goods transported in good order" does not mean that it cannot later satisfy its burden of showing that the received goods were damaged or lost while still in the possession of the bailee. This is particularly so where a bailment involves numerous (packaged) goods and the signature merely verifies the fact of delivery but does not represent an acknowledgement that the goods were received in good order. Where there is no opportunity for the bailor to verify that all its good have been returned to it in good order before signing the delivery receipt, the bailor should not be barred from bringing a bailment action on the mere basis of its signature.[282]

CC. CONCLUSION

Proving that the bailee caused the damage to or the loss of the bailed goods during the subsistence of the bailment is a necessary part of the bailor's onus of proof, and must be discharged by the bailor in all circumstances. This position is supported by Ziff, who states:[283]

---

281 This is required of a bailor to trigger the reverse onus on a bailee regardless of whether or not the bailee can actually effect the delivery of the goods. In *Priceville, ibid*, Riddell JA alluded to the fact that the foxes may have perished in the ordinary course of things, to the knowledge of the plaintiff (bailor), which is why the plaintiff chose *not* to make a demand for them in the first place. The rationale was that the demand would have been ineffectual, and the defendant would have been found to have met his standard of care in any a case, since no redelivery would be required in such circumstances: *ibid* at para 10. Even where goods have perished in such circumstances, the bailor must still prove that a demand was made before the bailee will have to offer an explanation for its inability to deliver the goods. See *contra*: *Baud Corporation, NV v Brook*, [1973] AJ No 8 at para 12 (SCAD).

282 See *Atlantic Furs*, above note 274 at para 27.

283 Bruce Ziff, *Principles of Property Law*, 4th ed (Toronto: Thomson Carswell, 2006) at 303–4.

> The presumption in bailment suits is not easily invoked. The plaintiff bailor must show that the acts complained of occurred during the course of the bailment, not before or afterwards. So, if the items have gone missing the presumption will not apply unless it is shown that the loss occurred while the goods were in the possession of the bailee.

A bailor's burden of proof includes a bailor pleading and proving that the goods were lost or damaged while in the possession of the bailee. While reference to the term "bailment" is not an absolute requirement, certainly the facts pleaded by the plaintiff must include the necessary ingredients of the action in order for it to be considered to be properly before the court. While the authorities are not completely consistent, this is the prevailing view. Merely requiring a bailor to plead that the goods were lost during the term of the bailment without having to prove that they were lost or damaged during the course of the bailment would water down the bailor's onus of proof to the point of absurdity. Bailees would essentially becoming insurers; nearly every bailee would have to disprove negligence any time loss or damage to a bailor's goods occurred, including in circumstances where the evidence suggests that the loss or damage occurred outside of the term of the bailment, circumstances that clearly do not merit putting such a heavy onus on the bailee. Unlike in times past, the bailee is no longer "strictly liable for just about any conduct that results in damage or loss,"[284] let alone for damage or loss that may well have occurred outside the bailment relationship.

284 *Ibid* at 300.

CHAPTER 4

A Bailee's Onus of Proof: General Considerations

A. INTRODUCTION

A bailee's onus of proof is more complicated than a bailor's in that there are varying levels of liability that can apply to a bailee, depending on how the bailment is classified and on the circumstances presenting. A bailee's onus of proof is triggered once a bailor meets its onus of proof—that is, when the bailor proves that its goods were lost or destroyed while in the custody of the bailee. The bailee's onus is a heavy burden indeed, as it presumes that the bailee's negligence caused the loss or damage at issue unless the bailee rebuts that presumption.[1] The duty of care on a bailee may last for a long period of time, such as in the case of a long-term storage, or may subsist only for a very brief time.[2]

---

1 James Crossley Vaines, *Personal Property*, 5th ed (London: Butterworths, 1976) at 96.

2 For an example of the latter, see *Evans v Northside Security Services Ltd*, [2002] NWTJ No 95 (Terr Ct). There, despite the very brief time the plaintiff's personal property was in the hands of a security company at the airport he was departing from, while he went through screening, enough time had passed to create a bailment and a relatively heavy duty of care on the defendant bailee to disprove that its negligence had caused the loss, which it ultimately failed to do when the plaintiff's property was stolen from the screening area by an unknown third party.

1) Rationale for a Bailee's Heavy Onus of Proof

The rationale for the heavy reverse onus of proof on a bailee was well described by Aikins J in *The "Ruapehu"*:[3]

> The original principle seems to be grounded on a common sense view of the facts. The bailee knows all about it: he must explain. He and his servants are the persons in charge; the bailor has no opportunity of knowing what happened. These considerations, coupled with the duty to take care, result in the obligation on the bailee to show that the duty has been discharged.

The above rationale certainly breaks down, as we have seen, where both the bailee and bailor have had possession of the goods at the material times, or have exercised control over the goods, and where the bailee is not, strictly speaking, the only party with information as to what happened to cause the bailor's losses.[4] A bailee for reward has often been said to owe a bailor a higher degree of care than does a gratuitous bailee. Indeed, different standards of care can sometimes apply during the course of the same bailment, requiring courts to apply a stricter or more relaxed onus of proof on the bailee, depending on when the loss in question occurred.[5]

2) Various Ways in Which a Bailee's Onus Has Been Described in Law

In law, a bailee's onus of proof has been described in a myriad of ways. This has been perplexing, if only because certain descriptions seem to posit a higher, or at least different, standard than others. Some state that a bailee must merely show that it took "reasonable care" of the bailor's goods during the course of the bailment in order to escape liability, or, alternatively, that any lack of reasonable care did not contribute to the bailor's losses.[6] Others have required the bailee to explain how the injury

---

3 (1925), 21 LL LR 310, as quoted by Thorson P in *R v Halifax Shipyards Ltd* (1956), 4 DLR (2d) 566 at 571 (Ex Ct) [*Halifax Shipyards*].

4 See, for example, *Kinsella v Club "7" Ltd*, [1993] NJ No 365 (SCTD) [*Kinsella*]; *Halifax Shipyards*, above note 3.

5 See, for example, *Ritchie Bros Auctioneers Ltd v Chabot & Levesque Logging Ltd*, [1982] BCJ No 1415 (Co Ct) [*Ritchie Bros*].

6 *Carpenter v Cargill Grain Co*, 1982 CanLII 1123 at para 12 (Alta QB) [*Carpenter*]. See further: *British Motor Corp of Canada Ltd v Ross E Judge Auto Transport Ltd*, [1966] NSJ No 11 at para 33 (SC) [*British Motor*].

of the bailed goods was caused, and then to negative negligence in relation to that cause.[7] As apparent, the latter standard is far more onerous than the former standards and may result in the bailee's being fixed with liability in circumstances where the cause of the loss of the bailed good cannot be ascertained. Many courts also speak of the bailee's standard of care as equalling what a prudent owner of the goods would have done in the circumstances. We shall explore these standards and descriptors in the discussions that follow and identify the prevailing trends in the caselaw.

3) A Bailee's Varying Levels of Liability Based on the Nature of the Bailment: *Coggs v Bernard*

That a bailee's varying levels of liability depend on the nature of its undertaking is traceable to the oft-cited and venerated decision of *Coggs v Bernard*,[8] decided by Sir John Holt CJ in the King's Bench. In that case, the plaintiff hired the defendant to transport several barrels of brandy from a certain cellar in which they were stored to a location a short distance away. There was no charge made for the transport—that is, it was done gratuitously. While the brandy was being unloaded at its new location, one of the casks carrying the liquor was broken and many gallons of brandy were spilt and lost. The chief justice refused to disqualify the bailment on the basis of a lack of consideration, finding that the trust reposed in the defendant (bailee) required him to take reasonable care of the goods. In the process, Holt CJ set out six classes of bailment[9] with varying standards of care:

1) *Depositum*: A bare-naked bailment where a bailee accepts a bailor's goods into its custody to keep them for the use of the bailor. This is a bailment without reward. Here the bailee is liable only if the goods are lost or damaged while in its care because of its gross neglect; common or ordinary neglect will not make the bailee chargeable.

---

7 See Laidlaw JA's discussion in *Stables v Bois*, [1956] OJ No 620 at paras 7–9 (CA). Paton rejects this standard as being too high, "to an absurd extent" (quoting Lord Halsbury), concluding that the onus *should not* require a bailee to explain "exactly" how the loss was occasioned, but instead only to prove definitively that the loss was not caused by any want of care on its part: Sir George Whitecross Paton, *Bailment in the Common Law* (London: Stevens & Sons, 1952) at 166–67 as cited in *British Motor*, above note 6 at para 33.

8 (1703), 2 Ld Raym 909 (Eng KB) [*Coggs*].

9 *Ibid* at 912–920.

2) *Commodatum*, or lending *gratis*: Where a bailee receives goods that are useful from a bailor for the bailee's own use without charge. Here the bailee is liable for slight negligence in the use and care of those goods and must prove that it used the utmost care to avoid liability.
3) *Locatio et conductio*: Where a bailee receives bailor property or goods for hire. This is a bailment for reward. Here the bailee is required to use the utmost care and diligence and to redeliver the goods to the bailor when the period of hire is completed.
4) *Vadium*: Where a bailee receives goods from a bailor as security for a loan or debt, or the fulfillment of an obligation. Here the standard of ordinary care applies, including in restoring the goods to the bailor.
5) Where the bailee receives goods from a bailor for carriage, or for the purpose of performing a service to the goods, for a reward. With respect to carriage carried on as public employment, strict liability applies; that is to say, save acts of God and the like, the bailee will be answerable. With respect to deliveries to private carriers and private persons, ordinary or reasonable care is the standard of care that applies.
6) *Mandatum*: Where the bailee receives goods from a bailor for carriage, or for the purpose of performing a service to the goods, without reward. Careful management of the goods is required here, irrespective of the lack of reward.

In *Coggs*, the bailment was found to be a *mandatum*, and liability was fixed against the defendant by the court accordingly. Careful management of the goods would not have resulted in one of the casks carrying the liquor being staved by the defendant, with the consequent loss of several gallons of brandy. While this case has no doubt greatly influenced the development of Canadian caselaw addressing a bailee's standard of care, its categorical approach has fallen out of favour with most Canadian courts, which prefer to discuss whether a bailee has taken reasonable care of the bailor's goods, or has negatived negligence in all the circumstances. Still, there is no question that there is an alluring quality to Holt CJ's legal framework and that a bailee's standard of care should be informed by the nature of the bailment and the particular circumstances in which it arises. It seems to make sense that in a *commodatum*, where goods are being held by a bailee for its own use and advantage without charge, such as where a bailor lends a bailee a shovel to use for his own benefit, a greater degree of care be placed on the bailee than might otherwise be the case in a bailment for reward situation. By contrast, in a *depositum*, where a bailee is holding goods as a favour to the bailor without recompense, such as where a bailee is storing a bailor's car in her own garage as a favour to the bailor without charge while he is away on vacation, a lower degree of care should be placed on the bailee than might otherwise be the case in a bailment for reward situation.

4) Conclusion: Significance of *Coggs v Bernard*

Certainly, Canadian caselaw demonstrates an abiding regard for the need for a distinction to be made between gratuitous bailments, on the one hand, and bailments for reward, on the other, in that, while reasonable care is required of the bailee in both circumstances, the degree of "reasonableness" in a reward situation will often be greater than in a gratuitous situation. Still, bailments cannot be classified along the lines of Holt CJ's framework for all purposes, as they arise in an infinite number of circumstances. Involuntary bailments, limited bailments, bailments at will, and suspended bailments have emerged in the caselaw and are not reducible, or do not seem easily amenable, to Holt CJ's six categories of analysis. Chief Justice Holt also makes mention of a bailee's keeping of a bailor's goods as it would keep its own[10] as a mode of analysis when it comes to determining whether a bailee has met its standard of care. The argument is that no more should be expected of a bailee than the standard of care it applies in caring for its own goods. This standard is a useful tool in determining what should be expected of a bailee in a given set of circumstances, it has been held to extend to sub-bailees,[11] and it does have an appealing quality to it. Nevertheless, it does not speak for itself in all circumstances, it requires much analysis to unpack, and it lacks in clarity, at least at first glance. Specifically, the subjective versus the objective quality of this standard leaves much to be desired. Is a bailee's actual treatment of its own goods prior to the commencement of the bailment relevant to a bailee's standard of care where the bailee is shown to have been unreasonable in caring for its own goods?[12] Or must the bailee

---

10 *Ibid* at 914.

11 *Punch v Savoy's Jewellers Ltd* (1986), 54 OR (2d) 383 (CA) [*Punch*].

12 Chief Justice Holt in *Coggs*, above note 8, seems to answer this question in the affirmative, stating "suppose the bailee is an idle, careless, drunken fellow, and comes home drunk and leaves all his doors open, and by reason thereof the goods happen to be stolen with his own, yet he shall not be charged, because it is the bailor's own folly to trust such an idle fellow": at 914–15.

be treated as the "reasonable person" in the circumstances, divorced from actuality? In considering how a prudent owner would have treated its own goods under similar circumstances, is a bailor's conduct in caring for its own goods, prior to the commencement of the bailment, relevant to the bailee's standard of care analysis? These questions and others will be explored in the discussions that follow with regard to the Canadian caselaw, which has not always strictly followed Holt CJ's mode of analysis.

B. STANDARD OF CARE ON A BAILEE: BAILMENTS GENERALLY

In the caselaw, the standard of "reasonable care in all the circumstances" appears to have emerged as the prevailing standard of care to be applied to bailees in most bailments and most circumstances, whether for reward or not, despite the more than appreciable amount of caselaw that has been produced over the years that wishes to maintain a strict distinction between the standard of care applicable to gratuitous bailments and that for bailments for reward. The gratuitous bailment for the sole benefit of the bailee requires the bailee to meet a heightened degree of care (that is, that it was not even slightly negligent in caring for the bailor's goods), while the gratuitous bailment for the sole benefit of the bailor requires the bailee to meet a lowered degree of care (that is, that it was not grossly negligent in its handling of the bailor's goods). Both of these circumstances contrast with the ordinary bailment for reward situation, where there is a mutual benefit flowing between the parties, requiring the bailee to do no more than negative ordinary negligence in relation to its handling of the bailor's goods. While the more generalized and flexible standard of "reasonable care" appears to have emerged as the predominant standard in the caselaw to be applied to all bailments, whether for reward or not, it should not be viewed as a repudiation of the distinction in standards of care between gratuitous bailments and bailments for reward, or of Holt CJ's categorical framework from *Coggs*[13] more generally. On the contrary, we shall see that the distinction between a gratuitous bailment and a bailment for reward is still drawn, and very much alive, and that the "reasonable care in all the circumstances" standard may still require an increased or decreased duty of care in gratuitous bailment situations — that is, either a negativing of slight or gross negligence

13 *Ibid.*

rather than a negativing of ordinary negligence required in a bailment for reward situation. This distinction applies *even in the same set of circumstances*. That said, the more flexible standard of reasonable care in all the circumstances allows for a degree of care to be specified by a court that perhaps cannot be strictly categorized as a negativing of ordinary negligence, gross negligence, or slight negligence. This, of course, may allow a bailee to escape liability more easily; conversely, it may make it easier for liability to be fixed against a bailee. Whatever the case may be, in light of the myriad and innumerable circumstances in which bailments can, and have, arisen, it is apparent that the more flexible standard, reasonable care in all the circumstances, will allow justice to be done more frequently than would a more categorical approach.

C. A BAILEE'S STANDARD OF CARE IS MORE ONEROUS THAN THAT APPLIED AGAINST THE BAILEE UNDER THE PRINCIPLE OF *RES IPSA LOQUITUR*

A bailee's standard of care is said to be more onerous than that required of a bailee under the principle of *res ipsa loquitur*. As discussed by the Supreme Court in *Taylor Estate v Wong Aviation Ltd*,[14] *res ipsa loquitur* only requires a bailee or defendant to produce an explanation equally consistent with negligence and no negligence in order to avoid liability where the circumstances include a dead bailee, no bailed goods, and no information as to what happened to cause the loss of the subject property. The ordinary onus on a bailee for reward requires much more than that— that is, in order to escape liability, the bailee must disprove that its negligence caused the bailor's losses.

D. A BAILEE'S STANDARD OF CARE IS LOWER THAN THAT OF AN INSURER AND A COMMON CARRIER

The caselaw is replete with statements by courts that a bailee's standard of care is not that of an "insurer." The implication is that a bailee does not have to meet the standard of perfection, or near perfection, in order to escape liability. Instead, the bailee just has to negative negligence, or show that it took reasonable care of the bailor's goods. An exception, of

---

14 [1969] SCR 481 [*Wong*].

course, exists where the contract provides for a higher duty of care to apply.[15] A bailee's standard of care is lower than that of a common carrier at common law, whose duty of care is equal to that of an insurer—that is, the standard of perfection. In *Northern Industrial Carriers Ltd v Jasper Millwork Ltd*,[16] the Alberta District Court, per Cormack DCJ, recognized as much but commented that a bailee's onus is a heavy one too, and that the distinction will sometimes be merely academic. A carrier, like a bailee, has to prove that the damage of goods in its care did not arise from its neglect. But this onus is triggered only once the bailor has proven that the goods were in good condition when the bailee received them and that the loss occurred while the goods were in the custody of the bailee.[17] In the case, the defendant shipper was able to prove the good condition of only one of its three loads when delivered to the plaintiff carrier. Therefore, the plaintiff, at common law, was answerable only for that load. With regard to the load, the carrier was found liable for the damage, since it called no evidence to negative negligence on its part, which was presumed to have caused the losses.[18] However, as Cormack DCJ underlined, the result of the counterclaim would not have been any different had the plaintiff been a bailee for hire rather than a common carrier:

> Had the plaintiff not been a common carrier but rather a bailee for hire it bears the onus of showing that while the goods were in its possession it handled them without negligence. Here again there is a preliminary onus on the Shipper to show the conditions of the goods when delivered to the carrier. This onus was not discharged in the case of the shipments of July 30 and August 23. In respect of the load of August 26th the Shipper gave evidence that the goods were in good condition and the Carrier adduced no evidence to negative negligence on his part. Therefore the result is the same as it would be with the plaintiff found to be a common carrier.[19]

---

15 See *Grant v Armour*, [1894] OJ No 99 (HCJ).

16 [1978] AJ No 720 (Dist Ct).

17 *Ibid* at paras 13–14.

18 *Ibid* at paras 18–22. The doctrine of *res ipsa loquitur* operates in this context too. If a loss or damage to a shipper's goods occurs while in possession of a common carrier, the law assumes that, if the property provided by the shipper was otherwise suitable, the fault must lie with the carrier—that is, that there must have been some lack of proper care in attending to the goods on the part of the carrier that explains the loss.

19 *Ibid* at para 23.

It is clear that both a common carrier and a bailee for hire face heavy onuses of proof that are not easily discharged. However, unlike a bailee, a common carrier *can not* exonerate itself from liability by showing that due care of the goods was taken, or that no negligence at all was committed.[20] It must show a standard of perfection (that no loss or damage occurred while goods were being cared for by it) or, alternatively, that it was not responsible for the loss or damage, due to an inherent defect or vice in the goods delivered, or for some other acceptable reason, such as the goods not being properly packaged by the shipper of the goods. Thus, a common carrier's escape routes are more circumscribed than a bailee's, although as was demonstrated in the case, it will be a distinction without a difference where a carrier offers up no explanation for the loss, since this will also not be an acceptable defence to a bailment action.

E. THE STANDARD OF CARE OF THE REASONABLY PRUDENT OWNER

Many bailment cases state that the bailee's conduct at the relevant times is to be measured against the care that the "reasonably prudent owner" of the same goods in the same circumstances would have provided. While determining this measurement is an art, not a science, much can be gleaned from the caselaw here. It indicates that both a bailee's actual treatment of its own goods prior to the start of the bailment and a bailor's own conduct in caring for its own goods prior to the start of the bailment can be relevant to determining what the bailee's standard of care is and whether it has been met. The rationale is that no more should be expected from a bailee than the care that it provides to its own similar goods, to the extent the bailor has knowledge of the standard of care employed by the bailee previously and explicitly or implicitly accepts same. Similarly, a bailee should *not* have to meet a higher standard of care than that employed by the bailor in looking after the bailed goods prior to the start of the bailment, to the extent that this standard is known by the bailee

20 The distinction extends and is relevant to exclusion clauses contained in common carrier rather than bailment contracts. In order for the common carrier to protect itself from liability for the acts of its servants, it must exempt itself from negligent and non-negligent acts of its servants, whereas bailees have to concern themselves with protecting themselves only from the negligent acts of their servants, but not all acts that may cause damage or losses to bailor property: see *Porter & Sons v Muir Brothers Dry Dock Co*, [1929] OJ No 109 at paras 60–61 (SCAD) [*Porter & Sons*].

and is not renounced by the bailor. A subjective rather than an objective analysis will, accordingly, sometimes be required.

What is required of a reasonably prudent owner in the circumstances is affected by whether the bailment is for reward or not. Where for reward, the standard of care is greater than that expected of a gratuitous bailee in the same or similar circumstances. For example, it might be acceptable for a gratuitous bailee storing a bailor's motor vehicle on an enclosed parking lot awaiting repair to leave the keys in the ignition switch of the bailor's vehicle, if this could be said to be consistent with a bailor's own practices, but the same conduct would probably not be acceptable for a bailee for reward. The latter might have to do more — namely, secure the keys to the vehicle in a locked premises — to meet its standard of care.[21]

1) A Bailee's Actual Treatment of Its Own Similar Goods

In *Queen Sales & Service Ltd v Smith*,[22] the appellant and respondent entered into a verbal agreement whereby the respondent would buy a 1963 Meteor motor vehicle from the appellant in exchange for the respondent's used 1959 Zephyr vehicle and $2,200 in cash. As the appellant (bailor) did not have the Meteor in stock but was desirous of the opportunity to sell the Zephyr, it arranged with the respondent (bailee) to have him borrow a 1957 Pontiac motor vehicle to be used (as a loaner vehicle) until the Meteor became available for purchase. This arrangement was put into place by a salesman for the appellant. The salesman advised the respondent that the brake on the right front wheel of the Pontiac was defective and that the Pontiac would veer to the right when the brakes were applied suddenly. The salesman was aware that the respondent let his girlfriend drive his own vehicle, the Zephyr, from time to time. Indeed, she had driven the Zephyr in the salesman's presence, and both the girlfriend and the respondent had test-driven the Meteor. As it happened, the respondent's girlfriend got into an accident with the Pontiac, crashing into a parked car when she applied the brakes on a narrow street, which caused the Pontiac to pull to the right, in an attempt to stop to allow an oncoming vehicle to pass.[23]

---

21 See *Manitoba Public Insurance Corp v Midway Chrysler Plymouth Ltd*, [1977] MJ No 87 (CA).

22 [1963] NSJ No 24 (SC).

23 *Ibid* at paras 22–28, Bissett J.

The appellant sued the respondent in bailment for the damage to its Pontiac, claiming that the respondent was strictly liable as insurer for its losses, since he had deviated from the terms of the bailment contract by allowing his girlfriend to drive the appellant's Pontiac without the appellant's express consent. The appellant further argued that the bailment between it and the respondent of the Pontiac (under which the respondent was a bailee) was terminated when the respondent's girlfriend was allowed to drive the Pontiac. Chief Justice Isley of the Nova Scotia Supreme Court rejected these arguments, holding that, in light of the appellant's actual knowledge, through its salesman, that the respondent's girlfriend drove the respondent's car (the Zephyr) from time to time, it was reasonable to imply a term into the bailment contract authorizing the respondent's girlfriend to drive the appellant's Pontiac (since the Pontiac had become the respondent's new, temporary mode of transportation until the Meteor became available for purchase). Based on the parties' discussions and previous history, it was reasonably foreseeable that the appellant's girlfriend would drive the vehicle and was not a deviation from the bailment contract.[24]

In the result, the only question left for determination was whether the respondent's girlfriend had been negligent in her driving of the Pontiac, in breach of her standard of care as agent of the bailee. Chief Justice Isley found that she had not: her driving qualities were impeccable; she had driven the respondent's vehicle (the Zephyr) on numerous occasions before the accident without incident; and the cause of the accident was not her careless driving but a recognized mechanical defect in the brakes of the Pontiac.[25]

This case demonstrates that a bailee's own treatment of similar property, in this case a car, can inform the standard of care analysis of the bailee by modifying what is and is not acceptable under the bailment contract. Since the respondent (bailee) had allowed his girlfriend to drive his own car, the Zephyr, prior to the commencement of the bailment, to the knowledge of the appellant, it was not unreasonable for the respondent to continue to allow his girlfriend to drive the Pontiac (as that was his new, temporary mode of transportation). However, it is submitted that a bailee's actual use of its own similar property, prior to the commencement

---

24 *Ibid* at paras 5–12.

25 *Ibid* at paras 15–37.

of a bailment, is only relevant to the standard of care determination to the extent that the bailor is aware of how the bailee treats or uses its own similar property, and tacitly or explicitly accepts such treatment, or where such knowledge can be reasonably imputed to the bailor in the circumstances. It would be asking too much to expect a bailor to know all the eccentric ways in which a bailee may treat its own similar or identical property prior to the commencement of the bailment without specific notice of same. For example, had the respondent allowed his cousin from another country to use his Zephyr when he was visiting him, unbeknownst to the appellant, then the cousin's use of the appellant's Pontiac with the permission of the respondent would have constituted a deviation from the bailment contract, such that the respondent would have been found to be strictly liable to the appellant for the damage to its Pontiac (perhaps even irrespective of the mechanical defect with the brakes). Where there is no knowledge or discussion of the ways in which a bailee has used its own identical or similar property prior to the start of the bailment, it is submitted that a standard of reasonableness should be applied.

In *MacDonald v Pro-Line Trailers Ltd*,[26] the defendant's (bailee's) treatment of its own property was referred to by Simonsen J in deciding whether it had met its applicable standard of care following the loss of the plaintiff's trailer, which had been left on the defendant's premises in the hope of a sale by consignment: "In this case, the trailer was placed in exactly the same position as other trailers owned or stored by the defendant."[27] Justice Simonsen found that the plaintiff must have been aware of the fact that the defendant stored its own trailers in the manner as the plaintiff's own property — namely, unguarded in an unfenced yard where there would be no monitoring of the comings and goings of the trailers and where there was no security system.[28] While it is true that a bailee's treatment of its own similar goods can be a relevant consideration when assessing whether it has discharged its applicable standard of care, this should be the case only where the practices are known by the bailor and have been either explicitly or impliedly accepted by the bailor in the bailment contract. Otherwise, it is not a relevant factor, and a bailee is entitled to exercise a standard of reasonable care as defined by the law based on the industry practice prevailing in the particular locale.

---

26 [1996] MJ No 318 (QB) [*MacDonald*].

27 *Ibid* at para 16.

28 *Ibid* at paras 9–10.

2) A Bailor's Own Treatment of the Bailed Goods or of Similar Goods

a) Where No Higher Standard of Care Is Given to the Bailed Goods by the Bailor Prior to the Start of a Bailment than by the Bailee During the Bailment

A bailor's own treatment of the bailed goods, or similar goods, can be relevant to the analysis of whether a bailee has discharged its applicable standard of care. In *MacDonald*,[29] the plaintiff (bailor) *had not* provided a higher level of security than the defendant in storing his own trailer on his own farmyard in an unfenced area without any security systems in place whatsoever. Justice Simonsen accordingly used this finding in support of the legal conclusion that the defendant (bailee) had met its applicable standard of care, since the plaintiff could not expect a higher level of care than he himself had provided over his own property while exclusively in his possession and control before the start of the bailment.

While a bailor's treatment of its own goods can be relevant to assessing whether a bailee has satisfied its standard of care, this will be the case only where the bailee can show that its level of care taken over the goods was at least equal to that of the bailor. Where the bailee's level of care is found to fall below that standard, this will strain in favour of finding that the bailee has breached its duty of care. In *Kinsella*,[30] Puddester J of the Newfoundland Supreme Court—Trial Division considered the treatment of the premises by the plaintiff prior to its transfer into the defendants' possession, focusing on the use of the area of the building where the plaintiff's items were stored and from which they had ultimately disappeared while in the exclusive possession of the defendants. Prior to the bailment, and while the plaintiff was in control of the premises, the areas had been used by two street vendors, with no prohibition on their access to the storage areas. The plaintiff did not take any special steps to secure the chattels in the premises, although he testified that external access to this portion of the premises was maintained secure by the vendors while he was in charge of the premises. Although access for the vendors to the area continued unimpeded under the defendants' control, and no steps were taken by the defendants at all to secure the plaintiff's goods, the defendants' actions

---

29 *Ibid.*

30 *Kinsella*, above note 4. This case is discussed more fully in Chapter 1, Section B(1)(b)(iv)(b).

had not (exactly) maintained the plaintiff's level of care: specifically, the defendants had permitted the area to be occupied by three additional tenants, two of whom undertook work and renovations in the immediate vicinity of the plaintiff's items. This was no small thing and increased the risk of loss of the plaintiff's goods. As well, the plaintiff had not consented to these changes to the storage areas of the premises. Indeed, the defendants never consulted at all with the plaintiff about the addition of the new tenants (although, admittedly, the plaintiff had attended the premises subsequently and did not object or protest when he saw the new tenants' use of the area or their activities, nor did he discuss any matter of concern with the defendants). The vendors, while under the plaintiff's charge, had generally been cautious about entering and exiting the storage areas in terms of ensuring that external access points were secure, while, on the defendants' evidence, that situation did not obtain after the plaintiff's departure. Justice Puddester, accordingly, rejected the defendants' argument that they had met their standard of care by taking the same degree of care of the plaintiff's chattels as had been taken before their takeover of the premises.[31] Where a bailee's standard of care falls below that of the bailor's treatment of the same or similar goods, this can contribute to a finding that the bailee has failed to meet its standard of care.

b) Where the Standard of Care Given to Bailed Goods by a Bailor Prior to the Start of a Bailment Exceeds Industry Standards

A more difficult question is how a bailor's own treatment of its goods should affect the bailee's standard of care where the evidence shows that the bailor's safekeeping measures exceeded those required by industry standards in the particular locale where the bailee's business was located. Should a bailee be required to meet those higher standards? In *Hertz Canada Ltd v Suburban Motors Ltd*,[32] the plaintiff (bailor) had stored the keys to its own vehicles for its business in a safe overnight, while the defendant (bailee) had provided less security than this to the plaintiff's vehicle left overnight with it for the repair of a seatbelt. Specifically, the defendant had placed the keys in a locked building on a turnstile with identifying information on it. However, the industry standard in the locale indicated that the defendant had met its applicable standard of care, despite the

31 *Ibid* at paras 50–60 and 103–4.
32 2000 BCSC 667. This case is discussed more fully in Chapter 5, Section B(11).

theft of and damage occasioned to the car by a determined thief who went to great lengths to gain access to the defendant's locked building and, more specifically, to the room within which the plaintiff's vehicle keys were located in order to steal the plaintiff's keys. Justice Warren of the British Columbia Supreme Court refused to use the other evidence in the record that indicated that higher standards of care were sometimes employed by others, including the plaintiff, since these were not reflective of industry practice.[33] As apparent, a bailor's treatment of its own similar or identical goods may not always be dispositive where they do not otherwise reflect the industry standard. As well, a bailee may not be aware of all the special or distinct security measures that a bailor has in place for its own goods, which may rise above industry standards, and, without a bailee being made aware of these by a bailor and agreeing to same, it would seem unfair to hold the bailee to them.

c) Where the Standard of Care Given to Bailed Goods by the Bailor Prior to the Start of a Bailment Is Substandard

The other challenge that may arise when comparing a bailor's treatment of the same or similar goods with the treatment afforded those same goods by a bailee is that a bailor may treat its goods in a substandard way. Does this mean that a bailee can emulate this treatment? The better view would seem to be to use industry standards to set a bailee's minimum degree of care owed to goods under a bailment, rather than to allow bailees to shirk their responsibilities by relying on a bailor's own shortcomings in its treatment of its own goods, which may or may not be known by the bailee and may or may not be relevant to the nature of the bailment at issue. Perhaps it is for this reason that Reid J of the Ontario Supreme Court—High Court of Justice in *Hamilton v Chris Marion Holdings Ltd (cob Servicemaster of Ottawa)*[34] rejected out of hand the notion that a bailor's own treatment of its own goods could have any relevance to an assessment of whether a bailee has met its standard of care: "A careless owner is entitled to expect a better standard of care from a bailee for hire than he might himself meet. I thus set aside the evidence of plaintiff's custody of the gun collection as irrelevant to the issue of Servicemaster's negligence."[35]

---

33 *Ibid* at paras 6–12.
34 [1981] OJ No 523 (HCJ).
35 *Ibid* at para 27.

Eliminating all consideration of a bailor's treatment of its own identical or similar goods would be contrary to the received view, which allows for such consideration. That said, certainly undue focus should not be placed on this factor, especially where the treatment of the goods by the bailor is not known by the bailee, the bailor and bailee are dealing with each other at arm's length, and the bailee's standard of care has fallen below the applicable industry standard for the locale.

F. FORM OF PLEADINGS

A bailee may have to defend against a bailment action, either as a defendant in the main action or as a defendant in a counterclaim. Either way, the bailee will need to show that reasonable care of the bailor's goods was taken at all material times, which may require more or less depending on whether the bailment is for reward or not, and on several other considerations.

G. SUMMARY JUDGMENT MOTIONS

While no case could be found where a bailor has met its onus of proof pursuant to the summary judgment procedure, bailees have not been similarly saddled. They have, on certain occasions, succeeded in having bailment actions against them dismissed. For example, in *Chiaravalloti v Leading Edge Auto Collision*,[36] the plaintiffs sued the defendants, alleging a bailment relationship between the owner of a motor vehicle and a vehicle repair shop. The plaintiffs argued that this bailment was breached by the defendants when the plaintiffs' vehicle was rear-ended by a driver employed by the defendants whose driver's licence was suspended, making the defendants liable to the plaintiffs. The defendants moved for summary judgment and a dismissal of the plaintiffs' action on the basis that no bailment relationship existed between them and the owner of the vehicle, one Mr Singh.[37] In dismissing the plaintiff's action, Edwards J of the Ontario Superior Court of Justice found that "a full appreciation of the evidence and issues" could be accomplished without the "full forensic machinery of a trial." This was so even though there was some conflicting evidence in the record with respect to *exactly* what transpired and what had been agreed upon when

36 2012 ONSC 4554.

37 *Ibid* at paras 1–10.

Singh deposited his vehicle with the defendants.[38] However, the evidence was clear that Singh had left his vehicle on the defendants' lot for over five months and had chosen not to proceed with the repair after receiving the repair quotation from the defendant repair shop. Indeed, he had chosen to abandon his vehicle on the defendants' premises. Thus, at most, a gratuitous bailment relationship existed between the parties at the material times. Since there was no evidence to establish "gross negligence" on the part of the defendant repair shop causally connected to the plaintiff's (bailor's) losses suffered in the rear-end collision, the defendants were relieved of all liability for the plaintiffs' losses.[39]

H. FORM OF EVIDENCE

A bailee does not necessarily have to call evidence to satisfy its onus of proof, although, needless to say, this will almost be required for a bailee to disprove that its negligence caused the bailor's losses. The bailee can rely on any reasonable explanation absolving it from liability contained in the evidence put before the court by the bailor, or the bailor's counsel, including the bailee's answers from examination for discovery.[40] The evidentiary standard that a bailee must satisfy in order to meet its onus of proof and avoid liability is to the balance of probabilities.[41] A bailee should not be required to meet a higher standard than this.

I. VICARIOUS LIABILITY: BAILEE LIABILITY FOR EMPLOYEE ACTS

It is difficult, if not impossible, for there to be a separation of personhood between employee and employer for the purposes of exclusive possession of company property required for a bailment to be found, since the employer usually commands or directs an employee's use of the property and is responsible for that use. What is more, the employer is usually the owner, hirer, or lessor of the property. It follows that, where an employee of a bailee is negligent and third-party bailor property is damaged during the course of a bailment, the bailee (employer) will generally be liable to the bailor for the employee's acts pursuant to the doctrine of vicarious

38 *Ibid* at paras 5–8.
39 *Ibid* at paras 14–17.
40 Andrew James, *CED* (Ont 3d), Supplement vol 2, title 13, Bailment at 41.
41 *627360 Saskatchewan Ltd v Bellrose*, 2007 SKQB 14 at para 16 [*Bellrose*].

liability. In other words, where a bailee entrusts an employee or agent with a bailor's goods to perform its duty as bailee, then the employer is liable if the servant is negligent or careless with the goods, and for other tortious acts occurring in relation to the goods during the course of the bailment, such as conversion or theft, as this will mean that a bailee *has not* fulfilled its duty to take reasonable care of the goods.[42] Bailees are also answerable where their employees decide to take bailor property on a "frolic of their own" and cause damage or loss to the property, such as where an employee tasked with repairing a car deviates from the bailment contract and takes it on a joyride and damages it. In other words, a mere delegating of duties by a bailee to its agent or employee should not erase the bailee's duty to take reasonable care of the goods, since a bailee who is not an individual or sole proprietor must always act vis-à-vis its employees to carry out its duties.[43] While, despite their best efforts, a bailee may not always be able to prevent or detect the dishonesty or criminality by an employee that causes losses to a bailor, a bailee should be the one held liable, as it has put its trust and confidence in the employee. The bailor may not even know the employee—he or she may be a complete stranger to the bailor—and the bailor will likely have very little control, if any, over the manner in which a bailee's employee treats the bailed property, beyond the general instructions that are given to the bailee and conveyed to its employees at the outset of the bailment. Thus, as between the two, the bailee is more deserving of bearing the burden of risk than a bailor for damage done to bailed goods by rogue employees, regardless of circumstance.[44]

It follows that an employer will usually be the party sued by the bailor and held responsible for bailor losses caused by employees charged with carrying out the duties of the bailment, including the duty of safekeeping. However, where an employer can show that the party who damaged the bailed property was an independent contractor (and not one of its employees) who lawfully took the property into its own exclusive possession and control and thus became bailee independent of the employer, liability may be avoided. However, where the party who takes control of

42 *Morris v CW Martin & Sons Ltd*, [1965] 2 All ER 725 at 732 (CA) [*Morris*], Diplock LJ. Lord Justice Diplock's rulings on these points were in complete accord with the other two honourable justices in the case, namely Lord Denning MR and Salmon LJ, and represent binding law from the case.

43 *Ibid* at 730, Denning MR.

44 *Ibid* at 735, Diplock LJ.

the property is an employee of an employer who assumed possession on behalf of the bailor, then the employer becomes bailee and the employee should not be regarded as having received the property in their personal capacity. As bailee, the employer will have to disprove negligence to avoid liability where damage to bailor property is committed by an employee during the course of the bailment.[45]

There do not seem to be many escape routes for an employer bailee here. In *Morris*,[46] Salmon LJ mentioned the possibility that an employer bailee might not be held liable for the loss of bailed property where a rogue employee who is not specifically entrusted with the goods by the employer, but who can gain access to the goods, were to take them or damage them: this would mean that the employee was clearly acting outside of the scope of their employment, as they were never supposed to have custody of the goods in the first place. For Salmon LJ, the mere fact that employment gives an employee the opportunity for nefarious conduct in relation to a bailor's goods should not be enough, without more, to hold an employer liable in bailment. The learned judge gives an example of furs being stolen from one business location of the bailee by an employee who works at another of the bailee's locations and who decides to break into the building at the other location and to take the property.[47] While Salmon LJ's view seems defensible enough, the specific facts of each situation will have to be examined, as they may indicate that a bailee has failed to discharge its duty of safekeeping owed to the bailor. For example, if the bailee in the previous example were careless in allowing employees from another location of its business to have access codes to the building in which bailor goods were stored at the other location, when there was no *bona fide* business reason for doing so (that is, no legitimate reason for the employees at the other location to have this information), and if a rogue employee from the other location takes advantage of the mishap, gains access to the building, and steals a bailor's goods, should a bailee be able to escape liability?

J. THE *WONG* EXCEPTION

Where bailed goods are lost and the circumstances surrounding the loss are a *complete* mystery—that is to say, where nothing is known of the

45 See *MacDonald*, above note 26 at para 11.

46 Above note 42.

47 *Ibid* at 740.

circumstances, the bailee is dead, and the bailed goods are missing—and there is no evidence of negligence or breach of contract by the bailee, the bailee will not face its ordinary onus of proof to disprove negligence. Instead, its onus will be a modified one, as set out by the Supreme Court of Canada in *Wong*,[48] a case where an aircraft and its (bailee) pilot vanished without a trace. In these circumstances of a dead bailee, no bailed goods, no one knowing what happened, and a complete absence of evidence of clear negligence or breach of contract by the bailee, the adjusted onus of proof will only require the defendant to provide an explanation to show that the happening may have occurred without negligence on the part of the bailee. The explanation consistent with no negligence must be equally convincing as any countervailing explanation that might be offered up by the plaintiff (bailor) in order for the defendant to avoid liability as bailee.[49] The defendant (bailee) should *not* be put to its ordinary onus of disproof of negligence in these circumstances.

In *Amo Containers Ltd v Mobil Oil Canada Ltd*,[50] however, it was demonstrated that the *Wong* exception is not easily met or triggered in favour of a bailee, and is highly circumscribed. There, the respondent rented some cargo containers from the appellant for the transportation of goods to oil rigs off the east coast of Canada. The containers were placed onboard a ship chartered by the respondent. This ship later sank in a severe storm, and everybody onboard the ship, including three representatives of the respondent, died. The cause of the sinking was unknown at the time of the loss and immediately thereafter. However, a royal commission was established to investigate the cause of the sinking, and the ship was later found on the ocean floor.[51]

The respondent took the position that it should be permitted to rely on the modified onus of proof as established by the Supreme Court in *Wong* for the purpose of explaining its failure to redeliver the containers to the appellant rather than having to show no want of reasonable care on its part.[52] The argument in support of this position was well summarized in the trial judge's comments about the state of the respondent's

48 Above note 14.

49 Once this is done, the plaintiff (bailor) is essentially left to prove negligence against the defendant in the ordinary way, in order to fix liability against it.

50 1989 CanLII 3947 (Nfld CA).

51 *Ibid* at paras 1–4.

52 *Ibid* at para 5.

knowledge regarding the appellant bailor's losses, in the court below, where the judge appears to analogize between the fact situation from *Wong* and the one before him:

> All of the people who could have explained or who could have offered some kind of explanation, all the people who may have known about it no longer live. They died with the destruction of the bailed articles and I think it would be just as unreasonable to call upon the corporate defendant to satisfy the burden which normally attends on bailees as it would be to require the testator/executor to explain.[53]

The Court of Appeal for Newfoundland, per Goodridge CJN, found that the trial judge had erred in finding that the *Wong* criteria had been met such that the respondent should be allowed to rely on the relaxed onus of proof, surmising that a great deal about the sinking might be gleaned from the public inquiry into the matter that involved 180 days of hearings and that this was a relevant fact that needed to be considered by the trial judge. The evidence before the trial judge did not establish "that nothing was known about the sinking," the threshold point that Goodridge CJN stated needed to be met by the respondent bailee in the case in order to enjoy the benefit of the modified onus carved out by the Supreme Court in *Wong*. In the result, the matter was ordered returned to trial for reconsideration of the question of the respondent's (bailee's) liability for the appellant (bailor's) losses.[54]

The *Amo* decision raises some important questions about the applicability of the *Wong* exception to the bailee's ordinary onus of proof. For one thing, it forces us to question whether the state of knowledge requirement as to what happened to cause the bailor's losses is to be assessed at the point of the loss and immediately thereafter, or whether it extends further to the point of trial. It seems to make sense to extend it to trial, since at that point in time the bailor's and bailee's onuses of proof come into play and must be satisfied. More significantly, however, Goodridge CJN's decision seems to mean that an absence of direct evidence as what happened to cause a bailor's losses might not be enough to trigger the modified, relaxed onus on a bailee as long as "what actually did happen," rather than "what might have happened," can be established by a

53 *Ibid* at para 16.
54 *Ibid* at paras 17–22.

third-party independent investigation such as a public inquiry.[55] But this seems to be possible only where there is some sort of physical evidence relating to the loss of the bailed goods that is in existence at the time of trial that might shed light on what in fact transpired to cause the bailor's losses. In *Amo*, had the ship housing the appellant's cargo containers perished without a trace, and not been found on the ocean floor, then it would truly have been a *Wong* situation, and the respondent would have been entitled to rely on the more relaxed onus of proof to try to escape liability for the appellant's losses.

It is to be observed that all the criteria from *Wong* must be met before the relaxed onus of proof will apply to a bailee. The fact that the precise circumstances surrounding the loss of bailor property remain uncertain is not enough to trigger exception to a bailee's ordinary onus of proof where the bailee is alive and well and available to provide an explanation for the loss of the bailor's property. For example, in *Drake v Bekins Moving and Storage Co*,[56] only purely speculative evidence was before the court on the circumstances surrounding the loss of a valuable Persian rug after it had been delivered by the plaintiff to the defendant's employees at her home for storage in the defendant's warehouse. While the *Wong* case was not specifically considered by the court, the defendant (bailee) *was not* given the benefit of a relaxed onus of proof and faced liability accordingly under the reverse onus, since there was no way for it to escape liability by showing that reasonable care of the plaintiff's property had been taken, given the lack of evidence on the circumstances surrounding the loss. In *Lifestyles Kitchens & Bath, a division of GVBS Inc v Danbury Sales Inc*,[57] it was recognized by Cullity J that, where the circumstances surrounding loss of bailor property remain a mystery or are highly uncertain at the point of trial, the placing of the reverse onus on the bailee may well result in liability against it, since there will be no way for it to escape liability. In sum, "mysterious disappearances" of bailor property that fall short of the *Wong* circumstances will not be enough to trigger the relaxed onus of proof on a bailee.[58] Thus, a bailee's failure in these circumstances to

55 The foregoing phrases were used in Goodridge CJN's reasons for decision to distinguish between the fact situation in *Wong* and that present in most bailment actions: *ibid*.

56 [1982] BCJ No 1020 (Co Ct) [*Drake*].

57 [1999] OJ No 3097 (SCJ).

58 See, for example, *Lakeside Commission Agency Ltd v Saskatchewan Wheat Pool*, [1990] SJ No 350 (QB) [*Lakeside*].

disprove negligence, or show that reasonable care was taken, should result in liability against it.

K. BAILMENTS FOR REWARD: THE QUESTION OF CONSIDERATION

In order for a bailment to be for reward, the bailee must have received consideration for the bailment, regardless of its nature or value. Establishing consideration for the bailment is important for a bailor, for, where it exists, a bailee will often owe the bailor a heightened duty of care, as compared with a gratuitous bailment. In most cases, the question of consideration will not be a controversial one and will be easily shown on the evidence. For example, and most commonly, a fee will be paid to the bailee to safeguard the bailor's goods, to perform a service to them, to transport them, or to use them, or to resell them. A bailor's delivery of goods to a bailee to be tested for adequacy of use, in the hope of making a sale (or lease)[59] or trade,[60] will also suffice.[61] A consideration will also be shown where a bailor has transferred goods, such as a computer, to the bailee to facilitate a contractual and commercial relationship already in existence between them[62] or in certain circumstances where the bailee (as the seller of the goods) is holding the goods for a bailor, subsequent to a completed sale and a passing of title in the goods to the bailor, but prior to the bailor (purchaser) having collected all of its goods from the seller (bailee) or its premises.[63] Any time or money saved by a bailee will also suffice as sufficient consideration to make a bailment for reward,[64] as will any money earned, however indirectly, from the bailment.[65] One court

59 See, for example, *Mobilex Ltd v Payne*, [1959] OJ No 81 (HCJ).

60 See, for example, *Fairley & Stevens (1966) Ltd v Goldsworthy* (1973), 34 DLR (3d) 554 (NSSCTD) [*Fairley*].

61 In *MacDonald*, above note 26, Simonsen J disagreed that the possibility of a bargain, in that case a sale on consignment, was enough, without more, to create a bailment for reward: see para 15. The learned judge's conclusion is at odds with the received view in the caselaw, which holds otherwise, and certainly is an outlier.

62 *Tech-North Consulting Group Inc v British Columbia (Minister of Skills, Training and Labour)*, 1997 CanLII 1797 (BCSC).

63 See *Lakeside*, above note 58.

64 See *Bellrose*, above note 41 at paras 21–22.

65 In *Robertson v Stang*, [1997] BCJ No 2022 at para 68 (SC), the court found that a bailment resulting from the removal of a tenant's goods from her apartment (a hoarder in a cooperative) by the landlord (bailee) to certain storage areas within the complex, so that the plaintiff's (bailor's) unit could be measured for the purposes of converting the

has gone so far as to find the removal of a fire hazard by way of bailment to be sufficient consideration to make a bailment for value.[66] "Consideration," then, is to be defined broadly to include any benefit to the bailee, however remote or incidental and whether financial or not. Future or present consideration is sufficient. Where there is a clear reward, or hope of reward, flowing to the bailee, such as where a bailee takes a bailor (seller's) car out for a test drive in the hope of making a trade of the bailee's own vehicle for the purchase of a new one, the standard of care of gross negligence, applicable to gratuitous bailments for the sole benefit of the bailor, *should not* be applied. This would be setting the bar too low in a reward situation. While it will not make a difference where the bailee is guilty of gross negligence,[67] it might well be consequential where a bailee's misconduct falls short of that. As a general rule, adequacy and sufficiency of the consideration will be irrelevant; its presence is all that will be required for a reward to be found.[68]

The Court of Appeal for Manitoba's ruling on the issue in *Martin v Town N' Country Delicatessen Ltd*[69] is therefore questionable. There, the appellant went to the respondent's restaurant for dinner and drove his vehicle to the parking lot located nearest to the restaurant. The restaurant was very busy, and the appellant could not locate a parking spot in that lot, so he drove his vehicle into one of the aisles between two rows of cars. A person that the appellant assumed to be a parking attendant suggested that the appellant leave his keys in his vehicle, which the appellant assumed meant that the attendant would park his car for him later, when a space became available, which he did. The appellant proceeded to go to dinner at the restaurant. The appellant had parked his car without charge on the lot and received no ticket for the parking (in accordance with the lot's usual practices), and there was no sign restricting parking there. Essentially the appellant had taken advantage of the respondent's courtesy parking facilities.[70] When the appellant returned to the lot to pick up his car, it was missing and presumably stolen. Chief Justice Miller, speaking

---

cooperative into a strata corporation, a deal apparently worth several million dollars, was for reward. This is because the deal could not have been completed without the said removal having occurred.

66 *Ibid.*

67 See, for example, *Fairley*, above note 60 especially at paras 14–15.

68 See *Carpenter*, above note 6 at para 11.

69 [1963] MJ No 78 (CA) [*Martin*].

70 *Ibid* at paras 1–8.

for the majority of the court, rejected the appellant's evidence that the attendant had assured him that his keys would be retained in his possession and would need to be picked up from him upon the appellant's return, finding that this was inconsistent with the appellant's other evidence, that he expected his keys to be in his car when he returned to the lot.[71]

Chief Justice Miller stated that, even if there were a bailment of the appellant's vehicle (which he did not find on the facts), relying on the agency and convenience-based arguments from the Court of Appeal for Ontario's decision in *Palmer v Toronto Medical Arts Building Ltd*,[72] it would have been a "gratuitous bailment" for which the respondent had received no consideration. Chief Justice Miller's words are apposite:

> The facilities of the parking lot were made available gratuitously for the convenience of plaintiff and others desirous of using the restaurant and arriving by car. The supply of a parking lot for the convenience of patrons was not a service covered by a consideration paid by patrons of the restaurant. Presumably the same prices would be charged people who walked to the restaurant, or who came by bus or taxicab, without any consideration for the furnishing of a parking lot for motorists.[73]

Chief Justice Miller was of the view that no profit accrued to the respondent as a result of its operating the courtesy parking lot for the temporary storage of cars. It was not in the parking lot operator business, it was in the restaurant business, and those bailment cases dealing with "parking facilities provided as a business venture" were distinguishable.[74] Chief Justice Miller's refusal to find a consideration was very consequential indeed, since, without consideration, the appellant (bailor), to succeed, had to show "gross negligence" on the part of the respondent, which he could not do. The respondent had presumably acted in accordance with the arrangement it had with the appellant, parking his car in a designated space when one became available and leaving the keys in the vehicle as was contemplated between them. The appellant's appeal was accordingly dismissed.

Chief Justice Miller's view here neglects to consider that the lot was being operated by the attendants on busy nights for the benefit of the

71 *Ibid* at paras 14–16.
72 [1960] OR 60 (CA).
73 *Martin*, above note 69 at para 13.
74 *Ibid* at paras 9–12.

restaurant. A more efficient use of the parking lot for those customers travelling by car, by taking certain vehicle owners' keys to optimize the parking facilities' use, as had occurred with the appellant, would presumably increase the patronage of the restaurant on those nights. Surely that was a consideration flowing directly to the respondent bailee, a point picked up on by the dissenting judges in their reasons for decision.[75] The words of Harris CJ, speaking for the majority of the Nova Scotia Supreme Court in *Murphy v Hart*,[76] a bailment case also involving a restaurant proprietor who provided a coat check to his patrons at no cost, are apposite and are to be preferred:

> The depositing of the overcoat in the place provided by the defendant for that purpose was for the benefit of both parties, and while no price was paid directly or specifically to the defendant for the care of the plaintiff's overcoat, it was part of the accommodation for which the defendant received his recompense from his customers. It is obvious that the defendant derived some advantage in the way of increased trade by making his premises attractive and the providing of a place in which customers could leave their coats and hats while eating was a necessary incident to the business just as it is in the case of a barber shop, or a bathing house.

If a bailment for reward was created between the parties, then it would seem that the respondent's actions in not safeguarding the appellant's vehicle from theft could well have made the respondent liable as bailee, irrespective of the discussions that may have occurred between the appellant and the parking attendant with respect to the disposition to be made of the keys following the parking. This is because a bailee for reward is under an obligation to take reasonable steps to protect bailor property under its care from theft. Leaving a vehicle unattended and unlocked with its keys inside can hardly be equated with the safeguarding of a vehicle and the exercising of reasonable care expected from a bailee (given the reasonable foreseeability of theft in such circumstances) and is more akin to behaviour one would expect from a licensor who owes no duty of care to a licensee.

---

75 *Ibid* at paras 45–52.

76 [1919] NSJ No 7 (SC). See further: *Larsen v 368884 Alberta Ltd*, [1990] AJ No 220 (Prov Ct Civ Div).

L. BAILEES FOR REWARD: THE APPLICABLE STANDARD OF CARE

In a bailment for reward scenario, the bailee, to avoid liability, must show that it took reasonable care of the bailor's property at all material times, meaning that it took the steps that a reasonably prudent owner would have taken in looking after its own property in the same circumstances. This is a heavy burden and is not easily discharged. At law, the bailee is responsible for the theft, negligence, or other wrongful acts of its servants and agents. That said, the bailee needs only to negative ordinary negligence to be successful in overcoming its standard of care here, rather than negativing either gross or slight negligence, the standards applicable to gratuitous bailments.[77] In *Punch*,[78] Cory JA, speaking for the Court of Appeal for Ontario, described the standard of care applicable to the bailee for reward as follows:

> The bailee for reward must exercise due care for the safety of the article entrusted to him by taking such care of the goods as would a prudent man of his own possessions. Significantly, a bailee is liable for the loss of goods arising out of his servant's theft on the grounds that he is responsible for the manner in which his servant carries out his duty. In the result, it matters not whether the servant is careless, whether the goods are stolen by a stranger, or if the servant himself steals them.

If we set aside the modified onus applicable to bailees recognized by the Supreme Court in *Wong*, a bailee for reward's standard of care has generally been expressed by the courts in one of four ways:

1) that reasonable or due care was taken in all the circumstances
2) that any lack of reasonable care did not contribute to the loss
3) a negativing or disproving of ordinary negligence in relation to the cause of the loss
4) the standard of care that a reasonable and prudent person would apply to their own possessions in the circumstances

---

77 "Gross negligence" is required to be shown on the part of the bailee, where the gratuitous bailment of the goods is for the sole benefit of the bailor, while "slight negligence" is applicable where the gratuitous bailment is for the sole benefit of the bailee.

78 Above note 11 at para 18.

Where the precise circumstances surrounding the loss of the bailor's goods are uncertain and a bailee has been put to its onus, it may be difficult, if not impossible, for it to marshal sufficient evidence to meet its burden of proof, regardless of the particular expressions utilized by the court to express and assess the bailee's standard of care. A bailee's ability to defend against the reverse onus will very much be affected by the circumstances in which the loss arises. Justice Laskin's words, from the Court of Appeal for Ontario's decision in *Wong*,[79] regarding the bailee's onus of proof continue to ring true: "the evidence offered in exoneration may be different in its thrust according to whether the cause of the loss is known or unknown."[80] The question of bailee liability can be disposed of without a court establishing *precisely* how a bailor's property was lost where it is not possible for a court to do so based on the evidence before it. Justice Wetmore's words in *Drake*[81] are apposite:

> I do not conceive it to be my duty to determine where and how this rug disappeared. I simply find on the probabilities that it was delivered by Mrs. Drake to the employees of Bekins when they arrived at her house and it was removed from that house. Where and when it disappeared is entirely speculative on the issues and the evidence before me and I need not determine this.

(In the case, the defendant's mere denial that the carpet had arrived at its warehouse was *not* enough for it to be excused of liability, irrespective of the learned judge's refusal to make a finding on how and when the rug disappeared, illustrating the distinct advantage that bailors enjoy in bailment actions. The defendant had to go further and show that the rug had been lost without negligence on its part.)

In expressing the bailee for reward's standard of care, courts most commonly use the expressions "reasonable care" or a "negativing or disproving of negligence," often interchangeably, regardless of whether the precise cause of the loss of the bailor's goods is known, unknown, or uncertain, or anything in between.[82] Where the required standard is met — that

79 [1966] 2 OR 182 (CA).

80 *Ibid* at para 5.

81 *Drake*, above note 56 at para 3.

82 In a bailment case, often the general cause of the bailor's losses will be known — for example, that the goods were destroyed by "fire" — however, the evidence will be lacking on the precise cause of the loss. That is to say, the evidence will be inconclusive on (exactly) how the fire originated: see *Hutchings v Loveless*, [1990] NJ No 411

is, where the bailee shows that it took reasonable care appropriate to the circumstances, or negatives negligence in relation to the cause of the loss — the bailee will generally be exonerated and will not need to rely on an exclusion clause to protect itself from liability.[83] It may also be acceptable for the bailee to show that any failure to take due, or ordinary, care was immaterial, in that it did not contribute to the bailor's losses. However, where the bailee's evidence offered in exoneration remains in doubt, or is evenly balanced with other equally credible evidence in the record that points toward negligence, the question of liability must be decided against the bailee.[84]

M. A BAILEE'S DUTY OF CARE TERMINATES WITHIN A REASONABLE TIME OF BAILMENT BEING COMPLETED (AND PERHAPS EARLIER)

At law, a bailee for reward's duty of care to a bailor is not indefinite — it applies for only a finite period of time. Indeed, as we have seen, it may terminate immediately upon the purpose of the bailment being completed, such as following a car wash once the vehicle is parked awaiting pickup by the bailor,[85] or perhaps after the expiry of a reasonable period of time to allow the bailor to pick up the goods, or perhaps on a specific date pursuant to the bailment contract.[86] Where a bailor in a reward situation continues to store goods on a bailee's premises but has stopped paying for safekeeping

---

(SCTD). In these circumstances, a bailee may still be able to avoid liability by showing that it took reasonable care at all the material times, such that its negligence could not possibly have led to the bailor's losses.

83 *Procinsky v McDermott*, [1955] AJ No 57 at para 13 (SCAD).

84 See *McCreary v Therrien Construction Co Ltd*, [1951] OR 735 at para 13 (CA); *Newell v Acme Farmers Dairy Ltd*, [1939] OR 36 at para 38 (CA).

85 See, for example, *Furbank v Andersen*, [1966] BCJ No 49 (Co Ct). Where the purpose of the bailment has not yet been completed and the bailee relocates the bailor's property for its own convenience, to later complete the job, which property happens to be next to or alongside other bailor property currently in the bailor's possession, this will *not necessarily* be indicative of a break in possession. Where the bailor does not interfere with the bailee's continued possession, the bailee will continue to owe a duty of safekeeping over the goods, which duty may include an obligation to watch over the goods to ensure they do not come into harm's way: see *Porter & Sons*, above note 20, especially paras 21–22.

86 In *Ritchie Bros*, above note 5, it was an express requirement of the contract that successful bidders at auctions remove items purchased from the defendant's premises within seven days of the date of sale. At the expiry of the seven-day period, subject to special arrangements being made between the parties, bailments were at an end.

by the bailee, a bailee may put the bailment to an end immediately.[87] In general, in determining whether a bailment is over, consideration will have to be given to the reasonable expectations of the parties, industry practice, and the bailor's knowledge of the bailee's capacity to continue to act as a bailee to protect the goods. That said, as a general rule, once a reasonable time has passed following the completion of the purpose for which the bailment was formed, and assuming that the bailor has been given a reasonable opportunity to collect its goods, a bailee's duty of care will be at an end. Should a loss of the bailor's goods occur after the expiry of the bailment, the bailor will generally be left without a remedy.

1) Termination of a Bailment Contract After a Reasonable Time of Completion of the Purpose of Bailment

In *Davis v Henry Birks & Sons Ltd*,[88] the plaintiff delivered a diamond brooch to the defendant for an appraisal for insurance purposes. A bailment was created between the parties, as the defendant bailee required possession of the brooch to effect the appraisal. This was not contentious. However, once the defendant advised the plaintiff that the appraisal was completed, conveying the written appraisal to the plaintiff and to the plaintiff's insurance agency accordingly, the plaintiff chose to do nothing. It did not attend the defendant's premises to pick up the jewellery by providing the numbered ticket it had been given when the jewellery was dropped off, nor did it contact the defendant to express its intentions one way or another. Almost seven years later, the plaintiff finally decided to attend at the defendant's premises to claim the brooch, presenting the claim ticket as required. The jewellery could not be found. The plaintiff sued the defendant in bailment for its losses.[89]

Not surprisingly, Taggart JA, speaking for the majority of the Court of Appeal for British Columbia, found that the bailment was at end, as a reasonable time had passed since the completion of the appraisal, and that the plaintiff (bailor) had failed to collect the property within that time. Justice Taggart of the Court of Appeal refused to accept the plaintiff's argument that the defendant had not, as was its usual practice, given a formal written or oral notice to the plaintiff for the brooch to be picked

87 See *Fong v Tinkess (cob Imperial Taxi)*, [1941] OJ No 198 (CA).
88 [1982] BCJ No 2128 (CA).
89 *Ibid* at paras 13–14.

up, so that the bailment should be viewed as having continued up until the time of the plaintiff's intended pickup, despite the letter of appraisal having been sent out. According to the learned judge, this position was self-serving: upon receipt of the letter from the defendant, the plaintiff should have realized that she had a reasonable time to secure the goods. Justice Taggart found this time to be one month, which was a far cry from the almost seven years it took the plaintiff to attend the defendant's premises to collect her property.[90]

The majority of the court was right to have rejected the conclusion of the trial judge, Proudfoot J, that, once the appraisal was done, the defendant became a gratuitous bailee of the jewellery. A bailment should not be foisted onto a bailee in these circumstances: once the purpose of the bailment is at an end, and the bailor has been put on notice and given a reasonable opportunity to pick up its property, there can be no bailment of any kind. A formal written notice or telephone call by a bailee should not be required where it is clear that the bailor has been advised that its goods are ready for pickup unless redelivery is necessary for such requirement being met by the bailee as per the contract between the parties. The dissenting appeal judge's desire in the case to fix bailees in these circumstances with an indefinite and absolute obligation to take reasonable care of the goods until clearly relieved of this obligation, without any contractual underpinning for such an onerous obligation, is equally misplaced. A bailee should not be required "to prove that the loss [of a bailor's goods] was not caused by his fault"[91] in all circumstances, including in circumstances where a bailor waits almost seven years after the service to its goods has been completed to decide to pick up those goods from the bailee's premises. Nor should the bailee be required to physically redeliver goods to the bailor before being relieved of bailee obligations in the absence of a contractual requirement to this effect; constructive redeliveries carried out in good faith can be sufficient to terminate a bailee's obligations in these circumstances.[92] A bailment is a voluntary relationship that places very heavy duties of safekeeping on bailees, and it does not continue in perpetuity unless agreed upon by the parties. While we have reviewed caselaw supportive of the dissenting judge's position, it is

90 *Ibid* at paras 2–11.

91 *Ibid* at para 16.

92 See, for example, *Calgary Transport Services Ltd v Pyramid Management Ltd*, [1976] AJ No 551 (SCAD).

submitted that the better view is that, unless a contrary intention can be found in the contract or circumstances between the parties, once a reasonable time has passed after a bailor has been put on notice that its goods are ready for pickup, a bailment is at an end, and the bailee owes no further obligations of safekeeping to the bailor. This means that the bailee will not owe a duty of care as a gratuitous bailee, or otherwise, to the bailor, and that the bailee should not be required to show that its negligence, or lack of reasonable care, did not cause the injury to the bailor's goods where the injury occurred after the bailment was terminated. Indeed, in many circumstances, the bailee will simply have become a licensor, with no duty of care at all to the bailor. A bailor's action, in these circumstances, will likely not be able to succeed.

2) A Bailor's Repudiation of the Bailment Contract

A bailment can also be terminated by a bailor's repudiation of the bailment contract in certain circumstances where all the necessary requirements are met. In *Van Dorne v North American Van Lines (Canada) Ltd*,[93] the plaintiff sued the defendant (bailee) after most of his household furniture and certain personal effects disappeared while in the possession of the defendants for storage. It was an express term of the bailment contract that the plaintiff's goods were to be stored for $60 a month, to be paid in advance, as confirmed in the warehouse receipt delivered to the plaintiff by the defendants. The goods were to be stored in a warehouse in Burnaby, British Columbia. The goods, however, unbeknownst to the plaintiff, were relocated to a warehouse in a building in North Vancouver then being leased by the defendants after the defendants decided, for business reasons, to dispose of the warehouse in Burnaby. The plaintiff had not consented to the relocation of his goods and did not discover that the goods had been relocated until after virtually all of them had been destroyed by fire after the new warehouse they were in burned down.[94]

However, at that time, the plaintiff (bailor) had long been in arrears on his storage charges. He had paid only the charge on the first bill and had not made a payment for storage to the defendants for over a year. The defendants relied on the plaintiff's continuing default in paying the

---

93 (1977), 79 DLR (3d) 42 (BCSC) [*Van Dorne*], aff'd (1979), 95 DLR (3d) 358 (BCCA).

94 *Van Dorne*, above note 93 at 43–44.

monthly charges to argue that the plaintiff had committed a fundamental breach of the contract amounting to a repudiation, such that the defendants were no longer bound by the contract. In other words, at the time of the fire, the defendants no longer owed the plaintiff a duty of safekeeping over the goods. They, therefore, could not be liable as bailees in damages to the plaintiff for his loss.[95] In considering the defence, Aikins J of the British Columbia Supreme Court had to decide whether the defendants had deviated from the contract, making them strictly liable in damages to the plaintiff. It is true that if the goods *had not* been relocated by the defendants, they would not have been destroyed. However, was the relocation an appropriate action in all the circumstances, based on the plaintiff's continuing default in making payments on the contract? Relying on the principle enunciated in *Lilley v Doubleday*,[96] Aikins J found that the defendants had not notified the plaintiff that they were electing to treat his failure to pay the monthly storage charges as a repudiation of the contract and had chosen to treat the contract as discharged. While the learned judge had no trouble finding the breach to be a fundamental one that went to the root of the contract, it did not relieve the defendants from having to communicate their decision in that regard to the plaintiff, which they did not do. There was no express communication to this effect at the time the change was made. Nor could the learned trial judge find an implied communication, since there was no mention of the legal consequences of the plaintiff's failing to pay the storage charges mentioned in the warehouse receipt—namely, that the defendants would no longer have to perform their obligations under the contract.[97] Nor was there anything in the course of dealings between the parties that indicated such intention, not in the letters or the statements of account delivered to the plaintiff, or otherwise. Letters ending with statements such as "It would be greatly appreciated if you would send in this remittance, and bring your account up to date" were not sufficient, without more, to indicate such intention, nor was the fact that the defendants

95 *Ibid* at 44.

96 (1881), 7 QBD 510.

97 Admittedly, there was mention of the defendants' right to a possessory lien over the goods for non-payment, which lien the defendants could realize on by sale. But even here, a notice of sale would have to be sent out by the defendants to the plaintiff before the defendants could realize on their security and complete the sale of the goods: *Van Dorne*, above note 93 at 51.

eventually stopped sending out monthly accounts to the plaintiff indicate that the defendants had elected to treat the contract as at an end. The judge found that the defendants were bound. In the result, the defendants were in breach of the bailment contract by reason of their deviation from the terms thereof,[98] and were held to be strictly liable in damages to the plaintiff for his losses.[99]

The failure of the defendants to give an express notice to the plaintiff (bailor) was fatal, since it meant they had deviated from the bailment contract improperly without the plaintiff's knowledge or consent. As apparent, a repudiation of a bailment contract by a bailor, without more, is not enough to relieve a bailee of its duty of safekeeping over the bailor's goods. The bailee must put the bailor on notice of the fundamental breach of the contract by the bailor constituting the repudiation and what (exactly) this constitutes and, further, the bailee must notify the bailor that it has elected to act on the breach by discharging the bailment and, with it, all its obligations thereunder. While an express notice is not necessarily required, it is the preferred mode of giving such notice, given the severe consequences that a bailee faces in these circumstances—namely, that they will be found to be strictly liable to the bailor in damages for the lost or damaged goods, notwithstanding the fundamental breach of contract by the bailor.

N. CONCLUSION

While a bailee's standard of care has been described in a myriad of different ways and operates on varying standards, depending on the nature and circumstances of the bailment, a bailee will generally need to show that it took reasonable care of the bailor's goods to avoid liability against it. Put another way, it will need to disprove that its negligence caused the loss at issue in order to avoid liability. This is the onus of proof that will generally apply to a bailee, where a bailment is proven to have existed between bailor and bailee, which will require a bailor to show that the

98 For the same reasons, the defendants were also found to be in breach of their obligations to the plaintiff under the provincial *Warehouse Receipts Act*: *ibid* at 52.

99 *Ibid* at 47–53. Nor was it a case where, through the defendant's own actions to the plaintiff, the plaintiff could be made aware of the legal consequences of the default, such as where the seller of goods by instalment deliveries, with payment to be made on delivery, or shortly thereafter, refuses to make further deliveries because they have not been paid for previous instalments: *ibid* at 48 and 52.

bailee had exclusive possession of the bailed goods at the time of the loss. Where the *Wong* criteria are met, which, to be sure, will be the great minority of cases, a bailee's burden of proof should be reduced: it should only be required to give an explanation of loss that is consistent with no negligence on its part, which explanation must be equally credible as any countervailing explanation offered up by the bailor in order for the onus of proof on a bailee in these circumstances to be met. Where a bailment is for reward, a greater degree of care should be required and expected from a bailee than where the bailment is gratuitous or without fee. While a bailee's and bailor's own previous conduct in relation to the bailed goods, or similar goods, will be a relevant consideration to establishing a specific standard of care owed by a bailee in a particular set of circumstances, where there is any doubt as to the intentions of the parties here, courts should fall back to industry practice and use that to set the standard of care. While a bailee's duty of care is high, it is not equal to the standard of perfection or to that which would be owed under a contract of insurance. Last, a bailee's duty of care will normally be at an end when the purpose for which a bailment was formed is at an end, or perhaps after a reasonable period of time has passed to allow a bailor to retrieve its goods. While a bailor's goods may remain on a bailee's premises following the end of a bailment at the consent of a bailee, this will not necessarily indicate the continuation of a bailment (gratuitous or otherwise) and the duty of safekeeping by a bailee over the bailed goods. Indeed, it may well represent nothing more than a licence between the parties, merely preventing that which would otherwise be a trespass.

CHAPTER 5

Bailees for Reward: Specific Considerations When Assessing the Standard of Care

A. INTRODUCTION

A bailee for reward is different than a gratuitous bailee, as, in the former case, the bailee is receiving recompense for the bailment. This generally means that the bailee will owe a more rigorous duty of care to the bailor. In a bailment-for-fee situation, there are many factors that a court considers, often in different contexts, in deciding whether the bailee has made out its applicable standard of care. While the contexts considered in this chapter should not be considered an exhaustive list, a review of the caselaw indicates that the considerations discussed here should form part of the standard of care analysis of bailments for reward.

B. SPECIFIC CONSIDERATIONS

1) A Bailee Needs to Disprove Negative Negligence and Show Reasonable Care Was Taken Only in Respect of Losses That Have a Proper Evidentiary Foundation

A bailee needs to disprove negligence only in relation to causes of loss that have a proper evidentiary foundation and not in relation to all possible causes of a bailor's losses, no matter how remote those causes may be. In *Riverview Truck Repair Ltd v Phillips*,[1] the respondent's truck was stolen after being left in the appellant's unsecured parking lot until replacement

1 2007 NBCA 60 [*Riverview*].

parts could be procured and repairs effected. Specifically, the respondent had contracted with the appellant to have it repair the diesel motor of its truck. After the vehicle was moved into the appellant's garage and brief work was done to it, it was realized that additional replacement parts had to be ordered to make the repairs. The parts were ordered from the appellant's usual supplier. In the meantime, the appellant, in accordance with its standard practices, placed the respondent's vehicle, unlocked, in an unsecured parking lot adjacent to the repair shop. This happened on a Friday. The vehicle was immobile and could not be moved from the premises except by tow truck. The keys to the vehicle were stored in the appellant's building in an unlocked case. The respondent testified that, prior to the theft on Saturday morning (the day following the appellant's placement of the vehicle in the adjacent lot), he had driven to the appellant's premises and observed that one of his vehicle's windows was down and that there were parts lying on the back of the truck and also on the ground. The respondent further testified that he had tried to address these issues with the appellant by knocking on the door of the workshop where he saw workers, but no one responded.[2] On the following Tuesday, the parts arrived at the defendant's premises and the appellant first became aware that his truck had been stolen. The keys to the truck were found undisturbed in the case they had been placed in inside of the appellant's repair shop.

The respondent sued the appellant in bailment for the loss of the vehicle, which he argued was wholly attributable to the appellant's failure to lock the truck's doors and store the vehicle in a secure area. The trial judge in the court below, while appearing to acknowledge that these allegations were not enough in and of themselves to fix liability against the appellant if the truck remained in a disabled state on the lot at the time of the theft, theorized that repairs could have been made on Saturday morning prior to the theft, allowing the truck to be driven away rather than towed.[3] In reaching his conclusion, the trial judge reasoned as follows:

> Although I find as a fact that the truck could not be started in its state of disrepair when parked on Friday afternoon, I am not satisfied that it could not be started after it had been further worked on Saturday morning. There is no evidence that the required parts could not have been obtained from some source other than the defendant's usual supplier

2 *Ibid* at paras 1–3.

3 *Ibid* at paras 2–4.

> and the evidence is that the qualified mechanics who had access to the building could have effected such repairs.[4]

The trial judge noted further that the appellant's repair shop was accessible to several persons on non-working days; that these persons could have had easy access to keys belonging to the respondent's vehicle; and that the keys had been found undisturbed following the theft. The trial judge accordingly fixed liability against the appellant, finding that it had not adopted appropriate procedures to protect the respondent's vehicle from theft. Essentially, it had not negatived theft by its employees or others involved in the possible removal of the vehicle.[5]

On appeal, Robertson JA of the New Brunswick Court of Appeal accepted the appellant's argument that the trial judge's finding of liability was based on erroneous and unreasonable inferences of fact that the evidentiary record simply did not support: "In my view, the trial judge made a palpable and overriding error in speculating that the appellant's mechanics or others might have ordered the needed parts from another supplier and that the truck's engine had been repaired such that the vehicle could have been driven off rather than towed."[6]

Justice Robertson of the Court of Appeal found that the appellant had met its applicable standard of care in the circumstances, that the respondent's vehicle had been disabled so that any failure to lock the doors was inconsequential; that the appellant had placed the keys inside of its repair shop, frustrating their use by third parties for nefarious purposes; and that imposing a greater standard of care on the appellant would be unduly burdensome on repair shop businesses.[7]

Justice Robertson of the Court of Appeal was correct to have overturned the trial judge's decision in favour of the respondent here. Bailees should not be required to provide an explanation negativing negligence as to a cause of loss that does not have sufficient and reasonable support in the evidentiary record and, instead, amounts to mere conjecture or speculation. To hold otherwise would place an unduly high burden on bailees. In *Riverview*, there was insufficient evidence to support the trial judge's theory of loss in the case, which was quite far-fetched, and bailees,

---

4 *Ibid* at para 3 (Robertson JA citing paras 30–34, inclusive, of the trial judge's reasons in the court below).

5 *Ibid* at paras 2–4.

6 *Ibid* at para 8.

7 *Ibid* at paras 7–9.

to avoid liability, should not have to negative negligence or, alternatively, show reasonable care was taken in respect of every theory of loss that can be hypothesized or has any remote speck of plausibility that is consistent with negligence on its part.

However, where there is the necessary factual underpinning in the evidentiary record to support a certain theory or cause of loss that is consistent with negligence on the part of the bailee, and the bailee fails to offer up a satisfactory explanation, liability should be fixed against it accordingly. In *Warbrick v Absolute Bailiffs Inc*,[8] the plaintiffs' action in bailment followed after damage was done to their tractor-trailer while in the possession of the defendant bailiffs, who had seized it from its then operator, McKinnon. Specifically, repairs had been made to the trailer, with the plaintiff's knowledge and consent, by two lessees, who had leased the trailer (with an option to purchase) from the plaintiffs after the plaintiffs' operator of the unit had become ill and could no longer operate it himself. The lessees *failed to pay for* the repairs, and the repair shop, Ted's Truck Trailer and Auto Repairs, filed a lien against the trailer. The plaintiffs took possession of the trailer from the lessees, as they had not made any of the lease payments on the vehicle. The trailer was then sold by the plaintiffs to a separate individual, one McKinnon, on the condition that the lien be satisfied by the buyer; the plaintiffs maintained their security interest in the unit pending the purchaser's satisfaction of the purchase and sale agreement. McKinnon failed to satisfy the lien or to make any payments under the agreement. McKinnon ultimately ended up leasing the unit to a trucking company (which became its new registered owner), but he continued to operate the vehicle. As Ted's Repairs had received an extension of its lien, it decided to realize on its lien and ultimately had a warrant issued for the seizure of the unit to the defendant Absolute Bailiffs Inc. After making some concerted efforts, the defendant located the trailer, seized it, and brought it to its yard in a fenced compound, as Ted's Repairs (its client) did not have room for the unit on its property. The defendant notified the plaintiffs that the vehicle would be advertised for sale on a date about a week later, in accordance with the *Repairers Lien Act*. Prior to the date for sale, the plaintiffs negotiated the release of the trailer upon their agreement to satisfy the lien and other associated fees of the bailiffs.[9]

8 2000 BCPC 47, aff'd 2001 BCSC 362.
9 *Ibid* at paras 1–6.

Prior to its obtainment of the vehicle, and the date of its intended sale, one of the plaintiffs (the former operator of the truck) had attended the defendant's premises to view the tractor-trailer and had observed that certain equipment in the car area of the unit had been pulled out, though not removed completely; that the tools and equipment in the sleeping area were damaged; and that three batteries were missing. Upon redelivery, it was also discovered by the plaintiffs that there was no coolant in the tractor-trailer's radiator and that significant damage had been caused to its engine because it had been run without the proper fluids. The plaintiffs testified that operating the engine without the appropriate fluids even for a short period of time could cause serious damage to the engine. McKinnon, the last (and sole) operator of the truck, in his evidence, stated that he had not caused any of the said damages or losses to the truck and that shortly prior to the seizure, the radiator had been replaced and the coolant had been topped up as required. McKinnon further testified that, shortly after the seizure, when he was collecting his personal items from the truck, he had inspected the truck and did not notice anything out of the ordinary (though he conceded he had not operated the engine at that time). The plaintiffs testified that they had no knowledge of the vehicle's condition at the time of seizure. The defendant, in its evidence, stated that it had not noticed any damage to the interior of the tractor-trailer upon its receipt at the yard; that it had not inspected the engine for any mechanical defects, or otherwise, even though it had moved the vehicle into position on the lot; and that the unit had been placed in a secure yard protected by barbed wire and a locked gate, in the care of a full-time yard person who tended to the vehicles it had in storage.[10]

Justice Bruce of the Provincial Court of British Columbia accepted McKinnon's evidence and concluded that the damage and losses must have occurred while the tractor was in the defendant's yard, in its custody, for approximately one month, before it had been redelivered to the plaintiffs. This resulted in the defendant, who was found to be a bailee for reward despite the lack of privity of contract[11] between the plaintiffs

10 *Ibid* at paras 8–17.

11 Even though there was no contractual relationship between the plaintiffs and the defendant, the defendant clearly gained a "financial benefit" from the storage in terms of the fees ultimately paid by the plaintiffs to the defendant to recover their tractor-trailer. The trial judge's finding of a bailment for reward was therefore fully justified, and the correct one to be made on the facts: *ibid* at para 27.

and defendant, being put to its onus of disproving that its negligent conduct had caused the plaintiffs' losses. While the defendant was successful at showing that appropriate care had been taken to prevent the *apparent vandalism* done to the truck, and the *apparent thefts* of the missing items from the truck, by keeping the unit locked up behind an enclosed fence and security gate, it had *not* negatived negligence with respect to a likely cause for the engine damage suffered by the tractor-trailer while it was outside of the plaintiffs' possession. Specifically, the defendant *had not* proven that it had checked to ensure a proper coolant level in the radiator prior to moving the vehicle into position on its lot, or prior to starting it to show the vehicle to prospective buyers, to protect the engine from damage. Thus, the defendant was held liable as bailee for the engine damage found by the plaintiffs upon the return of the vehicle to them.[12]

It is submitted that operation of the unit with a lack of coolant in the radiator was an alleged cause of the plaintiffs' (bailors') losses that had *reasonable support* in the evidentiary record before the court; it was not mere speculation, conjecture, or hyperbole. Thus, it was right for the trial judge to require the defendant to negative negligence in respect of this cause in order for the defendant to escape liability for the injury done to the engine of the plaintiffs' vehicle. Based on this decision, in order for a bailee to escape liability fully, where there are multiple plausible causes or explanations for the different injuries done to bailor property based on the evidence before the court, such as theft, vandalism, and improper use or operation of bailor property, a bailee must negative negligence in respect of all of them.

2) Unsatisfactory or Incomplete Explanations of Loss Offered Up by Bailees

Goods that are the subject of a bailment for reward are not uncommonly lost by fire or theft, or through some other cause. Where goods are lost and not returned to the bailor in good order, a bailee will need to offer up a satisfactory explanation for their loss to avoid liability. In *McCreary v Therrien Construction Co Ltd*,[13] the appellant Ross Therrien, or his company, leased a cabin trailer from the respondent for use as living

12 *Ibid* at paras 29–33.
13 [1951] OR 735 (CA).

quarters by himself and others. While it was in the possession of the appellant, the cabin trailer and its contents were destroyed by fire. The respondent sued in bailment to recover the value of the lost property. The appellant denied that his negligence, as alleged by the respondent, had caused the respondent's losses, and argued that "the said destruction was entirely accidental."[14] The appellant further argued that the trial judge had improperly placed the burden of proof on it to excuse the happening by negativing negligence, rather than requiring the respondent to prove negligence against the appellant affirmatively.[15] The jury at trial found that the appellant had not provided a satisfactory explanation for the loss that was inconsistent with negligence on its part, and liability was thus imposed against the appellant accordingly.[16]

Justice Laidlaw, speaking for a majority of the Court of Appeal for Ontario, disagreed with the appellant's position, stating that the onus was correctly placed on him by the trial judge, since he was a bailee and in possession of the bailor's property at the time of the loss. That said, the court found that requiring the bailee to discharge this onus on a "beyond a reasonable doubt" standard was misplaced.[17] Justice Laidlaw of the Court of Appeal found that the onus was on the appellant to satisfy the court below that the injury to the trailer and its contents was not caused by an absence of reasonable care and skill on his part on a balance of probabilities standard, which he failed to do:

> I reach the conclusion, on the authorities to which I have referred, that the learned trial judge in the present case properly placed the burden of proof on the defendants. The jury has found that the trailer was in the possession and control of the defendant Ross Therrien at the time of the fire, and that he did not satisfy them that the damage did not arise through his negligence or improper conduct. Those findings are good and sufficient in law to support a judgment for the plaintiff, as against the defendant Ross Therrien, and the appeal by him must therefore be dismissed.[18]

It was not enough for the appellant to simply show that the trailer had been destroyed by fire in order to meet its onus of proof as bailee, as

---

14 *Ibid* at para 1.
15 *Ibid* at para 4.
16 *Ibid* at para 11.
17 *Ibid* at paras 6–11.
18 *Ibid* at para 11.

was argued by the appellant, but instead, it also had to show that that fire was *not* as a result of its negligence or improper conduct, which it did not do. The appellant's argument that, once an explanation of how the bailor's goods were destroyed is given in a general way (i.e., the bailors property was destroyed by fire), some evidence of negligence on the part of the bailee must exist before the bailor can recover was quite properly rejected out of hand by Laidlaw JA in the case. That is a mischaracterization of the ultimate burden of proof in a bailment, which lies on the bailee to disprove that its own negligence caused the loss at issue. Where the cause is known, this must, of necessity, include the bailee disproving that its negligence contributed to the cause of the loss. Alternatively, the bailee can adduce evidence to show that it took reasonable care appropriate to the circumstances, such that its negligence could not possibly have led to the cause of the loss.[19]

In *A-1 Rentals Sales & Service Ltd v Alberta Arches & Beams Ltd*,[20] the respondent hired a lighting plant from the appellant for a fee. While the plant was in the possession of the respondent, it was stolen and never recovered. The plant not having been returned to the appellant, the appellant (bailor) sued the respondent in bailment for its losses, for the respondent (bailee's) failure to return the plant to it. The appellant made no allegations of negligence against the respondent.[21] The respondent argued that it was not liable, because it had advised the appellant of the theft, and because the plant had been stolen without negligence on its part. Justice Kane of the Alberta Supreme Court, Appellate Division, identified the problem with the respondent's case, as presented: "At the trial no evidence was given by or on behalf of the respondent relating in any manner as to where the plant was kept by it after it had received it. Nor was there any evidence which would tend to establish that it was stolen without default on the part of the respondent."[22]

As apparent, the respondent was duty-bound under its onus of proof to establish that the theft occurred without its negligence before its onus of proof could be considered to have been met. It had to show that it had

---

19 For accidental fires, there used to be some relief provided to a bailee in Ontario under the *Accidental Fires Act*, RSO 1990, c A.4 (see, for example, *Neff v St Catharines Marina Ltd*, [1998] OJ No 253 (CA)), but that statute has been repealed by SO 1997, c 4, s 85.

20 [1966] AJ No 85 (SCAD).

21 *Ibid* at paras 1–5.

22 *Ibid* at para 6.

taken reasonable care of the plant. It presented no evidence to this effect. This is a heavy onus and required it to explain the circumstances surrounding the loss, including information about where the plant was stored once in its possession and, specifically, the procedures that it had in place and had applied at the material times to protect and safeguard the appellant's goods from ordinary hazards, including theft, which it did not do.[23]

As demonstrated by these cases, a bailee must do more than simply assert that it was not negligent or careless in its handling of bailor property destroyed by fire, or otherwise, in order to escape liability. Explaining how the loss occurred in a general way,[24] whether by theft or fire, will be insufficient for a bailee to meets its onus of proof. The explanation must go beyond this. Indeed, it must include particulars showing where the bailor's goods were kept, and that the place where they were stored afforded them reasonable protection. The bailee must prove that there were sufficient measures in place to protect the bailor's goods from ordinary hazards, such as fire and theft, before it will be able to show that reasonable care was taken such that its negligence cannot be said to be the proximate cause of the bailor's losses. The explanation must clearly negative negligence on the part of the bailee for the bailee to succeed.[25] Where no evidence is presented by either party as to the circumstances surrounding the loss—that is, where the facts stand absolutely bare—but where it is clear that bailor property disappeared while in the bailee's possession, there will be no way for a bailee to escape liability, and

23 *Ibid* at para 15.

24 See *Lakeside Commission Agency Ltd v Saskatchewan Wheat Pool*, [1990] SJ No 350 (QB). Following a sale by auction, the defendant (bailee) seller could not account for the loss of one of nine animals sold to the plaintiff (bailor), *but not yet* picked up by the plaintiff's agent, upon his return to the defendant's premises to pick up the remaining animals that he could not deliver to the plaintiff on his first trip. The defendant's statement for the mysterious loss, "we have checked all our records and our stockyard and the animal cannot be found," was not enough to exonerate it from liability—that is, was not enough to prove that it had exercised reasonable care over the plaintiff's animals during the relevant period: see para 9 [paragraph number assigned by author].

25 In *Jenkins v Smith*, [1969] NSJ No 142 (SC), the defendant (bailee) damaged the plaintiff's truck, which he was driving for the first time, as bailee on a winter night; the night was clear and the road was bare except for ice patches. The defendant was aware of the possibility for jack-knifing in these conditions with a fully loaded truck. His explanation that he had "hit a frost bump in the road and some ice patches and his vehicle jack-knifed and slid off the road in a jack-knife position" was not sufficient, without more, to negative negligence on the part of the driver in the circumstances: see para 20.

a judgment will have to be entered against it accordingly. The rationale for liability being fixed against a bailee in circumstances where the bailee leaves damage or loss to bailor property unexplained was well explained by Lord Denning MR in *Levison v Patent Steam Carpet Cleaning Co Ltd*:

> [I]f he leaves the cause of loss or damage undiscovered and unexplained — then I think he is liable: because it is then quite likely that the goods were stolen by one of his servants; or delivered by a servant to the wrong address; or damaged by reckless or wilful misconduct; all of which the offending servant will conceal and not make known to his employer.[26]

There is no question that the doctrine of *res ipsa loquitur* is at work here and assists bailors greatly where the bailor can merely show that the goods were lost or damaged while in the care of the bailee, but where the bailee cannot provide a reasonable explanation, or any explanation, for the loss. This is because an inference of negligence will arise that can only be negatived by clear evidence negativing negligence, or showing that reasonable care was taken by the bailee at the material times.

3) A Bailee's Failure to Preserve Relevant Evidence Can Lead to Negative Inference Against It

Where a bailee destroys, or fails to preserve intact, physical evidence relevant to whether it has discharged its standard of care in the circumstances, in circumstances where litigation by a bailor ought to have been clearly contemplated by the bailee, this leads to a negative inference against a bailee, making it impossible for it to displace the burden on it to disprove negligence. In *Forsey v Burin Peninsula Marine Service Centre*,[27] the plaintiff (bailor) entered into a contract for the defendant to lift its ship out of the water and perform some routine maintenance to it. The vessel fell, on a windy day, some thirteen days after it was lifted out of the water and placed on a "cradle," the structure used to support the vessel and keep it upright while the work to it was being done. The cradle was composed of cross-bracing, cribbing, and wedges. No one witnessed the fall. Although the vessel was uprighted and recradled by the defendant using new cribbing materials and a new cradle, the vessel was rendered

26 [1978] QB 69 at 82, as endorsed by the Ontario Court of Appeal in *Punch v Savoy's Jewellers* (1986), 54 OR (2d) 383 at para 39 (CA) [*Punch*].

27 2014 FC 974, aff'd 2015 FCA 216.

a constructive loss by the fall, given the serious structural damage it had sustained. The plaintiff sued the defendant for damages for breach of bailment arising from the fall, among other causes of action.[28]

On the evidence, there was dispute between the parties as to who selected the cribbing and who constructed the cradle. These were important issues. There was clear evidence in the record that the cribbing materials used to construct the cradle had been left outside exposed to the elements. As well, because the cradle ultimately failed to prevent the fall, the question of who constructed the cradle was germane. The defendant's damaged cribbing materials relating to the fall had been removed from the defendant's premises before their fitness for the task could be examined by an expert who had been scheduled to attend at the premises, survey the damage to the vessel, and prepare a report. Thus, the court was left without the expert evidence.[29] The plaintiff also testified that he had not been warned about any insufficiency with respect to the defendant's cribbing materials.[30]

In the end, Heneghan J of the Federal Court, St John's, Newfoundland and Labrador, found that the cribbing and other materials used to construct the cradle were selected solely by the defendant and that the defendant was in charge of the operation of building the cradle. While plaintiff employees had assisted the defendant in the said task, this was only when they were called upon to do so. It was the defendant who was in control of the undertaking, and the plaintiff employees had only assisted in a "peripheral manner."[31] The defendant was the party who decided when the ship was ready to rest on the cradle and to be released from the travel lift and straps that had been used to pull it from the water.[32] In addition, the plaintiff's employees' mere painting of the vessel while it was stored on the defendant's premises did not revert possession back to the plaintiff.[33]

The learned judge found that the crushed cribbing material had been removed from the site by the defendant prior to the arrival of the inspector so that it would not be available for examination. A significant,

---

28 *Ibid* at paras 1–3, 12, 16, and 24–27.
29 *Ibid* at paras 33–34 and 57.
30 *Ibid* at para 56.
31 *Ibid* at paras 40–45.
32 *Ibid* at para 99.
33 *Ibid* at para 102.

negative inference as it relates to the fitness of the cribbing was drawn against the defendant since the adequacy or sufficiency of the cribbing materials could not be tested before the court, given the defendant's disposal of the materials when it knew, or ought to have reasonably contemplated, that litigation would be brought forth by the plaintiff.[34] The negative inference was powerful in the case, and the defendant's various arguments, including that the cribbing materials and cradle must have been sufficient, given that the vessel had been secured for thirteen days without incident, and that no other vessel under its care had fallen over during the subject period, was *not* sufficient to overcome the defendant's reverse onus in the case in light of the missing evidence.[35]

4) Affirmative Acts of Negligence by a Bailee Are Strongly Connected to the Loss of Bailor Property

Where clear, affirmative acts of negligence are found to have been committed by the bailee as it relates to bailed goods within its possession during the course of a bailment that are causally connected to the bailor's losses or damages, this will mean that a bailee will not be able to displace the presumption of negligence on it and will face liability accordingly. For example, where a fire destroys a vehicle in a repair shop and the evidence shows that the destruction was due to an employee's allowing gasoline from a vehicle to accumulate on the floor, which later igniting because of the anticipated use of a torch, the bailee will be liable. Similarly, where employees of a bailee do not follow the correct protocol, or are not properly trained on how to do their work safely and perform the work negligently, causing damage to

34 The defendant employee in charge of the operation had also given evidence at trial regarding the location of the cribbing materials following the fall of the vessel, as well as the date of its disposal, which evidence was inconsistent with the evidence he had given at his discovery: *ibid* at para 69. As well, the same witness had noted a change to company policy pertaining to the use of cribbing, namely that the defendant decided to no longer maintain the cribbing materials for customers, renting it out at no charge to them instead, which led to the reasonable inference that the materials must not have been adequately maintained by the defendant before the incident in question: *ibid* at para 75.

35 *Ibid* at paras 82, 111–13, and 123. The excluding clause in the signed statement of the plaintiff, as well the notices on the premises excluding liability, failed, because they did not expressly include negligence and because the limiting words in the statement that the plaintiff accepts responsibility for "securing and locking," strictly construed, did not mean that the plaintiff was responsible for the vessel while it was on the cradle: *ibid* at paras 127–35.

bailor property, the bailee is answerable. Such circumstances apply where an employee of a vehicle repair shop incorrectly secures a vehicle to a hoist, causing the vehicle to fall to the ground during the course of repairs. Finally, where the bailee leaves bailor property, or materials needed to secure bailor property and keep it safe and unharmed, exposed to the elements, and bailor property is damaged as a result, the bailee will be answerable.

The bailee's actions do not need to lead to a total loss or to damage to bailed goods that interfere with their mechanical functionality in order for the needed threshold to be met. Where significant deterioration to the appearance and condition of bailor property is caused by a clear lack of due attention and care by a bailee, which results in appreciable reduction in the market value of the bailor property, a bailee will be answerable. In *Canadian Imperial Bank of Commerce v Doucette*,[36] the plaintiff (bailee) had, among other missteps in the enforcement of its security, left the defendant's used tractor exposed to the elements over three winters and four summers on a third-party garage proprietor's premises. The plaintiff (bank) had seized the machinery pursuant to a statutory lien and claim for non-payment of a loan and was seeking to satisfy the deficit on the loan arising from the sale of the plaintiff's tractor.[37] The question for determination was whether the plaintiff's monetary claim should be reduced by reason of the plaintiff's negligence in leaving the plaintiff's machinery exposed to the elements (and for other improper actions that led to a reduction of the machinery's sales value but that are not pertinent to our discussions here). While the damage to the bailed property due to exposure to the elements was "a matter of external appearance rather than mechanical condition" (i.e., the tractor was still functional), Campbell CJ of the Prince Edward Island Supreme Court found that the defendant's actions still constituted clear negligence and that the defendant (bailor) was entitled to a reduction of the deficit on the loan that it owed to the plaintiff equal to the loss of sales value engendered by the plaintiff's own negligence. This is because the machine's worsened appearance, and the general public's knowledge that the machinery had been left exposed to the elements for a considerable period of time, would make the machinery much less attractive for purchase. This was borne out by the defendant's own unexplained admission that the tractor had sold for $300 in

36 [1968] PEIJ No 3 (SC).
37 *Ibid* at paras 3–8.

the spring yet that it had, itself, valued the equipment at $900 just the previous fall, before it had expended great sums of money on repairing the plaintiff's property for sale.[38]

The causal relationship between the plaintiff bank's negligence and the defendant's (bailor's) losses in the case were clear, and it was right for Campbell CJ to have reduced the judgment in damages on the loan made against the defendant accordingly. The fact that the plaintiff (bailee) had seized the machinery under a statutory lien and claim as security for the non-payment of a loan, and was storing it pending a sale, meant that it was in exclusive possession of the defendant's property and owed the defendant certain heavy responsibilities as a bailee for reward.[39] These duties required it to store the defendant's machinery inside, if the sale of the property was not going to occur for a long period of time, so that the property could be protected from the elements. By not doing so, the sales value of the machinery dropped substantially (which was reflected in the actual sale price obtained by the plaintiff), and the plaintiff's (bailee's) recovery of the remaining monies on the loan, owed by the defendant, was artificially and unfairly increased, to the detriment of the defendant. A set-off on the loan owed by the defendant to the plaintiff was, accordingly, the appropriate remedy for the plaintiff's breach of its standard of care as bailee to be made in the case.[40]

5) Breaches of Applicable Statute Laws and Regulations by a Bailee

Where a bailee is found to have breached duties set by statute during the course of the bailment, and damage or loss to bailor property results, the bailee should be found liable in damages to the bailor. In *Townsend Air Services Ltd v Hansen*,[41] the defendant pilot hired an aircraft from the corporate plaintiff, which aeroplane he was to fly from Orangeville to Minden, which was about an hour's flight away. The aircraft was to be returned to the defendant the same day it was hired, during the day in accordance with the pilot's flight restrictions; but, as it happened, the

38 *Ibid* at paras 18, 19, and 26.

39 *Ibid* at para 8.

40 For relevant discussion in the context of the carriage of goods: see *Commercial Bakeries Corp v Frasier Transport Corp*, [2000] OJ No 1119 (SCJ).

41 [1974] OJ No 2233 (Co Ct) [*Townsend*].

plane crashed on landing in atrocious winter conditions after nightfall by the pilot upon his return to Orangeville and was rendered a total loss.[42] The plaintiff, who did not have appropriate insurance cover on the plane, sued the defendant in bailment for damages to cover the loss.

Justice Hollingsworth of the Ontario County Court Judicial District of Peel agreed with the expert evidence that showed the cause of the crash to be carburettor icing,[43] rejecting the defendant (pilot's) explanations for the crash, including sudden white-out conditions upon his approach to Orangeville and arguments dealing with structural or mechanical deficiencies of the aircraft.[44] More pertinent for our purposes is that the defendant was found to have been negligent by, among other things, violating applicable regulations that he was bound by as a private licensed pilot during his flight under the *Aeronautics Act*, namely:

1) He engaged in night flying;
2) He failed to check the weather forecasts on leaving Orangeville, and especially on returning, which could have been done by making a simple telephone call, and which should have caused him to alter his flight path or to avoid flying altogether.[45]

The defendant had also failed to apply the carburettor heat equipment properly in icy wintry conditions; had flown into freezing rain, when this should have been avoided; and failed to use a timepiece in planning his departure and return trip.[46] All of this, for Hollingsworth Co Ct J, meant that the defendant had engaged in "gross negligence" and was therefore liable in damages to the plaintiff. The plaintiff's statement to the defendant, that there was insurance in place to cover such eventualities and that the defendant need not worry, was not made until after the crash, and had not become a condition of the bailment contract.[47]

It is submitted that, where a bailee (whether a pilot or otherwise) breaches applicable laws and regulations during the course of a bailment that are causally connected to the damage or loss done to bailor property, this will make the bailee liable to the bailor and will constitute "gross

42 *Ibid* at paras 1, 3, and 8.
43 *Ibid* at para 41.
44 *Ibid* at paras 30 and 41.
45 *Ibid* at para 53.
46 *Ibid* at paras 41 and 53.
47 *Ibid* at paras 56–57.

negligence" by the bailee, meaning that even a gratuitous bailee will be liable. In *Townsend*, even if defendant *had not* engaged in the other negligent acts outside of those involved in a breach of the air regulations, those acts alone were likely enough, without more, to make the defendant guilty of gross negligence and liable as a bailee for reward to the plaintiff. The question of insurance was a "matter of loss allocation" between the defendant and his insurer.[48] Prior to the hiring out of the aircraft, the plaintiff (bailor) had not agreed that the defendant (pilot) would be completely covered under its insurance policy in the event of a crash during his flights. Accordingly, there was no such term in the bailment contract and the defendant (bailee) was therefore liable.

6) A Heightened Standard of Care for Use of Dangerous Things by a Bailee

Where a bailee uses dangerous things on or around bailor goods, the bailee must exercise extreme caution. If loss or damage comes to bailor goods in connection with the dangerous equipment, the bailee will be liable where it can be shown that it did not use the utmost care. In *Stables v Bois*,[49] the plaintiff took his vehicle to the defendant's business premises principally to have certain repairs done to it. When the repairs were done, the vehicle was left inside the garage awaiting the installation of a minor part. During this time, a mechanic for the defendant was removing a muffler from another vehicle in the vicinity of the plaintiff's vehicle in the garage using a torch and other equipment. As it happened, an explosion and then fire occurred, burning the garage and its contents to the ground, including the plaintiff's car. While the trial judge had found that the explosion and fire were caused by "unusual circumstances of gasses backing up into the acetylene-tank," the Court of Appeal for Ontario found no support for this explanation in the evidentiary record, overruling the trial judge accordingly. Indeed, the evidence indicated that the torch had been mishandled and that the failure of the torch and flashback were quite common occurrences, which an experienced operator would contemplate and

48 See *Duckworth v Armstrong (cob Superior Autobody)*, [1996] BCJ No 1337 at para 25 (SC) [*Duckworth*] and further discussions on insurance in Section B(17), below in this chapter.

49 [1956] OJ No 620 (CA).

anticipate in the course of handling a torch.[50] The Court of Appeal found that the cause of the incident was due to the defendant bailee failing to use the utmost care in handling the torch, and that the explosion had been due to a spark from the torch resulting therefrom.[51] As to the heightened standard of care in these kinds of circumstances, Laidlaw JA, speaking for the court, had this to say: "The use of an acetylene-torch is the use of a dangerous thing. The operation undertaken by the defendant's employee was a dangerous operation. It placed upon him a duty to use consummate care to see that damage would not result."[52]

The defendant had failed to take the necessary precautions to prevent the occurrence. The torch and equipment had sat idle before use for some three weeks; there was no evidence that the equipment had been inspected before use to ensure that the gauges and valves on the acetylene tanks were properly seated to prevent explosion. Nor was there evidence that the mechanic had properly inspected the gas tank of the car he was removing the muffler from to ensure that no gas remained in the tank prior to beginning his work on it. While there was evidence that the floor of the garage was kept relatively clean, this was not enough without more, to negate all the other acts of negligence committed by the defendant.[53] As apparent, a more exacting standard of care will have to be met by a bailee when it is operating dangerous equipment, or using dangerous substances, on or around bailor property. Where a bailee fails to use consummate care, it should be held liable.

7) A Bailee Conveys Material Misrepresentations as to Safekeeping to a Bailor

a) Misrepresentations as to the Presence of the Bailee at the Bailee's Premises

A bailee's material misrepresentations as to safekeeping can be relevant to assessing whether the bailee has met its applicable standard of care. In *Bell v Tinmouth*,[54] the respondent Bell owned certain art works, namely paintings, and wanted to display them to a select group of buyers in the appellants'

50 *Ibid* at paras 2–3.
51 *Ibid* at paras 3–6.
52 *Ibid* at para 4.
53 *Ibid* at para 5.
54 1988 CanLII 3220 (BCCA) [*Bell*].

art gallery, and did so pursuant to a consignment arrangement with them. The gallery doubled as a residence for the principals of the gallery, Mowatt and Buschlen. The appellants had advised the respondent that, as a condition of accepting the artwork on consignment, the respondent would have to arrange for his own insurance cover. The respondent, accordingly, arranged for an insurance agent, one Adshead, who worked for a separate company, Harbord Company, to obtain the appropriate coverage. He was instructed by the respondent to procure the required specifics from the gallery for the purposes of securing that coverage.[55]

With respect to the security provisions at the gallery, which were of obvious importance to the insurer, Adshead was advised by Mowatt, upon inquiring with him, among other misrepresentations, that there was "always someone on premises," as it doubled as a residence, which information he then conveyed to the insurer, one Lloyds, via telex without independently inspecting the appellants' premises or verifying the information received. Thereafter, while the respondent's artwork was still in the appellants' premises, having been viewed by some potential purchasers only some twenty-four hours before, the two owners of the gallery, Mowatt and Buschlen, absented themselves from the gallery/their residence to make a trip to Seattle, taking the "watchdog" with them. Prior to their departure, Mowatt had secured the frames of two basement windows at the rear of the house. During their absence, which happened to coincide with Bell being out of the province as well, some of the respondent's paintings were stolen. The respondent's artwork had been left visible on the wall inside the appellant's house during the time the house was left unoccupied by Mowatt and Buschlen, which undoubtedly left the artwork at significant risk of theft. Because the statements that Bell had conveyed to Lloyds via Adshead, based on the specifics he had obtained from the appellants, were false with respect to the level of protections and security at the gallery, Lloyds denied coverage to the respondent (bailor) for its losses.[56]

Bell sued the gallery and its principals in bailment for his losses, in addition to bringing an insurance action against Lloyds, Adshead, and the Harbord Company. The trial judge found that Adshead had a strict duty of care to convey accurate information to Lloyds and that he had failed to do so, in breach of his contract with Bell, and that that was a failing

55 *Ibid* at para 6.
56 *Ibid* at paras 7–15.

of his personally, not of the respondent.[57] The British Columbia Court of Appeal disagreed. Justice Carrothers of the Court of Appeal, speaking for the majority of the court, placed the blame squarely at the feet of Mowatt as bailee:

> I do not consider Adshead negligently misrepresented the facts to Lloyds. I am of the view that the real falsity in the facts inquired into by Adshead, which made them inaccurate and misleading, was not an error of transmission but rather was an error of omission on the part of Mowatt to make any reference to the possibility of an unforeseeable exposure to the risk of theft through total desertion of the gallery.[58]

As Carrothers J observed, there would have been no way for Adshead on behalf of the respondent bailor, to have detected the possibility for substantial abandonment of the premises by Mowatt and Buschlen, even if he had had a duty to make an on-site inspection of the premises and had made one, which duty the court found he did not have, based on his agreement with Bell. Adshead had exercised reasonable care to obtain a policy in the terms bargained for and could not be liable for breaching his legal duties to Bell. It was incumbent on the gallery, as bailee, to *expressly* inform Bell (the bailor) as to this major shortcoming in its security protocols, if Mowatt and Buschlen expected they might be leaving the premises unattended and unsupervised. Because the appellants had completely and without notice deserted the gallery, leaving the plaintiff's artwork highly susceptible to theft, Carrothers J confirmed the trial judge's ruling finding that the appellants had breached their duties of care owed to Bell in the case.[59]

The rulings of Carrothers J in the case are eminently reasonable. A bailee's standard of care must be informed, in part, by any representations, including any misrepresentations, made by the bailee at the commencement of the bailment where loss or damage to a bailor's goods occurs. Mowatt had omitted to advise Bell that the gallery might be left unoccupied during a period of time when valuable artwork would be housed there, and the artwork was stolen during that time, making the misrepresentation quite material and effectual. The significantly increased risk of theft to which the artwork would be put by the absence must have

---

57 *Ibid* at paras 19–25.

58 *Ibid* at para 26.

59 *Ibid* at paras 30–39 and 44–48.

been contemplated by Mowatt, for, as noted, he had taken steps to secure some windows in the basement of the house storing the artwork before departing together with Buschlen for Seattle. There was no way for Bell to have known about this serious deficiency in the appellants' security protocols, even if an inspection had been conducted by the agent Adshead. Bailees, in these circumstances, must accordingly be completely forthcoming and should *not* be allowed to hide behind insurance agents who may intercede on behalf of bailors to obtain appropriate coverage against loss, but whose function or capability *may not* permit them to verify the accuracy of information received from a bailee regarding the safeguards to be in place to protect a bailor's goods from loss during the course of the bailment. It follows that Carrothers J was right to have rejected the appellants' argument that no bailment could be formed, as a condition precedent for the commencement of the bailment (i.e., the obtainment of proper insurance coverage for the paintings by Bell) had not been satisfied, as evidenced by Lloyds' denial of coverage. This contention by the appellants was self-serving, since the denial of Bell's coverage was solely the result of Mowatt and Buschlen's absenting themselves from the gallery after claiming that there was always someone on site, which wrongdoing they were now seeking to benefit from.

b) Erroneous Assurances of "Almost Absolute Safety" or a High Level of Security

In *Davidson v Three Spruces Realty Ltd*,[60] the plaintiffs entered into a contract with the defendant to store their valuables in bulk storage for safekeeping. The plaintiffs were promised "almost absolute safety" over their belongings, even though they were being placed in containers supplied by the plaintiffs and not in safety deposit boxes (which provided a much higher level of security) in bulk storage vaults. Consistent with the promise, the defendant told the plaintiffs that they need not concern themselves with getting insurance for their valuables for the period of the storage. The impression left was that the defendant would take due care to ensure that no stranger or customer could gain access to the valuables that had been placed in storage by the defendant's patrons. However, these were in fact misrepresentations, since the defendant did not take reasonable precautions to protect the plaintiffs' goods. Indeed, there

60 [1977] BCJ No 1239 (SC) [*Davidson*].

were many chinks in the defendant's (bailee's) armour. For example, the defendant failed to require individuals entering the vaults to identify themselves or to sign admission slips; it allowed customers and strangers to enter the bulk storage area without supervision by defendant employees; and it failed to adduce any evidence showing that any real security precautions at all had been taken to protect the plaintiffs' property from theft. Not surprisingly, the plaintiffs' items were stolen. Indeed, new locks had been placed on the containers, and the plaintiffs' gold and silver coins had been replaced with concrete bricks wrapped in plastic bags. The plaintiffs sued the defendant in bailment, among other causes of action.[61]

The defendant did not call any evidence to show that a high level of security had been taken over the plaintiffs' goods, consistent with the representations made at the start of the bailment. Justice Anderson of the British Columbia Supreme Court found that the defendant's failings in this regard were clearly connected to the plaintiffs' losses. Indeed, the plaintiffs had not merely proven that their property had disappeared from the containers in bulk storage but also that the defendant's failure to exercise proper precautions was the reason for the theft. Unauthorized persons, most likely strangers or customers of the defendant, had removed them due to the defendant's failure to take reasonable precautions. In the absence of an enforceable exclusion clause, which Anderson J did not ultimately find to be present in relation to any of the plaintiffs' bailment contracts with the defendant, for various reasons,[62] the defendant was liable as bailee.[63] The defendant's representations required it to implement a high level of security over the goods to meet the heightened standard of care set by those representations, which it did not do. Indeed, as underlined by Anderson J, the defendant "did not take any of the precautions normally taken by prudent persons engaged in this type of business."[64]

In *Robertson v Stang*,[65] false representations of a "safe and secure" storage area made by the bailee in specific reference to the plaintiff's (bailor's) goods, moved by the defendant (landlord) into two storage areas within the apartment complex, contributed to a finding of liability against the defendant (bailee) landlords. Specifically, one of the defendant managers

61 *Ibid* at paras 1–10.
62 *Ibid* at paras 17–38.
63 *Ibid* at paras 12–15.
64 *Ibid* at para 8.
65 [1997] BCJ No 2022 (SC) [*Robertson*].

of the premises, Mr Stang, on two separate occasions, told the plaintiff (bailor) that only he and the hydro representative had keys to one of the storage areas (i.e., the 300 block of the complex) in which some of her goods were being stored. This was not true. Indeed, several master keys to the area were unaccounted for, and each member of the board of the cooperative also had their own key with which they could access the area. In addition, the door in the 300 block hydro rooms was not well secured and could be opened easily with a screwdriver. Last, the plaintiff's misapprehension of the facts in terms of the level of security being provided to the goods was continued by the defendants' failure to advise the plaintiff expressly and clearly of thefts that had occurred in the 300 block on two separate dates, when the area was broken into by unknown third parties, during periods of time when the plaintiff's goods were being transported from her apartment to the storage areas. During these breaks-ins, it was very possible that some of the plaintiff's goods were taken by the thieves.[66]

Because the defendants' security precautions clearly fell below the expectations they had set for themselves, or any reasonable standard that could be applied in the circumstances, and the loss of the bailed goods was causally connected thereto, Parrett J of the British Columbia Supreme Court easily found the defendants to be liable to the plaintiff in bailment, since the thefts were reasonably foreseeable, given the large gaps in the defendants' security system. This was irrespective of the fact that an unknown third party was likely responsible for the thefts and the plaintiff's losses.[67] A *novus actus interveniens* will not inure to the benefit of the bailee here, since it is the bailee's own failings, or negligence, in meeting its own, or reasonable, standards of security that make the goods particularly susceptible to theft or injury by third parties, which a third party happens to exploit to the detriment of a bailor, who will then be able to look to the bailee for recompense.

As illustrated by the two previous decisions, a bailee's standard of care owed in a particular circumstance must always be informed by the representations that a bailee makes at the outset of a bailment, which may increase or decrease the level of care otherwise required by industry practice. Where a bailee does not follow its own promised security protocols and loss or damage to bailed goods results, liability should be fixed

66 *Ibid* at paras 1–17.
67 *Ibid* at paras 70–71.

against it, since it will not have met the very standard of care that it set for itself, which a bailor has reasonably relied on to their detriment.

8) A Bailee's Failure to Catalogue Items/Goods Received from and Redelivered to a Bailor

Where a bailee fails to adequately catalogue bailor goods in its possession at all times, including during all transports (pickups and drop-offs), it may not be able to stave off arguments from the bailor as to bailed goods that were allegedly lost while in the possession of the bailee but that the bailee claims were already returned to the bailor, or claims that the goods have been sold to third parties pursuant to the parties' agreement. Certainly, detailed, reliable, and complete records should be maintained by bailees at all times, particularly where there are numerous bailed goods involving numerous drop-offs and pickups by the bailor or bailee of the goods during the course of the bailment. Receipts or bills of lading should also be signed by the bailor at all times, if possible, confirming delivery or redelivery of the specific bailed goods. The bailor should be given the opportunity to verify the identity of all items received as least in a general and casual way before the signing of any document confirming delivery of same.

In *Painter v Waddington, McLean & Co*,[68] the plaintiffs sued in bailment for the loss and damage of certain paintings and frames that had been left for safekeeping with the defendants, namely Waddington, McLean & Company Ltd (Waddington) and SKR Moving Inc (SKR). The bailment in the case had arisen from an estate litigation process, whereby the plaintiff Painter had obtained an *ex parte* court order in Newmarket, Ontario, causing the sheriff of the court in that jurisdiction to seize 601 paintings from the residence of Painter and Jensen, who were a married couple and also art collectors, pending resolution of the legal dispute. Waddington, a prominent Toronto art dealer and auction house, was engaged by the sheriff to remove the paintings and store them. To assist them with the removal, Waddington employed SKR, with whom it had an ongoing working relationship.[69]

The paintings were stored at Waddington's premises on Queen Street in Toronto for over three years, at which time Waddington relocated its

68 [2003] OJ No 5458 (SCJ).

69 *Ibid* at paras 1–3.

premises to a new location in Toronto on Bathurst Street. Some of the paintings had been sold at auction, but the remaining ones were still in the possession of Waddington. Pursuant to a further court order made at that time, SKR became the custodian of the paintings at that time, and the paintings were moved from the Waddington premises to the SKR warehouse in Scarborough. There, the paintings remained for nearly eight months, at which time the legal dispute was settled, with the result that the paintings were to be redelivered to Painter and Jensen by SKR. The plaintiffs claimed that, upon receipt of the delivery, certain paintings were missing or were damaged and that the defendant Waddington had known about the missing items two years prior but had failed to make the necessary disclosure to the plaintiffs.[70] However, prior to the seizure of the paintings, the plaintiffs had created no catalogue or record of their art collection or any valuations or proofs of authenticity relating thereto.[71]

An initial detailed cataloguing of the 601 paintings had been done upon Waddington's attendance at the plaintiff's residence together with the sheriff. Each painting was given a number, tagged, briefly described, and roughly measured. The artist's name was documented as well, if it was apparent, in addition to significant damage present on any piece. Waddington did not have enough tags for all the pieces, so the last approximately 200 items were marked individually on each piece. A copy of the list was left with the plaintiffs upon Waddington and SKR's departure from the premises with the paintings. Approximately a month later, another list was created by Waddington, attributing values to each painting.[72]

Pursuant to the second court order, a further (third) version of the list was prepared by Waddington, indicating whether a painting had been sold on consent and when the sale had occurred.[73] The new list also contained checkmarks inserted by Waddington to indicate those paintings that had been left at Waddington's Queen Street location for SKR's Scarborough facilities. When SKR picked up the paintings from Waddington, upon assuming its duty of safekeeping over the goods, pursuant to the court order, Waddington's evidence was that all the paintings were transferred over except one, which was later located by the plaintiff Jensen at Waddington's new business premises. (Jensen and Painter's requests to be

70 *Ibid* at paras 4–7.
71 *Ibid* at para 13.
72 *Ibid* at paras 15–17.
73 *Ibid* at paras 18–19.

present when the paintings were moved from Waddington's Queen Street location to SKR's Scarborough location had been denied.) A Waddington employee who testified at trial could not say definitively whether SKR had the third version of the Waddington list previously prepared.[74]

SKR claimed that nothing was lost or taken from its own premises and that everything at Waddington's premises had been relocated to its own in Scarborough. SKR acknowledged that it had no inventory list of the paintings moved from Waddington to SKR, that none had been provided to it by Waddington, and that it would have been expensive to have done a cataloguing, which is why it was not done. It was admitted by SKR that there was no checking-off of the paintings delivered because SKR was never furnished with a list. There was only an SKR invoice, which showed that 350–400 assorted paintings had been shipped from Waddington's premises to SKR's Scarborough location.[75]

Given the lack of identifying information in the shipments, and because of some other limitations, it took the plaintiffs six weeks to go through the shipment. They created a checklist in the margin of Waddington's most recent version of its inventory list, noting the paintings that had been sold and those that had been located or were missing. They then corresponded with Waddington, preparing an amended list of missing paintings accordingly. A final summary was prepared by the plaintiffs, which indicated nineteen missing paintings, two missing frames, and one damaged painting.[76]

Justice DiTomaso of the Ontario Superior Court of Justice found that a bailment for reward had been formed between the plaintiffs and the defendants in the case,[77] "albeit created and directed by the Court in this instance."[78] In addition, DiTomaso J found that a high degree of care was expected of the defendants, signified by the second court order, which required that one year's insurance premiums were to be paid to insure the paintings from the monies held in trust by Waddington, which duties

74 *Ibid* at paras 21–22.
75 *Ibid* at paras 25–28.
76 *Ibid* at paras 28–31.
77 Even though Waddington was volunteering to help the sheriff in the seizure of the paintings without immediate recompense, it was doing so with a clear commercial expectation that it would earn fees from selling the paintings or from storing them for the plaintiffs. This clearly made the bailment one for reward, as found by the learned judge: *ibid* at para 35.
78 *Ibid* at para 38.

had been breached by the parties. Besides substantially reducing the measures that had been in place to protect the goods at Waddington's premises, without the knowledge of the plaintiffs, the defendants were also in breach of their duty because of their failure to ensure that an itemized cataloguing of paintings was used by SKR when it took custody of the paintings and transported them to the SKR warehouse and, again, when the paintings were redelivered to the plaintiffs. The boxes and crates containing the plaintiffs' items were not numbered and were generally without identification upon redelivery to the plaintiffs. The learned judge found this to be unacceptable and the reason why it took the plaintiffs a considerable amount of time to confirm the accuracy of the shipment.[79]

Justice DiTomaso found the one-page invoice maintained by SKR to be inadequate to discharge its duty of care when it came to cataloguing the goods. Waddington had failed in not providing its list to SKR, which SKR needed to verify the specific paintings and items it was receiving from Waddington for redelivery to the plaintiffs. And, without its own self-generated list, SKR had no idea what specific items and paintings it was delivering to the plaintiffs in its crates, boxes, and containers. In its evidence, neither SKR nor Waddington could identify the specific items delivered to the plaintiffs. Waddington ultimately admitted in its evidence that there were two missing paintings, but could provide no explanation as to why. There was also a notation on the SKR invoice that acknowledged some damage to the goods, which SKR could provide no explanation in relation to. These things proved to be fatal and demonstrated clear negligence by the defendants in their cataloguing and record systems, as well as in their methods of safekeeping.[80]

The trial judge found that, in attempting to move the items from Queen Street to Scarborough as quickly and cheaply as possible,[81] the parties had failed to ensure that proper safeguards were in place to ensure that the plaintiff's property would not be lost or damaged. Justice DiTomaso found the plaintiff Jensen's evidence as to what the plaintiffs discovered to be credible and convincing—the best evidence available—and awarded damages to the plaintiffs based on their own records accordingly.[82] The learned judge refused to accept the defendants' argument that the plaintiffs' own

79 *Ibid* at paras 46–51.
80 *Ibid* at paras 49, 51, and 56.
81 *Ibid* at paras 46–48.
82 *Ibid* at paras 54–56.

negligence in storing and handling the goods contributed to the plaintiffs' own losses, as it had inadequate support in the evidentiary record.[83]

This decision makes clear that bailees must maintain accurate records and a cataloguing of bailed goods in their possession at all times. This includes during all transports and all transfers of possession between different parties involving the bailed goods, whether involving other bailees or the bailor. The bailee, at the time of redelivery to the bailor, or at the time a transfer of possession of the goods to another bailee occurs, must be able to identify specifically and definitively, with reference to its own records created contemporaneously with the act of delivery, all goods and items returned to the bailor or delivered to another bailee, as the case may be. The bailee must also ensure that the form of shipment allows the bailor, within a reasonable time, to verify the accuracy of the delivery. Certainly an invoice lacking in detail and information, of the kind SKR put before the court, which does not accurately and fully reflect the goods received from another bailee on behalf of a bailor and redelivered to the bailor, will not be enough to displace the presumption of negligence on a bailee where there is a shortfall in the goods redelivered to the bailor, or where some of the bailed goods are inexplicably damaged. Bailees who are relinquishing control of bailed goods to another bailee, pursuant to legal authority, can also be liable in damages to a bailor where they fail to work with subsequent bailees in transferring inventory lists and maintaining a system of checks to ensure bailor property is fully and completely transferred in a safe and verifiable manner without any losses or damage occurring in the process. Finally, the case indicates that all terms of a court order applicable to a bailment must be strictly followed in order for a bailee to discharge its duty of care, including, if required, the purchase and provision of insurance cover for the goods.

9) A Highly Qualified Bailee or Bailee's Agents

Undoubtedly, it will be easier for bailee to meet its onus of proof—that is, to show that reasonable care of the bailor's goods was taken or that no negligence was committed with respect to care of the bailor's property—where the bailee or its agent is highly qualified or trained in the specific type of act that led to the damage or loss in question. In *Mobilex Ltd v*

83 *Ibid* at para 57.

Payne,[84] the parties reached a deal, whereby an agent (i.e., a driver) of the defendants' would test out a piece of equipment (a tractor-trailer unit) owned by the plaintiff, to see whether the unit was appropriate to the tasks required by the defendants for their excavating business, before deciding whether they wished to buy or lease it. The agent, after an abortive test, made the test, which required the unit to be tested under actual working conditions, off the plaintiff's premises, at a job site. As it happened, while being operated by the defendants' driver, the tractor-trailer unit tumbled over in the process of dumping a load and was seriously damaged. The plaintiff sued the defendants in bailment for the damage done to the equipment.[85]

Justice Spence of the Ontario Supreme Court — High Court of Justice, in finding that the defendants had met their burden of proof of showing that reasonable care of the equipment had been taken at the material times considered, among other evidence, the defendants' choice of driver, finding him to have impeccable credentials and demonstrable abilities:

> On any of the evidence submitted no criticism can be made of Payne in his choice of Ellis [the driver], for Ellis had driven trucks for eleven and a half years and in fact had driven an exactly similar unit carrying loads of rock, which I think one would agree would be a dangerous load, for two and half years. Some further evidence of the competence of Ellis may be obtained from the fact that he was able to drive this very large unit into the pit and up to the shovel on the morning of the 27th, without mishap, while the plaintiff's driver on the test of the 25th had been unable to do so.[86]

In light of the above, Spence J favoured the evidence in the record that showed the cause of the accident to be the result of an inherent defect in the equipment itself, rather than any negligence on the part of the defendants' driver. The learned judge refused to find that an experienced driver such as Ellis would have parked the unit on an uneven surface before dumping his load and causing the mishap. In the result, Spence J found that the defendants "were not even guilty of the slight degree of

84 [1959] OJ No 81 (HCJ).
85 *Ibid* at paras 1–6.
86 *Ibid* at para 11.

negligence which would be sufficient to hold them liable under the mandate type of bailment,"[87] let alone under a bailment for fee.[88]

10) A Bailee's Failure to Explicitly Warn a Bailor of Significant Risks to Bailor Property Arising During the Course of a Bailment

In *Bell*,[89] a failure by the appellant (bailee) art gallery, and its principals, to warn of the significant risks of theft associated with its absenting itself from the gallery where the respondent's valuable artwork was stored under a showing arrangement was found to be a breach of its duty of safekeeping as bailee. This is because the respondent (bailor) had been left with the impression that someone would be physically present in the house where its artwork was being stored at all times during the bailment. This did not happen, and much of the respondent's artwork was taken while the premises were left unattended by the appellant. A bailor must be told of significant risks that may be present based on the level of safekeeping to be provided by the bailee and must explicitly approve of those deficiencies (that is, agree to run the risk), in order for a bailee to avoid liability for any losses occasioned by such risks.

This principle includes advising of certain specific hazards that may arise from the work being done by the bailee itself to bailor goods and the nature and extent of the risk. In *Camire v Carlson*,[90] the plaintiff brought his motor vehicle to the defendant's premises for the installation of vinyl decals, among other work. During the course of the work, the plaintiff's vehicle was damaged by the defendant. Specifically, scratches were observed in areas where the decals had been installed, and the decals were "bubbling" after only a short period of time following their installation. The defendant claimed that the decals had been properly installed, but that they were not "custom fitted," were of poor quality, and needed to be cut directly on the automobile to be installed. In this connection, the defendant underlined that it had a sign in its premises that warned customers, including the plaintiff, of the requirement to trim decals with a razor blade to achieve a proper fit, the implication being that risk of

87 *Ibid* at para 18.
88 *Ibid* at paras 11–18.
89 Above note 54.
90 [2015] OJ No 1213 (SCJ Sm Cl Ct).

damage during such procedures was brought home to customers and made a term of the bailment contract. The plaintiff claimed not to have seen the sign but did acknowledge speaking with the defendant and authorizing it to cut the decals to ensure a proper fit, though he denied authorizing the extent of the cutting that was done. In any case, the defendant denied that it was responsible for the extent of the damage (i.e., the scratching) allegedly sustained by the plaintiff's automobile while it was in its care and custody, claiming it did not know how the damage was caused.[91]

Deputy Judge Cleghorn of the Ontario Superior Court of Justice Small Claims Court—Thunder Bay quite easily found that the damage consisting of the scratching had occurred while the vehicle was in the defendant's custody; there was no third-party intervention or other reasonable explanation for the damage. The defendant could not be saved by the sign, because it did not explicitly warn of the "scope and extent" of the cutting that would be done on the defendant's premises. Instead, it noted only that such cutting would be done, and so the plaintiff could not be said to have been put on express notice of the specific risk to which his vehicle would be put.[92] (The defendant seemingly could have also been saved if it had proven that it had communicated the "scope and extent" of the cutting to the plaintiff over the phone, when the plaintiff communicated with the defendant prior to the work commencing, and received the plaintiff's express instruction to proceed despite the stated risks with the work, which it did not do.) The defendant needed expert evidence to support its claim that the quality of the decals was to blame for the scratches, or at least a part thereof; its mere speculation, standing alone without more, not being sufficient to discharge its duty of care owed to the plaintiff as bailee.[93]

11) A Bailee's Failure to Secure Keys to Bailor Property

A bailee must generally safeguard bailor keys to bailor property, after locking up that property, in order to meet its standard of care. A failure to do so will often result in liability against it. Ideally, keys should be secured in locked and enclosed premises of the bailee's and should be protected from theft or improper use. The mere fact that a vehicle is stolen, or keys are

91 *Ibid* at para 7.
92 *Ibid* at para 11.
93 *Ibid* at para 10.

accessed, does not mean that the bailee will have violated its applicable standard of care. However, where keys are left unattended and unsecured, such as under the front seat of a vehicle accessible to a thief,[94] and bailor property is stolen or damaged, a bailee will very often be liable.

a) Securing Bailor Keys

In *Hertz Canada Ltd v Suburban Motors Ltd*,[95] an employee of the plaintiff delivered the plaintiff's new Lincoln Town Car to the defendant dealer in Vancouver to have a faulty seat belt repaired. The keys to the vehicle were left with the service department. In accordance with its standard practice, upon receipt of the plaintiff's property, the plaintiff's keys were tagged with a number, and a correspondingly numbered portion of the card was left on the rear-view mirror of the vehicle (in the interior of the vehicle) so that a service technician could locate the vehicle once servicing could begin. Because the work could not be performed by the defendant on the day the vehicle was received, the vehicle was left in the general, unsecured parking area of the defendant's business overnight when the premises were vacant, together with several other vehicles, and was stolen therefrom during the overnight hours. The plaintiff proceeded to sue the defendant as bailee for reward for the purchase price of the car and for other related damages.[96]

For the theft to occur, the keys of the plaintiff's vehicle had been obtained from the defendant's premises from the inside of a locked service building, and the inside of a locked room, where they had been stored, by person or persons unknown using concerted and determined efforts. Specifically, the third parties had gained access to the defendant's premises by using a tire iron, breaking through the locked rear entrance door of the service building (used for pedestrian traffic during the day), passing through another locked door inside and locating the appropriate key, and then gaining access to the separate room where the keys to the plaintiff's vehicle were housed. The defendant had another large parking lot behind its service building enclosed by a high wire fence topped with barbed wire. The thief, or thieves, had accessed the rear door after scaling this fence. The rear door leading into the rear of the service building was highly secure. It was steel-clad and dead-bolted and was hung on a steel

94 *Brown v Toronto Auto Parks Ltd*, [1955] 2 DLR 525 (Ont CA).

95 2000 BCSC 667 [*Hertz*].

96 *Ibid* at paras 1–4.

frame, yet the unknown parties still overcame it by way of a tire iron. Upon breaking the lock on the first door and passing through, the thieves had to force the lock on another door before gaining access to the room where the plaintiff's keys were located on a turnstile. As noted, the keys had a tag with a number on them that corresponded to a card that had been placed on the rear-view mirror of the vehicle, allowing the thieves to locate and steal the plaintiff's chattel thereafter. While a number of keys were stolen, only the plaintiff's car was taken by the thieves.[97]

The evidence indicated that the defendant had better security measures in place at some of its other business locations (although these were in Victoria, not Vancouver), where keys to vehicles were placed in a safe after hours. The evidence as a whole, however, showed that the plaintiff's measures were not unreasonable, or uncommon, and were employed by another similar business in Victoria, although that business also used a vehicle to block the entry to the parking area, due to its secluded nature, in order to protect its vehicles from theft. "Determined thieves," however, could still overcome reasonable obstructions to the entry of a parking area of a dealership's facility put into place by a dealership, by driving a car over the curb or crashing through a locked gate, and so such obstructions would not necessarily prevent a determined thief from gaining entry.[98]

The main question for determination by the court was whether the defendant had met its standard of care by taking the aforementioned precautions. The plaintiff (bailor) argued that it had not and relied on the following with respect to storage of the keys:

1) The defendant's security measures did not include an alarm system for the service building where the plaintiff's keys had been stored.
2) The plaintiff's keys were left out in the open in the room in which they were stored in the defendant's service building, on a turnstile (with vehicle identifying information on them), instead of being locked away in a safe.
3) The defendant had failed to block the entry of the driveway of the lot in question after hours to prevent or impede the removal of cars from that lot.[99]

---

97 *Ibid* at paras 6–7.

98 *Ibid* at para 8.

99 *Ibid* at para 9. The plaintiff (bailor) also argued that the vehicle should have been stored inside a locked building and that the defendant's failure to do so in the circumstances was a breach of the defendant's duty of care. This argument was rejected by Warren J

Justice Warren of the British Columbia Supreme Court found that the defendant had taken reasonable care of the plaintiff's vehicle and had implemented sufficient precautions to guard against theft by independent third parties:

> I hold that the defendant took reasonable steps to safeguard the plaintiff's vehicle and storing the keys of customers' cars in a locked room inside the locked premises was not negligence on the defendant's part. In my view, the loss was not the result of any negligence on the part of the defendant but the result of the efforts of a truly determined third party who surmounted all of the safeguards employed by the defendant.[100]

It is submitted that Warren J's decision was the correct one in the circumstances. Certainly, the steps taken by the defendant were adequate for it to discharge its minimal obligations at law and are commonly employed by comparable car dealers in the industry. The added measures, urged by the plaintiff (bailor), while they would certainly have enhanced safekeeping, would bring the bailee's standard of care to the standard of perfection or near perfection, and should not be required out of a bailee in these circumstances. Keys do not need to be placed inside a safe inside of locked premises overnight for a bailee to meet its standard of care in these circumstances. This is asking too much from a bailee and would most surely impede commercial expediency. It might also impair a bailee's ability to remove bailor property from its own premises in exigent circumstances such as fire, which might actually undermine its ability to discharge its duty of safekeeping. As was observed by Warren J, it is not clear that the additional precautions, suggested by the plaintiff, would have prevented the thefts in the case, given the determination of the thieves. A bailee should not have to make its premises impervious, or impenetrable, or "Fort Knox-like," to meet its standard of care in these circumstances, or in most circumstances. The exception, of course, would be if there were something in those circumstances to merit an increased standard of care, such as prior thefts of bailor property, the isolated nature of bailee premises, or the crime-ridden nature of the area in which the bailee premises are located. Otherwise the defendant's precautions with respect to

---

of the British Columbia Supreme Court, who, after considering the relevant caselaw, found the measures that the defendant had taken to safeguard the plaintiff's vehicle from injury to be reasonable in all the circumstances: *ibid* at paras 9–12.

100 *Ibid* at para 12.

vehicle keys taken in the case should suffice most of the time. Clearly, valuable or unique property or artwork may demand greater safeguards from a bailee at law or by contract, and those circumstances should be assessed differently than the storing of vehicles on dealers' lots awaiting repair under the present consideration.[101]

b) Bailee Company Policies on Bailor Keys

The mere existence of a policy or practice requiring bailor keys to be stored in locked premises, and not, for example, in the ignition switch of a vehicle on an open lot, is not enough to exonerate a bailee from liability where the policy is not followed in practice and damage or loss to bailor property results. This consideration applies even if the general security measures and general policies of the bailee in place are otherwise appropriate and usually implemented without fail. In *Manitoba Public Insurance Corp v Midway Chrysler Plymouth Ltd*,[102] an employee of the respondent (bailee) failed to remove the keys from the ignition switch of the appellant's vehicle, which vehicle was left on the defendant's enclosed parking lot, behind a six-foot chain-link fence topped with barbed wire, overnight awaiting repair. This employee of the respondent had departed from the established practice of the respondent, which required the keys of cars parked on the lot that were awaiting repair to be removed from the ignition and placed on a board in the respondent's locked office. As it happened, the appellant's automobile was taken by an unknown third party during the overnight hours, crashed through the locked metal gate of the respondent's compound and later recovered in a damaged condition. The vehicle had an anti-theft mechanism, but it could be, and was, overcome by the use of the keys by the unknown third party, making the decision by the court on the keys quite consequential in the case.[103]

The Court of Appeal for Manitoba, per O'Sullivan JA, overruled the trial judge in the case, finding that the departure from the established safety procedure meant that the respondent, as a bailee for reward, had failed to meet its applicable standard of care and was vicariously liable for its employee's failure to secure the keys to the appellant's vehicle. An

---

101 The rules regarding the securing of bailor keys to bailor property from *Hertz, ibid*, should be applied with equal vigour in the parking context where a bailment has been formed between the parties.

102 [1977] MJ No 87 (CA) [*Manitoba Public Insurance*].

103 *Ibid* at paras 1–4.

ordinary system of care would require keys in the circumstances to be secured and not left in the ignition switch of a vehicle that is parked outside and not in a locked building. The defence of *actus novus interveniens* was, accordingly, not available to the respondent (bailee), unlike in *Hertz*, where the minimum degree of care was taken by the bailee but where a "determined thief" was nevertheless able to overcome the reasonable precautions that were in place for the safeguarding of the vehicle.

In *Manitoba Public Insurance*, O'Sullivan JA properly cautions against equating every breach of a safety procedure adopted by a bailee as being indicative that a bailee has breached its applicable standard of care. Bailees may sometimes adopt extraordinary or special procedures, above those required by ordinary practice, which should not lead to higher standards of negligence being imposed against them at common law.[104] Certainly these are supportable statements of law; bailees should *always* be judged against the applicable industry standard where the parties' contract does not impose a specific (and higher) standard of care on the bailee, and they should not be punished for adopting higher standards of safety and security for a bailor's goods than are otherwise required at law. However, where that minimum standard has been identified and is clearly breached, liability should be fixed against the bailee accordingly. Clearly, safety procedures that are more honoured by bailees in the breach than in the observance should not be countenanced by the courts and should not be enough to allow a bailee to escape responsibility for a bailor's losses.

c) Leaving Bailor Keys Insecure in the Ignition of Vehicles

In many bailment cases, including parking cases, the issue of whether it is appropriate to leave keys in the ignition of a bailor vehicle that is the subject of a bailment has arisen for consideration. As just indicated, this practice will usually not be acceptable because the increased risk of theft that this engenders, in the absence of appropriate supervision or security by a bailee, will mean that a bailee has breached its applicable standard of care when a theft of a vehicle left so vulnerable in fact occurs. However,

---

104 This, of course, must be subject to the caveat that, where a bailee assures the bailor that certain safeguards will be in place to protect its property during the course of the bailment (where these representations can be said to have become part of the terms of the bailment contract) but does not deliver on such protections, this should lead to a finding that a bailee has breached its standard of care, irrespective of whether the missing precautions exceeded the requirements of industry practice in the particular locale in which the bailment arose.

context will always matter, and exceptions will arise where it simply may not be practical, or necessary based on the industry practice prevailing in the specific geographic locale, for a bailee to remove keys from a vehicle's ignition to meet its applicable standard of care. In *Duckworth*,[105] because the defendants' repair shop's policy of leaving keys in the ignition of vehicles in a locked garage, to allow for the quick removal of such vehicles in the event of fire, was consistent with established practice in the town, it was not viewed as a breach of the defendants' (bailees') standard of care when the plaintiff's vehicle was lost. Justice Wilson of the British Columbia Supreme Court pointed out that, while removing the keys to vehicles in such circumstances and securing them reduces the risk of theft, it concomitantly increases the risk of loss or damage by fire. Rather than determine which risk was more prevalent in deciding what the appropriate action was to be taken in such circumstances by the defendants, Wilson J focused on the standard practice in the geographical area in which the defendants operated their business; other repair shops generally did the same thing as the defendants did, and this was not unusual or unexpected. This supported the defendants' actions and meant that they had not been negligent and *had not* breached the standard of care by leaving the keys in the ignition switch of the plaintiff's vehicle.[106]

In *British Motor Corp of Canada Ltd v Ross E Judge Auto Transport Ltd*,[107] several thousand cars were being stored at one location at one and the same time, to the knowledge of the bailors. From time to time, certain cars needed to be moved out. It would have been impracticable for the bailee to retrieve hundreds of keys to move one car out, so the bailee chose to leave all the keys in the ignition switches of vehicles so they could be easily moved as needed. This was not found to have been a breach of the standard of care. In other words, the mere leaving of keys in the ignition switch of a vehicle that ends up stolen or damaged, in

---

105 Above note 48.

106 *Ibid* at para 29. However, the defendant bailees were still found to have breached their applicable standard of care, since they had failed to maintain a padlock on an overhead door latch leading into where the plaintiff's vehicle was located with its keys in the ignition. This made the vehicle too susceptible to theft, since it would not take much to "break one window, then open a latch" and take the vehicle out. The maintenance of a padlock was a standard practice in the town in which they operated and had not been followed by the defendants, making them liable as bailees: *ibid* at para 32.

107 [1966] NSJ No 11 (SC) [*British Motor*].

these circumstances, should not be enough, without more, to find that a bailee has been negligent such that it cannot meet its standard of care and should be found liable in bailment.[108]

Where the removal of the keys is a non-factor in the damage or injury done to bailor property, such as where a vehicle is immobilized or broken-down and the leaving of the keys in the ignition switch does not in any way enhance the risk of loss or injury to the vehicle, such an act should not be used by a court to find, or contribute to finding, that a bailee has breached its applicable standard of care and failed to take reasonable care of the bailor's property.

12) A Bailee's Failure to Provide Other Safeguards Against Loss by Theft or Vandalism

a) Fencing

Certainly the provision of fencing by a bailee on its premises, inside which bailor property is stored, will increase the probabilities of the bailee being able to meet its standard of care in circumstances where bailor property has been lost or damaged by third-party trespassers. However, there is no absolute obligation on a bailee to keep bailor property stored or housed behind a fence or inside a building at all times in order for it to meet its standard of care (although, admittedly, in some circumstances, these things may be required).[109] In *Igboji v Old Town Chrysler Ltd*,[110] the plaintiff left his car with the defendants in November for servicing. Some misunderstandings developed between the parties with respect to the particulars of the work to be done to the vehicle, and, as a result, work did not begin until the following May, upon receipt of a work order from the plaintiff. During the intervening period, very little contact was made between the parties, and the plaintiff's vehicle was stored in the corner of the defendants' unenclosed lot, enclosed behind other vehicles, in accordance with the defendants' usual practice. There was no charge made for the storage while the parties discussed what work was to be done to the

108 There was "more" in the case, however, since the watchmen of the defendant (bailee storer) were found to have been negligent in failing to prevent extensive vandalism done to the plaintiff's (bailor's) vehicles while stored on the defendant's premises, which, with due vigilance, the court found could not have occurred: *ibid* at para 43.

109 See, for example, *Parkinson v Saunders Sales & Service Ltd*, [1988] BCJ No 140 (Co Ct) [*Parkinson*].

110 [1991] NWTJ No 86 (SC).

turbo in the vehicle. In January, the defendants acknowledged that some of the vehicles parked on this same lot were broken into and some contents from those cars stolen.[111]

When the plaintiff picked up his car from the defendants' premises in May, a stereo was missing from the vehicle. However, as was found by Davis J of the Northwest Territories Supreme Court, the plaintiff had not expected the defendant to store his vehicle in a more secure way than it did (on an "open lot") and could not expect a greater level of care for his vehicle than he himself provided.[112] With this came certain risks, namely, the risk of vandalism or theft: "Any vehicle that is in an open lot is subject to possible vandalism. It would be unreasonable to expect more security from a bailee than that usually provided by persons for the protection of their own goods. Without some agreed upon terms requiring special security, a bailee must exercise no more than is reasonable under the circumstances."[113]

Therefore, Davis J found that the loss could just as well have occurred in any open lot in the city, while the vehicle was in the possession of the plaintiff or defendants, or anyone else for that matter, and that the defendants, as gratuitous bailees, had not been negligent in the way they had parked the vehicle for storage (awaiting repair after they had clarified the plaintiff's instructions). While the decision is undoubtedly correct in holding that the storage of a bailor's vehicle on an unenclosed lot may be enough for a bailee to meet its standard of care in the general circumstances presenting in the case, certainly the past thefts that had occurred on the open lot should have alerted the defendants to the need for greater safeguards. The types of failures on the part of the defendants — specifically, their failure to increase security, or to notify the plaintiff of the thefts and the specific risks to which his vehicle was now exposed in light of them — have been used as grounds for judges in other bailment cases to have found against, or contributed to findings against, defendants in similar circumstances. Still, it is true that there is no absolute obligation on a bailee in all situations to provide fencing to protect bailor goods in the absence of an industry practice or an agreement to the contrary, and, accordingly, bailors are well advised to ensure that such security features are put into place by contract where they feel they are needed but where the general law does not provide for them.

---

111 *Ibid* at paras 1–4 [paragraph numbers assigned by author].

112 *Ibid* at para 12.

113 *Ibid* at para 13.

Ken Ertel Ltd v Balan (cob Balan Motors)[114] is also supportive of there being *no absolute obligation* on a bailee to provide fencing when storing ordinary bailor property, even overnight, on its premises. There, the plaintiff corporation purchased a vehicle from the defendant car dealer for use by the principal of the business's wife, which vehicle was to be returned for resale by the defendant if the wife was not satisfied with the vehicle. No other terms were provided for. The vehicle was so returned by the plaintiff to the defendant, and the insurance that the plaintiff had placed on the vehicle was removed.[115] The vehicle was then stored on the defendant's unenclosed lot located in a well-lit part of town at the intersection of two extremely busy streets, and the keys to the vehicle were locked in the defendant's office. The defendant checked each night to ensure that the keys were still secure in the office. The lot was not equipped with an alarm system. The defendant had not experienced any prior thefts or breaches of its safeguards. Given its history of dealings with the defendant, the plaintiff was aware of the conditions in which the vehicle would be stored. Indeed, the defendant had stored its own vehicles in the same place and manner as the plaintiff's, presumably to the knowledge of the plaintiff. The plaintiff's vehicle was nonetheless stolen from the lot. The plaintiff sued the defendant in bailment for its losses.[116]

The plaintiff's bailment action failed. Justice West of the Ontario Court of Justice (General Division) found that the defendant had followed its system of checks dutifully, and that it had provided a standard of care for the plaintiff's property that aligned exactly with the standard that the defendant was providing to its own property, which standard was not unreasonable or uncommon in the circumstances. Justice West also found that there was no legal duty on the defendant (bailee) to advise the plaintiff to maintain insurance on the vehicle, although the learned judge found that the defendant had done so.[117]

This is a good ruling. To meet their standard of care, bailees do not need to provide fencing or alarm systems in circumstances like these without specifically agreeing to same in the bailment contract. Securing

114 [1995] OJ No 3163 (Gen Div).

115 The defendant and plaintiff had expressly agreed in the bill of sale that the defendant *was not* obliged to obtain insurance cover for the vehicle while in its possession but that it would assist the plaintiff to obtain such coverage for the vehicle if so requested: *ibid* at para 12.

116 *Ibid* at paras 1–11 and 15.

117 *Ibid* at paras 17–23.

keys to a vehicle in a locked building and parking that vehicle in an unenclosed lot would seem to be enough to meet the standard of care on a bailee, unless there are circumstances requiring enhanced security, such as prior thefts, the isolated nature of the bailee's premises, or the value of the bailor property being stored, or if a clear industry practice requires same. None of these circumstances were present in the case, and West J was right to have rejected the plaintiff's claims accordingly.

b) Lighting

Lighting is another factor that has been evaluated in assessing whether a bailee has met its standard of care in particular circumstances. Poor lighting, without more, will probably only rarely make a bailee liable in damages to a bailor. In *Parkinson*,[118] the defendant's (bailee's) premises were in a rural area on the outskirts of Victoria. The plaintiff had left his car there for resale under a consignment agreement. The vehicle was vandalized while on the defendant's premises, its steering wheel being removed together with a radio, while the vehicle was in the care of the defendant dealership, before a sale of the vehicle could be completed.[119] Justice Hutchinson of the British Columbia County Court was critical of the defendant's failure to have good lighting at the back of the premises, given the isolated nature of the premises, the prior acts of vandalism that had occurred to the defendant's vehicles on its own premises (which the plaintiff was not advised of, but that resulted in the defendant placing insurance cover on its own vehicles), and the only sporadic patrols of the area conducted by the RCMP to the knowledge of the defendant. The area in which the vehicle had been left on the defendant's premises was also unfenced. Together, these facts meant that the defendant had failed to satisfy its burden of proof to show that it had taken reasonable care of the bailed goods that had been entrusted to it.[120] The inclusion of the term "customer to supply own insurance" in the consignment agreement did not excuse the defendant's failure to take the steps necessary to fulfill its obligations to take due care of the plaintiff's vehicle while it was in its custody. Moreover, although the plaintiff was aware of some of the particulars of the defendant's premises and the level of safekeeping it would be providing, he was not told about the periodic acts of vandalism to which

118 Above note 109.

119 *Ibid* at paras 1–3 [paragraph numbers assigned by author].

120 *Ibid* at paras 4–6.

vehicles on the lot had been subjected to in the past. Such acts, according to the learned judge, presented an "unusual risk" about which the plaintiff (bailor) needed to be expressly notified.[121] In the result, the defendant had to pay the plaintiff the sum of $2,000, representing the loss of value to the vehicle engendered by the acts of vandalism. As apparent, poor lighting in certain circumstances can contribute to a finding that a bailee has failed to meet its standard of care and should face liability accordingly.[122]

c) Alarm Systems and Locked Vaults

For expensive bailor property, such as diamonds or jewellery, or property that is particularly liable to theft,[123] the bailee may need to maintain an alarm system on its premises where the goods are being stored to satisfy its standard of care. The goods may also need to be placed in a locked vault, and other security measures may need to be implemented.[124] The

---

121 Interestingly, the defendant had placed insurance coverage on its own vehicles stored on the premises because of the periodic vandalism done to vehicles located thereon but had not informed the plaintiff of this. Had he known that the defendant had done so, this may well have influenced the plaintiff and led him to secure insurance coverage on his vehicle during the course of the bailment, which he did not ultimately do presumably because of the lack of disclosure. Had full disclosure been made by the defendant and had it been brought home to the plaintiff that the storage would be solely at his own risk, then, per Hutchinson Co Ct J, the defendant (as bailee) might well have been able to avoid liability for the plaintiff's losses: *ibid* at para 10.

122 *Ibid* at paras 10–12.

123 It must be clear to the bailee that the property to be stored is "valuable" before a heightened standard of care by the bailee will be required. For example, in *Hamilton v Chris Marion Holdings Ltd (cob Servicemaster of Ottawa)*, [1981] OJ No 523 (HCJ), the defendant storage company was not aware that the gun collection it was storing for the plaintiff was of considerable value, as there was nothing in the guns' appearance to suggest this to them as laypersons. Moreover, none of the plaintiff bailor's agents in the case had advised the storage company of the high value of the goods. Indeed, the plaintiff's own relatives were not aware of the particularly high value of the guns; their concern for their continued existence centred on the goods' sentimental value. Thus, in these circumstances, the defendant was not required to meet a heightened standard of care to show that it had constructed or modified its premises appropriately to store items of high value: see paras 24–25.

124 In *Pazitch v Shaughnessy Antique Gallery*, [1997] BCJ No 1036 (SC), the respondent (bailee) who was a storer of jewellery, pieces of arts, and antiques for sale, also maintained video cameras, bars on the doors, and a system that restricted the number of items that could be removed from the display case and seen by a customer at any one time. Even though robbers were able to overcome these measures, which did not make the respondent's premises impervious to break-in, they nonetheless were found to meet the standard of reasonable care on the respondent in the case with respect to the bailor's items lost in the robbery: see para 8.

alarm system, like any system of security, is not expected to be foolproof, and a bailee should *not* be found to have violated its standard of care merely because the system did not prevent the theft or allow the thieves to be caught by police before making off with the bailor property.[125] That would be asking too much from bailees and is certainly not something that should be expected of them. Since these security features constitute special security, if the industry practice does not clearly require them from a bailee, then the parties should agree to them and incorporate them into the bailment contract before they become terms of agreement between parties. For ordinary property, such as the storage of cars awaiting repair, industry practice will not always require that a bailee maintain a monitored alarm system over its premises.[126]

13) A Bailee's Failure to Properly Supervise the Goods/Bailed Property

a) Publicly Accessible Areas

A bailee will sometimes need to have personnel supervise the bailor's goods in order to discharge its duty of care. In *Roy Foss Motors Ltd v Total Ford Sales Ltd*,[127] the plaintiff (bailor) left his vehicle containing certain chattels with the defendant for repair. The vehicle was placed in a bay for repairs during normal business hours, with the keys in the ignition. The bay was not secure, and access by the public could be made. As it happened, while the vehicle was in the bay still in the process of receiving repairs, a thief stole the vehicle. The defendant admitted that public access to the area could be made, that the area was not secure because the bay door was left open, and that the vehicle was not under constant watch by its personnel. The defendant argued that it would be impractical to keep members of the public completely out of the bay area but that personnel would question members of the public if they were observed in the area, and that this was a sufficient deterrent against theft. Any further

125 See, for example, *Giovanetti v GK Rose Appraisals Ltd*, [1994] NSJ No 44 (SC).

126 In *Duckworth*, above note 48, since repair shops in the particular locale did not maintain alarm systems, a security service, or a monitored entry service, the defendant was not required to have such systems in place to show that due care of the plaintiff's goods had been taken, even though they might well have prevented the theft of the plaintiff's vehicle: see para 27.

127 [1990] OJ No 1180 (Dist Ct).

precautions, the defendant argued, would have hampered commercial expediency.[128]

Justice O'Connell of the Ontario District Court — York Judicial District disagreed. The learned judge found that, given how precarious a vehicle was with its keys in the ignition, the defendant needed to supervise the vehicle at all times, which it failed to do, while allowing members of the public into the area. This permitted the vehicle to fall prey to a passing thief. Justice O'Connell accordingly awarded the plaintiff damages for the lost vehicle as well as for the personalty in the vehicle, which the learned judge found to be of the kind one would commonly expect to find in a vehicle undergoing repairs.[129] While O'Connell DCJ's decision is undoubtedly the correct one, it would seem that there are various ways in which a bailee could meet its duty of care in these circumstances without having an employee watch over the vehicle at all times, which is unquestionably very costly and not always necessary. The two simplest would be having the vehicle's keys secured each time a technician is away from the vehicle, either with the technician or in a secure area, or entirely prohibiting public entry into the repair area. The latter would allow a bailee to leave keys in ignitions for convenience while still allowing it to meet its duty of care. However, where a bailee fails to take these required steps, and instead chooses to leave keys in a vehicle unsupervised and susceptible to theft by members of the public, liability should be fixed against it accordingly.

b) A Bailee's Unilateral Removal of Agreed-Upon/Expected Supervision over Bailor Goods

Where a bailee has agreed as part of the bailment contract to have someone physically present to watch over the goods at all times but absents itself thereafter, liability should easily follow. In *Larsen v 368884 Alberta Ltd*,[130] two plaintiffs and a friend checked their coats at the defendant's restaurant and bar with the coat-check person (whom the plaintiffs recognized from previous visits and who was wearing a sweater with the restaurant name on it). In return, the employee gave the plaintiffs a ticket with a number on it representing the hanger on which all three of the plaintiffs' coats were placed. Near closing time, when a plaintiff went to retrieve the coats, she discovered that the coat-check area was no longer

128 *Ibid* at paras 1–4 [paragraph numbers assigned by author].

129 *Ibid* at paras 6–10.

130 [1990] AJ No 220 (Prov Ct Civ Div).

being staffed by restaurant employees (who would normally receive tickets in exchange for coats) and, upon finding the appropriate hanger on the rack, discovered that her coat and the other plaintiffs' virtually new coats were all missing. The three friends then searched the entire coat-check area, but to no avail: the missing three coats were never found. The restaurant proprietor denied all responsibility for the loss. Justice Moore of the Alberta Provincial Court disposed of the liability question in bailment quickly, concluding that the plaintiffs had not been notified that the coat-check employee was leaving and that customers therefore had to retrieve their own coats. This act of negligence by the bailee clearly put it in breach of its duty of safekeeping and clearly exposed the plaintiffs' coats, in a busy bar, to theft, which theft actually transpired.[131]

Industry practice, or the bailment contract, will sometimes require bailees to have security personnel in place to watch over the bailor's goods during the course of the bailment in order to meet their standard of care, especially where the bailor property is valuable and highly susceptible to theft or damage. Such a requirement must be fulfilled dutifully if the bailee wishes to avoid liability. There is no question that, in order for security guards to successfully carry out their duty of safekeeping under a bailment, they must be present in the area where the bailor's goods are being stored and must have the ability to monitor and check on the condition of the bailed goods at all times, to ensure they are still in good condition and have not come into harm's way. (Where this is not possible, it is unlikely that the relation between the parties is one of bailment.)[132] They must also exercise due vigilance at all times to prevent reasonably foreseeable damage, including by third parties, to the bailor property that is under their watch.[133]

c) Ticketing Systems and Parking Attendants

In the parking lot context, where there is a ticketing system and a bailment is found between patron and operator, there is no question that parking lot attendants, or employees, will have a duty to exercise due care in ensuring that vehicles that are in their charge are handed over only to those who present the correct ticket to them, confirming that the ticket-holder is the

131 *Ibid* at paras 1–11 [paragraph numbers assigned by author]. See further *Bell*, above note 54.

132 See *Seaspan International Ltd v The "Kostis Prois,"* [1974] SCR 920.

133 See *British Motor*, above note 107.

rightful owner or possessor of the vehicle. Attendants also must ensure that tickets are issued to drivers before this, as they come into the lot. When failings occur in this regard, such as arose in *Ashby v Tolhurst*,[134] where a man masquerading as the vehicle's owner was given custody of an owner's (bailor's) car improperly and the vehicle was lost or damaged, the parking operator will be responsible in the absence of a clause exempting the bailee from liability. Parking attendants are responsible for safely parking, relocating, and moving bailor vehicles on a parking lot, and for securing keys to bailor vehicles to prevent the theft or damage of those vehicles. In short, parking attendants must ensure that a certain minimum level of security, consistent with industry practice, is maintained on the parking lot if a bailee is to avoid liability for loss or damage to vehicles stored thereon.

14) Secure Locks to Access Points on Bailee Premises: Doors and Gates

A bailee certainly has a duty to ensure that gates and doors leading to areas where bailor goods are kept are properly locked and secured, especially after hours and overnight, to meet its duty of care. Failure to do so (for example, by inadvertently leaving a door or gate unlocked), leading to theft of bailor goods should amount to liability against the bailee.[135] Where a bailee does not properly secure doors or gates when returning property to the possession of a bailor, and the evidence is unclear on when the disappearance of the bailor's goods occurred, a bailee should be required to disprove that its negligence caused the bailor's losses to avoid liability.[136] Bailees should take care to ensure that all gates and doors leading to areas where bailor goods are stored are properly locked at the end of each day, particularly where no agent or employee of the bailee will be remaining with the goods overnight to monitor their security and protect them from theft. If the bailee's premises are left vulnerable to theft due to a failure to secure a lock or door, and theft of bailor property results therefrom, liability should be fixed against the bailee, and the bailee should be denied the defence of *novus actus interveniens*.

134 [1937] 2 KB 242.

135 See *Kieller v Sentinel Self-Storage Corp*, 2008 ABQB 783 at paras 53–55.

136 *Lifestyles Kitchens & Bath, a division of GVBS Inc v Danbury Sales Inc*, [1999] OJ No 3097 at para 44 (SCJ).

a) Inadequate Locks

In *Duckworth*,[137] a failure by the defendant (bailee) to secure the latch of the deadbolt with a padlock, allowing the windows in overhead doors to the garage (storing the plaintiff's vehicle awaiting repair) to be broken and the doors of the garage to be opened, proved to be fatal. It was foreseeable that a theft could happen in the circumstances. Despite the absence of a "rash of break-ins" in the area, they were not completely unheard of, and the necessary precautions had to be put into place to ward them off.[138] Industry practice in the locale indicated that a padlock on deadbolts inside overhead doors that could be broken was necessary to prevent, or at least minimize the risk of, such occurrence.[139] In *Robertson*,[140] the fact that the door to one of the storage areas in which the plaintiff's (bailor's) goods were being stored could be easily overcome by a screwdriver contributed to a finding of liability against the defendant bailees in that case when the door was overcome by thieves, who stole some of the plaintiff's goods.

b) Prior Thefts or Breaches of a Bailee's Premises

Where there have been prior breaches into a bailee's premises and bailors' goods have been previously stolen or damaged, there may be a heightened duty of care on bailees to protect bailor goods, at least in those areas of its premises where the thefts occurred. There may also be a duty to inform the bailor of such thefts or breaches[141] and to advise the bailor of the additional precautions that have been, or are to be, put into place by the bailee to ensure the security of their goods in light of such instances. It may also be advisable for a bailee to strongly recommend that a bailor obtain insurance in these circumstances to protect the bailor's goods from loss by theft, where no such coverage has been placed on the goods by either the bailor or the bailee.

---

137 Above note 48.

138 *Ibid* at para 34.

139 *Ibid* at para 28.

140 Above note 65 at para 86.

141 In *Davidson*, above note 60, the defendant storer's failure to advise the plaintiffs, who were storing their valuables with the defendant in containers in its bulk storage vaults, of a prior theft from a container in those vaults was viewed as both negligence and as a breach of the bailment contract, contributing to a finding that the defendant (bailee) had failed to meet its standard of care in all the circumstances: see para 9. See further: *Robertson*, above note 65 at paras 15–16.

15) A Bailee's Failure to Provide Appropriate Safeguards Against Loss by Fire

a) Failure to Maintain Equipment/Systems in Good Working Order

A bailee's failure to maintain equipment in good working order can result in liability being imposed against it where there is a reasonable causal connection between such a failure and a bailor's losses caused by fire (or another cause, for that matter). Conversely, where a bailee can show that all of its equipment was in good working order prior to the loss, this can constitute disproof of negligence such that a bailee will be exonerated from liability. *Hutchings v Loveless*[142] is instructive. There, the plaintiff left his motorcycle at the defendant's facility for repair. The motorcycle could not be repaired immediately, as the mechanic on duty was too busy, so it was parked, with the plaintiff's agreement, inside the defendant's garage near the small motor repair room awaiting repair. The plaintiff left the defendant's premises and promised to return later to check on the vehicle and the status of the repair. The next day, and prior to the plaintiff's intended return to the defendant's premises, a fire started suddenly in the ceiling of the small motor repair room and spread very quickly, while the mechanic was performing some welding about twenty to twenty-five feet from where the plaintiff's bike was parked. The mechanic was unable to remove the plaintiff's bike from the burning building. The building and all of its contents, including the plaintiff's motor vehicle, were destroyed.[143]

The fire and police investigation, as well as the physical evidence, indicated that the fire had originated in a fluorescent light in the ceiling of the small motor repair room. The welding being performed by the defendant at the material time was not viewed as a possible cause of the fire, as that work had occurred a distance away from the origination of the fire. Nothing else was revealed in the investigation to indicate any other possible causes. The defendant's premises were kept as clean and organized as possible, and there were three or four fire extinguishers in the building in accessible areas. The gasoline in the small motor room was stored correctly, in appropriate and approved containers.[144] While a bailment in the case was easily found by Easton J of the Newfoundland

142 [1990] NJ No 411 (SCTD).

143 *Ibid* at paras 1–5.

144 *Ibid* at paras 6 and 13.

Supreme Court, Trial Division, the question of the bailee's standard of care was not as easy to resolve. This is because the evidence showed that the fluorescent light was new, that there had never been any problems with it in the past, and that no challenge was made by the plaintiff as to its installation. Still, the plaintiff's motor vehicle had been destroyed, and the defendant's evidence did not explain *exactly* how the fire had started, which, plaintiff counsel argued, was the required standard that needed to be met by it as bailee.[145]

Justice Easton disagreed. The learned judge found that the defendant had kept its shop and the fluorescent light in good working order at all times and that nothing had occurred with respect to the light to alert the defendant to any "peculiarities or malfunctionings" requiring the defendant's attention or concern. As explained by Easton J, "It was quite simply an ordinary light fixture which operated as such until the night of the fire. It is neither fair nor correct in law in this case to place on the defendant the burden of demonstrating *exactly* what caused the fire. In my view, the defendant has come far closer here than in many other cases in explaining what happened and in discharging the onus."[146]

This case illustrates that a bailee is not an insurer and is not required to meet the standard of perfection. Where the bailee can show that it had proper systems in place to protect a bailor's goods, and maintained those systems at all relevant times, the fact that harm comes to a bailor's goods by fire will not be dispositive. This is because a bailee only has to show that reasonable care of the bailor's goods was taken to escape liability; this is enough to rebut the presumption of negligence on bailees in bailment actions. While Easton J did not have to go this far, it is clear that if the defendant (bailee) showed reasonable care, this must mean that the cause of the fire was probably an inherent defect in the light, rather than any failing on the part of the defendant. This is what distinguished the case from the many other bailment cases involving fire, and other mishaps, discussed by Easton J, where liability was fixed against bailees because a lack of proper care by the bailee was apparent and clearly the cause of the bailor's losses. Such circumstances included allowing gasoline to leak onto a garage floor while repairs were being made to a motor vehicle, causing a vehicle's damage or destruction. That was not the case

145 *Ibid* at paras 7–18.
146 *Ibid* at para 18.

before Easton J, and the learned judge was right to have dismissed the plaintiff's action accordingly.

b) Businesses That Are Potential Fire Risks

A more robust system to protect against loss by fire will be called for where the bailee's business is considered to be a potential fire risk. In these circumstances, fire extinguishers and the steps taken by the bailee (defendant) in *Loveless* to protect against loss from fire will not be sufficient for a bailee to meet its standard of care. In *Falcon Lumber Ltd v Canada Wood Specialty Co Ltd*,[147] the defendant (bailee) accepted delivery from the plaintiff, as it had been hired to do many times in the past, of its lumber in order to have the wood kiln-dried to a certain moisture content in accordance with previous instructions conveyed by the plaintiff. The lumber would usually be stored first by the defendant for a period of time to achieve a certain moisture content before being placed into the defendant's kilns. As it happened, in the early morning hours, while the plaintiff's lumber was still inside the defendant's facility and the kilns were operating (as they did twenty-four hours a day), a powerful fire ripped through the defendant's building, destroying all the lumber in the kilns as well as all the lumber being stored in the building at the time. The building was a total loss. The evidence showed, at the time of the fire, every available space in the building was filled with lumber, that there was no watchman service on weekends or after business hours and the building was usually left unsupervised during these periods of time, and that the building contained no operative sprinkler system or alarm system, even though there had been two recent fires in the same building.[148]

While Griffiths J of the Ontario High Court of Justice found the cause of the fire to be accidental and unexplained (there was no evidence of arson), this did not exonerate the defendant (bailee) in the case. This is because inadequate protections were in place to protect against loss by fire, given the potential risk that was engendered by the defendant's business as a kiln-drying company that stored 600,000 board feet of lumber in its kiln building and operated its kilns twenty-four hours a day.[149] This was a high-fuel load that "imposed upon the defendant a duty of care

---

147 [1978] OJ No 3693 (HCJ) [*Falcon*].
148 *Ibid* at paras 1–18.
149 *Ibid* at paras 14–17.

commensurate with that risk."[150] Moreover, the two previous fires that had occurred in the kiln building, one of which had caused tens of thousands of dollars in damage, should have brought home to the defendant the importance of having rigorous protections in place. Justice Griffiths accordingly ruled that the defendant was negligent in failing to maintain either a sprinkler system, a firm alarm system, or a night watchman, irrespective of the fact that no municipal bylaws, regulations, or the like, required them. If the costs of the former two precautions were prohibitive, which was not shown on the evidence, the learned judge was of the view that the third needed to be put in place by the defendant.[151] In the words of Griffiths J, "Had this precaution been taken, then it is probable that the fire could have been detected and extinguished at an early stage and the loss to the plaintiff averted."[152]

These are reasonable holdings and conclusions, and illustrate that the degree of fire protection systems that a bailee needs to have in place will be commensurate with the risk of fire generated by the bailee's business. Certainly kiln-drying facilities will owe a greater duty in that regard than the average car or jewellery repair shop and will very likely need to have a sprinkler or fire alarm system in place, or a night watchman in lieu thereof, in order to meet their standard of care. Where the proper systems are in place, the mere occurrence of a fire that damages bailor goods in mysterious, or unexplained, circumstances need not lead to an automatic finding of liability against a bailee. A bailee should be provided with the opportunity to show that it had the necessary systems in place to protect the bailor's goods from loss in order that it may escape liability. To be sure, those systems need to be demonstrative of reasonable care being taken over the bailor's property, such that bailee negligence is unlikely to be the cause of the bailor's losses.

c) Allowing a Fire to Spread

Even where a bailee is found to have not been negligent in causing a fire to begin, such as in the case of an accidental fire, it may still be found negligent for allowing a fire to spread, by reason of a failure to have the proper systems in place to minimize the spread of fire. In *Hogarth v Archibald*

---

150 *Ibid* at para 17.

151 *Ibid* at paras 16–19.

152 *Ibid* at para 19.

Moving and Storage Ltd,[153] the defendants were in the business of storage but had not equipped their warehouse with sprinkler or alarm systems to protect against loss by fire. Indeed, the defendants had only very minimal preventive measures in place to protect against loss by fire; there may have been fire extinguishers on the premises; but there were no smoke detectors, heat detectors, fire doors, fire alarms, sprinklers, or watchmen. As it happened, the plaintiffs' goods were destroyed after an accidental fire caused significant damage to the defendants' building.[154]

The fire department, which attended on the scene, was unable to put the fire out. As a consequence, the plaintiffs' goods were destroyed.[155] Justice Oppal of the British Columbia Supreme Court found that the existence of a sprinkler system, or protective system, would have contained the fire such that the damage caused would have been "minimal,"[156] and that the defendants' failure to provide such systems had contributed to the spread of the fire. However, the key issue, on which liability rested, was whether there was a legal obligation on the defendants (as bailees) to provide such systems. There was such a duty, according to Oppal J, under statute by virtue of the defendants being warehousemen; but could such a duty be extended to the defendants as bailees under the common law by way of industry practice? That is to say, did the industry practice of the community require the defendants to have an operational sprinkler system at the time of the loss? There was conflicting evidence on this point,[157] leaving Oppal J to conclude without any reference to judicial authority that "[t]he defendants are not afforded any defence by virtue of other warehousemen in the jurisdiction not having adequate fire detection or preventive means. In any event the evidence on this point is equivocal in that there are other warehouses which are equipped with detection and alarm systems."[158]

Justice Oppal went on to fix the defendants with liability as bailee accordingly. With respect, the crux of the issue was the adequacy of the defendants' protection measures in place, and the issue under the common law of bailment had to be resolved with reference to the industry practice in the community. On the evidence before the court, it was clear

153 [1991] BCJ No 2321 (SC).
154 *Ibid* at paras 1–6 [paragraph numbers assigned by author].
155 *Ibid* at para 3.
156 *Ibid* at para 22.
157 *Ibid* at paras 22–25.
158 *Ibid* at para 25.

that there were other warehouses that used sprinkler and alarm systems in the jurisdiction, but that was not the issue; neither was whether the systems would have substantially reduced the damage to the plaintiffs' goods — clearly, they probably would have. The issue was whether such systems represented an "industry practice in the community," such that the defendants should be found to have breached their applicable standard of care by failing to have such systems in place at the material times. If the evidence was "equivocal" on this point, this should have inured to the benefit of the defendants. Certainly, bailees should not be held to higher standards of care merely because such standards would have better protected the bailor's goods from destruction or damage. At law, bailees do not owe bailors a standard of perfection, or near perfection, but only the standard that is considered to be in accordance with industry practice or is required by the contract of bailment, no more, no less.

16) Geographical Location of the Bailee's Premises: Urban v Rural Areas

A bailee's standard of care may be impacted by whether its facilities where bailor goods are being stored or repaired are in a well-developed town or city or in a rural area. In particularly isolated areas, the bailee may need to employ greater security measures to meet the same level of safekeeping as compared with their urban counterparts. This, however, is a factor that would seem to cut both ways. In some urban areas, thefts and crimes will be higher than in rural areas, militating in favour of more rather than fewer security precautions against theft and vandalism. Contrariwise, the isolated nature of some bailee premises in rural areas might require more rather than less security. While no bright line test is therefore possible here, it would seem, based on the prevailing caselaw, that the greatest emphasis, in setting a bailee's standard of care, should be placed on industry practice in the particular locale as well as on prior thefts or acts of vandalism at the business premises of the bailee. However, this should not be interpreted as meaning that minimum degrees of care should not be required of all bailees in all geographic locations. For example, keys to automobiles left parked overnight on bailee premises will normally need to be secured in locked premises in order for a bailee to meet its standard of care, regardless of the location of bailee premises, since a failure to do so will leave a vehicle highly susceptible to theft and will usually equate to gross negligence by a bailee. In these circumstances, a bailee will always be liable to a bailor in damages for any losses occasioned by such negligence, at least in the absence of an enforceable exemption clause, regardless of whether the bailee's premises are located in a rural or urban geographic area.

17) Insurance

a) No General Duty on a Bailee to Obtain Insurance Against Loss over Bailed Goods

As a general rule, bailees do not need to obtain insurance to protect a bailor's goods in order to meet their standard of care. However, some exceptions apply to this rule.

i) Exception 1: Where an Undertaking to Insure Is Made an Express Term of the Bailment Contract

To meet their standard of care, bailors need to obtain insurance if the contract between the parties *expressly* requires them to do so. The terms of a lease of expensive equipment, such as a crane, may require the lessee (bailee) to obtain insurance to indemnify the lessor against all losses and damage to the equipment arising during the course of the rental.[159] Where this is the case, a bailee will *not* be able to rely on a lack of negligence to exonerate itself from liability to pay damages to the bailor for its losses where no such insurance is maintained. That is to say, where a bailee clearly agrees to indemnify a bailor against all loss and damage to the equipment, it will owe the standard of perfection to the bailor and nothing else, including reasonable care, will suffice. In most cases, however, as Wilson J aptly noted in *Duckworth*,[160] the question of whether a defendant (bailee) has insurance over the bailed goods will be "a matter of loss allocation" between the defendant and its insurer, and not an obligation owed by the defendant to the plaintiff (bailor).

Where a bailee undertakes to insure goods as part of the bailment contract, a failure to do so, or a failure to make a claim under the policy obtained where a loss or damage to the bailed goods is occasioned, will amount to a breach of that bailee's duty of care owed to the bailor. In *Jakobashvili v*

159 See, for example, *Tobin Tractor (1957) Ltd v Ideal Crane Rentals Ltd*, [1971] SJ No 311 (CA) [*Tobin Tractor*].

160 Above note 48 at para 25.

Gem-Well Ltd,[161] the plaintiff left diamonds (among other things) in the defendant's possession at its business premises, on a sell-or-return basis. As it happened, a little less than a month later, the premises were broken into and most of the plaintiff's diamonds were stolen from the vault in which they were stored. The thieves were determined; they had come through the roof of the premises and were not caught in spite of an alarm system and the prompt arrival of police to the premises. At the point of loss, title to the diamonds had not passed to the defendant, and ownership remained throughout in the plaintiff and at his risk under the applicable rule in the *Sale of Goods Act*.[162]

However, even though a sale had not occurred between the parties, since title to the diamonds remained with the plaintiff, a bailment had been formed between them because a transfer of possession had occurred. As part of the terms of the storage, the defendant had accepted a duty of safekeeping over the diamonds and said that they would be insured for the duration of the storage. The evidence before the court did not establish whether such insurance cover against theft was ever obtained by the defendant. Certainly, no payout from insurance proceeds was ever made by the defendant to the plaintiff following the loss of the diamonds, despite the defendant's assurances to the plaintiff that said payment would be made. Instead, the defendant merely offered the plaintiff a nominal amount for the lost diamonds, which the plaintiff refused, and an action in bailment for the value of the lost diamonds followed.[163]

Justice Cromarty of the Ontario High Court of Justice found that the defendant, as bailee, had agreed to insure the diamonds and was responsible for the uninsured losses. According to the learned judge, the defendant "either did not insure them or . . . he wilfully failed to make a claim under his policy, and . . . in either event he failed to carry out the obligation which he had assumed."[164] If the breach of the obligation was merely a result of the defendant's not reviewing the insurance policy received to ensure that it covered what it was intended to, he was still answerable as bailee. Certainly the bailee is obligated to ensure that the desired coverage has been obtained. Had the defendant in the case applied himself to the task, the desired coverage could likely have been obtained and the plaintiff's losses

161 [1977] OJ No 2470 (HCJ).
162 *Ibid* at paras 1–8.
163 *Ibid* at paras 9–19.
164 *Ibid* at para 19.

would have been covered under the policy. There was no requirement at law requiring the defendant to insure the goods, but, having assumed such obligation by contract, the defendant had to strictly carry it out.[165]

ii) Exception 2: Where Valuable Goods Are Placed in Transit by a Bailee with Untried Third-Party Carriers

Where bailed goods are "valuable," a heightened standard of care will often be placed on bailees. This will sometimes include an implied term that the bailee appropriately insure the goods, at least where they are placed in transport with an untried third-party carrier and much more susceptible to theft, since a bailor's goods would otherwise be left at an unacceptably high risk of loss. This would seem to be an absolute duty on a bailee unless clearly relieved of such duty by a bailor. In *Punch*,[166] a case of sub-bailment, the defendant bailee and defendant sub-bailee both failed to ensure that appropriate insurance cover was placed on valuable jewellery while it was being transported by untested third-party carriers between Toronto and Sault Ste Marie in connection with some repair work. These combined, and repeated, failures made the defendants liable in bailment to the plaintiff when the jewellery was later lost while left in the hands of a final third-party carrier for transport back to the defendant (bailee) for redelivery to the plaintiff (bailor) owner of the valuable ring. This was so even though the practices of the defendant bailee and sub-bailee did not appear to be inconsistent with the relevant industry practices of jewellers who would transport such items by registered mail without suffering a loss.

b) No General Duty on a Bailee to Ascertain Whether a Bailor Is Aware of a Lack of Insurance Cover over Goods in Its Care

Consistent with there being no general legal duty on bailees, outside of valuable goods being transported during the course of a bailment by untried third-party carriers, to place insurance on bailed goods, there is no duty on a bailee to ascertain whether the bailor is aware that a bailee

165 *Ibid* at paras 20–22. While there was some evidence offered by the defendant in the record (see para 16) that the reason that he could not obtain the insurance is because the diamonds were obtained illegally and were therefore uninsurable, Cromarty J must not have found this to be the case. Such a finding would have meant that the obligation assumed could not have been carried out by the defendant and may have meant that the contract was criminal and unenforceable.

166 Above note 26.

has not placed insurance cover over the goods in storage under a contract of bailment.[167] In *Mason v Morrow's Moving & Storage Ltd*,[168] the respondents sued in bailment after their household furnishings and effects were destroyed by fire after being delivered and stored in the appellant's warehouse for two years under a bailment for reward. At the time of the loss, the respondents' goods in storage with the appellant were not insured by the appellant against the risk of fire. However, the respondents were not aware of this and did not believe that it was their responsibility to inquire about the matter. The respondents had moved to Chilliwack, British Columbia, from out of province and had taken up temporary residence there, while they looked for permanent residence.[169]

The appellant's normal protocols to communicate to owners of goods that storage rates did not include fire insurance, that goods were at the owner's risk in the event of fire, did not result in the respondents becoming aware of the condition. The appellant had not mentioned the lack of fire insurance on the goods in his discussions with the respondents or that the risk associated with fire belonged to the respondents.[170]

The trial judge found in favour of the respondents, finding that the appellant had been "negligent in failing to assure that the plaintiffs (respondents) knew that there would be no fire insurance unless they placed it themselves."[171] However, on appeal, the Court of Appeal for British Columbia, per Carrothers J, disagreed, noting that there was no authority whatsoever in support of there being a general legal duty on a bailee to advise the owner of goods placed in storage that the fire risk lay with a bailor, or to determine whether the bailor was aware of the lack of insurance on the goods. The respondents' argument that there was an "exceptional risk" of fire, given the lack of fire prevention systems in place at the appellant's premises, requiring the appellant to expressly warn of the lack of fire insurance, was rejected by the appeal court on the basis that the precautions in place, while quite minimal,[172] must have

167 Nonetheless, it is advisable for a bailee to advise a bailor to supply its own storage insurance where the bailee has no intention of doing so, so that the bailor is made aware that the storage is at its risk to an extent: see *Parkinson*, above note 109.

168 [1978] BCJ No 1230 (CA).

169 *Ibid* at paras 1–6.

170 *Ibid* at para 8.

171 *Ibid* at para 9.

172 There was no watchman service, no fire alarm system, no heat or smoke detection system, and no sprinkler or fire suppression system: *ibid* at para 10.

met the minimum requirement set by law, since the premises had passed recent fire, security, and warehouse inspections only six weeks before the fire. This meant that the risk to the respondents' goods was ordinary, not exceptional, such that no special warning was required.[173]

Two questions as to the bailee's standard of care arose in the case, which need to be sharply distinguished from one another. One was whether the bailee had breached its standard of care by not advising the bailors that the risk of damage to their stored goods by fire lay with them, or by not ensuring they knew this. The Court of Appeal found no breach in the case, which is not surprising, given that, in most bailments, there is no legal duty on the bailee to maintain insurance against loss of a bailor's goods. However, to avoid too sweeping a conclusion in this regard, it is submitted that industry practice should always be consulted, which may make insurance over the goods, or a bailee's advising of the lack of such insurance, a general requirement of the bailment. The second question was whether the measures the bailee had in place to protect the goods against loss by fire were adequate or constituted an "exceptional risk" that required the bailee to advise the bailor as to the lack of insurance in order to meet its standard of care. Again, here, the appeal court found in favour of the bailee, given that the bailee had passed recent fire, security, and warehouse inspections of its premises despite the lack of several safeguards. The appeal court's conclusion here seems to be maintainable only if the passing of the inspections meant that the bailee had met the standard set by industry practice. Equating the two seems to be a mistake, or too sweeping a rule, since industry practice may set a higher standard of care on a bailee than the one set by a particular municipality's laws.[174] Surely if the fire prevention measures themselves were less than those required by industry standards, a failure to warn the bailor as to the risk generated by this would have put the bailee in breach of its standard of care, in the absence of explicit consent by the bailors to run the risk.

173 *Ibid* at paras 11–14. As well, the cause of the fire was arson committed by an employee acting outside the scope of his employment. The court found that the employee's determined efforts would have likely overcome many, if not all, of the additional precautionary measures that could have been put into place, as suggested by the respondents. For example, the employee could have presumably shut off any fire alarm or smoke detection systems and any automatic fire suppression equipment: *ibid* at para 12. Thus, there was no causal relationship between the lack of precautionary measures and the loss at hand.

174 See *Falcon*, above note 147.

18) The Value of the Subject Property

a) The Need for Increased Security Measures

Where a bailor's property is unique, valuable, or special, and is more liable to theft, a bailee's standard of care will likely be increased. In *Lundrigan v Pierce*,[175] the plaintiff took his high-performance vehicle to the defendant's garage in an isolated area, in accordance with earlier discussions between the parties, to have body work and other work done to the vehicle. The defendant agreed to do the work immediately, but this did not occur, and the plaintiff's (bailor's) vehicle was left locked outside the garage on the defendant's lot for an extended period of time until the work on it could proceed, including overnight. During that time, parts were stolen off the plaintiff's engine and were never recovered. The engine, as it happens, could be (and was) accessed without the benefit of keys. The plaintiff assumed that his vehicle would be stored inside the defendant's garage during the period of the repair. The defendant did ask the plaintiff if his vehicle was insured and did not advise the plaintiff that vehicles were left at the risk of the owners. The plaintiff did not have insurance on the vehicle at the time it was damaged. The defendant testified that he relied on owners of vehicles to carry their own insurance coverage. The defendant further stated that thefts from his lot were relatively rare and that he had some minimal security precautions in place as a protection against theft.[176]

Justice Jones of the Nova Scotia Supreme Court Trial Division disposed of the liability question in the case quickly, finding that the leaving of a valuable and attractive vehicle on the lot in an isolated area for an extended period of time was negligent, as the likelihood of theft in these circumstances was readily foreseeable. The fact that the vehicle was *locked* was not enough for the defendant bailee to overcome its burden here. The vehicle should have been left inside the station and not on an open lot, or, alternatively, the defendant should have demanded that the plaintiff remove the vehicle from the lot until the work could be commenced and should not have left the vehicle on the lot for such an extended period of time. The defendant's failure to do either of these things made it liable as a bailee for reward to the plaintiff for his losses.[177] As was acknowledged

---

175 [1978] NSJ No 658 (SCTD).
176 *Ibid* at paras 1–9.
177 *Ibid* at paras 10–13.

in the court's reasons for decision,[178] it is not uncommon for bailees in the position of the defendant to leave bailors' vehicles locked outdoors on unenclosed lots awaiting repair. However, it is submitted that this practice should be avoided for valuable vehicles or vehicles with special equipment. Further, it is submitted that, if work on a bailor's vehicle can not begin for a prolonged period of time, then the bailor should be required to pick up the vehicle from the bailee's premises and bring it back when the work can be commenced, as leaving bailor's vehicles in exposed positions outside, especially overnight, can make bailees negligent should a theft or damage to the vehicle occur. Bailees can also reduce their exposure to liability in these situations by insisting that owners of vehicles that are left in locked positions outside of buildings on open lots awaiting repair carry their own insurance against theft and other possible losses and by warning them of the significant risks of not doing so.

b) Unsupervised Bailor Property

In *Tech-North Consulting Group Inc v British Columbia (Minister of Skills, Training and Labour)*,[179] the court found that the plaintiff bailee for reward's leaving of the plaintiff's computer case containing a laptop computer in plain view at the back of his car for fifteen minutes on a busy downtown street while he ran a personal errand breached his duty of reasonable care as bailee for reward to the defendant. In the result, the defendant was entitled to a set-off against money owed to the plaintiff for computer services rendered by the plaintiff but not paid for by the defendant, equal to the value of the computer and parts loss as a result of the plaintiff's failure to take reasonable care.

In *Bell*,[180] the defendants' failure to supervise the plaintiff's expensive artwork at all times, failure to provide an alarm system, and failure to provide a watchdog at all times to guard against theft resulted in liability being fixed against them when pieces of the plaintiff's artwork were stolen from the defendants' premises. Certainly the fact that the artwork being stored by the defendants in the case exceeded their insurance coverage, and was of greater value than all their other inventory combined, required them to apply a much higher degree of care than they did.

---

178 *Ibid* at para 9.

179 1997 CanLII 1797 at paras 16–17 (BCSC).

180 Above note 54.

c) The Need for Insurance on Valuable Bailed Goods Placed in Transit with Untried Third-Party Carriers

In sub-bailments, where valuable goods are placed in transit by a bailee with a third-party, untried carrier, there is an implied duty that a bailee will insure the goods against loss. An appropriate level of insurance should be placed on the goods by the bailee, ideally one that reflects the true value of the goods. Attributing a lesser value to the goods for insurance purposes, even where in line with industry practice, may not exonerate the bailee from liability where the goods are subsequently lost or damaged. Failing to place insurance cover at all on valuable goods left for transport with a third party will also make a bailee liable. The mere fact that a previous bailee in the chain of bailments failed to instruct a subsequent bailee on the need for such insurance will not exonerate a subsequent bailee who comes into possession of goods, where that bailee is clearly aware of the high value of the goods yet fails to ensure appropriate cover has been placed on the goods before transferring them into the possession of a third-party carrier with whom it has privity of contract but with whom it has had no previous dealings.[181] Such a practice would be inconsistent with a bailee's over-arching duty of safekeeping, which requires it to ensure that appropriate precautions are in place to protect the bailor's goods during the course of the bailment, including during the act of redelivery of the goods.

d) Need for a Bailee to Convey to Sub-bailees the Value and Nature of the Goods

Where goods are valuable or unique, there will be a clear requirement on bailees to advise sub-bailees of the valuable nature of the goods, upon their transfer, so that an appropriate level of care can be taken over the goods by the sub-bailee. A failure to do so can contribute to a finding that a bailee has failed to meet its standard of care.[182]

19) Industry Practice

Industry practice in the particular locale where the bailee operates its business is relevant to determining whether a bailee's standard of care has

181 See *Punch*, above note 26.
182 See *Duncan v Allen*, [1983] SJ No 759 at para 25 (QB).

been met in a specific circumstance. The theory is that no more should be expected from a bailee than the standard of care commonly employed by other bailees in the same industry, in the same area, and therefore reasonably expected of them by bailors. In *Hertz*,[183] the industry practice indicated that the defendant's actions in placing the plaintiff's locked automobile on its unenclosed lot for a short period of time while awaiting repair, together with the storage of its keys in a locked service building, were consistent with the minimal standards of care expected from a bailee in the circumstances in the industry. While the measures in place were not infallible to theft, nor were they the maximal measures that could be employed in the circumstances, this was not a bar to the bailee meeting its onus of proof, as the industry standard had been met. The fact that a few members in an industry might employ a higher general standard or a lower standard than the majority of others should not be enough to transform the standard of care on the bailee. Only reasonable standards that are practised by a majority of members of the industry should be enforceable against bailees, not the highest, or higher, standards being employed by members in that industry.

a) Appropriate Systems and Equipment

In *Babin's Distributing Co v Masco Enterprises Ltd*,[184] the plaintiff and defendant entered into an oral agreement whereby the defendant would receive deliveries of the plaintiff's canary seed (bought from various producers), would clean it to industrial standards, and would deliver it to the plaintiff's customers on the direction of the plaintiff and would store it if necessary, all for a charge. The importance of the defendant's following industry standards was key to it meeting its standard of care, since the plaintiff's customers could refuse to accept deliveries of seeds that were not properly cleaned. The plaintiff claimed a shortfall in excess of 231,000 pounds of seed, being the difference between what it delivered to the defendant (based on Canadian Grain Commission figures it had received)[185] and what the defendant delivered to the plaintiff's customers.

183 Above note 95.
184 [1985] SJ No 735 (QB).
185 These figures were based on samples from loads of seed delivered by various producers to the plaintiff and sent to the Canadian Grain Commission for analysis, where the seed was cleaned by the commission, but to different standards than that employed by the defendant and agreed upon by the parties. This resulted in different yields from the cleaning process: *ibid* at paras 10–18.

The plaintiff sued the defendant in bailment for the shortfall, leaving the defendant to disprove that its negligence had caused the loss.[186]

The defendant had recently purchased, and used, the latest, top-of-the-line, and most modern seed-cleaning equipment in North America, allowing it to meet the industry standards involved in commercial seed cleaning. This proved to be dispositive in the case. Justice Hrabinsky of the Saskatchewan Court of Queen's Bench found that the defendant had met its onus of disproving negligence: "On the basis of the defendant's evidence, I conclude that the equipment was properly operated and that the total amount in equalled the total amount out."[187]

The equipment had been used properly by the defendant, and had cleaned nothing else but canary seed since it was purchased. Justice Hrabinsky found, based on the evidence, that the Canadian Grain Commission figures were not reliable indicators of inputs and outputs, since they did not correspond with the actual amounts of pure sound canary seed produced by commercial cleaning. In short, the commission standards did not reflect the commercially prevalent standards.[188] This case indicates the importance that industry standards play in assessing a bailee's standard of care, including whether the bailee has redelivered the correct quantities of goods to the bailor, or to its customers or agents. Certainly no more should be expected of a bailee than what is required by industry standards, unless the bailee agrees to more in the bailment contract. The defendant had not agreed to be bound by Canadian Grain Commission figures and matrixes, and Hrabinsky J was accordingly right to have not held the defendant to them. Bailors who wish for bailees to meet heightened standards of care—that is, standards above and beyond those required by industry practice—must make that explicit in the bailment contract for those standards to prevail.

A lack of certain systems to protect against loss will not necessarily mean that the bailee has breached its standard of care, where such absence is consistent or in line with industry practice, even where such systems may have prevented the bailor's losses or lessened them. These additional precautions, if they are to exist in the bailment relationship, must be negotiated by the parties into the bailment contract. In

---

186 *Ibid* at paras 1–7.
187 *Ibid* at para 23.
188 *Ibid* at paras 10–18.

Mochinski v North American Van Lines (Canada) Ltd,[189] warehouse facilities not equipped with a sprinkler system were not necessarily in breach of bailee obligations, since the industry practice in the geographical locale indicated that many warehouses were similarly ill equipped.

b) Specific Actions and Procedures

Sometimes industry practice will require the bailee to perform a very specific action, or to follow a very specific procedure meticulously and fully in order to discharge its standard of care in the particular circumstances in which the duty arises. In *Bowker v Coquihalla Towing Co*,[190] the defendant (bailee) towing company arrived at the scene of an accident and was tasked with removing, safely, a damaged tractor-trailer that was no longer road worthy. The vehicle was sitting on its side in a ditch in foul weather. The steps taken by the defendant employees, using two tow trucks, caused the trailer to fall back into the ditch and to sustain further damage above and beyond what it had already sustained, including to its cargo.[191]

Not surprisingly, Saunders J of the British Columbia Supreme Court focused on the appropriateness of the manoeuvre that had been attempted, albeit unsuccessfully, by the defendant tow truck drivers in using recovery lines and two tow trucks to extricate the trailer, in its current state, from the ditch. The question was whether this action was in line with what a reasonably prudent person in the towing industry would have done in the circumstances. The learned judge, based on the evidentiary record before the court, found that the recovery lines had not been used correctly, that the "perpendicular tension" that had been applied by the defendant employees using their pulley systems had been applied to the wrong areas of the trailer, and that the recovery lines themselves may have been improperly located. In the result, the defendant was found liable as bailee to the plaintiff for the additional damage caused to the trailer.[192] As apparent, industry standards must be followed even where they require complex manoeuvres from a bailee, where such manoeuvres are practised by experienced and qualified members of the trade. Where the manoeuvre is overly complex, or particularly risky, even where performed by experienced persons, it

189 [1977] BCJ No 926 (SC) [*Mochinski*].
190 [1998] BCJ No 1072 (SC).
191 *Ibid* at paras 1–2 and 17–18.
192 *Ibid* at paras 31–36.

is wise that bailors and bailees negotiate the risk rather than leave it to chance to be determined by the common law.

20) Temporary Lapses in Judgment

When, during the course of the bailment, a bailee makes a temporary lapse in judgment that any reasonable bailor could have made in dealing with its own property and that lapse results in losses to the bailor, the bailee may escape liability. In *Gavin v Douglas Securities Ltd*,[193] the plaintiff's (bailor's) car was seized by a bailiff acting for a finance company under the terms of a conditional sales agreement, which company was an assignee for value under the agreement and seeking to realize on its security. The vehicle was ultimately transferred into the possession of the defendant towing company for storage for the period of redemption. The towing company received the keys to the vehicle and the vehicle from the plaintiff in an immobile condition, with specific instructions from the plaintiff that the vehicle was to be kept inside a garage with the keys removed. The towing company adhered to these instructions dutifully. Indeed, it exceeded them, parking the vehicle tightly between two vehicles in its parking garage such that a person could not get into the plaintiff's vehicle and drive it away.[194]

The garage was accessible only by a door at the side of the towing company's dispatch office, fronting onto the street. If a person could make it past the office, there was a stairwell leading down into the garage where they would not be heard by those in the dispatch office. A dispatcher was on duty twenty-four hours a day. During the material times when the plaintiff's vehicle was on the premises (that is, from 4:00 PM to 12:00 AM and 12:00 AM to 8:00 AM, over the two dates in question), two dispatchers were on duty. They both stated that they had not left their post at any time during their respective shifts and had not heard or observed anything untoward occurring. Certainly they had not observed a stranger walk by them and make their way down to the parking garage. Nonetheless, the plaintiff's vehicle was stolen from the premises and later found in a damaged condition, with the plaintiff's tools missing. One of the dispatchers, in their evidence, had conceded that, if a dispatcher was on the phone or the radio, a person might be able to get past them and down

193 [1958] BCJ No 12 (SC).
194 *Ibid* at paras 3–4.

the stairs into the garage to steal the vehicle. There was evidence in the record that indicated that employees and drivers would walk past the dispatch office and that, perhaps, a noise or disturbance that would have been occasioned by a stranger in walking past the office might have gone unnoticed by the dispatchers.[195] The towing company could not explain (exactly) how, or when, the plaintiff's vehicle was stolen, which the plaintiff argued meant that the defendant could not disprove negligence as bailee to exonerate itself from liability.[196]

Based on the evidence heard, taking the car out required the thief, or thieves, to have undone some bolts inside the parking garage to gain access to the outside, and to have taken great time and effort to remove the immobile vehicle from the garage (and to have been quite gutsy and determined in walking past the dispatcher office). In these circumstances, McInnes J of the British Columbia Supreme Court was unwilling to find the defendants liable under bailment law, since a dispatcher of the towing company had, at most, made a "temporary lapse" in judgment in permitting a stranger, or strangers, to walk past them and gain access to the garage where the plaintiff's motor vehicle was located and then leave undetected, such as any prudent person could do while safeguarding their own property: "At best if there was a lapse of duty it was a mere temporary lapse and one that anyone safeguarding his own property might quite reasonably and conceivably be guilty of and I do not consider it to be sufficient to come within the rule so as to render the defendants liable."[197]

As can be seen, bailees do not owe a standard of perfection to bailors. Mistakes, including temporary lapses of duty, happen and *do not* necessarily indicate that due care of goods has not been taken by the bailee, even if a bailor has incurred losses arising therefrom. This may be the case even if a bailee is not able to account precisely for the disappearance of the goods. Still, it is submitted that the system of security otherwise present must itself be reasonable in order for a bailee to escape liability based on temporary lapses of judgment. Justice McInnes's decision presupposes that the defendants' system in place for safeguarding the plaintiff's vehicle — which

195 While the defendants raised the possibility that perhaps a break-in had occurred from the outside, by a third party who had broken the door down resulting in the theft of the plaintiff's vehicle, this was mere conjecture, with no support in the evidentiary record and was dismissed by the learned judge out of hand: *ibid* at para 12.

196 *Ibid* at paras 4–9 and 12.

197 *Ibid* at para 12.

relied on dispatchers stopping strangers or suspicious individuals who, once inside the premises, if they could get past a "distracted" dispatcher sitting in the dispatcher office, could proceed unimpeded to a stairwell leading to the parking garage where the vehicles stored therein would be highly vulnerable to theft—was, itself, a reasonable system of security, based on industry standards. It also presupposes that the happening of theft itself did not bespeak negligence on the part of the defendant bailee. This does not seem at all self-evident and probably should have been the subject of commentary by the court.

21) Unavoidable Accidents

Not all accidents that result in damage to bailed property mean that a bailee has been negligent or has failed to meet its standard of care. Some accidents are unavoidable, or may occur even where reasonable care has been exercised by the bailee over the bailor's goods at all material times. Sometimes an accident may be due to faulty equipment or very hazardous conditions that the bailee finds itself operating in, with the explicit or implicit consent of the bailor. Or it may be the result of an unknown third party with whom the bailee comes into contact and who is acting recklessly and negligently while the bailee is carrying out its duties. In these circumstances, bailees should be able to exonerate themselves from liability. However, where the evidence shows that, if the bailee had used proper care, then the accident in the "ordinary course of things" could have been avoided, liability against the bailee should follow.[198]

In *Chief Construction Co v McDonald*,[199] the defendant (bailee), a private carrier for the plaintiff, was using a tractor to transport molten sulphur in trailers for the plaintiff when an accident occurred. Specifically, the tractor being driven by the defendant employee overturned and went off the road, resulting in substantial damage to the trailers and the loss of the molten sulphur being transported. The accident was found to be solely the result of passenger-type vehicle having come around a blind curve in a road (with an uneven grade) with one half-width of the vehicle over the centre line (on the defendant driver's side of the road), forcing the defendant driver to swerve quickly to the right to avoid a collision.

198 See *Tobin Tractor*, above note 159 at para 14.
199 1987 CanLII 3337 (Alta QB).

The driver was unable to identify the other driver. The tractor driver's credentials were impeccable and he was found not to have ingested drugs or alcohol on the day of the accident or to have driven negligently at any of the material times. Most pertinently, the driver was not found to have sped or driven too closely to the centre line in the road. Nor were the weather conditions harsh, requiring the driver to exercise extreme caution when driving or not drive at all. Accordingly, Stratton J exonerated the defendant from liability as a bailee for reward for the accident:

> I have concluded that the accident occurred through the actions of the unknown driver who was proceeding at the critical time to the left of the centre of the road. Having been confronted with that situation, McDonald's reaction was not negligent. His failure to react as he did, namely, by swerving quickly and sharply to the right, could well have resulted in a collision with potential loss of life and substantially greater property damage.[200]

As apparent, bailees cannot prevent all damage to bailed property at all times. Bailee drivers who do not make an error of judgment but who happen upon a third party who is breaking the law, such as driving over the centre line of a road, instead of on the proper side of the highway, especially where the road is of a winding and uneven nature, must make a quick decision to minimize losses involved in an unavoidable accident. As long as that decision is reasonable, bailees should be exonerated from liability for damage done to the bailed property.

22) Deviance from a Bailment Contract

Where a bailee deviates from the bailment contract[201] and harm is done to the bailor's property, the bailee will be strictly liable. The applicable law was well described in the English authorities by Grove J in *Lilley v Doubleday*, as follows: "If a bailee elects to deal with the property entrusted to him in a way not authorized by the bailor, he takes upon himself the risks

---

200 *Ibid* at para 35.

201 There are many bailments where the bailee is entitled to make a sub-bailment, either expressly or impliedly under the contract of bailment. The repairer of a motor vehicle, for example, is often authorized to send away a part of it to another business for repairs: *DW Pellant and Associates Ltd v Resnick's Automotive Specialties Ltd*, [1986] BCJ No 726 at para 24 (Co Ct) [*Pellant*].

of so doing, except where the risk is independent of his acts and inherent in the property itself."[202]

a) Clear Departures from the Bailment Contract Without Bailor Consent

In *Blumenthal v Tidewater Automotive Industries Ltd*,[203] the respondent brought his vehicle to the appellant's shop on a Thursday to have some rustproofing repair work done on it and left it at the appellant's premises together with a set of keys to the vehicle. The respondent had instructed the appellant to keep the car inside, and the appellant had agreed to do so. When the respondent contacted the appellant on the following Monday, as he said he would do, to find out whether the work had been completed, he was told that his vehicle was missing from where it had been left following its servicing on the Friday, namely, outside the appellant's shop in a paved parking area. The appellant had not, in fact, kept the respondent's vehicle inside as promised. The appellant testified that, when he did not notice the respondent's vehicle in the lot upon his return to the garage on Monday, he had assumed that the respondent had come and picked up the vehicle from the parking area. He also testified that cars were customarily left outside so that customers could come and pick them up for their own use over the weekend.[204]

The trial judge in the case rejected out of hand the appellant's evidence that the respondent or his wife had contacted him on the Friday asking that the vehicle be left outside, presumably so that it could be used by the respondent over the weekend, and found that no such communication had ever been conveyed. The trial judge, accordingly, found the appellant to be strictly liable on the bailment for breaching the term of the bailment, which required the appellant to keep the respondent's vehicle inside his building at all times. On appeal, Cooper JA upheld the trial judge's decision in all respects,[205] summarizing the act of deviance as follows: "The appellant dealt with the respondent's motor vehicle 'in a manner not authorised' by leaving it outside instead of putting it inside his building and therefore is liable for the loss of the car and its contents."[206]

---

202 *Lilley v Doubleday* (1881), 7 QBD 510 as quoted in *Pellant*, above note 201 at para 23.
203 [1978] NSJ No 620 (SCAD) [*Blumenthal*].
204 *Ibid* at paras 1–5.
205 *Ibid* at paras 5–8.
206 *Ibid* at para 8.

Justice Cooper of the Court of Appeal was right to have affirmed the trial judge's decision in this case. Bailees must abide by the terms of the bailment in order to discharge their standard of care. Serious departures, as occurred in *Blumenthal*, will make a bailee strictly liable for the loss of bailor property, including the contents thereof, at least where there is a causal connection between the departure and the loss. However, it is submitted, consistent with other discussion, that the bailee be held liable for the loss only of contents that it had actual or constructive notice of, and not all contents.

b) A Question of Deviation Must Always Be Assessed with Reference to the Terms of the Bailment Contract in Existence at the Time of the Loss of the Bailed Goods

Whether a deviation has occurred is, of course, related to the bailment contract, which can fluctuate and change over time. A deviation will not have occurred where the bailee deals with the bailor property in a way not permitted under the original bailment contract but in accordance with modifications made thereto subsequently, after the commencement of the bailment, on the agreement of the parties. In *Mochinski*,[207] the plaintiff stored his furniture and other household effects with the defendant companies while he was engaged in a project for his employer in the Philippines. The storage was done pursuant to an ongoing arrangement that his employer had with the defendants for the storage of its employees' goods while they were engaged in projects in various parts of the world. Before entering into the arrangement, the employer had verified that the condition of the premises where the goods would be stored was satisfactory. The employee's goods would be stored in a relatively new building with a complete sprinkler system. Upon a visit by the defendants' representative to the plaintiff's residence, the plaintiff was assured that the goods that he had expressed concern about would be safe. The plaintiff did not discuss specifically with the representative the particulars of the arrangement, including the location of the warehouse where his goods would be housed or the details of the insurance coverage. These things the plaintiff left to be worked out by his employer, who dealt directly with the defendants with respect to the storage arrangements. As it happened,

207 Above note 189.

the goods were significantly undervalued for insurance purposes by the plaintiff's employer who operated under a policy of minimum coverage.[208]

During the course of the storage, the defendants sought the permission of the plaintiff's employer to relocate all the employee's goods to a relatively new warehouse complex. This complex did not have a sprinkler system. The employer consented to the new storage arrangements without examining the new proposed warehouse, unlike at the outset of the arrangement with the defendants, stating that so long as "it was good storage," the relocation of the goods was fine. The plaintiff's employer later formally accepted the relocation in writing. The plaintiff's property was accordingly moved following the initial approval, without his knowledge, and was later destroyed by fire without any particular negligence on the part of the defendants. Indeed, the cause of the fire could not be established.[209]

Since the warehouse used by the defendants was found to be up to the standard required by industry practice (the majority of buildings used for the warehousing of household effects in Canada were not sprinkler-equipped), to have been in accordance with the national building code for federal government-approved buildings, was approved by the fire department of the district of the province in which it was located, and was of fire-resistant construction, the only pertinent question left for determination with respect to the standard of care analysis was whether the defendants had deviated from the terms of the bailment in relocating the goods such that they should be held strictly liable.[210] Justice McKay of the British Columbia Supreme Court found that they had not. The judge found that the employer, as an authorized agent of the plaintiff, had expressly and formally accepted the new storage arrangement proposed by the defendant: "This is not a case of the warehouseman agreeing to store the goods at a certain place and then moving them elsewhere without authority. Commonwealth [the employer], as the authorized agent of the plaintiff, expressly agreed to the move."[211]

As apparent, a bailment is not frozen in time, and its terms can be changed by the parties, or their authorized agents, on consent, as occurred

---

208 *Ibid* at paras 1–10.
209 *Ibid* at paras 8–9.
210 *Ibid* at paras 13–16.
211 *Ibid* at para 18. For an example of deviance in this context, see *Van Dorne v North American Van Lines (Canada) Ltd* (1977), 79 DLR (3d) 42 (BCSC).

in the case. The question of deviation must always be answered with reference to the terms of the bailment in existence at the time the purported act of departure from the bailment contract occurred, and not before or afterwards.[212] Certainly, material misrepresentations by a bailee that induce a bailor to agree to a change of terms of a bailment relationship, such as advising a bailor that a warehouse into which its goods are being moved is sprinkler-equipped when in fact it is not (to the knowledge of the bailee), should be enough to disqualify a bailor's consent to the change, such that a bailee should be held strictly liable for any losses to bailor property occurring thereafter in the new facilities.

c) A Bailee Must Have Received Express or Implied Authorization from a Bailor to Deal with Goods as It Has

A bailee must show that it was authorized to deal with the bailor property in the way it did pursuant to the bailment contract. There must be either an express or implied authorization[213] given by the bailor for the act carried out by the bailee that is said to be in deviation from the bailment contract. Where there is neither, the bailee will be strictly liable for the bailor's losses. In *Pellant*,[214] the plaintiff had taken his high-end vehicle to the defendant's workshop numerous times over several months to have modification work done to it to significantly increase the car's power and speed.[215] On the particular occasion in question, the plaintiff left his vehicle with the defendant shop for a tune-up while he travelled out of town on business. The defendant agreed that the plaintiff could leave his vehicle on the defendant's premises overnight, which were proximate to the airport, as he had done many times in the past. The plaintiff departed for his trip. However, unlike past times, the shop was full and could not

---

212 For a further example, see *Bowes v Super-Service Stations Ltd*, [1955] NSJ No 17 (SC).

213 In *Cook and Jones Motors Limited v Walsh*, [1983] NJ No 188 (Dist Ct), since the plaintiff (bailor) car dealership had not placed any restrictions on the use by the defendant bailee Walsh (the father) of the loaner vehicle given to him, he was not in deviation of the bailment contract when he lent the vehicle to his son while his son's vehicle was in the plaintiff's shop for repair. This was the case even though the defendant sub-bailee Walsh (the son) had previously been refused use of such a car by the plaintiff. The defendant bailee Walsh (the father) had essentially received an implied consent from the plaintiff to allow members of his family to occasionally drive the loaner car, in accordance with the instructions he had received from the plaintiff: see paras 73–74.

214 Above note 201.

215 *Ibid* at paras 1–18.

accommodate the defendant's vehicle. The defendant did not think a location outside of the shop would be safe, and so he asked the father of one of his employees, who lived in a neighbourhood nearby, on a quiet cul-de-sac, to transport the car there and park it on the street in front of his house.[216]

As it happened, during the night a drunk driver collided with the vehicle and damaged it. The plaintiff's losses were only partially covered by his company's automobile insurance policy, and so he sought the remaining compensation for the balance of his losses from the defendant. The key question for determination was whether the defendant had dealt with the vehicle in an unauthorized fashion such that he should be held strictly liable for the plaintiff's losses. Justice Hutchinson of the British Columbia County Court could find no express or implied authorization to move the vehicle to the new location. The defendant had not advised the plaintiff, prior to his departure for the airport, that the defendant had insufficient space in his shop to store the plaintiff's vehicle there overnight. Therefore, there was no express authorization for the defendant's actions. There was no implied authorization either, because on none of the previous occasions had the defendant stored the plaintiff's vehicle in the same or similar fashion or advised the plaintiff of the possibility that, if the shop were full, the vehicle might have to be parked on a nearby street for safekeeping. Thus, the defendant was found liable for its deviant act and ordered to pay the plaintiff damages representing his uninsured losses.[217]

As apparent, there is a need for bailees in these circumstances to seek authorization from a bailor prior to committing to a course of conduct with respect to bailor property that has not been impliedly or expressly authorized by the bailor. Where the bailee seeks to deal with the bailor's property in a new way that is not contemplated by the contract of bailment, the bailee should seek the bailor's express approval before proceeding, based on a consideration of both the parties' past dealings with each other as well as the terms of the agreement.

d) Where the Bailment Is to Be Performed Personally, a Sub-bailment Will Amount to an Act of Deviation by the Bailee

Where goods are left with a bailee to be worked on, or stored, "personally" by them, then any sub-bailment of those goods to a third party would

216 *Ibid* at paras 19.

217 *Ibid* at paras 19–26.

amount to a fundamental breach of the bailment contract and a clear breach of the standard of care owed by the bailee.[218] However, context and the intention and expectations of the parties will always matter: an implied authorization, in addition to an express authorization, can make a sub-bailment authorized such that no requirement of personal service can be viewed as applying to the underlying bailment relationship between bailor and bailee. In *Banks v Dennis*,[219] an expensive fur jacket had been left with the defendant bailee personally for an appraisal for insurance purposes and thereafter for storage purposes. However, since the bailee *did not* have cold storage facilities of his own, to the knowledge of the plaintiff (bailor), it was implied that the bailee could sub-bail the jacket to complete the latter purpose of the bailment. This was not viewed as a deviation from the contract of bailment when the jacket was subsequently lost during the sub-bailment, which indicates that a bailment may require personal service for one purpose but not for another. Thus, when assessing deviation from a bailment contract, the actions of the bailee will always need to be measured against the different purposes of the bailment, which may or may not authorize different actions to be taken by the bailee, including a sub-bailing of the goods.

23) Remedial Security Measures Taken by a Bailee After the Fact of Loss or Damage of Bailor Property

Increased security measures and other remedial measures taken by bailees for reward after bailor property is lost or damaged will be relevant to the question of whether a bailee has met its standard of care. However, improved measures taken after the fact will not always mean that a bailee did not meet its applicable standard of care at the material times. In *Hertz*,[220] the theft of the plaintiff's vehicle from the defendant's premises after hours occurred despite the defendant car dealer's quite reasonable precautions in place to prevent against such an occurrence, including securing vehicles parked on its unenclosed lot and locking the keys to those vehicles in a locked building while they awaited servicing. Although the break-in led the defendant to implement new and improved security

218 See *Banks v Dennis*, [1956] OJ No 621 especially at para 10 (HC).
219 *Ibid* at paras 13–15.
220 Above note 95.

measures,[221] the court found the security measures that the defendant had in place at the material times to have been sufficient to meet its standard of care.

However, in *Robertson*,[222] the opposite result obtained. There, the improved measures, namely the installation of metal plates onto the doors to the storage areas to more effectively prevent people from overcoming the locks, helped illustrate the great inadequacy of the defendant bailees' previous security measures in place to protect the plaintiff's (bailor's) goods, leading to a finding that the defendants had breached their duty of care to the plaintiff. Doors to storage areas could be easily opened with a screwdriver at some of the material times, which made theft of the plaintiff's goods "reasonably foreseeable," making the defence of *novus actus interveniens* unavailable to the defendants.

24) Terms of the Bailment Contract

In a bailment, a written contract is relevant only to the extent that it contains terms, implied or express, that depart from the bailment relationship and its ordinary obligations and rules as established by the common law. Otherwise these rules, by default, will apply. For instance, a contract may increase a bailee's standard of care to the standard of perfection or to a higher standard than the one that the bailee would otherwise face under bailment law principles, being reasonable care in all the circumstances.[223] In *Edwards on Bailments*,[224] the applicable law is well set out:

> The bailee may bind himself by an express contract for the absolute return of the property in as good a condition as it was when he received it. He may assume a greater obligation than the law would impose upon him under the circumstances; that is to say, the law will enforce against him the very terms of his contract, in their fair meaning.

---

221 While these are not enumerated in the case, it is likely that they included the security measures that were lacking in the case, namely an alarm system, securing keys to vehicles in a safe in a locked building on the defendant's premises, and perhaps blocking the driveway giving access to the front lot of the premises to prevent or inhibit thefts of vehicles parked thereon.

222 Above note 65 at paras 14, 18, 70, and 90.

223 *Marine Construction Ltd v Metro Engineering and Construction Ltd*, [1978] NJ No 146 at para 29 (SCTD).

224 3d ed, s 380, as cited in *Grant v Armour*, [1894] OJ No 99 at para 21 (HCJ) [*Grant*].

In *Grant v Armour*,[225] during the course of the bailment, a pile driver and a scow hired out by the defendants were washed away and sunk in a violent storm, of almost hurricane-like proportions. The defendants, by contract, had put themselves under an absolute obligation to return the goods to the plaintiff, save for wear and tear, which they could not do. Thus, they were liable to the plaintiff, irrespective of the impossibility of redelivery of the property because of the intervening storm. In other words, absolute liability can be placed on a bailee by contract, meaning that a failure to return goods to a bailor in the same condition as they were received will result in liability,[226] irrespective of acts of God or occurrences of *novus actus interveniens*. A finding of no negligence will not be enough to save a bailee in these circumstances, since a bailee in these circumstances owes a bailor a standard of perfection.

Conversely, a contract of bailment may reserve some aspects of the duty of care to the bailor, which means that the bailee will not be answerable for not carrying them out. In *JD Irving Ltd v Mojan Ltée*,[227] the terms of the contract of bailment involving the hiring out of a crane indicated, among other things, that the plaintiff (bailor) was responsible for supplying the defendant (bailee) with an experienced crane operator who could follow the general directions of the defendant foreman; providing the defendant with a competent oiler for the crane; levelling the crane for use; delivering the crane to the site; and warming up the crane for it to operate at functional capacity. Thus, the defendant (bailee), in discharging its onus, did not have to disprove negligence in these areas.

A bailment contract between parties may also only *partially*, rather than exclusively, govern a bailment relationship between the parties, meaning that there will be room for the default regime at common law to operate. This may be because the contract is under-inclusive, in that it addresses only certain aspects of the bailment relationship but not others, or because the contract is transaction- or date-specific, applying only to certain bailment transactions and events between the parties but not to others.[228]

---

225 *Grant*, above note 224.

226 See *Insurance Co of North America v Redi-Rentals Ltd*, [1975] AJ No 138 at para 11 (Dist Ct).

227 [1983] NBJ No 386 at paras 35–36 (QBTD).

228 See, for example, *Halbauer v Brighton Corp*, [1954] 2 All ER 707, as cited in *British Motor*, above note 107.

C. CONCLUSION

The question of whether a bailee has met its standard of care depends on consideration of a number of factors as well as the type of bailment under consideration. Some of the factors will be dispositive of bailee liability. For example, where a bailee breaches applicable law or regulations governing the bailment, or deviates from important terms of the bailment contract, a breach of the standard of care will usually be easily made out, and the bailee will be liable to the bailor in damages. However, there will be closer calls. Many cases will require context to be looked at very closely, including the industry practices prevailing in the locale in which the bailment arises, before any decision on liability can be made. The nature and value of the bailment will be relevant too. Where the value of the bailed goods is high, or the bailee is using dangerous substances or equipment around bailed goods, a heightened degree of care will be expected of the bailee. For example, a bailee may need to store an expensive, or particularly attractive, vehicle inside a locked building rather than outside on an unenclosed lot. While provision of insurance will not generally be required of a bailee, it will be required in certain circumstances, such as where a bailee puts valuable bailor goods in transit for transport to another location by an untried third-party carrier.[229] A failure to provide insurance in such a case should make a bailee liable where the goods are damaged or lost during the course of the bailment. Lastly, a standard of perfection should never be applied against a bailee unless it is clearly required by a term in the bailment contract.

229 *Punch*, above note 26.

CHAPTER 6

Bailee Defences and Limitations on Bailee Liability

A. INTRODUCTION

A plaintiff's (bailor's) right to recover damages from the bailee may sometimes be taken away or reduced, even if the bailor is able to prove a bailment and shift the onus of proof onto the bailee. For example, the bailed goods themselves may contain a latent defect that ends up destroying the goods or other bailed goods with which they are stored, or the bailor may have voluntarily assumed certain risks upon the commencement of the bailment, which risks then manifest themselves into injuries to bailor goods or property. In all such cases, the bailee may be completely or partially exonerated. Yet the defence of contributory negligence arising in a bailment action will constitute only a partial defence, meaning that the bailee will only have its liability to pay damages to a bailor reduced by a certain percentage as a result of the plaintiff's (bailor's) negligent actions, or lack of reasonable care, taken in respect of its own goods.

B. LIMITATION PERIODS

1) Statutory Overlay

The question of limitation periods in a bailment action specifically arose for consideration in *Sobota v Kleider*[1] in the British Columbia Supreme Court. The action was brought by the plaintiff for the loss of his horse

1 *Sobota v Kleider*, [1986] BCJ No 2059 (SC) [*Sobota*].

while in the custody of the defendant (veterinarian). The action had been brought two years and two months after the date of loss. The applicable rules in the *Limitation Act*[2] in effect in British Columbia at the time were contained in sections 3(1)(a) and (4), which read as follows:

> 3. (1) After the expiration of 2 years after the date on which the right to do so arose a person shall not bring an action
>
> (a) for damages in respect of injury to person or property, including economic loss arising from the injury, whether based on contract, tort or statutory duty; . . .
>
> (4) Any other action not specifically provided for in this Act or any other Act shall not be brought after the expiration of 6 years after the date on which the right to do so arose.

Not surprisingly, the plaintiff (bailor) in the case, wishing to preserve his action against expiry, argued that, since bailment was *not* a transaction in the realm of contract, tort, or statutory duty, he should receive the benefit of section 3(4) of the Act, a six-year limitation period, and that section 3(1)(a) should *not* apply. While not dismissing the notion that a bailment is *sui generis* and does not neatly sound in either tort, contract, or statutory duty, Macdonell J concluded that the bailment action, which was based on breaches of common law duties rather than contractual ones, fell into the category of tort, as it was not a class of wrong that clearly fell outside the ambit of tort law, such as a civil wrong based solely on breach of contract or some other equitable obligation.[3] "Whether that tort is simple negligence, detinue, conversion, or a specialized tort of breach of bailment, it is caught by s. 3(1)(a) of the *Limitation Act*."[4] In the result, the plaintiff's action was found to be barred by statute.[5]

If a bailment is truly *sui generis*, it is not clear why this is the result that should have obtained. Little, if any, authority exists for the proposition that a bailment represents nothing more than a "specialized tort." For one thing, it reverses the ordinary onus of proof otherwise applicable to negligence actions and is much broader and elaborate than can be captured by either the torts of conversion or detinue. It also can, and does, exist independent of contract. It follows that a bailment does not

---

2 RSBC 1979, c 236.

3 *Sobota*, above note 1 at paras 1–12 [paragraph numbers assigned by author].

4 *Ibid* at para 12.

5 *Ibid* at paras 13–14.

neatly, or properly, fit into contract, tort, or statutory duty, even though it may originate from, or overlap with, one or all of these categories of law in a given set of circumstances. If this is so, then it seems that the plaintiff's argument in *Sobota* should have carried the day and that section 3(4) should have prevailed, extending the limitation to six years and thus preserving the plaintiff's bailment action from expiry.[6]

Curiously, the *Limitations Act, 2002*[7] currently in force in Ontario contains a very open-ended general limitation period of two years (see section 4). This avoids the difficulties involved in precisely characterizing the nature of a bailment transaction for the purposes of determining an applicable limitation period, an issue that plagued the court in *Sobota*. It presumably captures bailment actions, since it captures all claims in relation to "injury, loss, or damage" and *does not* specifically exempt bailment actions in any of the categories mentioned in either section 2, which explicitly deals with the applicability of section 4,[8] or section 16,[9] which eliminates limitation periods for specific kinds of proceedings. As for the ultimate limitation period of fifteen years set out in section 15 of the Ontario Act, it does not appear to have any application to bailment actions, except perhaps in the case of an involuntary bailment, where a bailee might be able to rely on it to save itself where it chooses to abandon bailed goods before it is relieved of its duty of safekeeping by a bailor who collects them, since section 15 is not made subject to a discovery principle (unlike section 4).

2) Involuntary Bailments

"Involuntary bailments,"[10] which have occasionally been recognized in the caselaw, are another area that may pose difficulty for limitation laws.

---

6 Section 3(4) has been held to include claims for return of property, or damages for breach of a consignment agreement, as well as breach of fiduciary duty: *Hamilton v Lepin*, 2005 BCSC 1824 at paras 15–17; *Seibold Holdings Ltd v Wilson & Kofoed Ltd* (1990), 45 CCLI 253 (BCSC). Given that a claim for return of property can be a claim in detinue, and detinue can be a species of bailment (see *Kinsella v Club "7" Ltd*, [1993] NJ No 365 (SCTD) [*Kinsella*]), it is not clear why bailments could not fall within s 3(4) based on the aforementioned caselaw.

7 SO 2002, c 24, Schedule B.

8 For example, s 2(1)(a) states that s 4 does not apply to "proceedings to which the *Real Property Limitations Act* applies."

9 For example, s 16(1)(a) states that no limitation period under the Act applies in the case of "a proceeding for a declaration if no consequential relief is sought."

10 Although the term "involuntary bailments" is a misnomer, since it implies the lack of a key ingredient of a bailment, namely, voluntariness, some courts have nonetheless

Since a defendant (bailee) may not be able to make a plaintiff (bailor) aware of its losses arising from an involuntary bailment at the time that they arise, as the whereabouts of the bailor may not be known, at least one judge[11] has identified the serious concern that a bailee in such circumstances may not be able to avail itself of a limitation period subject to a discovery principle. Such a situation would lead to the absurd result that an involuntary bailee or gratuitous bailee (at common law) may owe greater standards of care than bailees for reward, including under some of the applicable provincial statutes dealing with warehousing of goods. In Ontario, there may be an escape route for involuntary and gratuitous bailees by using section 15 of the *Limitations Act*.

3) Discovery Principle

In *Rose v Fishery Products International Ltd*,[12] the question of when a bailment action should be discovered by a plaintiff for limitation purposes was front and centre before the Supreme Court of Newfoundland and Labrador Trial Division (General), albeit by way of application for summary judgment brought by the defendant to have the plaintiff's action dismissed as being outside the time permitted by the applicable limitations act.[13] There, the plaintiffs had purchased a large seine (fishing net) in 1992 and received the permission of the defendant to store it for them gratuitously that year, until they needed it and sought delivery of it. The seine was first placed at the defendant's plant at Port Union and then transferred to its facility at Burin after 1998. Before the property went to Burin, the plaintiffs had checked on the condition of the seine on several occasions and been told that it was in fine condition. According to the plaintiffs, they first learned that the seine was missing in 2003, when they say they sought its collection from the defendant for use, after the conditions of the fishing industry changed, causing the plaintiffs to re-evaluate their mode of fishing. That is when they actually made a demand for redelivery

---

been willing to recognize the existence of such bailments: *Duet Marketing Corp v Spetifore*, [1986] BCJ No 3173 (SC); *Martin v Stephens*, 2002 BCPC 196 [*Martin*]; *Landry v Grunwald*, [1986] BCJ No 1889 (SC); *Whash v Chigani*, [2012] OJ No 3329 (SCJ Sm Cl Ct).

11 See reasons of Romilly Prov Ct J in *Martin*, above note 10, especially at paras 43–47.

12 [2016] NJ No 106 (SCTD) [*Rose*].

13 The parties agreed, however, that, if the limitations issue were resolved in favour of the plaintiffs, then liability by the defendant was admitted and the only issue left for determination was assessment of damages: *ibid* at para 74.

of the property. They were told it was *not available* and knew that the defendant had lost the seine and that it could not be returned.[14]

There was conflicting evidence before the court indicating that the plaintiffs may have learned that their property was missing, or that there was a problem with it, much earlier in time, that is, before 2001, perhaps in 1998. One defendant employee testified that, before he left the employ of the defendant company in 2001, he had told one of the plaintiffs that the seine could not be located. But the witness was not able to say *definitively* that he told the plaintiff that the company did not have the property in its possession. Another witness's evidence, upon which the court placed more importance, indicated that the seine had been at the Burin location for anywhere between five and seven years before it went missing.[15]

Based on the totality of the evidence, Faour J of the Supreme Court of Newfoundland and Labrador Trial Division (General) accepted that the seine had been at Burin for five or six years and that the cause of action had not crystallized until 2003, when the plaintiffs indicated that they had first made a demand for the seine. The learned judge rejected the defendant's alternate argument, that the limitation period should start earlier in time when the plaintiff may have learned about a possible breach of the defendant's duty of safekeeping, since there was no evidence of conversion, which might trigger a limitation period, but only evidence that the defendant had failed to redeliver when called upon to do so. This made the action *only* actionable in detinue, which required a demand for the property to be made by the plaintiffs (bailor) and a failure to deliver up by the defendant before the cause of action arose. Mere knowledge of a possible loss not being enough, without more, to trigger a limitation period with regards to a bailment action.[16] In any event, Faour J buttressed his legal conclusion by pointing to the lack of certainty in the information that may have been conveyed to the plaintiffs earlier in time: they were told that the property held by the defendant could not be found, not that the defendant did not have it in its possession.[17]

---

14 *Ibid* at paras 11–19.

15 *Ibid* at paras 20–43.

16 *Ibid* at paras 48–55. Presumably, had the plaintiff learned in the late 1990s that the seine had fallen victim to conversion, then the bailment action would have been time barred, since the Newfoundland and Labrador *Limitations Act*, SNL 1995, c L-16.1 set a six-year limitation period for damages for conversion: *Rose*, above note 12 at para 68.

17 The limitation period of ten years applicable to trust actions in the province was properly found not to be applicable, since a bailment is not a trust and is legally

Accordingly, since the bailment action was commenced in 2008, and the limitation period applicable to actions for damages in detinue, or for recovery of goods, was six years, the action *was not time-barred*, and the plaintiffs' action could succeed.

While it is true that a demand for goods and a concomitant failure to deliver them up can trigger a limitation period, this should be the case only where the bailment is conditioned upon such request. In other words, this should apply only to bailments at will, where there is a "demand obligation" requiring the bailor to demand return of the goods. Otherwise, a bailor's knowledge of a possible loss will be required to trigger a limitation period, particularly where the limitation period is made subject to a discovery principle. Thus, the lack of due diligence that may have been committed on the part of the plaintiffs in *Rose*, after they were alerted that there may be a problem with their goods — namely, that the seine might be missing — but chose not to look into it further, may not bode well for bailors in most circumstances. Ontario's *Limitations Act, 2002*[18] is supportive of this view, where a bifurcation is recognized between actions dependent on a demand obligation and those that are not, with only the former receiving the benefit of a delayed commencement of a limitation period and the latter being subject to a discovery requirement. Finally, a bailor's failure to make the needed enquiries where serious concerns have been raised with regards to the condition of the goods may mean that a bailor will be viewed as having failed to mitigate its damages.

C. ACCORD AND SATISFACTION

The defence of accord and satisfaction can be a complete defence to a bailment action where the defendant bailee can show that the plaintiff (bailor) intended to release it from any and all liability arising on the bailment in exchange for the payment of some consideration. The release must cover all losses and injuries to bailor property caused by the bailee occurring during the course of the bailment. In *Ware Chemical of Canada Ltd v Cosmos Chemical Ltd*,[19] the plaintiff's materials and goods

---

distinguishable from that legal relationship, not least of which because title in a bailment is not normally transferred to the bailee, who only has possession of the property that is the subject of the bailment: *ibid* at paras 62–66 and 72.

18 Above note 7, s 5(3).

19 [1973] OJ No 2013 (HCJ).

bailed with the defendant Cosmos, and stored on its factory premises, were destroyed in a fire and explosion at those premises. The plaintiff brought an action in bailment against the defendants to recover the value of the property lost. One issue before the Ontario High Court of Justice was whether, irrespective of the defendant Cosmos's possible negligence or breach of the bailment, the plaintiff had effectively released the defendant from liability by virtue of an agreement that had been signed between the parties shortly after the incident in question.[20] While the release was drafted in general, broad language and did not make mention of the goods lost by the plaintiff by reason of the fire at the defendants' premises, Fraser J found that the surrounding circumstances were such that the release clearly contemplated those losses and did not apply *solely* to the other contractual obligations in existence between the parties at the material times. The release had been signed after the incident; it was being executed to avert a possible legal claim by the plaintiff with respect to the losses of property occurring as a result of the fire; the plaintiff had intended for it to be a complete release; and the release was signed for good consideration (a payment of $5,000 by the defendant Cosmo to the plaintiff). Clearly, the parties had arrived at a *consensus ad idem.* Thus, the release in favour of Cosmos was effective as against the plaintiff. As well, since Cosmos did not have any knowledge (or notice) that an insurer had become entitled to be subrogated to the claim of the plaintiff with respect to any matters in the action, the release was also effective as against the insurer, notwithstanding that the insurer did not know about the settlement entered into between the parties until months after the agreement had been executed.[21]

D. CONTRIBUTORY NEGLIGENCE

The defence of contributory negligence will arise relatively infrequently in a bailment action.[22] It can arise during the course of a bailment, although this will be very rare, as the bailee will have exclusive possession of the goods, and there will be little opportunity for a plaintiff's (bailor's) negligence to intervene to cause, or to contribute to causing, loss of or damage

20 *Ibid* at paras 1–11.

21 *Ibid* at paras 30–42.

22 *Letourneau v Otto Mobiles Edmonton (1984) Ltd*, [2002] AJ No 825 at para 61 (QB) [*Letourneau*].

to the bailed goods. Acts of contributory negligence by a bailor are also possible during an act of delivery by the bailor and also toward the end of a bailment where a bailor fails to act prudently in collecting its property from a bailee, leading to its subsequent damage. In all these instances, contributory negligence will be *only* a partial defence,[23] meaning that the bailee's negligence will also remain a cause of the bailor's losses. The bailee will still have to pay damages to the bailor, but those damages will be *smaller* than the bailee would otherwise have to pay, due to the bailor's own contributions to its losses.

1) Bailor Negligence at the Time of the Delivery of Bailor Property to the Bailee

a) Failing to Leave Bailed Goods in a Secure or Proper State

The defence of contributory negligence is possible at the time the bailor delivers the goods to the bailee, provided that the bailor engages in an act of negligence that leaves the goods in an insecure state with the bailee, which state, together with subsequent bailee negligence, later contributes to loss of or damage to the goods while in the possession of the bailee. *Edelson v Musty's Service Station*[24] is instructive. There, the plaintiff left his car with the defendant service station (with the keys in the ignition) who subsequently parked the plaintiff's vehicle all day on a public street (due to a lack of space on the defendant's premises) without locking the vehicle's doors. The vehicle was positioned in such a way that the defendant could not view it from inside its premises (to keep it under surveillance at all times) but only by going to the front of its premises. The defendant had removed the ignition keys from the vehicle, which had been provided by the plaintiff, but, unknown to them, another set of keys was locked in the glove compartment of the vehicle. Injury befell the vehicle after access was gained to the vehicle by virtue of this second set

23 Contributory negligence, like *ex turpi causa*, was once an "absolute defence" to an action put in negligence or bailment. However, this is no longer the case. By reason of statute in most, if not all, common law provinces and territories, namely the *Negligence Act*, damages for losses caused jointly by the negligent acts of plaintiffs and defendants, including in bailment actions, are now apportioned between the parties based on degree of fault or negligence for the losses: see, for example, s 3 of the *Negligence Act*, RSO 1990, c N.1. See further: *Lewis v Sayers*, [1970] OJ No 1577 (Dist Ct) [*Lewis*], discussed in the context of *ex turpi causa* in Section I below.

24 [1956] OJ No 334 (CA).

of keys. Justice Roach of the Ontario Supreme Court—Court of Appeal agreed with the learned trial judge that the defendant (bailee) had been negligent in parking the vehicle all day on a public street in the manner it did—namely, without the doors locked and under no watch—which precipitated the incident in question and that contributory negligence *had not* been committed by the plaintiff. Contributory negligence was not found to have been committed by the plaintiff (bailor) because the second set of keys had been locked away in the glove compartment and while the plaintiff's brother was aware of some method by which the compartment could be opened from the bottom, the keys in the compartment were not readily accessible and had not been left *sufficiently* susceptible to theft.[25] However, where ignition keys are left in an unlocked glove compartment, or similar area in a vehicle, or in plain view, and are left sufficiently accessible to rogue thieves or vandals without the knowledge of the bailee in similar circumstances, it is submitted that contributory negligence should be found on the part of the plaintiff and liability in damages on a bailee reduced accordingly.[26]

b) A Bailor's Leaving of Bailed Goods in a Precarious Position at the Time of Delivery, in Accordance with Bailee Instructions

A finding of contributory negligence will not be possible where a plaintiff (bailor) delivers its property to the defendant (bailee) strictly in accordance with its instructions, perhaps even where the property is left in a "precarious position."[27] In *Letourneau*,[28] the plaintiffs left their trailer in a parking lot located adjacent to the business premises of the defendant repair shop for collection by the defendant the next morning, when the repair would be performed. As it happens, the property was stolen overnight before the work could be commenced the next morning. The

25 *Ibid* at paras 3–6.

26 In *Anderson v LeBlanc*, [1983] NBJ No 409 (QBTD), the plaintiff bailor was found guilty of contributory negligence after leaving his truck with the defendant repair shop with accumulated grease and oil on its body, including in areas proximate to the area of the truck to be repaired and in areas that would not be readily apparent to the defendant repairer upon receipt of the truck or during subsequent repair. In the result, the defendant (bailee) had its liability in damages reduced by 20 percent, when a fire later destroyed the vehicle while some welding was being done on the vehicle by the defendant.

27 However, this may mean that the bailor has accepted the bailment subject to certain risks or limitations, preventing it from succeeding in the bailment action.

28 Above note 22.

plaintiffs had relied on, and dutifully carried out, the defendant's express instructions in the manner in which they had delivered the trailer to the defendant: they had padlocked the hitch of the trailer and had hidden the key in a locked compartment.[29] Nonetheless, the defendant argued contributory negligence by the plaintiffs in their act of delivery, stating that they left the trailer in the manner they did at their own risk and had not taken any measures to safeguard the trailer prior to leaving it where they did, nor had they inquired about security measures in existence on the part of the defendant for the protection of the trailer.[30] The defendant, in its own evidence, did not deny that the area in which the trailer was parked may have lacked proper lighting and security.[31] Justice Johnstone of the Queen's Bench of Alberta Judicial District of Edmonton rejected the contributory negligence argument:

> I find that Mr. Faryna [defendant's service manager] at no time indicated to the Plaintiffs that they were parking in the Intuit Lot at their own risk. To the contrary, I accept the evidence of the Plaintiffs that the direction by the Service Manager to park in the designated spot assured them that the Trailer could be left safely in that location. This factor is corroborated by the testimony of Mrs. Provencher [another customer]. For these reasons, I find no contributory negligence on the part of the Plaintiffs.[32]

In the result, the defendant was found liable for the value of the lost trailer.[33] While the issue of voluntary assumption of risk on the part of the plaintiffs did not arise in the case, the circumstances do raise the following questions: Did the plaintiffs voluntarily assume the risks associated with leaving the trailer in the manner they did, even though this was at the specific behest of the defendant? If so, could this have been a defence that the defendant (bailee) could have used?[34]

---

29 This meant that an act of delivery from the plaintiffs to the defendant had occurred, despite the fact that the defendant *had not* taken physical possession of the goods and the plaintiffs still retained a set of keys providing ongoing access to the trailer: *ibid* at paras 21 and 37–41.

30 *Ibid* at paras 22 and 64.

31 *Ibid* at para 62.

32 *Ibid* at para 64.

33 *Ibid.*

34 The defence of voluntary assumption of risk is addressed in Section K, below in this chapter.

A bailor's actions in delivering goods to a bailee must be assessed based not only on verbal, express instructions received from a bailee before an act of delivery is made or during an act of delivery, but also on instructions conveyed to a bailor through other forms of communication, such as express directions contained in signage on a bailee's premises. In other words, the question of contributory negligence will always need to be contextual when it comes to assessing whether a bailor committed an act of negligence in the manner in which it left its property with the bailee at the time of delivery of the goods. In *Minichiello v Devonshire Hotel (1967) Ltd*,[35] the plaintiff (bailor) deliver his vehicle, which contained expensive jewellery in an attaché case in its trunk, to the defendant parking operator in an outdoor parking lot. Upon entry to the parking lot, the plaintiff was approached and given a parking ticket by the defendant attendant, who took custody of his vehicle. Upon the turnover of his vehicle, the plaintiff had left "his keys" in the ignition switch of the vehicle, as required by signage on the defendant's premises, and expressly told the parking attendant that he had valuables in the vehicle (before attending to business he had at an adjoining hotel also located on the defendant's premises). The attendant accepted custody of the vehicle and the keys, despite the plaintiff's caution.[36] The plaintiff had left *two* keys in the ignition switch: one was for the ignition and the other for the trunk of the vehicle where the valuables were located. As it happened, upon his return to his vehicle, he found his vehicle with the doors unlocked and the keys still in the ignition.[37] When he returned home, he discovered that the attaché case and jewellery were missing from the trunk.[38]

In the bailment action that followed, it was found that the manner in which the attendant had left the vehicle, even though within view of the attendant's office, constituted negligence on the part of the defendant, who was a bailee for fee. It was also found that the contents of the trunk

---

35 (1976), 66 DLR (3d) 619 (BCSC) [*Minichiello*], aff'd (1978), 87 DLR (3d) 439 (BCCA).

36 The defendant had alternative options: it could have refused to accept the valuables, limited its liability with respect to the valuables, or required an extra charge to be made for the inclusion of the valuables before the parking fee would apply to them. Having done none of these things, it did not lie in the defendant's mouth to take the position that the valuables *had not* become part of the bailment: *Minichiello*, *ibid* at 624.

37 On previous occasions, the keys would always be housed in the attendant's office during the course of the parking, together with the part of the ticket to which the plaintiff's car pertained: *ibid* at 621. Had this protocol been followed, it is not clear whether the theft in the case would have occurred.

38 *Ibid* at 620–21.

had become part of the bailment, since the plaintiff had put the attendant on express notice of them. The defendant, however, argued that the plaintiff had been negligent in leaving the trunk key in the ignition, when the key was not needed for any purpose relating to the parking, and that this act constituted contributory negligence by the plaintiff. Justice Rae of the British Columbia Supreme Court disagreed, focusing both on requirements of the signage to which the plaintiff was dutifully adhering and the intention of the parties as revealed by the exchanges that had occurred between the parking attendant and the plaintiff:

> I have already indicated that a sign on the lot required those parking vehicles to leave the keys (plural). Customarily customers left whatever keys they had which related to the car. The attendant in his evidence said he did not need the key to the trunk. But, in fact, he took the key to the trunk into his possession after being told there were valuables in the car. . . . In leaving the trunk key the plaintiff was doing so in response to a requirement on the sign. What the surrendering of the trunk key amounted to was a complete surrender of control and possession of what was in the trunk.[39]

As an exclusion clause present on signage in the parking garage *was not* found to be binding on the plaintiff, since the terms had not been drawn to his specific attention, the defendant was held liable to the plaintiff for the loss of the jewellery.[40]

Justice Rae's ruling is certainly consistent with the duty of safekeeping that a bailee owes to all parts of a bailor's property that the bailment applies to during the course of a bailment. Once it is found that a bailee has accepted custody of keys as a bailee for reward, for the duration of a bailment, then its duty of safekeeping applies not only to the property to which those keys give access but also for their safekeeping as a general matter. The scope of a bailee's duty of safekeeping must be adjudged in relation to the duties it accepts (or does not accept) at the commencement of the bailment. If the bailment for reward in the case truly included the jewellery, as was found by the learned judge, then the inclusion of the trunk key in the plaintiff's (bailor's) act of delivery *was not* surplusage, it was absolutely essential for the defendant (bailee) to have in order that

39 *Ibid* at 625–26.
40 *Ibid* at 621–22.

the valuables could be accessed and protected against certain risks of loss, including by fire, which might not be sufficiently guarded against with the ignition key alone. That being so, the plaintiff's (bailor's) handing over of the trunk key could not be classified as contributory negligence; instead, it was merely an act that enabled the bailment to proceed on certain terms.

c) A Bailor's Act of Delivery Affects the Extent of the Damage

What should the state of the law be where the bailor's act of delivery, or alleged act of contributory negligence, only increases the "extent of the damage" that would be done to bailor property in the event of fire, or similar ordinary risk of loss, arising from bailee negligence during the course of a bailment? In *Procinsky v McDermott*,[41] the plaintiff had a mechanical problem with the left rear wheel of his vehicle. He delivered said vehicle to the defendant's garage for repair and, with the assistance of a defendant (Rogers) and a third party, hoisted the vehicle and removed the problematic tire with a view to ascertaining which parts would be required to do the repair work. The plaintiff then advised Rogers that the vehicle had a gas leak and instructed the defendant to fix it while he left his vehicle with the defendant to go in to town to buy the needed parts. In the course of using a trouble light to effect an immediate repair of the gas line, which Rogers believed should be fixed immediately to prevent gas from leaking onto the floor and presenting a hazard, a fire was ignited, destroying the garage and rendering the vehicle a complete loss.[42] The Alberta Supreme Court, Appellate Division, did not find any negligence to have been committed on the part of the defendant Rogers in handling the trouble light (even though there was no other apparent source of the fire), making the matter of contributory negligence strictly an academic one, since no negligence was found to have been committed by the defendant in his handling of the vehicle.[43] The majority, accordingly, did not address any of its reasons with respect to the issue. In dissent, however, Johnson JA did. The learned judge's comments, while strictly *obiter dicta*, nonetheless raise an important issue with respect to the defence: assuming that negligence had been committed by the defendant during the course of the bailment, had the plaintiff been contributorily negligent in parking the vehicle inside the garage and removing the wheel, given

41 [1955] AJ No 57 (SCAD).
42 *Ibid* at paras 1–6.
43 *Ibid* at paras 7–13.

the gas leak, when he could have parked the vehicle outside in the same jacked-up manner, which would have presumably reduced the degree of damage done to the vehicle by fire? In answering in the negative, Johnson JA found that the procedure being performed by Rogers to address the gas leak was as hazardous outside as within the garage, meaning that the plaintiff's actions, or act of delivery, had not enhanced the risk. "The extent of the damage only would have been affected."[44] In the result, the defence of contributory negligence was not available to the defendant.

d) A Bailor Leaves Extraneous Personal Property in Larger Bailed Property When Concerned About Theft

In *Leong v Victoria Nissan Ltd*,[45] the plaintiff brought his vehicle, which had an expensive stereo system and high-end alarm system, to the defendant dealership for repair. The repairs could not be completed immediately, and the vehicle was left overnight on the defendant's open lot in a well-lit area in plain view. The plaintiff had expressed his concerns about the safety of his vehicle to the defendant, given the significant value of the stereo in his vehicle, and had made the defendant aware of his alarm system. As it happened, the car was broken into overnight and the stereo equipment as well as music CDs, CD cases, and cameras were stolen.[46] Justice Higinbotham of the British Columbia Provincial Court found that the defendant (bailee) had been negligent in disconnecting the vehicle battery, which disabled the alarm system of the vehicle, given how vulnerable a vehicle with such expensive equipment would be to thieves in such a state.[47] However, while the learned judge found that the defendant should be liable for the loss of the stereo equipment, was it equally liable for the CDs, CD cases, and cameras, which were also taken but which could have been removed by the plaintiff prior to delivering the property to the defendant in light of his concerns of theft? On this score, the judge found that the plaintiff had been contributorily negligent in not removing the items, since (unlike the stereo equipment) it would have been easy to do so, finding him 50 percent responsible for the loss of these items accordingly.[48]

---

44 *Ibid* at para 30.

45 2004 BCPC 179.

46 *Ibid* at paras 1–6 and 14.

47 *Ibid* at paras 16–18.

48 *Ibid* at para 26. While the question of notice of the items in question was not pursued by the court, if the defendant did not have actual or constructive notice of the CDs and other items and did not accept them as part of the bailment, then no duty

2) Bailor Contributory Negligence During the Course of a Bailment

Although rare, it is possible for a bailor to commit an act of contributory negligence during a bailment. In *St John's (City) v Holden's Transport Ltd*,[49] the plaintiff had contracted with the defendant to bring a boom truck to remove an undamaged excavator from a hole it had fallen into at a construction site. The defendant brought the truck that had been requested by the plaintiff, instead of a wrecker (which was available and would have been preferable for the task). During the removal procedure, one of the plaintiff (city) employees present at the scene assisted the driver of the defendant truck during the towing process by acting as a "spotter." As it happened, when the excavator was partially pulled out of the hole, the towing strap being utilized snapped and the excavator fell back into the hole, sustaining damage.[50] Justice Orr of the Newfoundland and Labrador Provincial Court found the defendant to be negligent, since the truck had been used by a defendant employee, who was a licensed crane operator who had never utilized the truck for towing before, and since there was no supervisor to oversee the operation, which might well have led to improper use of the vehicle by the driver and his failure to perform the needed manoeuvres to the needed acceptable standards. The question arises, however, whether the plaintiff had been contributorily negligent in the direction that it had provided to the defendant driver during the towing process? Justice Orr found that it had. This, together with the plaintiff's other act of contributory negligence in requesting the wrong truck (a boom truck rather than a wrecker), reduced the defendant's liability by one-third, meaning that the plaintiff received two-thirds' of its losses as damages.[51] As apparent, where bailors, or bailors' agents or employees, assist bailees in their work in relation to the bailed goods during the

---

of safekeeping was owed to them whatsoever. If there was such a duty, then, as we have seen, it becomes difficult to justify a finding of contributory negligence against a plaintiff (bailor) at all since the defendant (bailee) accepted the bailment on certain terms. These terms may have included allowing a bailor to leave property, at the time of delivery, in a certain state, which may make the goods more or less vulnerable to injury and the bailee's duty of safekeeping more or less exacting, depending on the circumstances.

49 [2017] NJ No 181 (Prov Ct).

50 *Ibid* at paras 1–6.

51 *Ibid* at paras 16–22.

course of a bailment, they put themselves at risk of being found guilty of contributory negligence where minor interferences together with other bailee negligence result in damage or loss to the goods.[52]

3) Bailor Failure to Collect Goods in a Prudent or Timely Fashion

The defence of contributory negligence has been recognized where goods are being held by a bailee, usually gratuitously and involuntarily for the bailor, and the bailor fails to collect them within a reasonable time of the commencement of the bailment.[53] In *Hynes v Hynes*,[54] a bailment action was brought by a plaintiff (bailor) against a defendant (bailee) following loss of some of her personal clothing from the matrimonial home following her being ordered out of the home by her husband after revealing her infidelity to him. The clothing was solely the wife's and had not been made the subject of a previous family law proceeding that had been resolved between the parties. She had left the clothing there in May of the year of her separation from the plaintiff. Although she returned to the home on numerous occasions, she did not remove all the clothing, claiming that, on at least one visit, she found some of the clothing was missing and not removable. While some of the missing clothes removed from the home by the defendant were collected by the plaintiff from the defendant's family lawyer, other items of the plaintiff's clothing remained missing. Because the husband had ordered the wife out of the house and items of her personal clothing remained in the home that were not the subject of the matrimonial proceeding, the husband had become a bailee and had to negative negligence.[55]

This he could not do. However, Justice Orr was not prepared to hold the defendant fully responsible, finding that the plaintiff's own negligence had contributed to her losses: she had made several trips to the

52 It is also possible, where the bailor interferences are substantial, that a bailment may be severed or terminated, since exclusive possession will no longer reside with the bailee, a prerequisite to the finding and continuing of a bailment. For relevant discussion, see Chapter 3, Section F(8).

53 There may be a heightened duty on a bailor to collect its goods from a bailee in a very timely manner in circumstances where the bailor has been put on express notice that there is exceptional risk of loss to the goods that cannot be sufficiently ameliorated by the bailee: see *Backmirzie v 1500569 Ontario Ltd*, 2006 CanLII 40669 (Ont SCJ).

54 [1995] NJ No 8 (Prov Ct (Sm Cl Div)).

55 *Ibid* at paras 1–16.

residence yet *had not* removed all the clothing; moreover, the parties had moved out of the residence on different dates, which raised the possibility of items going missing during these periods for reasons other than the defendant's sole negligence. In the result, the defendant was held to be liable for 70 percent of the value of the plaintiff's missing items of clothing while the plaintiff was found 30 percent liable.[56]

E. A BAILOR'S FAILURE TO MITIGATE LOSSES ARISING ON BREACH OF THE TERMS OF THE BAILMENT

The principle of mitigation applies to bailment actions. Where a breach of bailment occurs, a bailor's failure to act reasonably to minimize its damages arising on the breach can lower damages otherwise payable by a defendant (bailee). The onus is on the defendant, of course, to prove a failure to mitigate on the part of a plaintiff.

1) A Bailor's Failure to Make a Demand for Return of Its Property

The caselaw is reluctant to hold a bailor's failure to demand a return of its property against it when it comes to a bailor's duty to mitigate damages arising on the breach of a bailment. Part of the reason for this is that, in most bailments, a bailee's redelivery obligation is not conditioned upon the making of a demand. In other words, a demand is not a *condition precedent* to a bailee having to redeliver goods to a bailor, which is usually required upon the completion of the purpose for which the bailment was made. Until the redelivery occurs, there is a duty on the bailee to safeguard the bailor's goods. Another reason is that, where a bailment is subsisting and there is nothing (or insufficient information) alerting a bailor that there might be a problem with the goods, or with their continued retention by the bailee, there is no need for a bailor to make a demand for the immediate return of the goods.[57] The bailor, instead, can safely assume that the goods continue to be the subject of the bailment and that the bailee is taking sufficient steps to protect them for the bailor in accordance with its

---

56 *Ibid* at paras 18–27. For a further example of contributory negligence in these circumstances, see *McCarthy v Matthews*, [1987] BCJ No 3163 (Prov Ct (Sm Cl Div)).

57 Until the bailor might need them for a particular purpose such as to sell them, use them, or perhaps hire them out.

duty of safekeeping until the bailment is concluded and the bailor is given a reasonable opportunity to collect them from the bailee.

a) Circumstances Where a Bailor Is Not Alerted That the Goods May Be in Danger

In *Equirex Leasing Corp v 2028260 Ontario Ltd (cob Ocean Bay Restaurant and Night Club)*,[58] the defendant (bailee) had used the plaintiff's equipment in its nightclub for a period of time. The equipment, pursuant to the parties' agreement, was to be used in the club. That was the sole purpose of the bailment. As it happened, when the nightclub closed some time later, the equipment went missing. It was unclear on the evidence whether the equipment was removed from the club before it went missing.[59] In any case, Prattas Deputy J for the Ontario Superior Court of Justice Small Claims Court found that the defendant bailee's redelivery obligation was triggered when the defendant closed its nightclub, since the equipment was no longer needed to be used in the club, which was no longer operational. The redelivery obligation *was not* conditioned on a demand, and the defendant's failure to notify the plaintiff that the equipment was no longer needed and failure to redeliver the plaintiff's property to it did not allow the plaintiff, if it had any duty to do so, to mitigate its damages arising on the breach of the bailment. There was nothing in the circumstances to alert the plaintiff (bailor) that its goods might be in danger, or that the business might be closing, requiring the plaintiff to make a demand for the return of its property from the defendant. In the result, the defendant was put to the reverse onus and was unable to advance evidence to negative negligence on its part in relation to the loss.[60]

It is submitted that the mere fact that the defendant was in breach of the terms of the bailment, in that it was in arrears to the plaintiff on the lease payments for the equipment, was not enough in the circumstances, without more, to require the bailor to make a demand for a return of its property. The plaintiff was hoping that the defendant's club would generate income for the defendant, which would allow it to repay the outstanding monies, and not a long enough period of time had elapsed to make this belief an absurd one requiring the plaintiff to make a demand for the return of the equipment and to determine the bailment.

---

58 [2010] OJ No 3646 (SCJ Sm Cl Ct) [*Equirex*].

59 *Ibid* at paras 7–25.

60 *Ibid* at paras 59–63.

b) Circumstances Where a Bailor Is Alerted That the Goods May Be in Danger

In *Kinsella*,[61] the situation was different from that in *Equirex*. The plaintiff (bailor) was alerted that there might be a problem with the goods, as he had made a visit to the defendants' (bailees') premises during the course of the bailment, which led to certain discoveries. Specifically, the plaintiff observed that a table saw of his was being moved out of the storage areas in which his goods were being stored, for delivery to the dump by the defendants, and interfered to prevent this, indicating to the defendants that none of his property was junk and none of it was to be taken to the dump. As well, the plaintiff noticed that some of his other items might be missing. However, following assurances from a defendant that the goods would be relocated and segregated into a new storage location, since the areas in which they were stored were the subject of a cleanup, the plaintiff took no further steps to ensure that the goods were in fact relocated or secured by the defendants. The plaintiff made no formal demand for the goods at that point in time and did not ask for an accounting of his items, not at that time or subsequently, and did not communicate with the defendants about the matter again.[62]

The plaintiff had essentially assumed (albeit wrongly) that the goods would be relocated by the defendants and secured. When the plaintiff retook the premises, including the areas in which the goods had been stored, following the end of the defendants' sublease, he categorically discovered them to be missing. There was some evidence, albeit tenuous, that the plaintiff may have made a report to the police several months after his visit to the defendants' premises, reporting that some of his personal items at the subject premises had been stolen. Still, the plaintiff did not know definitively that any of his items might be missing until he retook the premises after the defendants' sublease had come to an end.[63]

Justice Puddester of the Newfoundland Supreme Court Trial Division found that the defendants (bailees) *had not* relocated and resecured the goods during the cleanup, as promised, and had instead disposed of the plaintiff's items, accordingly breaching their duty of safekeeping as gratuitous bailee owed to him. While the learned judge refused to use the plaintiff's failure to make a formal demand, or the plaintiff's "lack

61 Above note 6.
62 *Ibid* at paras 61–64 and 80.
63 *Ibid* at paras 73–83.

of pointed action," against him on the general question of liability, the plaintiff's conduct did lead to a reduction in damages. This is because his conduct supported the contention that the property left was in a "much depreciated state" and not all that valuable. It is submitted that, since the plaintiff probably did not know definitively that his property was missing at the time of his visit to subject premises, no formal demand was required by him to meet his onus of proof. There was no need to mitigate his damages either, because it was not clear that any losses had occurred by that point in time requiring actions in mitigation. The plaintiff had stopped the removal of the table saw and brought his concerns to the defendants for immediate remediation and could have a reasonable expectation that the defendants would follow through on what they promised.[64] In the result, a defendant (bailee) in these circumstances will not be able to be exonerated on the basis of the plaintiff's failure to make a formal demand for the return of the goods.

F. THE DEFENCE OF ABANDONMENT

1) Abandonment or Involuntary Bailment?

While the defence of abandonment of bailor property by a bailor has been recognized in the caselaw, its ability to operate will depend largely on a court's degree of willingness to recognize the relationship of "involuntary bailment." Where an involuntary bailment is recognized in its highest form, the defence of abandonment may have little, if any, room to operate, since, until clearly relieved of possession by a bailor, an involuntary bailee remains duty bound to safeguard the bailor's goods. However, not all courts have been willing to recognize involuntary bailments as having independent existence as actual bailment relationships, as bailments are meant to be consensual and voluntary relationships. They are *not* to be

64 Consistent with this view, it is unlikely that a limitation period in the case could have arisen until a retaking of the premises occurred, since the plaintiff's antecedent knowledge of whether the items might be missing was too uncertain or tenuous to conclude that the plaintiff had discovered his losses as at that point in time. However, if the plaintiff had in fact made a police report several months after his visit to the premises, alleging that some of his items had been stolen from the premises at that time, which was not found by Puddester J to have occurred definitively, certainly that action could have well triggered a limitation period and a requirement on the plaintiff to make a formal demand for the return of his property in mitigation of his damages arising from a breach of the bailment.

foisted on others, given the extensive duty of safekeeping they involve. Given the inimical nature of involuntary bailments, it is not surprising that some courts have outright rejected them. In *Visscher v Triple Broek Holdings Ltd*,[65] the plaintiff (bailor) parked his trailer containing bakery equipment on land owned by the defendant, from which location the defendant ultimately had the goods removed as scrap after having concluded that the property had been abandoned by the owner. The plaintiff was a salesperson for a company, LP Sales, that had subleased the defendant's land from a lessor of that land, one Broekhuizen, which land included, among other things, two adjacent lots for parking. The plaintiff erroneously believed Broekhuizen to be the owner of these lands, and he approached him, asking him for permission to park his trailer on one of the parking lots. The plaintiff assured Broekhuizen that he would remove the trailer on twenty-four hours' notice. Broekhuizen acceded to the plaintiff's request, with no charge made for the parking. From time to time, the plaintiff would attend the trailer to drop off bakery equipment for storage or to pick up some equipment for resale as a part of a sideline business he was operating on his own account. As it happens, Broekhuizen's lease was terminated on consent, and LP Sales was evicted from the premises thereafter. The premises thus became vacant as of April 2000, save and except for the plaintiff's trailer. The plaintiff acknowledged his awareness of the second event but not the first. Still, the plaintiff, who continued to work for the company out of his own private residence, left his trailer on the premises and continued to attend to his sideline business. The plaintiff submitted that Broekhuizen never gave him notice to move the trailer.[66]

When the plaintiff attended the premises in late August or early September 2000 after a three-week vacation (which he had not notified Broekhuizen that he was taking and during which time he did not attend the defendant's premises to check on the trailer), he found his trailer to be missing. He subsequently discovered that it had been towed from the premises by one Pertman, who oversaw the defendant's property and who had engaged a towing company to remove the trailer. Pertman refused to surrender the trailer to the plaintiff, or to tell him where it was, without him paying the towing charge incurred, which the plaintiff refused to

65 [2006] AJ No 626 (QB) [*Visscher*].
66 *Ibid* at paras 1–10.

do. The plaintiff did not advise Pertman that there were items of value contained in the trailer. Eventually, the plaintiff found the trailer in a salvage yard associated with the defendant's property management company, although he observed the vehicle only from a distance. He returned to the premises a few days later and discovered that the trailer had been damaged and that its contents had been placed on various recycling piles. The plaintiff decided not to salvage any of the contents of the trailer, as he (erroneously) believed they could not be salvaged.[67]

The evidence indicated that Pertman had requested in April or May that Broekhuizen remove the trailer from the defendant's property, as the defendant was trying to re-lease the premises. Broekhuizen advised that the trailer belonged to a friend and that the trailer would be removed within two weeks, which Pertman did not object to.[68] Two weeks later, this was not done, and Pertman again contacted Broekhuizen, asking that the trailer be removed, otherwise they would remove it. This second request was to no avail: the trailer remained on the property, and Broekhuizen did not give the plaintiff any notice to move it, despite Pertman's two communications. Pertman thus eventually, in late August or early September, treated the trailer as abandoned and had it removed from the defendant's premises and made no further efforts to ascertain who the owner of the trailer was.[69]

Justice Marceau of the Alberta Court of Queen's Bench Judicial District of Edmonton found that the plaintiff must have been aware that the premises were totally vacant as of April and that he could not force a bailment on the defendant:

> Given that bailment is created by the "voluntary" taking into custody of someone else's goods, the Plaintiff in the present case could not foist bailment on 122 [Pertman's company] by his failure to remove the trailer from 122's property after the Broekhuizen lease ended. Bailment is a voluntary relationship and cannot be imposed. The term "involuntary bailee" is an oxymoron. The bailee must agree to the bailment. In any event, there is nothing in the evidence to suggest that either Broekhuizen

---

67 *Ibid* at paras 11–13.

68 Justice Marceau stated that, even if this created an implied licence for the trailer to remain on the defendant's property, the licence extended only for two weeks, which time period had long elapsed by August or September, when Pertman had the trailer removed from the property: *ibid* at para 34.

69 *Ibid* at paras 18–19.

> or 122 took possession of or had any control over the trailer prior to late August 2000.[70]

Justice Marceau went on to find that the necessary indicia of abandonment in law were present on the facts of the case, even if the plaintiff had no intention in fact to actually abandon the trailer and even though neither Pertman nor Broekhuizen had given the plaintiff notice to remove the trailer from the defendant's property. The learned judge noted that the passage of time, the nature of the transaction, and the owners' own conduct were relevant, but not exhaustive, factors to consider when it comes to finding a reasonable inference of intention to abandon, citing the following facts in support of abandonment:[71]

1) The plaintiff had failed to give Broekhuizen notice he was going on vacation for three weeks, which would make it impossible for him to remove the property on twenty-four hours' notice, which condition he knew the licence given by Broekhuizen was subject to. The plaintiff should have contacted Broekhuizen to ensure he could continue to park the trailer on the property, but had failed to do so.
2) When he found the trailer damaged in a salvage yard connected to Pertman, the plaintiff had failed to collect any items from the trailer that had been placed on various heaps of recycling, even though it was not clear at the time that any of the items had been damaged beyond repair.
3) The plaintiff had treated his property throughout in a casual manner,[72] waiting several days after his vacation was over before checking on the trailer. Then, even after learning that the trailer was missing, he made enquiries *only* in his spare time and did not apparently place sufficient importance on its disappearance.
4) Despite Broekhuizen's communication to Pertman that the trailer would be removed from the property, it remained there from April to August, inclusive.

---

70 *Ibid* at para 31.

71 *Ibid* at paras 35–46.

72 Even if a bailment were findable on the facts, it is submitted the plaintiff's actions — namely, his "casual" treatment of the trailer and its contents, and his failure to collect the contents of the trailer that had been placed on piles of recycling (which were not damaged beyond repair) — probably made him contributorily negligent in his own losses. Alternatively, they constituted a failure by him to mitigate his damages arising on a breach of the bailment caused by the defendant's removal of the trailer from the property.

5) The trailer was old and decrepit and was secured only by two padlocks.
6) The parking lot was open to the public and was not well secured.
7) There was no reason for Pertman to believe that the trailer contained valuables.

This is the correct analysis to be applied in these circumstances. Bailments must be assessed based on all the circumstances and facts presenting in a given situation. Exercising voluntary control over the subject property, for the purpose of safekeeping, is the *sine qua non* of bailment. Neither the defendant nor Broekhuizen exercised such control at the material times. Pertman's limited actions, to remove the trailer from the property, were merely self-help measures and were not enough, without more, to create a bailment relationship. Nor was the property of such clearly high value to impose a duty of continued storage on the defendant. In the result, no bailment of any kind was findable. However, where a party in the position of the defendant or Broekhuizen in the case does exercise control over the subject property and assumes a duty of safekeeping over it, then the finding of a gratuitous bailment might be appropriate and seemly. Whether abandonment can thereafter be found by a court is a question rife with difficulty, since the law is not always definite on when a gratuitous bailment ends and abandonment begins. Still, where the owner of the bailed goods is not known and cannot be contacted, an indefinite duty of safekeeping on a defendant as a gratuitous and involuntary bailee, who is not being compensated for its work, seems far too onerous to be a maintainable and defensible rule. Perhaps the answer to this dilemma lies in the defence of self-help, to be discussed next.

2) Defence of Self-Help as an Alternative to the Defence of Abandonment

Justice Marceau in *Visscher* qualified his legal conclusion by stating that, even if it was incorrect to treat the trailer as abandoned in the circumstances, those same circumstances certainly gave the defendant the right to take the steps necessary to remove the trailer once reasonable notice to do so had been given, to end a continuing trespass and nuisance on the property.[73] Such notice had been given in the form of two phone calls placed by Pertman to Broekhuizen, and so the self-help measures employed

73 Above note 65 at paras 40–46.

by the defendant in removing the trailer were entirely reasonable in the circumstances. While it is true that Pertman had not given any notice directly to the plaintiff, the defendant did not know who the owner of the property was. In any case, Pertman had been assured by Broekhuizen that he would contact the plaintiff and facilitate the removal. In these circumstances, certainly a constructive notice given by a defendant, via an agent such as Pertman, should be enough to meet the necessary notice requirements here.[74]

3) Where the Purpose of a Bailment Has Been Completed

As we have seen, where the purpose for which a bailment was formed has been completed, a bailment may be brought to an end immediately or, alternatively, within a reasonable period of time thereafter, allowing a bailor a reasonable opportunity to pick up the property before a bailee's duty of safekeeping terminates. Where a bailor fails to collect the property within a reasonable time, but instead chooses to leave it on a bailee's premises indefinitely, the most that can arise is a licence (or perhaps a gratuitous and involuntary bailment), usually based on an express or implied authorization conveyed from a bailee, with *no*, or a reduced, duty of safekeeping being owed by the bailee. However, the property may eventually be considered to be "abandoned," allowing the bailee to remove the property from the premises, and ending the duty of safekeeping on a bailee. For example, in *Cole v Mark Lively Welding Ltd*,[75] the plaintiff delivered his truck to the defendant for repair in September 2010. The plaintiff did not reclaim the truck until March 2012, even though the truck was ready for pick up long before that time. On collection, the plaintiff found the truck to be in a severely deteriorated state (it would not start). The defendant had been forced to park the vehicle on its outdoor yard awaiting the plaintiff's collection and payment of the bill for the repair, where the vehicle may have fallen victim to vandalism. The defendant did not have a secure facility in which to store the vehicle. The plaintiff's vehicle had not been driven in the intervening time (for almost

---

74 Broekhuizen's omission in failing to give the plaintiff any notice to remove his property may have made him negligent or possibly breached the licence arrangement he had with the plaintiff. However, these were not legal determinations that were before Marceau J for consideration, and no rulings on these possible liability issues arose.

75 [2012] NSJ No 357 (Sm Cl Ct).

two years), explaining its significant deterioration. However, the defendant was forced to relocate it numerous times during this period of time, causing him some inconvenience. Even though he had significant health problems, the plaintiff's reasons for the delay in the pickup were found not to be *substantial enough* to have prevented him from picking up the truck. He could have had someone else pick up the truck or he could have called the defendant to try to make alternate arrangements; instead, he essentially did nothing. The defendant had made numerous attempts to contact the plaintiff to pick up his vehicle and to pay the outstanding bill, including visiting the plaintiff at his business premises, where the plaintiff advised that his wife would deliver a cheque to pay the bill the next day. This never happened, and the vehicle remained on the defendant's lot. The plaintiff nonetheless sued the defendant in bailment for the damage done to his vehicle upon collection.[76]

Adjudicator Slone of the Smalls Claims Court of Nova Scotia found that a duty of safekeeping, strictly speaking, applied only during the brief period of time when the work was being done and for a short time thereafter. After this period of time, the plaintiff basically abandoned his vehicle and there was no bailment or, alternatively, there was only a gratuitous one. In either case, the defendant had not been grossly negligent in permitting the plaintiff's vehicle to be vandalized. The plaintiff was essentially the author of his own misfortune, by abandoning his vehicle on the defendant's premises for nearly two years. The defendant had given notice to the plaintiff of the need for the vehicle to be collected, yet these communications went unheeded. In the result, the defendant was exonerated from liability for the damage that had been occasioned to the plaintiff's vehicle.

This decision demonstrates that a bailor cannot foist an "indefinite duty of safekeeping" on a bailee. Once a bailment has been completed and a reasonable period of time to allow a bailor to pick up its goods has passed, a bailment is at an end and the duty of safekeeping should be viewed as being terminated. Bailed goods left on bailee property thereafter for long periods of time, without the bailee's consent, should be considered abandoned where the bailee has made reasonable efforts to contact the bailor to have the property removed from the premises but where such communications are unavailing. This is especially true where it is clear that the bailee lacked the facilities for storage of the bailed goods, to the

---

76 *Ibid* at paras 6–17.

knowledge of the bailor, and through its actions cannot be said to have accepted a gratuitous bailment, or a licence when the bailment came to an end. Unless a special contract is in place, a bailee is not an indefinite custodian of bailor goods, whether as a gratuitous bailee or licensor. Bailees should be able to exercise self-help and remove goods from their property once a bailment is over and reasonable efforts have been made to contact the bailor to avoid a continuing trespass.

4) Express Terms in a Contract Requiring Removal of Bailor Property from Land by a Certain Date

What should the state of the law be where a contract, by an express term agreed upon between two parties, requires bailor property to be removed from land by a certain date? If the property is not removed by such date, is abandonment immediately findable and any previous bailment that was in existence between the parties at an end? In *J & V Ashfield Village Ltd v Starkell*,[77] the parties entered into two agreements, one of which involved the purchase of a parcel of land from the plaintiff by the defendants. The relevant provision of the agreement stated:

> There shall be included in or with the Property all fixtures and in particular all such electric light fixtures, heating and plumbing fixtures, T.V. antennae, fitted carpets, curtain rods, drapery tracks, screen and storm windows and doors as are now on the Property, but excluding these fixtures: any fill or soil piles shall be removed by vendor as soon as possible, prior to June 15, 2014.[78]

After the defendants took possession of the land on 1 May 2014, the plaintiff did not collect its property by the deadline date of 15 June 2014. Indeed, the first attempt came in September, three months afterwards, when the plaintiff sought authorization to enter the defendants' land to collect the piles of soil. By then, the defendants, pursuant to their landscaping and sodding obligations and deadlines under a different agreement also with the plaintiff, had levelled the land on which the mud was located and it was no longer retrievable. The defendants had not given the plaintiff any notice before doing this. However, the plaintiff had not

77 2015 MBQB 174.
78 *Ibid* at para 2.

asked for an extension to pick up its property. Nor had it granted the defendants additional time to satisfy their landscaping obligations. In the result, the defendants believed they were within their rights in taking the self-help actions they did. The Court Officer in the Small Claims Court below agreed, dismissing the action by finding that the plaintiff had breached its obligations under the Offer to Purchase Agreement by failing to remove the soil by the stipulated deadline.[79]

On an application for leave to appeal, the plaintiff argued that the court officer in the Small Claims Court had erred in failing to consider bailment law principles and the matter of ownership of the soil in question, both of which they argued were questions of law permitting leave to appeal from the decision to be given. While the application was dismissed, as Schulman J for the Manitoba Court of Queen's Bench found these issues to be questions of mixed fact and law,[80] the decision raises an important question: where a vendor (bailor) in these circumstances fails to pick up its property by a stipulated deadline in a contract, but where that agreement *does not* indicate any clear adverse consequence for not doing so, should "abandonment" nevertheless be inferred without the need for a notice by the bailee to be given, giving the bailee free rein to do what it wishes with the property? It is submitted that such a rule would be too harsh and that a notice from the bailee to the bailor asking for it to pick up its property, to avoid its disposal, be required before abandonment can be found, even where a reasonable time since a deadline date for the pick-up of the bailed property contained in a contract has elapsed. In the meantime, a gratuitous bailment or, at the very least, a licence, should be applied to the property, preventing that which would otherwise be a trespass and concomitantly preventing a bailee from removing the property from its premises.

G. THE BAILEE AS A MERE FORWARDING AGENT

The relevant caselaw indicates that, where a party receiving goods acts strictly as a freight forwarder, or forwarding agent, for the bailor and only makes arrangements for transport of the shipper's property, no bailment will arise. However, this defence will not be available where the would-be

79 *Ibid* at paras 5–6.
80 *Ibid* at paras 7–11.

forwarding agent actually obtains possession of the goods in the process.[81] For example, in *Costa Cartage*, the plaintiff (carrier) transported the defendants' two trucks to a carrier twice under a contract between the parties, for further transport between two cities within the same province (first, from Winnipeg to Churchill, Manitoba, then, from Churchill to Winnipeg). When the trucks reached their last destination, the defendants discovered that some chattels were missing from one of the trucks.[82]

In the court action that followed, Barkman J found that, in the circumstances, the plaintiff had taken possession of the goods even though its role was confined to loading the trucks obtained from the defendants, once in Winnipeg and the once in Churchill, onto flatcars (obtained by the plaintiff) and subsequently delivering the loaded flatcars to a railway company, at which point it lost all control of the defendants' property. The foregoing actions, which involved the plaintiff's use of the trucks' keys belonging to the defendants, showed that the plaintiff was exercising custody and control over the goods. The mere fact that the bulk of the actual transporting was done by a railway (which was the principal carrier of the goods) and not by the plaintiff *did not* mean that a bailment was not created in the interim. It meant that the bailment was at an end once the plaintiff had given up possession to the railway company.[83] Even though this did not make a difference in the ultimate analysis, since the plaintiff was found to have exercised reasonable care at all times, the point remains that a forwarding agent *must not* obtain possession of the bailor's goods if it wishes to avoid becoming a bailee of the goods, with all the obligations and duties that come with that classification.

In *Alcan Canada Products Ltd v Schenker Warehousing, a division of Schenker of Canada Ltd*,[84] a defendant in the business of warehousing was properly denied the defence of freight forwarder by the British Columbia Supreme Court, since possession of the goods was received by the defendant, and this brought with it a duty of safekeeping indicative of a bailment. This duty of safekeeping was found to continue, based on the actions of the defendant (bailee), even after the goods had been physically placed on a third party's trailers by the defendant on the defendant's premises,

---

81 *Costa Cartage Ltd v Turner Roto Rooter (1970)*, [1985] MJ No 491 at para 21 (QB) [*Costa Cartage*].

82 *Ibid* at paras 1–2.

83 *Ibid* at paras 11–21.

84 [1985] BCJ No 1256 (SC) [*Alcan*].

with its imprimatur, for a later transport to the plaintiff's premises. Thus, there was no room for the defence to operate, because the defendant had assumed possession and a duty of safekeeping over the goods at all material times and was not simply making arrangements to have the plaintiff shipper's goods transported, as a mere freight forwarder would do.

H. A DEFENCE OF IMMEDIATE TAKE-BACK OF POSSESSION OF GOODS BY A FIRST BAILEE FROM A SECOND BAILEE

Where a first bailee immediately takes back possession of a bailor's goods, including the duty of safekeeping from a second bailee for an interim period, after purportedly making an act of delivery of the goods to a second bailee, it may be possible for the second bailee to rely on this as a defence to a bailment action brought against it where the goods are damaged during this interim period. In such a case, the second bailee would, essentially, argue that it owed the bailor no duty of safekeeping during this period of time, as this duty had been transferred back to the first bailee and never crystallized to bind it. In *Alcan*,[85] aluminum products ordered by one plaintiff from another were transported to a warehouse from which they were to be picked up by a carrier and transported to the purchaser's premises. However, when the carrier showed up at the warehouse, and after the warehouse employees had, over a two-day period, loaded the goods onto the carrier's flatbed trucks for transport from a railcar, it was discovered by the parties that the purchaser's business was closed due to the holiday season. It was then agreed by the warehouser that the goods on the flatbed trucks would be left at the warehouse until after the new year, when the plaintiff's business would reopen. As it happens, the goods were not properly covered with tarpaulins in the open-bed trucks during the intervening period by either the defendant carrier or the defendant warehouse (even though the warehouse employees had covered them with a tarp at an earlier point in time) and were damaged by the elements.[86]

While there was some dispute before the court in the bailment action that followed as to whether an act of delivery had occurred at all, Oppal J of the British Columbia Supreme Court was prepared to accept that, if one did occur, the defendant warehouse, by its own evidence, had accepted

85 *Ibid*.

86 *Ibid* at paras 1–7.

the goods back into its possession. With possession came a duty of safekeeping, irrespective of the lack of direct benefit for the additional storage.[87] As a bailee, the defendant warehouse had a duty to properly tarp the plaintiff's goods to protect them from damage, which it did not do, despite having the ability to do so. This was not a duty it could foist onto the defendant carrier, since the warehouse had reassumed possession. In the result, the defendant warehouse was guilty of gross negligence, and liability in bailment law was properly fixed against it.[88] However, it is submitted that, had the defendant not admitted to having taken back possession, the mere fact that the goods remained on the defendant warehouse's premises, as a favour to the defendant carrier, was not enough, without more, to create a continuing bailment. As we have seen in many other cases herein, such a situation can lead to a licence, and a constructive act of delivery can be found to have occurred that divested the bailee of its duty of safekeeping and ending the bailment. Indeed, there was evidence in support of same in the case, including the likelihood that the defendant warehouse had removed its own tarp from the goods in anticipation of the goods being removed from its premises for transport by the carrier (which admitted to having its own tarps for use during the transport).

I. *EX TURPI CAUSA NON ORITUR ACTIO*

The common law defence of *ex turpi causa* states that an action can not arise from a dishonourable cause. It applies where both the plaintiff's and the defendant's conduct can be said to be at fault for the plaintiff's losses or damages. Where the defence is engaged, it will bar a plaintiff from recovering recompense for injuries. In *Hall v Hebert*,[89] the Court of Appeal for British Columbia, albeit in the context of a negligence action, laid down the general circumstances in which the defence is available to defendants:

> [T]he principle underlying ex turpi causa is not limited to circumstances where the injuries were sustained during the course of a joint criminal enterprise. The compass of the defence is much broader. It will be available wherever the conduct of the plaintiff giving rise to the claim is

87 Interestingly, the motor carrier was earning fees for the use of its trailer during this intervening period of time: *ibid* at para 8. Still, consideration without possession by a would-be bailee is not enough for a bailment to be formed.

88 *Ibid* at paras 9–21.

89 [1991] BCJ No 242 (CA).

> so tainted with criminality or culpable immorality that as a matter of public policy the court will not assist him to recover. The joint criminal enterprise ground is merely an example, and perhaps the most common example, of public policy at work.[90]

In a bailment action, the defence arose for consideration in *Lewis*.[91] There, Gould DCJ of the Algoma District Court stated that, in Ontario, the *Negligence Act*,[92] while passed primarily to reduce contributory negligence to a partial defence rather than an absolute defence, had, in effect, also abrogated the defence of *ex turpi causa* and that there was no room left for it to operate. The relevant section of the Act, now contained in section 3 (rather than section 4), continues to provide that "In any action for damages that is founded upon the fault or negligence of the defendant if fault or negligence is found on the part of the plaintiff that contributed to the damages, the court shall apportion the damages in proportion to the degree of fault or negligence found against the parties respectively."[93]

That said, facts relevant to the defence of *ex turpi causa* still matter and still have to be accounted for in applying the rule contained in the above section. However, the effect of the rule in the statute here is that, where a plaintiff (bailor) is guilty of conduct *formerly* giving rise to *ex turpi causa*, that conduct will no longer provide the defendant (bailee) with an "absolute defence." Instead, where there is fault on the part of both the plaintiff and defendant that has contributed to the plaintiff's losses, damages are to be apportioned based on the degree of fault or negligence of each party.

In *Lewis*,[94] the plaintiff, an owner of a vehicle (who himself was highly intoxicated by alcohol at the time), allowed a friend of his, the defendant, who was also highly intoxicated by alcohol to the knowledge of the plaintiff, to drive his vehicle, for the purposes of a short trip that the friend wished to make. The defendant was *not* found to have been too intoxicated at the time to know he had assumed the role of driver as between them when the plaintiff had passed the keys to him to take over the driving of the vehicle. During the course of the trip, the defendant ran into a parked truck while in an impaired state, damaging the plaintiff's vehicle

90 *Ibid* at para 18 [paragraph numbers assigned by author].
91 Above note 23.
92 RSO 1960, c 261.
93 *Negligence Act*, RSO 1990, c N.1.
94 Above note 23.

and the truck. Later, the plaintiff settled the truck owner's court action that had been brought against him and the defendant. The plaintiff then sued the defendant for negligence, for the injuries done to his vehicle[95] and to recover the sum he had paid to the owner of the truck by way of indemnity under section 3 of the *Negligence Act*.[96]

Even though a bailment had not been pleaded by the plaintiff, Gould DCJ recognized that the facts as pleaded gave rise to a bailment, albeit one that could not be easily classified. While the defendant's driving was the immediate cause of the accident and clearly breached the duty of care over the vehicle that he owed to the plaintiff, the plaintiff's actions were not without fault. This fact was relevant to the defendant's pleading of the defence of *ex turpi causa*, which fact, according to the learned judge, had to be adjudicated under section 4 of Ontario's *Negligence Act*, rather than at common law, since it dealt with situations where both a plaintiff and a defendant are jointly at fault for a plaintiff's losses.[97] Applying that rule to the facts of the case, Gould DCJ opined:

> [I]t is clearly an action for damages that is founded upon the fault or negligence of the defendant in driving an automobile while his ability to drive it was impaired by alcohol and in negligently and without reasonable excuse running into and damaging a parked truck, as wll [sic] as damaging the plaintiff's car. I have found that the plaintiff was at fault in turning over the operation of his automobile to an intoxicated driver and that by so doing he contributed to the damages. It follows that the statute directs me to determine what degrees of fault or negligence should be found against the parties respectively and to apportion the damages in proportion to those degrees of fault.[98]

Based on the parties' respective degrees of fault, Gould DCJ proceeded to allocate damages equally between the parties, one-half to the plaintiff and one-half to the defendant.[99] Even though *ex turpi causa* is no longer an absolute defence to a negligence action or, by extension, to a bailment

95 Curiously, the plaintiff's automobile insurance had expired at 12:01 AM on the day in question and was not in force at the time of the accident, making the liability questions in the case even more pressing and consequential for the plaintiff (bailor): *ibid* at para 7.

96 *Ibid* at paras 1–12.

97 *Ibid* at paras 22–23.

98 *Ibid* at para 23.

99 *Ibid* at para 24.

action, section 3 of the *Negligence Act* will still result in a discount to a bailee where a bailor's own negligent act or fault is partly responsible for its own losses, even where the bailee's actions are the immediate cause of the plaintiff's (bailor's) losses. In terms of the challenges in determining an appropriate degree of fault on a given set of facts as between plaintiff and defendant, section 4 of the current *Negligence Act*[100] provides some relief. It states as follows:

> *Where parties to be deemed equally at fault*
>
> 4. If it is not practicable to determine the respective degree of fault or negligence as between any parties to an action, such parties shall be deemed to be equally at fault or negligent.

J. INHERENT VICE OR DEFECTS IN THE BAILED GOODS

1) No General Bailee Duty to Remediate Defects in Bailor Property Left for Repair Where These Defects Were Not Included in the Undertaking to Repair

Where a bailor's losses are found to be the result of an inherent vice or defect in the goods themselves, rather than caused by any want of care by the bailee, a bailee should be able to escape liability. In *Georgia-Pacific Building Materials Ltd v Apex Kenworth Ltd*,[101] the respondent's truck was destroyed by fire while in the appellant's repair shop for repairs. The vehicle had been in the shop at different times previously for other repairs, including for headlight and brake repairs, and most recently for a tune-up. A few days following the tune-up, the vehicle experienced an oil leak and had to be returned to the appellant's shop so that the leak could be remediated. The leak was repaired by the appellant and the vehicle taken for a test drive by the mechanic, who returned to the shop around 11:00 PM, closed the doors of the truck, and left it parked inside the shop. During the night, the truck was destroyed by fire. The fire was found to have originated in the truck itself. The truck was equipped with battery boxes on both sides of its cab. There were cables in very close proximity to the battery box covers, which wires were worn, likely due to rubbing on the battery box. This situation was well known by the respondent bailor, who used rags, rubber

100 Above note 93.
101 [1983] NBJ No 154 (CA).

tubing, or a board to cover the cables to try to prevent a shorting should contact between the wires and battery box covers be made. The trial judge found that this should have been apparent to the appellant from previous work that had been done by it on the truck, namely, the work that had been done to correct a problem with the lights.[102]

At trial, the cause of the fire was found to be a prolonged short circuit caused by the bad wiring, brought on by attrition to the wires and cables of the electrical system. These conclusions were supported by the appellant's expert evidence, which the trial judge accepted. The trial judge found fault in the appellant, in light of its knowledge of the poor condition of the wiring, for failing to take "particular care to guard against the possible dangers and consequences of the bad wiring," which the learned judge concluded was incongruent with an absence of negligence on its part.[103]

On appeal, Angers JA of the New Brunswick Court of Appeal found the trial judge's conclusion with respect to what ought to have been observed by the appellant when it was performing work to the lights — namely, the deteriorated condition of the wires — to be too sweeping and not clearly inferable from the evidence. In any case, Angers JA found that the appellant, as bailee, should owe no greater duty than the owner of the vehicle, who, through its employees, was clearly aware of the problem and the possible dangers of the shorting (as they had placed rags around the cables), yet took no steps to report to the appellant any wiring problem when the truck was brought in for the oil leak to be corrected. The judge found that the appellant's employees had not committed any acts of negligence for which the appellant should be held responsible.[104] Justice Angers of the Court of Appeal isolated the particular error committed by the trial judge as follows: "In my opinion, the error of the trial judge in the instant case was to add to the duties of a bailee a duty to repair what the trial judge found to be an obvious defect in the wiring. Such a duty to repair, if it is to exist, must be found in the undertaking to repair, not in the bailment."[105]

The conclusion of Justice Anger of the Court of Appeal here is well founded. A bailee's duty of care must be informed by undertakings that it assumes, or does not assume, by contract at the outset of a bailment relationship when taking possession of a bailor's property for repair or

---

102 *Ibid* at paras 1–7.
103 *Ibid* at paras 7–10.
104 *Ibid* at paras 8–14.
105 *Ibid* at para 11.

servicing. It would be asking too much from a bailee to expect it to safeguard against hazards it is not aware of that may arise due to latent defects in bailor property, or that it is aware of but has not been contracted to address. It is not enough, merely, for a bailor to show that property has been damaged while in the possession of the bailee, as bailees do not owe bailors a standard of perfection. However, it is submitted that bailees be cautious about accepting bailor property that has clear and obvious defects that do not form part of the undertaking to repair assumed by the bailee, since such defects could create unacceptable risks of fire or loss that could make the bailee liable, if not to the bailor for damage to its property, then to other bailors who may have property on the premises as well. Where the defect is latent, and does not form part of the undertaking, bailees should easily be able to escape liability, as will be seen in the case discussed immediately below.

2) No General Duty on a Bailee to Take Impracticable Steps to Protect Against Bailor Losses Caused by Unknown Inherent Defects in Other Bailor Property

In *University of New Brunswick v Murdoch*,[106] the plaintiff's vehicles were damaged by fire while parked inside of the defendant's locked repair building together with some other customers' vehicles in the immediate vicinity. The damaged vehicles included a Subaru that suffered heavy damage as a result of the fire and was considered a total loss. The building was well constructed and fenced, but it was not protected by a fire alarm system or equipped with smoke detectors. A night guard was also not employed, though the garage was fenced and protected by two guard dogs, and fire extinguishers were located at key locations. The defendant was found to have left no lights on and to have created no fire hazards before securing the building at the end of the business day, which might serve as a possible explanation for the fire. He had maintained his premises, as an auto body repair and painting shop, adequately.[107]

Based on expert evidence before the learned judge, Creaghan J of the New Brunswick Court of Queen's Bench found the fire to have originated in the motor area of the Subaru. Since the Subaru's motor had not

106 [1987] NBJ No 227 (QBTD).
107 *Ibid* at paras 1–15 [paragraph numbers assigned by author].

been worked on by the defendant or his employees, and the vehicle had only been painted and was awaiting pickup at the time of the fire,[108] the learned judge concluded that the engine must have, unbeknownst to the defendant, had an "inherent defect" in it that caused the fire and that this cause was not attributable to any want of care on the part of the defendant: "In my opinion, the cause of the fire was a defect in the power source of the Subaru, an inherent vice and not due to a lack of care on the part of the defendant."[109]

While this fire hazard could have been prevented had the Subaru's battery been disconnected prior to the defendant's leaving the premises, it would have been impracticable for him to do so, given that seventeen customer vehicles were inside the building, and all would have required the same treatment. As well, there was no reasonable need for a guard or other systems to be in place to protect the plaintiffs' property from fire in these circumstances, since the defendant's business was not found to be a "potential fire-risk." The fact that a guard or certain acts (in this case a disconnecting of the bailor vehicles' batteries) might have saved the plaintiff (bailor) property (or reduced the damage arising from the inherent vice to other bailors' property stored with it) is not enough, without more, to fix a bailee with liability in these circumstances where due care was taken by the bailee and where the bailors' losses are due to an inherent and undetectable defect in other bailor property received. While a higher standard of care on the part of the bailee might increase the odds of such vices in other bailor property being uncovered and addressed by the bailee, or the damage from them being mitigated, a bailee does not owe a standard of perfection, or near perfection, to a bailor. Such standards, if they are to exist in these circumstances, must be contracted for by the parties.

3) Bailee Duty to Remedy Obvious Defects in Bailed Goods Based on Expected Regular Inspection of Bailed Goods Under the Contract of Bailment

Where the bailee owes the bailor a duty to inspect its goods regularly to ensure their safekeeping during the bailment, it may *not* be able to escape liability by relying on an "inherent defect" in the bailed goods

108 *Ibid* at paras 17–20.
109 *Ibid* at para 25.

themselves, at least not where the bailee fails to do required and anticipated inspections and the evidence shows that such inspections would have revealed an obvious inherent defect that could have been easily remediated by the bailee so as to have minimized the losses to the bailor. In *SHL Corp v Harvey Hooper Lobsters Ltd*,[110] the plaintiff lobster pound entered into a contract with the defendant in the fall season to store a large quantity of live purchased lobsters for it in New Brunswick, pending their delivery in February and March of the following year to Maine, where the plaintiff's business premises were located. It was agreed that the defendant would place the lobsters in the water, provide them with sustenance from a nearby fish plant, and remove them from the water by dragging when delivery to the plaintiff was required the following year. The defendant was to be paid thirty-five cents per pound for the storage. The plaintiff's lobsters were to be segregated and stored separately from the defendant's lobsters, in section 3 of the defendant's three-section tank. The plaintiff placed insurance on the lobsters to be housed in the defendant's facilities, which insurance required segregation of the lobsters to be effective. The plaintiff made several shipments of lobster to the defendant on various dates in the fall, which included purchases of several thousand pounds from the defendant itself, which was then stored by the defendant in its storage tanks.[111]

When February of the new year arrived and the plaintiff received delivery of thousands of pounds of lobster from the defendant, it discovered that many of the lobsters were infected with a disease, which disease caused both the plaintiff and the defendant to lose several thousand pounds of lobster (even after anticipated shrinkage due to water loss was taken into account). The plaintiff sued for its losses, arguing that the defendant had breached its duty of care as bailee. The defendant, for its part, argued that the plaintiff had introduced into its pound the disease via one of its October lobster shipments, purchased from a third party, and that it could not be held liable for losses that the plaintiff had caused to itself. The defendant argued that it was this inherent defect that caused the losses sustained by the parties, and not any failing on the part of the defendant.[112]

Justice Barry of the New Brunswick Court of Queen's Bench, Trial Division, considering the expert evidence before him, acknowledged the

110 [1980] NBJ No 42 (QBTD) [*SHL Corp*].
111 *Ibid* at paras 1–13.
112 *Ibid* at paras 19–38.

presence of the disease as being the culprit of the parties' losses while at the same time concluding that the cause of the infection was not as "clear-cut" as argued by the defendant. He noted that the disease could have arisen from either the plaintiff's or the defendant's stock, especially so in light of the fact that the defendant had not, as agreed, stored the plaintiff's lobsters in a segregated tank, instead mixing the plaintiff's and the defendant's stock together.[113]

Justice Barry found that, as part of its duty of care, the defendant had a duty to inspect the lobsters that it was storing by using divers, on a far more frequent basis than it did, except in the winter when the ice was covering the pound preventing such inspection. This duty was particularly pertinent, since it had chosen, contrary to the plaintiff's instructions, to store the plaintiff's lobsters together with its own in sections 1 and 2 of its storage tanks, instead of in section 3, as had been agreed upon between the parties. On the evidence, the defendant had examined the condition of the lobsters in sections 1 and 2 of its storage tanks, where both the plaintiff's and the defendant's lobsters were stored together, using its divers, only twice over the course of the storage, even though the depth of the tanks was no more than six to eight feet and such inspections by the defendant could easily have been performed. More consequentially, the defendant had allowed three months to pass from the beginning of the storage before examining the lobsters in the tanks. The "danger signs" caused by the disease would have been patently obvious upon such inspection (the lobsters infected with the disease would be dead very shortly after their arrival and placement in the tanks); the problem could have easily been rectified (the dead and diseased lobsters could have been removed from the tanks); and the issue needed to be rectified immediately to minimize the damage done to the other lobsters, including the plaintiff's. Had the defendant been truly concerned about the plaintiff's lobsters' possibly being infected with disease upon receipt, Barry J found that it should have placed the plaintiff's lobsters in section 3 of its tanks, where such an infection could have easily been spotted and remediated before any significant damage was done to the plaintiff's lobsters, or its own, which could result in possible liability for the defendant as bailee. In the result, the defendant was found liable as bailee to the plaintiff.[114]

---

113 *Ibid* at paras 33–41.

114 *Ibid* at paras 42–44.

This decision illustrates that, where a bailee has a duty, and the ability, to check on the condition of the bailed goods, this will sometimes require it to find and remedy "obvious defects" discovered in the bailed goods, at least where the correction is not overly burdensome. A failure to do so can amount to a breach of the bailee's duty of care. Bailees in the position of the defendant in the case should take care to reject bailors' goods that are clearly contaminated or defective, given the obvious dangers receipt of such property entails. Bailees, where required by the bailment contract, also need to ensure that regular inspections of bailed goods are made during the course of the bailment to prevent or minimize damage to those goods. Lastly, to ensure that defects that may arise in bailor property during the course of a bailment can be properly identified and attributed solely to the property, bailees will sometimes need to segregate bailor property from their own.[115]

K. *VOLENTI NON FIT INJURIA*

The defence of *volenti non fit injuria*—that is, voluntary assumption of risk by the bailor—can be a complete defence to a bailment action, at least where all the damage done to the bailor's goods can be directly traced to a bailor's voluntary assumption of certain risks that it can be said to have clearly and unequivocally agreed to accept upon the commencement of the bailment.[116] Acceptance can be indicated either expressly, through an express waiver, or impliedly, through a bailor's conduct. The risks accepted by a bailor may involve, among other things, accepting the use of bailee premises subject to certain limitations; bailor insistences that goods be stored in a particular part of the bailee's premises, which is less secure than elsewhere; or agreements to allow goods to be transported in sub-optimal manners or conditions.[117] Certainly acceptance of such

115 The defendant's failure in *SHL Corp, ibid* to segregate the plaintiff's lobsters, as required by the bailment contract, was a clear deviation from the contract. The breach was probably enough, without more, to have made the defendant strictly liable to the plaintiff for its losses, irrespective of the defendant's subsequent failures in inspecting the plaintiff's stock after the act of deviation had occurred.

116 However, a bailee's subsequent failure to immediately notify a bailor as to damages to its property caused by certain risks assumed by the bailor upon the commencement of the bailment, in order that steps may be taken by the bailor to minimize the losses, may limit the protection afforded by the defence: see *Branton v Maritime Moving and Storage Inc*, 2003 NLSCTD 156 [*Branton*].

117 *Ibid* at paras 19–21; *Quigley v Rands*, [1982] BCJ No 367 (Co Ct) [*Quigley*].

risks entails acceptance of the foreseeable damages and losses arising from them, be it from theft, vandalism, fire, or an increased likelihood of property damage. It would seem, since the analysis of whether a bailee has met its standard of care is always contextual, that the defence may allow a bailee to drop below the level set by industry practice. However, it is submitted that there must be clear acceptance of the risks by the bailor; any uncertainty here should inure to the benefit of the bailor and the standard of care should be the one set by industry practice. Where it is impracticable for a bailor to observe or discover certain deficiencies in a bailee's premises where goods will be stored, such as where a thorough inspection or extensive efforts would have to be taken, the bailor should not be assumed to have agreed to such deficiencies.[118] Where such deficiencies drop below the standard of reasonable care, or the industry standard, and this leads to damage to bailed goods, liability should be fixed against the bailee accordingly.

1) Bailor Consent to Use Bailee Premises Subject to Certain Limitations

Where a bailor has had the opportunity to observe a bailee's premises where their goods are to be stored, or equipment that is going to be used by a bailee on their goods, should the bailor be taken to have agreed to any risk of injury to their goods based on any apparent or evident defect or shortcoming in the bailee's equipment or premises? This is a question rife with difficulty, because the history of the relations between parties to a bailment can be a relevant consideration in determining the nature of a bailment in a given set of circumstances. Where a bailor has taken goods to a bailee with clear knowledge of shortcomings in the bailee's facilities or equipment, it would not be fair not to consider this fact in establishing the terms of the bailment, including the reasonable expectation of the parties as to the applicable standard of care to be applied to the bailment. In

---

118 For example, in *Furness-Withy & Co Ltd v Ahlin* (1917), 35 DLR 150 at 153–54 (NSCA), it was not practicable for the defendant (bailor), the master of a ship coming to a certain port for repairs to be made to its ship, to inspect the underside of the plaintiff's (bailee's) dock using divers to uncover that some of the supporting piles had been substantially weakened by worms, which had eaten part of them away. Thus, when the plaintiff's goods were later damaged after the wharf under the shed in which the defendant was storing the plaintiff's goods collapsed, liability was properly fixed against the plaintiff.

Quigley,[119] the plaintiff and the defendant entered into an agency agreement in order for the defendant to sell the plaintiff's truck in return for a commission. The plaintiff transferred possession of the truck to the defendant (bailee) agent. The parties agreed that the truck was to be stored in a third party's yard, also used by the defendant to store his own equipment. The defendant accordingly transferred possession to the third party's yard, well known to him to have little to no security. As it happened, the truck was stolen and never located. While the defendant was clearly found to have breached his standard of care (as bailee) in storing the plaintiff's vehicle in a yard with such minimal security—especially in light of the assurances of greater security that he had given to the plaintiff[120]—could the third party be found in breach of a sub-bailment and liable to the plaintiff in damages for the little-to-no security that it had provided to the plaintiff's vehicle prior to the vehicle's theft from its yard under its arrangements with the plaintiff and the defendant?

While McTaggart Co Ct J of the British Columbia County Court doubted that a sub-bailment could be created between the parties, given the lack of security and control exercised by the third party over the plaintiff's vehicle at the material times, even if a sub-bailment were created, the learned judge found the bailment would have been subject to certain limitations. Namely, that the plaintiff and defendant had agreed (based on a visit they had made together, prior to the commencement of the storage) to use the third party's property to store the plaintiff's vehicle despite the evident lack of security measures in place on the property to ensure the vehicle's safekeeping. This was supported by evidence given by the plaintiff's son (acting as agent for the plaintiff) who testified at trial that, based on the visit he had made to the third party's premises with the defendant, he "was satisfied it was a reasonably safe yard."[121] The acquiescence by the parties to use the third party's yard in its present (imperfect and insecure) state was also supported by a sign on the premises that read: "Private Property. All items left at owner's risk." The learned judge found that the defendant knew or ought to have known (given his previous and ongoing use of the third party's premises for storage of his own equipment) that property left on the premises was subject to the terms contained on the signage, which was present on the premises when the plaintiff's vehicle was left there

119 Above note 117.
120 *Ibid* at paras 1–16.
121 *Ibid* at para 12.

for storage and apparent safekeeping.[122] Thus, the court was right to have refused to fix liability against the third party as sub-bailee or otherwise for any failings in the services it had provided to the parties with respect to the storage of the plaintiff's property.[123]

Despite the ruling in *Quigley* it seems reasonable for a bailee, especially one who is being paid a fee presumably for their expertise, to have to meet a certain minimum standard of care, in accordance with industry practice in the trade, by the very nature of the transaction (being one of bailment), irrespective of a bailor's opportunity to have observed certain clear defects in the bailee's premises.[124] While no absolute rule, therefore, is possible or desirable here, where the evidence is equivocal on whether certain limitations in a bailee's premises and security were observed or acquiesced to by a bailor, so as to make the bailment subject to certain limitations, it is submitted that the standard of care applicable be determined by the industry standard.

2) A Bailor's Agreement to Allow Bailed Goods to Be Transported in Sub-optimal Conditions

Sometimes a bailor may agree to run the risk of having its goods moved or transported by a bailee in dangerous conditions by instructing them, for example, to begin the transport despite its clear awareness of the risk of damage consequent upon such transport. Such an agreement will often be a matter of convenience for the bailor, creating some kind of cost or time savings. For example, in *Branton*,[125] the plaintiff (bailor) and defendant entered into a moving and storage agreement for consideration, involving certain household goods and furnishings owned by the plaintiff. The goods were moved by the defendant onto its truck and transported to the defendant's premises, where they were stored until redelivered to the plaintiff. Upon their return, the plaintiff found that her furnishings were damaged. On the day of the move, it was found that the plaintiff had instructed the defendant, clearly and unequivocally, to move the goods in rainy weather (of consequence), despite the unavailability of an enclosed

---

122 *Ibid* at para 9.

123 *Ibid* at paras 18–22.

124 See reasons of Lord Watson in *Brabant & Co v King*, [1895] AC 632 at 641–42 as cited in *British Motor Corp of Canada Ltd v Ross E Judge Auto Transport Ltd*, [1966] NSJ No 11 at para 32 (SC) [*British Motor*].

125 Above note 116.

defendant vehicle for the move. The plaintiff's residential tenancy was at an end, and she wanted to avoid having to pay another month's rent and so proceeded to have the defendant move the goods in an open-back pickup truck. The defendant did employ a tarpaulin to shield the goods during their transport to the defendant's premises but admitted that the goods were soaking wet when he spread them out in the middle of his storage unit to enable them to dry.[126]

Justice Dunn for the Newfoundland and Labrador Supreme Court—Trial Division found that it was raining for at least 50 percent of the move, during which time at least two loads of the plaintiff's furniture were being placed aboard the defendant's vehicle and transported to the storage unit. This had clearly led to some of the damage to the goods present on their redelivery to the plaintiff after the storage period had elapsed. The plaintiff had proceeded with knowledge of the risks of moving her goods in inclement weather in an unenclosed truck. However, voluntary assumption of risk was not a complete defence in the circumstances, since the defendant (bailee) had failed to notify the plaintiff as to the state of her furnishings upon depositing them in the storage unit so that the plaintiff could immediately take whatever measures might be necessary to mitigate the damage. As well, the defendant's apparent methods for minimizing the damage to the plaintiff's furnishings post-transport had proven unsuccessful.[127] Accordingly, Dunn J apportioned only 25 percent of the damages to the plaintiff, holding the defendant liable for 75 percent of the damages.[128] As this case demonstrates, for a bailee to discharge its standard of care based on voluntary assumption of risk by a bailor, it may still need to take steps to minimize or prevent damage that is developing in bailor property arising from the risk being realized or, alternatively, give a bailor the opportunity to address damage arising from the risk being realized, immediately and without delay. To be sure, to allow a bailee to avoid all possibility of liability, a better option for a

---

126 *Ibid* at paras 1–13 and 27–28.

127 *Ibid* at paras 27–33.

128 *Ibid* at para 33. Justice Dunn also mentioned that the defendant could have avoided all liability if it had refused to transport the goods, or had obtained a disclaimer and confirmation from the plaintiff confirming her instructions to proceed with the move despite the clear dangers of doing so: *ibid* at para 30. However, if the defence of voluntary assumption of risk is available impliedly based on a party's conduct, why was a written waiver necessary? Clearly, the conduct of the plaintiff had evinced the necessary intention.

bailee might be to refuse to move goods in circumstances where damage to them is unavoidable or highly likely, or where the efforts to ameliorate such damage are too burdensome or are not guaranteed to resolve the damage. Moving goods where damage is assured does not seem conducive to a bailee's duty of safekeeping.

L. WHERE BAILEE LIABILITY IS EXPRESSLY COVERED BY A BAILOR'S INSURANCE POLICY?

Where the bailment contract contains an express term protecting a bailee from all liability arising from the bailment, the bailee will not be liable for losses incurred during the bailment. In *Joseph Abrams Ltd v Coady*,[129] an agreement was made between the plaintiff and the defendant Coady, whereby Coady would find an able and trustworthy driver to transport the plaintiff's vehicle from Toronto to California and would deliver the plaintiff's vehicle to the driver for transport to California. The defendant Coady had conveyed to the defendant Vint that he would be assuming no liability whatsoever in driving the vehicle from Toronto to Los Angeles, since he would be fully covered under the plaintiff's insurance policy. As it happens, Vint was involved in an accident with the vehicle en route to California, and the vehicle was damaged, together with damage being occasioned to the other vehicle involved in the collision. The amount of the damage to both cars was paid by the insurer, who subsequently, in the name of the plaintiff, brought an action against the defendants in bailment alleging negligence and seeking a damage award equal to the amount of the repairs paid out.[130]

Justice Laidlaw of the Court of Appeal for Ontario found that a very limited bailment had been created between the plaintiff and Coady, which bailment terminated when Coady delivered the vehicle to the defendant Vint for transport to California, pursuant to a separate and further contract entered into between Coady and Vint. During the course of the bailment, Coady had not been negligent in either delivering the vehicle to the driver or in selecting the driver, since he had done a thorough background check and had safely delivered possession of the vehicle to Vint. The argument that Coady had assumed a greater duty of safekeeping

129 [1963] OJ No 864 (CA).
130 *Ibid* at paras 1–7.

that extended beyond finding a driver for the plaintiff and delivering the vehicle to that driver on behalf of the plaintiff was rejected, as his role as agent for the plaintiff was explicitly limited to doing these things. In any case, possession, safekeeping, and control had been relinquished to Vint, and, as a result, the bailment was at an end.[131]

More pertinent for our purposes was whether Vint was liable in bailment for the damage of the vehicle, or whether he was protected from liability under the plaintiff's automobile insurance policy. Justice Laidlaw of the Court of Appeal found that the representation that had been made by Coady to Vint that he would be covered against any risk of loss under the plaintiff's insurance policy was consistent with the information that Coady had received from an employee for the plaintiff company. Indeed, it had become an express condition of the bailment between Vint and the plaintiff, and Vint was accordingly not liable in bailment for the damage caused to the vehicle.[132]

As apparent, where the bailor has an appropriate insurance policy in place on its vehicle and expressly agrees to cover a bailee who is driving the vehicle with their consent under the policy, pursuant to a bailment contract, a bailee will be covered for all losses occasioned during the bailment and will not be liable.[133] A bailee *will not* have to disprove negligence to avoid liability, as it would have to ordinarily. The issue of negligence does not need to be addressed if there is a term in the bailment contract that completely indemnifies the bailee from all liability arising from the bailment under the bailor's insurance policy.

---

131 *Ibid* at para 13.

132 *Ibid* at paras 14–15. The decision to find the bailment between the plaintiff and Coady to be at an end at the time Vint received the vehicle into his possession was the proper one to be made in the circumstances. Bailments require possession and physical control. These things were surrendered by Coady upon handing possession of the vehicle over to Vint. Since Coady had delivered the vehicle safely into Vint's possession and had not been negligent in selecting him as a driver, it was right to allow the appeal with respect to Coady as well, and to exonerate him from liability.

133 In these circumstances, a subrogated action by an insurer will likely not succeed. This is because it is a standard term under many automobile insurance contracts that an insurer waive subrogation against third-party drivers of a vehicle, so long as the driver of the vehicle received the insured's consent to drive, abides by the conditions of the policy, and is not otherwise excluded by the terms of the insurance contract: *Cecconi v State Farm Automobile Insurance Co*, [1991] OJ No 1059 (Gen Div).

M. EXTRANEOUS CAUSE: THE DEFENCE OF *NOVUS ACTUS INTERVENIENS*

1) Bailees Must Have Adequate Safeguards in Place Against Reasonably Foreseeable Risks of Loss to Bailor Property to Rely on this Defence

Where the bailor's losses can be shown to have been caused by a determined third party, outside of the bailment relationship, who overcame a bailee's reasonable safeguards in place to protect the bailor's goods, the bailee should be exonerated pursuant to the defence of *novus actus interveniens*. In *Brook's Wharf and Bull Wharf, Ltd v Goodman Brothers*,[134] a case dealing with the theft of a bailor's goods from a warehouse in which they were being stored, Lord Wright MR, stated the following:

> In the present case, the stealing of the goods being admitted, the plaintiffs have given evidence that they have taken all reasonable precautions to protect the goods against the risk of theft, and they say that they have satisfied the burden of proof which rests upon them . . . .
>
> Their explanation is, then, that the thieves must have shown ingenuity and daring against which reasonable precautions could not avail. Hence, I think the plaintiffs discharge the burden of proof upon them if they can show that the theft took place notwithstanding that they had taken all reasonable precautions to guard against the danger.[135]

Yet where the occurrence — the vandalism, theft, fire, or other occurrence — is found to have been likely preventable based on the taking of reasonable precautions, the bailee should face liability accordingly.[136] In *Turkitch v Ford Motor Credit Co of Canada*,[137] such a circumstance was present. There, the defendant assignee under a sales contract repossessed the plaintiff's automobile, by reason of the plaintiff's failure to make some remaining payments on a vehicle he had purchased, and stored it in a third party's compound. When the plaintiff attended at the defendant's premises to tender payment to the defendant, he was directed to the third-party compound, where the vehicle was being stored. There, the plaintiff

---

134 [1937] 1 KB 534 at 539 [*Brook's Wharf*] as cited in *British Motor*, above note 124 at para 35.

135 *Brook's Wharf*, above note 134 at 539.

136 See, for example, *British Motor*, above note 124.

137 [1978] MJ No 301 (QB).

learned that his vehicle had been destroyed by fire and refused to accept delivery of it.[138] The plaintiff's action in bailment against the defendant succeeded, as the defendant did not have the right, under statute, to repossess the vehicle, as less than 25 percent of the cash price of the vehicle remained to be paid.[139] Of more relevance, for our purposes, however, is the defendant's (bailor's) third-party claim against the compound, arising from the sub-bailment that arose between those two parties, in which the defendant alleged negligence against the compound for the loss of the vehicle. The compound succeeded in defeating the defendant's bailment claim because the evidence showed it had adequate security in place to protect the bailor's goods from damage by fire or otherwise at the time of the loss, including an eight-foot fence, topped with barbed wire and equipped with flood lights, surrounding the compound; locked gates; and an unleashed guard dog. Moreover, the cause of the fire was "a deliberate act of vandalism by an unknown but determined person."[140] The defendant, in its own evidence, had testified that it had regularly deposited vehicles in the compound and had never in the past had any concerns about the compound's security. Certainly bailees do not owe a standard of perfection to bailors and, to exonerate themselves from liability, must show only that reasonable care to prevent against reasonably foreseeable risks of loss by third parties was taken. Bailees should not be required to show that a greater standard of care could have prevented the happening but only that *reasonable care* was taken to protect the bailor's goods.

In *627360 Saskatchewan Ltd v Bellrose*,[141] the respondent was hired to renovate a building for the appellant. The respondent owned tools used in the job and was eventually requested by the appellant to leave the tools at the site where the work was being done for the greater convenience of the parties, rather than bringing them back and forth from that business's garage offsite as they were needed. The tools were stored in the maintenance building located on the appellant's property. The locks to the building were changed by the respondent, based on instructions received from the appellant, upon the respondent's voicing concerns to the appellant about the unfettered access to the building by its employees obtaining at the time. As a further precaution against theft, the appellant requested that

138 *Ibid* at paras 1–7.
139 *Ibid* at para 6.
140 *Ibid* at paras 14–17.
141 2007 SKQB 14 [*Bellrose* QB], leave to appeal refused, 2007 SKCA 23.

the respondent change the locks to the building once every three months. The number of keys giving access to the building was eventually whittled down to two or three. Subsequently, the respondent built an office in the maintenance building for the principal of the appellant business to perform his duties, while the tools still remained housed in the building. Thereafter, the respondent's tools were stolen from the building.[142]

The door had been pried open by unknown thieves, as evidenced by splinters on the inside. The respondent's position was that the installation of the office had made the building a more attractive target for theft and that the appellant had failed, as bailee, to exercise reasonable care in the circumstances to protect the tools from theft. In these circumstances, the pertinent question was whether the steps taken by the appellant were adequate to establish that a break-in would not have been a reasonably foreseeable event. The trial judge, in the provincial court below, found they were not:

> I find that a break-in is a reasonably foreseeable event. For example, many people in Saskatoon try to protect their homes and buildings by security alarms and other security devices. The question then becomes, did the Defendants exercise reasonable care for the Plaintiff's tools? This was for the Defendants to show. They did not. They called no evidence. I am unable to conclude that a deadbolt with a lock in a wood door and a burning light over the entrance constitutes reasonable care. Perhaps a steel door with a reinforced door frame and a motion detector might have been considered[143]

The fact that no break-ins had occurred in the past[144] was not enough to disqualify the intervening act here. The learned judge's decision was upheld on appeal. As can be seen, a bailee's failure to exercise reasonable care in relation to the cause of the loss at issue, such as a failure to properly secure a door leading to a break-in and theft, will make the defence of *novus actus interveniens* unavailable to the bailee, since it will not be possible, in these circumstances, to say that the lost was not reasonably foreseeable.[145]

---

142 *Bellrose* QB, above note 141 at paras 1–10.

143 *Ibid* at para 23.

144 *Ibid* at para 10.

145 While this was not addressed in the case, surely the respondent must have been aware of the deficiencies with the door, since he had done much work in the building and, while he had made other objections to the appellant's security measures, he *did not* raise these deficiencies with the appellant. Should the respondent, thus, have been seen as having acquiesced to this limitation on the use of the appellant's premises for the storage of his tools?

2) Industry Practice and Context

In *Hamilton v Chris Marion Holdings Ltd (cob Servicemaster of Ottawa)*,[146] while the plaintiff was away on a winter vacation, pipes and radiators in her home burst following the failure of the furnace in the house, causing the house to become drenched with water. When the caretaker of the home attended there and discovered the water damage, he contacted the plaintiff's daughter and insurance agent. Ultimately, an independent insurance adjuster attended at the house in the plaintiff's absence and a meeting was convened with the plaintiff's daughter and other interested parties. It was decided by the plaintiff's daughter, on the recommendation of the independent insurance adjuster, that the large gun collection housed in one of the rooms in the house be moved out for cleaning, storage, and safekeeping, since a firm would have to be engaged to come and clean up and restore the house. The measure was to prevent against the risk of theft to the guns in a vacant house where various workers would have to attend for cleanup purposes as well as of water damage to the guns that could be occasioned if the guns were not removed from the house. The adjuster specifically recommended a firm with which he was very familiar, Servicemaster of Ottawa. He was aware that one of their employees was knowledgeable about guns. This recommendation was accepted by the plaintiff's daughter, who had no business experience or expertise in these matters.[147]

As a consequence, the plaintiff's property was transferred into the possession of Servicemaster and moved to their premises. When the house was restored, the adjuster recommended that the guns still not be returned to a vacant house, where they would be subject to the real prospect of theft. The caretaker of the house, an agent of the plaintiff's, accepted this recommendation, and the gun collection accordingly remained with Servicemaster. A few days later, half the gun collection was stolen from Servicemaster's premises at night following a break and enter. The guns were taken away by stealth: the thieves had removed a metal fire door from the rear of Servicemaster's premises to gain entry to the stockroom where the guns were stored.[148]

The plaintiff sued Servicemaster in bailment for damages for the lost property (as well the insurance adjuster in negligence for damages

146 [1981] OJ No 523 (HCJ) [*Hamilton*].
147 *Ibid* at paras 1–13.
148 *Ibid* at paras 13–14 and 20.

for having recommended Servicemaster, among other reasons). The bailment action was based on a deficiency in the security at Servicemaster's premises, namely that the premises did not have an alarm system and, more important, that the back door was not properly secured, as well as on the fact that the defendant (bailee) had not advised the plaintiff that it would not be putting insurance on the goods while in its possession. The hinge pins on the fire door were on the exterior surface of the door rather than inside the door. The case put by the plaintiff essentially was that, because of these failings, the defendant had no great difficulty in gaining access to the defendant's premises and, ultimately, the guns that were in the defendant's possession for safekeeping.

In determining the applicable standard of care, Reid J of the Ontario Supreme Court—High Court of Justice underlined that Servicemaster was not in the moving and storing business; that the company did not realize that the gun collection was of high value[149] and therefore particularly susceptible to theft; and that the company would be storing the guns only for a brief period of time.[150] All of these things militated toward a lower rather than higher standard of care. In any case, Reid J concluded that, even if the additional measures had been in place—that is, even if the hinges were on the inside of the fire door—this would not have prevented the theft:

> It seems to me that the guns might well have been stolen if the hinges were on the inside. I say that because the circumstances suggest that the guns were the real object of the thieves' interest. True, the premises were disturbed, and files were open and papers thrown about and liquor was taken but nothing else of real value was stolen. The thieves appeared to know that the guns were in the storage room and broke in to get them. In other words, this was not a random theft. The premises were not burglarized simply because they were easy to break into. It seems to me that the thieves had a definite object, the burglary was clearly carefully planned, and I doubt if altering the door as plaintiff suggests would have deterred them.[151]

149 While Servicemaster might not have had specific awareness of the high value of the guns, it was an extensive collection, and the insurance adjuster had entrusted the guns to the company in large part because of its general experience and trustworthiness, and also on the basis that one of its employees, to the specific knowledge of the adjuster, had knowledge about guns. These things, while not adverted to by Reid J, could have been used by the court to support a higher rather than lower standard of care.

150 *Ibid* at paras 23–25.

151 *Ibid* at para 28.

While it is true that loss or damage by determined third-party thieves can exonerate a bailee, this should only be where the bailee can demonstrate that it had the minimum security precautions in place at the material times to show that it was taking reasonable care of the goods to prevent against reasonably foreseeable losses, including theft.[152] This is the key issue, not whether the precautions, if in place, would have actually deterred the thieves and prevented the theft. That enhanced security measures would have successfully prevented the theft can never be known definitively and so is setting the bar too high. While Servicemaster was not in the business of storing goods, it still should have been required to meet a minimum standard of care for a bailee for reward in the circumstances, which certainly required reference to be made to the industry practices in the locale. It should not have received a pass based on the isolated nature of its foray into the area. All that said, Reid J's finding, based on the evidence heard, of "little conformity"[153] in the industry on the practice at issue suggests that having hinge pins on the inside of fire doors *was not* a standard practice of storers in the industry, meaning that Servicemaster's lack of adherence to this practice did not mean that it had breached its standard of care in the circumstances. Interestingly, Reid J made no explicit finding on the lack of an alarm system but, given that the locks were found to be adequate in the circumstances and that Servicemaster was found to have owed a relatively low standard of care in the circumstances, it is doubtful that the lack of an alarm system would have had any effect on the learned judge's conclusion that the defendant had satisfied its standard of care.[154]

---

152 This case is distinguishable from *Hertz Canada Ltd v Suburban Motors Ltd*, 2000 BCSC 667, since there, the precautions taken by the defendant (bailee) easily met the minimum standard of care required in the circumstances even though they were still overcome by the third-party thieves. Thus, a finding in support of the defendant was clearly warranted.

153 *Hamilton*, above note 146 at para 23.

154 Relying on *Mason v Morrow's Moving & Storage Ltd*, [1978] BCJ No 1230 (CA) [*Mason*], Reid J also found that the failure of the defendant (bailee) to inform the plaintiff that it would provide no insurance cover on the goods was not viewed as a breach of the standard of care, since there is no general duty on bailees in most circumstances to inform: *Hamilton*, above note 146 at para 30. The plaintiff also failed to fix liability against the insurance adjuster in negligence, as he had based his opinions and recommendations on his long-term relationship with Servicemaster, on reasonable grounds, and had nothing to "gain personally" from the advice given. Since there was no general duty on Servicemaster to advise the plaintiff as to the lack of insurance cover on the goods while in its possession, there could be no correspondent antecedent duty on the adjuster to inquire into it. The agent owed his allegiance to the insurance

3) Clear Situations of Duress

Giovanetti v GK Rose Appraisals Ltd[155] also involves the taking of bailed goods by unknown third parties, albeit by determined robbers rather than determined thieves. In this case, Gruchy J underlines where the focus needs to be in cases involving the loss of bailed goods by extraneous cause such as theft—that is, on the actual level of care provided by the bailee and whether it met the minimum threshold, not on whether the additional precautions might have prevented the theft. In that case, the defendant (bailee) maintained very tight security with respect to the plaintiff's jewellery being stored at its premises. The merchandise was kept in a safe when not displayed, which safe was kept in a room the access to which was monitored at all times; there was an alarm system and only those patrons who were recognized by the principals of the business, and had a scheduled appointment, were permitted access to the premises; and there was a camera at the entrance of the premises to monitor all those entering or approaching the entrance. Despite all these measures, a principal of the business was accosted by armed robbers as he was opening the business on the day in question. The principal was forced at gunpoint to disengage the security system and to open the safe, and was subsequently gagged and bound, allowing the robbers to make off with the plaintiff's jewellery.[156]

The plaintiff (bailor) argued that the defendant was liable as bailee because, after the robbery, it did not redeliver the jewellery when the plaintiff demanded his jewellery back.[157] Notwithstanding the robbery, Gruchy J found that the defendant had taken more than reasonable precautions to prevent the crime and that the principal had no choice but to obey the robbers' commands in the circumstances. While this clearly prevented the

---

company he worked for. Absent a "special relationship," he owed the plaintiff no legal duty at all and was simply acting as a good Samaritan in assisting the plaintiff's daughter, who was clearly out of her element: *ibid* at paras 33–37.

155 [1994] NSJ No 44 (SC).

156 *Ibid* at paras 2–6.

157 *Ibid* at para 3. The plaintiff also argued that, prior to the robbery, the defendant had *not* notified the authorities of a sighting of a suspicious person lingering in the area around the jewellery store, which notification might have prevented the robbery, and that this amounted to a breach of its standard of care. Justice Gruchy found there was no such duty on the defendant in the circumstances, since there was nothing of any significance that could have been reported to police. In any case, there was no causal connection between the robbery and the mysterious individual, beyond a mere suspicion, and thus any failings on the part of the defendant (bailee) were immaterial in the final analysis: *ibid* at para 13.

duty to redeliver on demand from being carried out, it did not amount to negligence. A mere happening of the loss was not enough, without more, to fix liability against the defendant in the circumstances in the absence of a special contract.[158] As apparent, a bailee does not owe a standard of perfection, or near perfection, to a bailor, and, while a failure to redeliver on demand by a bailee will be enough, *prima facie*, to trigger the presumption of negligence on a bailee (where the bailment is at will), it should not make the presumption an irrebuttable one. Where a bailee can show that reasonable care was taken at all material times, it will be entitled to be exonerated from liability, even where it can be shown that additional precautions beyond the ordinary duty of care might have prevented the loss.

4) Bailee Responsibility for Third-Party Losses Arising from Preventable Intervening Negligence of a Third Party

Where the systems a bailee has in place to protect a bailor's goods are clearly deficient (e.g., a bailee leaves a gate of a fenced area containing bailor goods unlocked or the door of a vehicle under its care unlocked) and a determined third party takes advantage of the shortcoming, liability should be fixed against a bailee. It makes sense to fix liability against a bailee in these circumstances, since it is the bailee's own failures to take reasonable care that subjected the bailor's goods to an increased and unacceptable (and foreseeable) risk of loss to a third party, which a third party happens to exploit or becomes the fortuitous beneficiary of. The words of Schroeder JA in the Court of Appeal for Ontario's decision in *Martin v McNamara Construction Co Ltd*[159] are apposite:

> I hold it to be an established principle that damage is recoverable if, despite the intervening negligence of a third party, the person guilty of the original negligence ought reasonably to have anticipated such subsequent intervening negligence and to have foreseen that if it occurred the result would be that his negligence would lead to loss or damage.[160]

In *Spagnolo v Margesson's Sports Ltd*,[161] the plaintiffs were injured when they were sideswiped by a vehicle being driven by a thief, who had

---

158 *Ibid* at paras 9–15.
159 [1955] OR 523 (CA).
160 *Ibid* at 527.
161 [1981] OJ No 3323 (Co Ct) [*Spagnolo*].

appropriated the vehicle from the defendant parking garage where it had been left by one of the employees of the corporate defendant. The defendant employee, when he arrived at the defendant parking garage, could not find a parking spot where he could park without blocking in another vehicle, thus not allowing him to lock his doors and take his keys with him. The company's assigned parking spots with the parking operator, based on an arrangement for valuable consideration with the operator, were occupied by other company vehicles, and none of the other spaces that would allow for same were available. So, the employee approached the parking hut, where he communicated with the parking attendant for the lot, who instructed him to leave the keys in his vehicle's ignition, which instructions he followed. The employee received a parking stub or ticket back from the attendant for the parking. Upon his return to the lot, the employee could not locate the vehicle. The vehicle was later involved in an accident, causing significant damage to the plaintiffs' vehicle. The defendant parking operator did not have a key rack in the parking hut for the storage and protection of keys to unlocked vehicles, or any security system in place to protect the unlocked vehicles from theft. The keys were simply left in the ignition of unlocked vehicles at the decision of the parking attendant, presumably to maximize the space in the lot, allowing locked vehicles blocked in by the unlocked vehicles to be moved easily by parking attendants when required.[162]

The question of liability as regards the defendant company who owned the vehicle and the defendant employee who drove it to the parking garage was easily resolved, since they had not consented to the third party driving the vehicle and were not in possession of the vehicle at the time of the plaintiffs' losses, which were caused by an extraneous cause, namely, the reckless driving of the unknown third-party thief of the vehicle.[163] However, could the defendant parking operator who had received the defendant company's vehicle as a bailee for reward under an existing parking arrangement with that company, be held liable as bailee for the third-party plaintiffs' losses, in relation to whom it did not have a direct contractual relationship? Justice Rapson of the County Court, Judicial District of York, Ontario, addressed whether the defendant parking operator had met its standard of care with respect to the vehicle in its possession. The learned judge found

162 *Ibid* at paras 1–3.
163 *Ibid* at para 9.

that it had not, as it maintained no policy of security with respect to the unlocked vehicles in its lot, leaving them exposed to a substantial risk of theft. However, this was not the end of the matter, as the parking operator had argued that it should not be liable, even if it was negligent in caring for the defendant's vehicle, in light of the fact that the plaintiffs' losses were caused by an independent third party and not by it directly.[164]

Justice Rapson found that, despite the intervening negligence of the third party, the negligent conduct of the defendant parking operator through its parking attendant had "precipitated the theft of the motor vehicle," which was then followed by the damage to the plaintiffs' vehicle. Therefore, unless the defendant's actions could be said to be a remote cause, they were liable. Since it was reasonably foreseeable for a parking operator to know that leaving the keys in a vehicle in an unlocked state on its lot without any security precautions or security system in place could lead to a vehicle being stolen by an irresponsible person who could then become involved in an accident, the defendant could not rely on remoteness to exonerate itself from liability. The learned judge found that the precise nature of the loss did not need to be foreseeable, just its general nature. The preventative actions required would not have cost the defendant parking operator much in dollar terms and therefore were required by it in order for it to discharge its duty of safekeeping as bailee over the defendant employee's vehicle. In the result, the defendant parking operator was held liable to the plaintiffs in damages for the substantial damage done to their vehicle.[165]

This case demonstrates that, where bailee negligence precipitates a theft of bailor property in its possession by an unknown third party, who causes injuries to another third party because of its own subsequent negligence, the bailee can be liable for a plaintiff third party's losses and should not be automatically exonerated because of the unknown third party's actions. However, the bailee's negligent actions cannot be too remote a cause of the plaintiff's losses — indeed, they must be reasonably foreseeable. As well, the cost of the preventative actions required by the bailor to have averted the loss must not be prohibitively expensive, unless the bailment contract requires otherwise. It is possible that bailees who find themselves in circumstances such as those in *Spagnolo* will be found liable

---

164 *Ibid* at paras 15–16.
165 *Ibid* at paras 18–27.

to both a plaintiff bailor and a plaintiff third party, where the bailee's original negligence leads to foreseeable theft of or vandalism to bailor property by a rogue third party, which is then followed by a foreseeable act of negligence by the rogue that causes losses to a plaintiff third party.

5) Where an Extraneous Cause Is Only Partially Responsible for a Bailor's Losses

Not all cases of legitimate extraneous cause will fully exonerate a bailee. Sometimes the extraneous cause will apply only to certain bailor losses, while the other losses will be due to a bailee's lack of due care. Where this is the case, the bailee should face liability accordingly. Bailees should not be able to hide behind extraneous causes in these circumstances, even where those causes are responsible for most of the bailor's losses. In *Pazitch v Shaughnessy Antique Gallery*,[166] the appellant transferred rings over to the respondent for sale, in return for a commission if a sale was made. Some time later, the appellant terminated the relationship and claimed that twenty rings transferred over to the respondent had not in fact been returned and were missing and had not been accounted for by the respondent. The respondent did not deny that these items were delivered to it; rather, it claimed that the missing items were either sold or that the appellant's recordings in her stock book (which had been housed in the respondent's store) were, in certain instances, in error. The respondent also relied on a robbery at its premises, which occurred prior to the respondent's redelivering the appellant's rings, in which two trays of rings were taken from a display case, including nine rings belonging to the appellant.[167] Justice Spencer of the British Columbia Supreme Court found that nine rings had in fact disappeared because of the robbery and that the respondent had taken due care of those rings and should be relieved by reason of the extraneous cause. However, this did not end the standard of care analysis, because the respondent (bailee) still had to account for the remaining eleven rings by showing that reasonable care of those rings had been taken. This it could not do, as it had not used an adequate inventory system to track the comings and goings of items during the course of storage. Bailors were allowed to deposit items and make their own record of what was left. The respondent did not independently verify those records.

166 [1997] BCJ No 1036 (SC) [*Pazitch*].

167 *Ibid* at paras 5, 7, 8, 9, and 14.

Bailors were also allowed to remove items from display cases for their own use with no record of such removal being made by the respondent. The only record maintained by the respondent related to sales, on the basis of which monthly statements were prepared and delivered to bailors. Specifically, when an item was sold, a bailor's customer number and stock number would be recorded from the sales tag by the respondent and would appear on its sales statements. However, in the case of the appellant (bailor), some items *had not* been assigned a stock number, and stock numbers for sold items had been reused by the appellant, at the suggestion of the respondent, for other items. As a result of the latter problem, in some instances, a ring that the appellant claimed to be lost was recorded as an entirely different item sold by the respondent. These deficiencies made an accounting by the respondent practically impossible.[168] That is to say, it could not show which items were returned to the appellant and which were not, other than based on its limited recollection, and whether the appellant's records were accurate or not.

Accordingly, as the appellant had the only reliable record, Spence J rejected the respondent's argument that the appellant had received certain items back but failed to strike them off her own stock list. The respondent's evidence that it could not afford to maintain the desired system was found not to be a legitimate justification for not maintaining such a system from the standpoint of bailees having to disprove negligence: "In my opinion, the duty of care over goods bailed for reward includes a duty to keep track of them in the bailee's hands so that they may be accounted for. If the bailee decides not to use an adequate inventory system, it does so at its own risk."[169]

As can be seen, proof of an extraneous cause can completely exonerate a bailee from liability for a bailor's losses, but only where the outside cause relates to all the losses incurred by the bailor, and only where the bailee can show that it had an adequate system of precautions in place to protect a bailor's goods from loss at all material times during the course of the bailment. A demonstration of such reasonable care *will not be possible* in circumstances such as those arising in *Pazitch*, where the bailee fails to maintain accurate written records to show that the bailor's items were properly secured, redelivered, sold, or otherwise dealt with appropriately by the bailee at all material times.

---

168 *Ibid* at paras 11–14.

169 *Ibid* at para 12.

6) No Requirement for a Bailee to Provide Insurance Against Losses Caused by Third Parties on Bailee Premises

There is no requirement that a bailee maintain insurance against loss of a bailor's goods by a third party from its premises in order to be able to rely on the defence of *novus actus interveniens* where goods are damaged or lost due to the intervening acts of a third party. In *Petriew v Tricom Electronic Ltd*,[170] each of the respondents alleged that they took their personal property to the appellant's business premises for repair and that when they returned to pick up their property they discovered that the appellant's place of business had been destroyed by fire together with their chattels. The respondents sued in bailment. The evidence indicated that a third party had forcibly trespassed on to the appellant's premises and deliberately set the fire.[171]

The bailee did not have any liability insurance providing for coverage for the destroyed chattels belonging to customers. The trial judge, in the court below, used this fact, together with the fact that the bailee did not have an operable fire system, to find that the appellant had not met its standard of care as a bailee for reward in the case, fixing liability against the appellant accordingly. On appeal, Hrabinsky J of the Saskatchewan Court of Queen's Bench found that the trial judge had erred in law, for, among other things, using the absence of insurance against the bailee as part of the standard of care analysis and in failing to consider the defence of *novus actus interveniens*: "Whether the bailee carries insurance coverage covering the bailor's chattel is not a factor to be considered in determining the liability of a bailee for reward."[172]

In other words, an absence of insurance did not mean the appellant had breached its standard of care by exposing the goods to a reasonably foreseeable risk of loss by fire by third-party arson such that it could not rely on the defence of *novus actus interveniens*. Indeed, an unauthorized third party had caused the respondents' losses; they were not the result of a lack of due care by the appellant. As we have seen, outside of the circumstance where an untried bailee carrier is transporting valuable bailor chattels, such as jewellery, for a bailee, there is no duty on a bailee to

---

170 [1987] SJ No 341 (QB) [*Petriew*].
171 *Ibid* at paras 1, 2, and 7.
172 *Ibid* at para 11.

arrange for insurance cover over a bailor's goods.[173] Nor is there a duty to advise a bailor of the value of placing such cover on goods during the course of a bailment.[174] It would be contradictory to use this absence against a bailee to disqualify the defence of *novus actus interveniens* by finding that a bailee thereby did not exercise reasonable care of the goods. The defence is meant to apply to protect a bailee, who, despite using reasonable precautions to protect a bailor's goods and generally meeting all of its obligations with respect to the goods, is the victim of third-party intervention that leads to damage or loss of the goods. The question of insurance is really a question of loss allocation in any case, and does not make theft or fire by a third party more or less foreseeable. Instead, the focus of the analysis needs to be on whether the bailee had reasonable precautions in place such that it can be said that the act of the third party was not reasonably foreseeable in the circumstances. The question of insurance cover is irrelevant to this inquiry. Justice Hrabinsky was right to have refused to allow the absence of such cover to disqualify the defence of *novus actus interveniens* otherwise presenting on the facts, after finding that the appellant had the necessary safeguards in place to protect the goods from loss by fire.[175] In other words, where a bailee is found to have met its standard of care, any third-party intervention leading to loss of bailor goods will not be reasonably foreseeable and, instead, will constitute a *novus actus interveniens*, entitling a bailee to be exonerated.

N. EXCLUSION CLAUSES

Exclusion clauses in a bailment contract can exonerate a bailee from all, or some,[176] liability arising on the breach of a bailment, including for fundamental breach. However, the following requirements must generally be met:

1) The bailor must be put on notice of the clause (whether by signage, a car park ticket, written contract, etc.).[177]

---

173 *Punch v Savoy's Jewellers Ltd* (1986), 54 OR (2d) 383 (CA).

174 *Mason*, above note 154.

175 *Petriew*, above note 170 at paras 11–14.

176 In *Minichiello*, above note 35 at 622, one of the conditions on the car ticket stated: "Reasonable care by our employees constitutes full discharge of our liability." Because the theft of the bailed property arose from negligence, the clause did not exempt the defendant (bailee) from liability for the plaintiff's (bailor's) losses since negligence is antithetical to the exercising of reasonable care.

177 See *Williams & Wilson Ltd v OK Parking Stations Ltd*, [1971] 2 OR 151 (Co Ct).

2) The language in the clause must cover the loss at issue—that is to say, the loss must fall within the scope of the clause, which clause will be strictly construed pursuant to the doctrine of *contra proferentem.*
3) The bailee *must not* indicate to the bailor at any material time that it will not rely on the clause at issue.
4) The clause must still be in legal effect at the time of the bailor's losses—in other words, it could not have expired.[178]

While the above represent the basic considerations with respect to exclusion clauses, the Supreme Court of Canada's decision in *Tercon Contractors Ltd v British Columbia (Transportation and Highways)*[179] certainly has muddied the waters. In light of this decision, the legal test as to enforceability of exclusion clauses will be highly contextual and will need to consider as well, whether, by reason of unconscionability or some other overriding public policy reason, the clause should not be enforced.

O. THE STATUTORY OVERLAY

A bailee's ability to defend itself from a bailment action will be affected by applicable statute law in force at the time that the bailment was alive and in existence. For example, statutes can displace the otherwise sometimes impossible burden placed on bailees at common law to disprove negligence in circumstances where the precise details surrounding the loss of a bailor's goods are not known. Certainly, this was the case in the past in Ontario for bailed goods lost by accidental fires, where the *Accidental Fires Act* (now repealed)[180] in section 1 provided:

> 1. No action shall be brought against any person in whose house or building or on whose land any fire accidentally begins, nor shall any recompense be made by that person for any damage suffered thereby; but no agreement between a landlord and tenant is defeated or made void by this Act.

---

178 See *McKinnon v Acadian Lines Ltd* (1977), 81 DLR (3d) 480 at 484 (NSSCAD), where the contract of carriage containing the exclusion clause in favour of the defendant had ended by the point of loss of the plaintiff bailor's goods, which occurred at the bus terminal after transport of the bailor's goods had been completed.

179 2010 SCC 4.

180 RSO 1990, c A.4, as repealed by SO 1997, c 4, s 85.

In *Neff v St Catharines Marina Ltd*,[181] the Court of Appeal for Ontario made clear that Ontario's *Accidental Fires Act* then in force applied to bailment actions where bailed goods are damaged due to a fire determined to be "accidental" in nature, as defined in that Act, as "one that cannot, on a balance of probabilities, be traced to a particular cause" such as oily rags or vandalism.[182] In other words, where goods were destroyed by fires of unknown cause and the Act was invoked by the defendant (bailee) to defend against a bailment action and found to apply to that action, ordinary bailment law principles *would not* apply. In the case, a bailment action was brought by the plaintiffs (bailors) after their three boats being stored with the defendant marina (bailee) for safekeeping were destroyed by fire of unknown origin. While there was some evidence before the trial court, including the remains of the boat and positive evidence showing no cause for the fire could be determined, the circumstances of the loss remained largely unknown.[183] The central issue, as identified by the appeal court, was whether or not the Act applied and prevailed over "the broad liability" created by the common law of bailment when it came to determining the question of liability before the court. If so, the defendant (bailee) should be exonerated. If not, there would be no way for the bailee to escape liability, since there would be no way for the bailee to disprove negligence, given the mysterious circumstances surrounding the loss. No explanation, or a purely speculative one, would not suffice in the circumstances to rebut the presumption of negligence otherwise on the bailee.

The trial judge in the court below had concluded that the Act had no applicability to the action that had been brought: "I reject the application of the Accidental Fires Act. This is not an action for damages arising from a fire but in respect of rights and obligations arising from a bailment arrangement. The nature of the cause of action renders this legislation

---

181 [1998] OJ No 253 (CA) [*Neff*].

182 *Ibid* at paras 6 and 21. The trial judge's definition of accidental fire, as being one that is proved to be "accidental," was roundly rejected by the appeal court. Rather, where a specific cause such as vandalism or falling objects cannot be attributed to the fire and remains unknown, then it will be deemed "accidental" and a bailee entitled to be exonerated from liability pursuant to the Act.

183 *Ibid* at paras 2–4. Having said that, it was *not* a *Wong* scenario (see *Taylor Estate v Wong Aviation Ltd*, [1969] SCR 481), since the bailee was still alive and well, and the bailed goods *had not* been completely obliterated by the occurrence. In other words, it was not possible to say that no one knew what happened, which would have entitled the defendant (bailee) to a reduced burden of proof: see Chapter 4, Section J for further discussion.

irrelevant."[184] The Court of Appeal for Ontario, per Carthy JA, disagreed, finding that the Act has broad applicability and does not "carve out an exception to the general law as to liability for negligence, rather it was intended to make the general law applicable to fires be originating on the property of a landowner."[185] Accordingly, the common law of bailment could not displace the clear language of a statute made by Parliament. In the result, since the fire was established in evidence to be "accidental" in nature, it could not be said that the defendant's (bailee's) actions, or lack of due care, had contributed to the bailor's loss. In the result, the defendant was entitled to be exonerated.[186]

It is to be noted that the court still left open the possibility of the Act's not saving a bailee from liability in all circumstances for loss or damage to bailor property arising from "accidental fire" on its premises. The exceptions are the following:

1) where the fire started accidentally, but where the bailee fails to contain or put the fire out after it could have reasonably learned about it based on prevailing industry practices that it should have had in place at the material times;[187] and
2) where the parties, as allowed by section 1 of the Act, have an agreement in place defeating the intent of section 1 of the Act, and do not waive the application of same.

The issue of the applicability, scope, and legal effect of the *Accidental Fires Act* on bailment actions is now moot since the Act has been repealed by Ontario's Parliament. That said, it would seem that "accidental fires," as defined in the repealed act, in Ontario, will *now* inure to the benefit of bailors since bailees will have to demonstrate due care was taken in the case of bailed goods damaged or loss by "accidental fire" while in their custody, where no cause for the fire can be identified or ascertained. This

184 *Ibid*, quoted at para 5.

185 *Ibid* at para 11.

186 In any case, the appeal court was not in agreement with the trial judge on the finding that the precautions and procedures put into place by the defendant (bailee) to protect the plaintiffs' goods were inadequate, finding that they were consistent with industry practice and showed that due care had been taken by the defendant: *ibid* at para 10. The trial judge, effectively, was improperly attempting to hold the defendant to the standard of perfection.

187 See *Hogarth v Archibald Moving and Storage Ltd*, [1991] BCJ No 2321 (SC), discussed in Chapter 5, Section B(15)(c).

will be difficult, if not impossible, on a set of facts such as those arising in *Neff*, where the precise circumstances surrounding the loss are unknown and a specific cause such as vandalism cannot be attributed to the fire, meaning that a bailee *will likely not* be able to rebut the presumption of negligence upon it and will have to face liability accordingly.

P. CONCLUSION

Even if a bailor succeeds in proving a bailment, and sometimes even where it shows that a bailee has been negligent in caring for the bailor's goods, a bailee may be able to avoid liability by proving a defence or justification existed (or exists) excusing its conduct. This is equivalent to a bailee showing that reasonable care was taken at all material times, as all liability arising on the bailment can be avoided. For example, a certain provision of care over a bailor's goods, while deficient or substandard in some respects, may be acceptable if it was clearly agreed upon by the bailor at the commencement of the bailment, pursuant to the maxim *volenti non fit injuria*, or, alternatively, if the industry practice can be shown to have required no more than was provided in the circumstances. *Novus actus interveniens* may be availing where a third party overcomes a bailee's otherwise reasonable precautions in place to protect a bailor's goods, but that principle should not relieve a bailee of liability arising from the bailee's own shortcomings that precipitate the injury to the bailor property caused by the third party. A limitation period, and the defence of accord and satisfaction (where a bailor receives a payment from a bailee in exchange for release of all liability arising from a bailment), can be complete defences to otherwise meritorious bailment actions, too. Statutes, much like contracts of bailment, can increase or decrease a bailee's duty of care, or merely confirm that a bailee's duty of care at law continues to operate in the particular circumstance and can be quite determinative of bailee liability as was the case under the *Accidental Fires Act* in *Neff*. Therefore, applicable statutes in force in the particular jurisdiction in which the bailment arises will always need to be consulted in determining whether the bailee's onus of proof has been met on any given set of facts.

CHAPTER 7

Sub-bailment

A. INTRODUCTION

A sub-bailment is a second bailment of a bailor's goods. A sub-bailment would occur where a bailor takes a vehicle to a bailee such as a body shop for a paint job in circumstances where the vehicle needs to be subsequently transferred to another bailee (the sub-bailee) for a further secondary or ancillary purpose, such as to a repair shop for a small light repair, by the implied or express consent of the bailor. A sub-bailment can also arise where the bailee, while contracted to look after the work, is unable to perform some or all of the work or services under the contract of bailment itself but is authorized by the bailor to sub-contract or delegate the work to a third party for completion.[1] As a second bailment of the bailor's goods, a sub-bailment is no more defeasible than a first bailment of the goods and can be for reward[2] or gratuitous. Where for reward, the standard of care owed will be a higher one; the sub-bailee will have to disprove that its negligence caused the loss at issue. Alternatively, the sub-bailee may show

1 See, for example, *Purolator Courier Ltd v Nav Air Charter Inc*, 2002 BCSC 965.

2 For a sub-bailment to be for reward, there must be an exchange of value between bailor, bailee, and sub-bailee. In *FR Smith Towing Co v JM Swaine (The)*, [1980] FCJ No 105 (TD), the defendant bailee paid to charter a barge from the plaintiff (bailor). The defendant sub-bailee also received recompense from the defendant bailee for transporting the ship by tug to a certain location. Thus, the sub-bailment was for the advantage of all three parties and was thus for reward: see paras 26–28 of the decision, Collier J, for relevant discussion.

that reasonable care was taken at all material times.[3] Many of the same general considerations will apply when considering whether a sub-bailee has met its applicable standard of care as were considered in the cases of gratuitous bailments and bailments for reward,[4] such as whether the sub-bailee took the appropriate care as measured against what a prudent owner would have done in the same or similar circumstances.[5] Similarly, a failure by a sub-bailee to offer up any explanation for the loss of bailed goods, or merely stating that the goods may have been stolen by one of its own staff under its own charge, will make it liable.[6] A sub-bailee who fails to maintain proper records showing that injury to the goods did not occur as a result of the sub-bailee's negligence, or lack of reasonable care, during times when the goods were in the exclusive possession or control of the sub-bailee, will also be liable.[7] However, a sub-bailment is necessarily a more complex relationship than a mere bailment relationship, as it involves no fewer than three parties who owe legal duties to one another:

1) the owner of the goods (the bailor who delivers possession of the goods to the bailee);
2) the bailee of the goods (the party who receives possession of the bailor's goods directly from the bailor, or its assigns, for a particular purpose, and who transfers possession of those goods to a further bailee, called a sub-bailee, to carry out a further purpose); and
3) the sub-bailee of the goods (the party who receives the bailor's goods directly from the bailee, or its assigns, to carry out a further particular purpose involving those goods).

As a result of the more multilayered nature of sub-bailments, in order for the sub-bailee to discharge its standard of care and show that

---

3 See *Webb v Tyldesley's Ltd*, [1998] BCJ No 2978 at paras 33–34 (Prov Ct (Civ Div)) [*Webb*].

4 Many of the same considerations from the general law of bailment will also apply when determining whether the legal relationship of sub-bailment has been created at all, or whether a lesser legal relationship such as a licence should be found. For example, have the keys to the property been relinquished? Does the sub-bailee possess the ability to control the bailed goods, or at least to control access to the property on which they are situated? Does the sub-bailee have reasonable security precautions in place to protect the bailed property from theft or other ordinary hazards? See *Quigley v Rands*, [1982] BCJ No 367 (Co Ct), especially para 18.

5 See, for example, *Punch v Savoy's Jewellers Ltd* (1986), 54 OR (2d) 383 at para 20 (CA) [*Punch*].

6 *Ibid.*

7 See, for example, *Webb*, above note 3 at paras 38–39.

it has not deviated from the terms of the bailment contract, different considerations will apply than in your ordinary bailment involving two parties (i.e., the bailor and bailee). The communications between the sub-bailee and bailee will always need to be considered, including whether the sub-bailee has acted within its authority. In this connection, the bailee's actions in delivering the goods to a further bailee in a sub-bailment will always need to be considered where the goods happen to be damaged thereafter or in the process of the transfer being made.

Sub-bailments have presented problems for bailors and bailees alike where loss of the bailed goods occurs. This is because there is *not* generally a direct line of communication between bailors and sub-bailees. While the sub-bailee, in order to owe a duty of care to the bailor, must be aware that a bailor (who owns the goods) exists, the sub-bailee may try to rely on the terms of agreement entered into between it and the head bailee in defending against a bailment action and does not have to communicate with the bailor in carrying out the bailment. This does not necessarily make the actions or decisions taken by sub-bailees unauthorized or unlawful, so long as they are acting in accord with implied or express authority received from the bailor, via the bailee, and otherwise in accordance with their applicable standard of care. Direct consent from bailors, or bailees, to every action taken in relation to the bailed goods by the sub-bailee would not be practical, possible, or even desirable. Still, when a loss occurs, the question of consent and proper authorities is one that the law must grapple with in determining questions of liability arising between the relevant parties. To complicate matters further, acts of negligence, or breaches of the bailment contracts, by some or all of the bailees and sub-bailees that lead to loss of or damage to bailed goods, require the law to come up with rules to apportion liability between the various bailees. The applicability, reach, and enforceability of exemption clauses in sub-bailment contracts can present a challenge here.[8] In sorting out these questions, the law must determine the contractual relations between each set of parties and the extent to which those relations should affect standard-of-care and liability questions as between the various parties in the chain of bailments and sub-bailments, including between bailors and sub-bailees who may never

8 See, for example, *Punch*, above note 5 at para 27ff.

have met and who, in all likelihood, have no direct contractual relationship, yet still owe duties and obligations to one another.[9]

In a sub-bailment, the usual statuses possessed by a bailor and bailee are altered and turned on their head, since it is the bailee who transfers possession to a sub-bailee and, in essence, takes on functions traditionally reserved to, or performed directly (and solely) by, the bailor. These functions include transferring possession of the goods to the sub-bailee and often setting the specific terms of the sub-bailment within the authorities granted by the bailor. This can cause problems, as the bailor, while granting the authority for the sub-bailment, may not be aware of the specific terms of the sub-bailment, including, in particular, terms that may limit the liability of the sub-bailee in the event of loss of the bailed property. Even though the bailee acts on authorities received from the bailor in making the sub-bailment, no contractual relationship is created between the sub-bailee and bailor.[10] As well, the law does not view the bailee as acting as an agent for the bailor in the making of a sub-bailment but instead as a principal in its own right, which means that a contract is normally created between the sub-bailee and bailee, of which the bailor is not a party.[11]

In a sub-bailment, the bailee may take legal action against the sub-bailee directly, where the sub-bailee breaches the terms of the sub-bailment by committing negligence against the goods, misdelivering them, or otherwise deviating from the terms of the bailment. The bailor may also move against the sub-bailee, despite the lack of privity of contract between them.[12] At

9 *Morris v CW Martin & Sons Ltd*, [1966] 1 QB 716 at 734, [1965] 2 All ER 725, Diplock LJ [*Morris*].

10 See *Scott Maritimes Pulp Ltd v BF Goodrich Canada Ltd*, [1977] NSJ No 456 at paras 42–44 (SCAD) [*Scott Maritimes Pulp*].

11 See *Morris*, above note 9, Diplock LJ. However, as in the case with a head bailee, the sub-bailee's employees will act as agents for the sub-bailee and will generally be answerable for losses caused by those agents where they do not take due care of bailor goods entrusted to them, or engage in tortious acts in relation to those goods, which causes damage or losses to the goods: *ibid* at 738. Lord Salmon, in *Morris*, was of the view that if the tortious act, such as theft, is committed by an employee of the bailee who was not employed to do anything in relation to the bailed goods, then the doctrine of vicarious liability would not apply to make a bailee, or sub-bailee for reward, liable for such losses: *ibid* at 740.

12 *Ibid*. See, further, *Punch*, above note 5; *Scott Maritimes Pulp*, above note 10 at para 46. For English authority, see *Pioneer Container (The)*, [1994] 1 Lloyd's Rep 593 at para 10 (PC) [*Pioneer Container*]. There is older Canadian caselaw to the contrary: see, for example, *Bank of Montreal v Bay Bus Terminal (North Bay) Ltd*, [1963] 1 OR 561 at paras 12–13 (HCJ), but it should be viewed as having been repudiated by the previously cited authorities.

law, the sub-bailee owes duties to the bailor by virtue of taking into its custody the property of another. Where the bailee makes a sub-bailment without proper authorization, the bailor may rely on the bailee's act of deviation to hold the bailee strictly liable for its losses, even where those losses occur while the goods are in the possession of a sub-bailee under an unauthorized sub-bailment.[13]

B. THE CREATION OF A SUB-BAILMENT BY EXPRESS OR IMPLIED AUTHORITY RECEIVED FROM A BAILOR

A sub-bailment is formed when a bailee acts on express or implied authority received from the bailor and transfers possession of the bailed goods to the sub-bailee for a further purpose.[14] In *Punch*,[15] a leading Canadian case on sub-bailment, the plaintiff's ring (a family heirloom) was in need of repair, so the plaintiff delivered it to a jeweller in Sault Ste Marie for repair. However, the defendant Savoy was not capable of making the repairs itself. So it sent the ring by registered mail, with a value of $100 shown for insurance purposes, to a jeweller out of town, namely the defendant Walker in Toronto. The ring was subsequently lost after Walker had completed the work on it and surrendered it to an untried third-party carrier for redelivery to Savoy. At the time the ring was surrendered to the carrier, its value was again listed as $100 on the bill of lading. No insurance cover against loss had been placed on the ring. As well, the terms of the carrier contract agreed to by Walker limited the carrier's liability to $50.[16] The carrier gave no explanation for failing to deliver the ring to Savoy after it

---

13 See, for example, *Chapman v Robinson*, [1969] AJ No 59 (Dist Ct) [*Chapman*], discussed in Section D(2), below in this chapter. In these circumstances, however, the bailee may seek indemnity from the sub-bailee.

14 The goods may then become the subject of a further sub-bailment, or may be returned directly to the bailor, or to a bailee for redelivery to the bailor. It is also possible that, upon receiving the goods back from the sub-bailee, the bailee makes yet another transfer of the goods at the behest of the bailor. The further transfer may or may not amount to a bailment, depending on whether control over the goods is transferred to the further party. Thus, the duty of safekeeping on the bailee over the goods may persist even if the goods are no longer physically present at the bailee's premises and are being housed by a storer under a licence elsewhere: see, for example, *Webb*, above note 3.

15 Above note 5.

16 *Ibid* at paras 5–7 and 11–14.

had been entrusted to do so, other than conceding that the ring may have been stolen by its own driver.[17]

The sub-bailment between Savoy and Walker was *not* explicitly authorized by the plaintiff, but, in the bailment action that followed, after the loss of the jewellery, the Court of Appeal for Ontario found that the necessary implied authorization for the sub-bailment had been conveyed by the plaintiff. In particular, the plaintiff had testified that, if the defendant were not able to carry out the repairs itself, she would have expected it to contract out the work such as it did. As well, upon being notified by the defendant that her ring had been sent to Toronto for repair, the plaintiff did not express any objection or protest.[18] Thus, despite the lack of express authorization for the sub-bailment, it was still valid, and the defendant bailee Savoy had not acted improperly in transferring possession of the jewellery to Walker for repair.[19]

As indicated, there was a further sub-bailment between Walker (a sub-bailee) and a carrier (a further sub-bailee). This situation had been necessitated by virtue of a postal strike that had intervened, preventing the jewellery from being sent back from Toronto to Sault Ste Marie the way it arrived (i.e., by registered mail), as had been contemplated by Savoy (the bailee) and Walker (the sub-bailee). Thus, Savoy and Walker discussed the use of a specific (and reputable) carrier, Rapidex, a division of Canadian National Railway (CN). The Savoy employee who discussed the matter of alternate transport with Walker agreed that CN be used. The details or terms of the carriage were not discussed between Savoy and Walker and

---

17 *Ibid* at para 8.

18 *Ibid* at paras 3–4 and 10.

19 Similarly, in *Banks v Dennis*, [1956] OJ No 621 (HC) [*Banks*], possession of the plaintiff's (bailor's) expensive jacket was transferred by the defendant to a storage business with whom the defendant was familiar, because he had no appropriate facilities for the storage of the garment himself. While the plaintiff had not expressly approved this, she had been told by the defendant (bailee) and knew that he did not, himself, have appropriate cold-storage facilities for the storage of garments. The plaintiff had not objected to this information. Indeed, in her testimony at trial, she conceded that it was immaterial to her where the jacket was to be stored, as long as it was stored in appropriate facilities. The defendant had used a reputable company for this purpose. Thus, the contract of sub-bailment was found to be an authorized one and was not a deviation from the bailment contract that had been entered into between the plaintiff and the defendant. However, the plaintiff's recovery for the loss of the jacket while in the possession of the sub-bailee was limited to $500, based on the undervaluation that the plaintiff had herself attributed to the jacket in the storage receipt/agreement that she had signed with the defendant at the outset of the bailment: see paras 13–15.

were set entirely by Walker without the input or involvement of Savoy. The plaintiff (bailor) was not privy to these discussions; was not a party to the further sub-bailment contract that had been entered into between Walker and CN (and that had been authorized by Savoy); and, as in the first contract of sub-bailment entered into between Savoy and Walker, had not expressly approved of the arrangement or any of its specific terms.[20] Still, the appeal court, per Cory JA, *did not* find the second sub-bailment to be unauthorized: "Since Walker advised Savoy of its intention to use C.N. as the shipper and Savoy agreed to that method of carriage, this was a duly authorized sub-bailment of the ring to C.N."[21]

As apparent, where a further sub-bailment comes into being without the express and direct approval of a bailor,[22] there will need to be a consent conveyed by the bailee to the sub-bailee for the further sub-bailment of the goods to be authorized. This had clearly occurred in the case, and the second sub-bailment was properly found by the court to have been authorized.[23] However, as we shall see, in the further discussions of the case in Section E, below in this chapter, just because a sub-bailment is found to be consented to by a bailor, and is not viewed as unauthorized as a general matter, does not mean that all the terms of the sub-bailment will be binding on a bailor, including those that it does not have specific awareness of, including any limiting terms.

20 *Punch*, above note 5 at paras 4–10.

21 *Ibid* at para 30.

22 Sometimes a bailor, at the outset of a bailment, will sign a contract with a bailee that will give the bailee an express authorization, a *carte blanche*, to enter into sub-bailments for it in order to complete the purposes of the bailment. As long as the contract of sub-bailment is in furtherance of these purposes, it will be considered to be authorized: see *Pioneer Container*, above note 12.

23 The plaintiff's implied consent to Savoy to sub-bail the ring must be seen to have included, impliedly as well, the right to ensure that the necessary arrangements were in place to allow for the ring to be returned from Toronto by Walker (a sub-bailee) to Savoy (the bailee) in Sault Ste Marie, so that the ring could eventually be returned to the plaintiff by Savoy in a relatively timely way. The arrangements could be accomplished only by way of another sub-bailment by Walker to a carrier, namely CN (a further sub-bailee), due to the intervening postal strike, since Walker was not itself a carrier of goods and could not effect a redelivery of the goods to Savoy personally.

C. NO SUB-BAILMENT OF THIRD-PARTY (BAILOR) PROPERTY POSSIBLE BETWEEN AN EMPLOYER AND EMPLOYEE

It will likely not be possible to establish a sub-bailment where property is transferred from a third-party bailor to a bailee (employer) for use by the bailee's employees, who subsequently cause losses or damages to the property. In these circumstances, the employer bailee will be responsible. The employer will not be able to fix the blame on the employee by establishing a contract of sub-bailment between it (as bailee) and the employee (as sub-bailee). In *Alliance Truck Rental & Transport Ltd v MPHA Topographics Ltd*,[24] the plaintiff (bailor) leased a truck to the defendant corporation pursuant to a written agreement. The rented truck was later damaged when it was hit by a snowplow while being driven by a defendant employee of the defendant corporation in the usual course of business, who was accompanied by another employee. The employee driver pled guilty to careless driving, having driven the truck in breach of his standard of care owed to the plaintiff.[25] There was an express term in the contract of bailment that limited the liability of the customer to $100 in the event of damage to the truck, but only if certain stipulated conditions were met, including that any driver of the truck on behalf of the defendant (employer) was not to be younger than twenty-five years of age. As it happens, the driver was younger than twenty-five when the truck was hired out and driven by him, with the at least tacit consent of the employer.[26]

A clear breach of, and deviation from, the bailment contract had been committed by the defendant, as the plaintiff did not consent, impliedly or expressly, to a driver under twenty-five driving the truck;[27] indeed, the contract expressly prohibited it.[28] This lack of consent disqualified the limiting terms and the insurance coverage on the vehicle protecting the defendants from third-party damage claims. Still, the defendant tried to

---

24 [1984] OJ No 2360 (Co Ct).

25 *Ibid* at paras 1 and 37.

26 *Ibid* at paras 34–45.

27 *Ibid*. This deviation from the terms of the bailment contract was probably enough to make the defendant company strictly liable for the plaintiff's (bailor's) losses, even in the absence of its being shown that the defendant employee driver had not taken reasonable care of the truck.

28 There was, however, a waiver of the insurer's subrogated claim in accordance with the Ontario Standard Automobile Policy (as regards collision damage), since the defendant employee was driving the truck with the consent of the employer: *ibid* at paras 47–48.

foist the blame onto the individual employee who was at the wheel at the time of the collision, arguing a sub-bailment between him and the company. Justice Honey of the Ontario County Court—Judicial District of York refused to accept that such a legal relationship could be created in the circumstances:

> Topographics could only have the care, custody or control of the truck through its agents. In this case the agents were its employees Iley and Radford. At all times they were acting within the scope of their authority from Topograhics.... In my opinion the plaintiff delivered the care, custody or control of the truck to Topographics and it was still in that corporation at the time of the accident.[29]

Justice Honey accordingly found that the defendant (as bailee) was vicariously liable for the damage to the truck that had been occasioned by its driver. The learned judge's decision is consistent with other rulings we have considered herein. As between employer and employee, there can be no sub-bailment when it comes to use or operation of third-party property hired out by an employer. In such circumstances, the employer is the only bailee and cannot be divested of this legal status in favour of an employee. A judgment in bailment in favour of the employer (as head bailee) against the employee himself or herself (as sub-bailee) is not possible in these circumstances. This is because the employer is the one with the care, custody, and control of the bailor property and cannot be divested of this status in favour of an employee during the course of the bailment merely because the employee is using or operating the bailor property. As between employer and employee, there can be no demarcation or separation between the use or operation of bailor property, on the one hand, and the care, custody, and control of bailor property, on the other. As pointed out by the learned judge, this is because corporations or companies cannot operate (third-party) bailor property themselves; they must use and rely on living, breathing employees or agents, acting under their charge and on their behalf.

---

29 *Ibid.*

D. ENFORCEABILITY AND VALIDITY OF SUB-BAILMENT IN OTHER CIRCUMSTANCES

1) Deviation from Terms of Bailment in Making a Sub-bailment May Make the Head Bailee Strictly Liable to the Bailor for Any Losses Arising Therefrom

Where goods are transferred from a bailor to a bailee in order for the bailee to *personally* store them or work on them, in accordance with the parties' contract, then unless the contract between the parties is changed after the bailment has begun, no authorized sub-bailment to a third party may be possible. Any attempt at such sub-bailment should amount to deviation on the original bailment contract and should result in strict liability against the bailee. In *Duncan v Allen*,[30] the plaintiff left a unique and expensive watch and gold bracelet with the defendants, who were professional jewellers, to have the cracked crystal in the watch replaced. As the part had to be ordered by the defendants from a third party (supplier) for the work to be done, as the defendants did not have the crystal in stock, it was agreed between the parties that the plaintiff's property would be stored in safekeeping at either the defendants' business premises or at the personal residence of a principal of the defendants' business until the work could be effected. As it happens, the crystal had not been received from the supplier by the time the busy Christmas season hit, so the defendants decided unilaterally, without communicating with the plaintiff, to transfer some of the plaintiff's jewellery to the supplier to have the required work done by them directly.[31] The plaintiff's property was then lost after it had been repaired by the third party, on its redelivery to the defendants via regular mail.[32]

30 [1983] SJ No 759 (QB) [*Duncan*].

31 *Ibid* at paras 1–15.

32 The third party was not a professional jeweller and had not been told by the defendants of the high value of the plaintiff's property. It had, accordingly, proceeded to use regular mail, as it had always done, to redeliver the items to the defendants. The trial judge found that the defendants' failure to notify the third party of the uniqueness and valuableness of the goods, as well as failure to require the return of the goods by recorded mail, to be breaches of their standard of care as bailees, fixing liability against them accordingly: *ibid* at paras 12 and 25ff. Even in the absence of these breaches, it is submitted that the act of deviation by the defendant bailees in relinquishing the plaintiff's property to a third party without authority, was enough, without more, to make them strictly liability to the plaintiff for his losses.

On the facts, Grotsky J of the Saskatchewan Court of Queen's Bench Judicial Centre of Regina *did not* find that an authorized sub-bailment had been created between the supplier and the defendants because no authority by the plaintiff for such a bailment had been given. Indeed, the agreement was that the defendants were to carry out the work *personally* and to store the jewellery *personally* until such time as they could carry it out. Their failure to do so made them strictly liable to the plaintiff for his losses.[33]

2) Must a Sub-bailment Made Without Authority Be Rejected by a Bailor Before It Will Cease to Have Legal Effect?

Must a bailor repudiate the contract of bailment upon learning of an unauthorized sub-bailment before the sub-bailment will cease to have legal effect? Or does the act of deviation alone determine both bailments (i.e., predicate bailment and sub-bailment) by terminating them in favour of the bailor? In *Duncan*, Grotsky J seems to have accepted that the act of deviation by the defendant (bailee) meant that no sub-bailment could be created between the defendant and the third party, and that the underlying bailment had been determined by the act of deviation, such that the defendant (bailee) was strictly liable to the plaintiff (bailor) for his losses. As a consequence, presumably, only the defendant could be sued and not the third party (i.e., the putative sub-bailee). This finding is based on the premise that a bailee cannot give a sub-bailee that which it does not have—that is, lawful possession of bailor property in fundamental breach of the terms of the bailment.

There is, however, a different view that appears in the caselaw. It states, consistent with contract law principles, that, where a bailee parts with possession to a sub-bailee in deviation from the terms of the bailment, a sub-bailment is still created, however invalidly, by the virtue of possession in fact passing from bailee to sub-bailee, which sub-bailment may then be accepted or rejected by the bailor once the bailor learns of it. In other words, it is not the breach of a bailment, or a bailment contract, that causes a sub-bailment to cease to have legal effect, but rather a bailor's decision to accept the bailee's repudiation of the terms of the bailment and the bailor's choice to determine the bailment that are the decisive factors. While strict liability will still flow to the bailee for breach of the

33 *Ibid* at para 10ff.

bailment by virtue of the illegal delivery to the sub-bailee, the allowing of the sub-bailment protects a bailor's ability to sue the sub-bailee, and any further sub-bailees down the chain of sub-bailments, where loss or damage to goods occurs during those subsequent bailments.

In *Chapman*,[34] the plaintiff mother left the keys to her automobile with her daughter, Marlene, for her personal use while the plaintiff and her husband went out of the country on vacation. Under their agreement, the daughter was not to drive the vehicle to school. There was no discussion of whether others could drive the car, although the plaintiff stated in her evidence that she would not have permitted this.[35] As it happens, the daughter allowed a male friend, the defendant Robinson, to drive her vehicle almost daily, acting as a chauffeur for her and her friends. Marlene held a party at the parents' house where alcohol was consumed by the guests, including by Robinson. Ferguson, a friend of Robinson and another guest at the party, ended up borrowing the car from Marlene, with her consent, and took it for a drive, purportedly to sober Robinson up, with the specific restriction that Robinson was not to drive the vehicle as he was too intoxicated. Ferguson, too, had consumed significant alcohol. As it happens, Ferguson drove the car away to drop off a couple of other boys who were also in the car with him and Robinson. Following this, Robinson was permitted to drive the vehicle by Ferguson (in breach of Marlene's express direction against this), and, ultimately, an accident ensued, damaging the plaintiff's vehicle beyond repair. Robinson's negligence causing

---

34 Above note 13.

35 *Ibid* at para 1. In *Ertan v Thomas*, 2014 CanLII 7161 (Ont Sm Cl Ct), the defendant (bailee) should have been aware that the plaintiff had a girlfriend who might well drive the car (a Jaguar) that was the subject of the bailment. Indeed, at the outset of the bailment, she had accompanied the defendant in picking up the Jaguar from the defendant's premises for the outgoing trip. The evidence was inconclusive on who had driven the vehicle away from the defendant's premises. However, since the defendant *had not* expressly forbidden her from driving the vehicle on the parties' retrieval of it from his commercial premises, Deputy Judge Winny of the Ontario Small Claims Court found that an implied consent had been given to the boyfriend for her to drive the vehicle, and it was not a deviation from, or breach of, terms of the bailment for the boyfriend to have allowed the girlfriend to drive the vehicle. In the result, no strict or general liability was imposed against the defendant (bailee) when the vehicle was damaged when the girlfriend (sub-bailee) backed the plaintiff's vehicle into another vehicle on a car dealership's lot prior to returning to the plaintiff's business premises. The defendant had not breached his duty of care to the plaintiff on this basis and could not be held liable for the damage done to the plaintiff's vehicle: see paras 5–6 and 19–20.

the accident and damage to the vehicle was clear on the record: in driving while impaired by alcohol; in driving too fast and losing control of the car; and in failing to keep a proper lookout.[36]

The central question with which the court had to grapple was whether any bailment relationships were created beyond the clear, gratuitous bailment that had been generated between Marlene and her mother. That is, was possession transferred by Marlene to Ferguson and, further, from Ferguson to Robinson? Or was Marlene's deviation from the bailment contract entered into with her mother, in not obtaining consent from her mother (the bailor) for others to drive her vehicle, fatal to her ability to transfer possession of the vehicle to Ferguson for the purposes of creating a sub-bailment? These questions were of great consequence in the case, as the court action had been framed in sub-bailment by the plaintiff mother (bailor) against the defendants Ferguson and Robinson, whom she argued were sub-bailees who had breached their obligations owed to her as bailor.[37]

Justice Belzil of the Alberta District Court rejected the argument advanced, that the first bailment (between Marlene and her mother) had been determined by Marlene's violation of it, instead finding that Marlene could, and did, in fact and in law, sub-bail the vehicle to Ferguson in spite of the lack of consent received from her mother (the bailor). The transfer of physical possession of the vehicle from Marlene to Ferguson was enough to create a sub-bailment between them, there being no absolute requirement that an underlying lawful possession in the sub-bailor/head bailee (that is, Marlene) exist in the circumstances in order for a sub-bailment to be made lawfully. In the learned judge's words:

> I do not think it is necessary that the bailor should be the legal possessor of the chattel to create bailment. A bailment being in essence the delivery of possession of a chattel, it seems to me that any person in *de facto* possession, be he a lawful or unlawful possessor, or even a thief, can create a valid bailment as between himself and his bailee by delivering that possession on recognized bailment terms, although a contract grafted on the bailment may be invalid.[38]

---

36 *Chapman*, above note 13 at paras 2–8.
37 *Ibid* at para 10.
38 *Ibid* at para 24.

While Marlene was acting in breach of the terms[39] of the underlying bailment with her mother in transferring possession of the vehicle over to Ferguson, this was not enough, without more, to defeat the sub-bailment. As at that time, the plaintiff (mother) had not repudiated the bailment because she did not know of Marlene's breaches, and thus Ferguson assumed the duties of gratuitous sub-bailee upon his receipt of possession of the vehicle from Marlene. When Ferguson breached the terms of his sub-bailment with Marlene by allowing Robinson (a further sub-bailee) to drive the vehicle, he became insurer of the vehicle and strictly liable to Marlene for the losses caused to the vehicle and, by extension, to the plaintiff mother (bailor).[40]

Justice Belzil found that the plaintiff (bailor) was within her right to sue the defendant (sub-bailee) Ferguson for her losses, and to plead a sub-bailment against him, and to succeed against him on that basis in spite of the lack of privity of contract between them. The mother's actions in pleading a sub-bailment had essentially ratified Marlene's sub-bailment to Ferguson, since she was relying on and condoning an unauthorized act by Marlene in helping her as plaintiff make out her action against the defendant sub-bailees. Accordingly, a judgment in damages was entered against both Ferguson and Robinson in favour of the plaintiff, with Robinson being ordered to indemnify Ferguson, as his negligent acts, not Ferguson's, were the immediate cause of the plaintiff's losses.[41]

While this was not stated explicitly in the case, it is clear that the court accepted the validity of the second sub-bailment to Robinson, for the same reasons as the first sub-bailment to Ferguson, in making a judgment in damages against both defendant sub-bailees. Based on *Chapman*, a plaintiff (bailor) may ratify a sub-bailment by relying on it and properly pleading it, such that a deviation of the underlying bailment by a head bailee in the making of the sub-bailment without authority may be cured, foisting, however unfairly, all liability on the subsequent sub-bailee or sub-bailees for losses that may be caused to the bailor property thereafter. By virtue of the plaintiff's refusing to determine the first bailment contract based on Marlene's breach of it, the defendant sub-bailees were put to the reverse onus and were required to disprove negligence — that is, to

---

39 Justice Belzil found the term that Marlene not permit others to drive the vehicle to be an implied term of the bailment contract between her and her mother.

40 *Ibid* at para 23ff.

41 *Ibid* at paras 35–39.

show that they had taken reasonable care of the plaintiff's vehicle while in their possession. This, clearly, could not be done in the circumstances, and liability was fixed against them accordingly.

3) Ratification

As was seen in *Chapman*, an otherwise invalid sub-bailment made by a bailee may be saved by a bailor by subsequently and properly pleading and relying on the sub-bailment made without authority in asserting its case. The bailor is not required to determine the initial bailment based on a breach of it by the bailee in the making of a sub-bailment, as long as the sub-bailment is made on usual terms. That is to say, the bailor may elect to condone the bailee's breach and accept the sub-bailment, and then sue the sub-bailee on the terms of the sub-bailment. Such an election to ratify by the bailor will essentially free the bailee from liability[42] and result in the reverse onus being placed on the sub-bailee, or sub-bailees, to disprove that their negligence caused the loss at issue. To be sure, such an election by plaintiffs (bailors) will be rare, since this election will reduce the chances of plaintiffs' making out their bailment actions as well as reducing their ability to enforce their judgments jointly and severally against more than one bailee. Still, in the special circumstances presenting in *Chapman* (that is, where the underlying bailment is between a parent and their child) or in similar circumstances, the plaintiff may, in the preparation of its case and pleading, choose to pursue only the sub-bailee, or sub-bailees, as the case may be, by relying on the sub-bailment(s) and a breach thereof in making out their bailment action against the defendant(s) rather than relying on a breach of the underlying bailment by the bailee in the making of the sub-bailment(s) without authority. Such a right, based on the applicable caselaw, seems indefeasible so long as:

1) the bailor *does not* determine the initial bailment by acting on the breach of it by the bailee—that is to say, does not accept the repudiation of the bailment contract committed by the bailee once learning of it;

---

42 This would seem to mean, by extension, that any subrogated action brought under a bailor's insurance policy would have to be brought against the sub-bailees too, since the bailor, by its election, *would no longer* have a valid cause of action against the bailee for loss or damage to the property for the insurer to be subrogated to. For relevant discussion, see *Cecconi v State Farm Automobile Insurance Co*, [1991] OJ No 1059 (Gen Div).

2) the bailee *has not* defrauded the bailor in such a way as to be considered to no longer be acting as the agent of the bailor but instead as owner of the property in its own right in the making of the sub-bailment without express authority (such as would bar the possibility for ratification); and[43]
3) the bailor *has properly pled its bailment case* relying and ratifying the sub-bailment(s) made by the bailee and wishes to pursue liability against only the sub-bailee or sub-bailees, and not the bailee.

E. ESTABLISHING THE VALIDITY OF SPECIFIC TERMS OF THE SUB-BAILMENT WHERE SUB-BAILMENT IS GENERALLY AUTHORIZED

Where there is an express or implied authorization from a bailor for a sub-bailment to be created and the bailed goods are lost during the sub-bailment, the terms of that bailment need to be established in order for a court to determine questions of liability between the bailor and bailees. To be sure, where the contract of sub-bailment is *not* in writing, this will be a more difficult task. While the terms of any agreement are ultimately set by the parties to the contract, those terms will not necessarily apply to a bailor who is unaware of them even if it is the sub-bailee's intent that they should. In other words, establishing the terms of the sub-bailment as between the contracting parties will set out the relationship as between them, but not necessarily as between those parties and the bailor. This issue, of course, will be most controversial where the bailor is objecting to the application of a term in the contract of sub-bailment that denies them recovery for their losses.

In *Punch*, the first contract of sub-bailment between Savoy and Walker was verbal, yet its terms were not contended at all by the plaintiff (bailor) in the action that followed; indeed, the plaintiff was found to have approved of them. This contrasts with the second bailment between Walker and CN, which contained an exclusion clause in favour of CN and attempted to deny the plaintiff all recovery for the loss of the ring by CN. This second contract of sub-bailment between Walker and CN was express and confined to writing, but the plaintiff did not have specific awareness of its terms, in particular its limiting terms in the event of the loss of her

---

43 *Chapman*, above note 13 at para 35.

jewellery, and challenged its enforceability. The terms that the plaintiff was found not to have been aware of—namely, the limiting terms—were found not to be binding on her. Nor were they found to be binding on Savoy, which was similarly unaware of them.

1) Enforceability of Particular Terms of a Sub-bailment Against a Bailor

a) No Absolute Requirement That Privity of Contract Exist Between a Bailor and Sub-bailee for a Sub-bailee to Owe Duties to the Bailor Under the Contract of Sub-bailment

There is no requirement that a contract of sub-bailment be signed between the bailor and sub-bailee in order for that contract to be created. Even though the bailor would have more specific awareness of the terms of agreement if this were so, and there would be privity of contract between the bailor and sub-bailee, such a requirement would be quite unworkable and commercially unfeasible. Instead, the contract of sub-bailment is usually signed between the bailee and sub-bailee, with the bailee acting on proper authorities from the bailor. At law, the sub-bailee will still owe duties to the bailor vis-à-vis other bailees and sub-bailees with whom it may need to interact, or receive necessary authorities from, to complete the purposes of the sub-bailment, provided, of course, that the sub-bailee is aware of the existence of a bailor and that the necessary incidents of a bailment are present.[44] The sub-bailee may try to rely on any limitation of liability clauses, or limiting terms, contained in the sub-bailment contract to try to escape liability, as against both other sub-bailees and bailees coming before it in the chain of bailments, as well as bailors, where loss or damage should occur to the bailor's goods.[45] As well, the sub-bailee may be able to rely on any Himalaya clauses[46] contained in the principal or underlying contract of bailment between bailor and bailee.[47]

---

44 *Punch*, above note 5 at paras 29 and 32.

45 Thus, Cory JA in *Punch*, after finding that the sub-bailment between Walker and CN was authorized, due to the express approval for that sub-bailment that had been received by Walker from Savoy, stated: "[I]t would follow that C.N. would owe the same duty and enjoy the same limitations of liability with regard to Savoy as it did with regard to Walker." *Ibid* at para 30.

46 For a definition of these clauses, see below note 57.

47 See, for example, *Cami Automotive, Inc v Westwood Shipping Lines Inc*, [2009] FCJ No 1064 (FC) [*Cami Automotive*].

b) Sub-bailee Awareness of a Bailor: Actual or Constructive Knowledge Is Required Before a Sub-bailee Will Owe a Bailor a Duty of Care

In order for a sub-bailee to owe a duty of care to the bailor, instead of just to the bailee with whom it has privity of contract, the sub-bailee must be aware of the possibility of an owner of the goods who might make a claim in respect of them in the event that the goods subject to the bailment are lost. However, constructive, in addition to actual, knowledge of an owner will suffice. In *Punch*, neither the plaintiff nor CN were aware of the other. No contract had been entered into between them, and neither had had any dealings or communications whatsoever, directly or indirectly, that would have given them actual knowledge of the other.[48] However, the contract of carriage between Walker and CN clearly contemplated an owner of the goods in the event of the loss of the bailed goods, since its limitation of liability provisions stated that they were binding on "all persons claiming any right to the ownership or possession of the shipment."[49] Thus, by virtue of the wording of the provision, the sub-bailee CN was constructively aware of the plaintiff's existence and accordingly liable to the plaintiff for the clear acts of negligence that it had committed during the further sub-bailment of the jewellery.[50]

c) A Bailor's Lack of Specific Awareness of Terms in a Sub-bailment Contract May Invalidate Them Despite the Otherwise General Validity of the Sub-bailment

Where a sub-bailment is found to be authorized, should all the terms of that sub-bailment apply to a bailor, even those it may not have specific awareness of? The answer would seem to sometimes be "no." That is to say,

48 The absence of these things was not a bar to finding a sub-bailment to have existed between the plaintiff (bailor) and the sub-bailee (CN) in the case. The commentator, Norman Palmer, has found a similar development in the jurisprudence in England to be a true marvel of bailment law, as it "marks the final stage in the emancipation of bailment from contract, for it enables the former relation to arise not only without consideration but without communication or agreement of any kind": Norman Palmer, *Bailment* (Sydney: Law Book Co Ltd, 1979) as cited in *Punch*, above note 5 at para 33.

49 *Ibid* at para 32. For the full text of the limiting provision adverted to, see para 12 of the decision.

50 Similarly, in *Morris*, above note 9 at 729 [cited to All ER], the defendant (sub-bailee) cleaner knew that the fur given to it by the bailee furrier was not the furrier's, but instead one of its customers. While the defendant did not know the customer's name, this knowledge was enough, without more, to give it the requisite knowledge to create a sub-bailment between it and the plaintiff (bailor).

the fact that a sub-bailment is generally authorized does not necessarily mean that a bailor is bound by all the terms of the sub-bailment, including the limiting terms. The analysis must go further and consider the bailor's specific knowledge and awareness of each specific term in the contract of sub-bailment.[51] If the bailor can be said to have expressly or impliedly consented to the term, then the bailor will be bound, otherwise it will not be.[52] It will always be necessary to consider, in this connection, whether the bailee, acting on behalf of the bailor, consented to the specific terms in the contract. In *Punch*, neither the bailee (Savoy) nor the bailor (Punch) were aware of the limitation of liability clause contained in CN's contract of carriage with Walker, nor had they consented to the clause or to the other terms of the carriage. Indeed, Savoy had not discussed the terms with Walker at all, including whether sufficient insurance against loss for the true value of the goods would be placed on the jewellery to be transported. While this was found to constitute clear negligence on the part of Savoy to make it liable to the plaintiff (bailor) as bailee, neither Savoy nor the plaintiff were to be bound by the limiting terms in Walker's contract with CN, since they had no knowledge of them, actual, constructive, or otherwise. Savoy's negligence certainly did not change this basic fact.

However, there is an important proviso: where the bailee receives a *carte blanche* from a bailor to enter into sub-bailments on any terms it chooses, so long as the contracts are in furtherance of the head bailment, then a bailor's lack of knowledge of the specific terms of the sub-bailment cannot be used to try to invalidate the sub-bailment. The caselaw indicates that the bailor will be bound by all terms entered into by the bailee, at least where they are not unusual and are in accordance with industry practice. In *Cami Automotive*, the defendant bailee, an ocean carrier, was given a *carte blanche* to enter into any contract of sub-bailment for the inland transport of the plaintiffs' goods that it saw fit. Since none of the terms in the contract of sub-bailment, including the limiting terms, were found to be unusual, but instead were in accordance with industry practice, they were found to apply to the plaintiffs despite their lack of specific awareness of them.[53]

51 *Cami Automotive*, above note 47 at paras 74–82.

52 See *Morris*, above note 9 at 733 [cited to All ER].

53 *Cami Automotive*, above note 47 at paras 74–82. See, further, *Pioneer Container*, above note 12.

F. ALTERNATIVE CONTRACTUAL REGIMES: A SUB-BAILEE MAY ELECT THE MOST BENEFICIAL LIMITING TERMS FROM EITHER THE CONTRACT OF BAILMENT OR THE CONTRACT OF SUB-BAILMENT

In sub-bailments, the question sometimes arises as to whether a sub-bailee may take advantage of certain provisions limiting liability contained in the contract of bailment entered into between the bailee and bailor. This is particularly the case where those terms are more beneficial than the applicable terms contained in the contract of sub-bailment entered into between the bailee and sub-bailee. Sometimes those terms are in writing; sometimes not. Certainly, the intention of the parties (i.e., the bailor and the bailee) will be paramount here, and any consideration of that intention must consider closely the wording of any contract entered into between the bailor and bailee. In *Cami Automotive*,[54] the Federal Court was tasked with determining a preliminary issue between the parties, namely, the applicability of a limitation of liability clause contained in a shipping document (a waybill) as pertaining to the liability of the final sub-bailee carrier in the case. The plaintiffs (bailors) made a claim against the defendants with respect to damage done to their cargo arising from the derailment of train cars while the cargo was being shipped from Vancouver to Toronto, among other claims advanced by parties in the proceeding. Relations between the parties began when an ocean carrier (WSL), under a contract with the plaintiffs, chartered a ship to transport the plaintiffs' goods from Japan to Toronto. One of the two plaintiffs, Cami, had an existing business relationship with WSL, which included an annual service contract between them and a specific WSL shipping document, which the other plaintiff, AW, was also a party of and signatory to. As anticipated by the parties, as WSL was an ocean carrier, it was authorized to sub-contract rail transport to a third party, which it did in contracting with CN Rail, which was to transport the goods by land from Vancouver to Toronto. A contract on specific terms was entered into between CN and WSL, which was completely separate and apart from the waybill entered into between WSL and the plaintiffs. Both the waybill governing WSL's relationship with the plaintiffs and the contract

54 Above note 47.

between WSL and CN contained limiting clauses, albeit on substantially different terms.[55]

In the waybill, liability for each lost pallet of goods was limited to US $500,[56] while the written agreement between CN and WSL limited liability for loss on CN's part to those rules contained in the *Railway Traffic Liability Regulations* under the *Canadian Transportation Act*. Since CN did not qualify for any of the defences under the said regulations to limit its liability, such as acts of God, and faced substantial liability for the damage done to the plaintiffs' goods, CN sought to rely on the limiting clauses contained in the waybill entered into between WSL and the plaintiff bailors. If the clause was deemed to be a "Himalaya clause,"[57] which had the effect of extending all benefits of the contracting parties under the waybill, including the limiting provisions, to third parties, then Blanchard J found that CN would be so able.[58] The operative words of the particular clause of the waybill read:

> INLAND CARRIER and others used and employed by the OCEAN CARRIER in the performance of services in relation to the GOODS and the goods of others, shall be beneficiary of the bill of lading and shall be entitled to all defenses, exemptions, and limitations of liability to which the OCEAN CARRIER is entitled hereunder and under the applicable laws.[59]

Based on the language, the learned judge easily found that CN could take the benefit of the limiting clauses in the waybill, and that this was not a violation of the *Canadian Transportation Act*'s requirement that a rail carrier only be able to limit its liability by way of a written agreement signed by a shipper, since the waybill constituted such an agreement between WSL (a shipper) and CN (a rail carrier). Thus, CN was able to become the beneficiary under an upstream Himalaya clause contained in the contract of bailment between the plaintiffs and WSL, even though it was not a party to the contract. Justice Blanchard, following English

55 *Ibid* at para 6.
56 For text of the limiting clause in the waybill, see *ibid* at para 48.
57 A "Himalaya clause" is designed to protect third parties. This clause extends the benefits of the contract of carriage to any third party engaged by the carrier to satisfy the carrier's obligations under the contract of carriage. It was specifically triggered when a sub-contract was signed between WSL and CN: *ibid* at paras 85 and 92.
58 *Ibid* at paras 84–90.
59 *Ibid* at para 85.

authority,[60] refused to disqualify the limiting clause on the basis that it was inconsistent with what was contained in the contract of sub-bailment. As a consequence, both WSL and CN's liability to the plaintiffs was limited to $500 per package, a far cry from the plaintiffs' actual losses.[61]

It follows from this decision that, if a bailor does not wish sub-bailees to benefit from the terms of contract it has entered into with bailees previously, that it specifically bar such benefit and *not* give bailees with whom they contract a *carte blanche* to enter into sub-bailments on any terms they so choose. While Himalaya clauses may serve to simplify liability questions and are quite common in the shipping industry, they will likely substantially reduce a bailor's total recovery for losses arising from the negligence of a sub-bailee in a bailment case, sometimes to a very minimal amount, as was seen in the case just under consideration.

G. LEGAL EFFECT OF PREVIOUS BAILEE NEGLIGENCE ON LOSS OF BAILED GOODS ARISING IN A SUBSEQUENT BAILMENT

The treatment of a previous bailee's negligence, or a previous bailee's breach of the bailment contract, in dealing with liability of a sub-bailee under a contract of sub-bailment is an interesting affair. A first act of negligence by a head bailee can have lasting effects and can be very consequential when it comes to the future safeguarding of the bailed goods by sub-bailees further down the chain of bailments. Indeed, its "domino effect" can lead to the loss of the bailor's goods or to a bailor's goods not having appropriate insurance cover when a loss or damage to them does occur. In *Punch*, Savoy (the head bailee) accepted a new method of transportation for the goods without obtaining the plaintiff's (bailor's) consent to same, in agreeing to allow Walker to use CN (an untried carrier) to transport the plaintiff's (repaired) jewellery back to Savoy for redelivery to the plaintiff rather than sending the jewellery back via registered mail (the usual practice). While this action was necessitated by an intervening postal strike, it was a serious breach of Savoy's contract of bailment with

60 *Ibid* at para 93, referencing and endorsing *Pioneer Container*, above note 12 at 603, wherein Lord Goff of Chieveley states: "If it should transpire that there are in consequence two alternative regimes which the sub-bailee may invoke, it does not necessarily follow that they will be inconsistent; nor does it follow, if they are inconsistent, that the sub-bailee should not be entitled to choose to rely upon one or other of them as against the owner of the goods."

61 *Cami Automotive*, above note 47 at paras 85–93.

Punch. In the end, this new mode of transportation led to the demise of the goods. Savoy had also failed to make important and needed enquiries of Walker with respect to the terms of the carriage. In particular, there was no discussion of insurance for the valuable goods while in transit. Given that CN was an "untried" carrier, it was incumbent on Savoy to ensure that insurance cover was placed on the goods for their true value by Walker, if Savoy was to meet its standard of care to the plaintiff by acting as a prudent owner of the goods would have in the circumstances. Savoy did not do this. Instead, it failed to broach the topic with Walker at all, and the goods were severely and negligently underinsured for $100 by Walker, the value it had ascribed to the ring in its contract of carriage with CN. Savoy's negligence certainly contributed to Walker's not having appropriately insured the ring prior to its transport from Toronto back to Sault Ste Marie. This, however, did not completely exonerate Walker, with whom Savoy had a contract of sub-bailment, for its negligence in making the contract with CN in the manner it did.

Indeed, Walker was found to have breached its standard of care to the plaintiff in the manner it cared for the goods, particularly, in failing to discuss insurance cover for the jewellery to be transported with Savoy and in ultimately failing to place appropriate cover on the ring as a prudent owner would have done. In the words of Cory JA, "A prudent owner, when asked whether he would wish to insure a ring valued at $11,000 during transportation, would answer in the affirmative."[62] Alternatively, Walker or Savoy could have checked with the owner of the ring to see if she was prepared to run the risk of the ring being transported without insurance cover, given the lack of any losses experienced by Savoy in handling jewellery in its care in the manner it did, which was in accordance with the customs of the trade. This did not occur, and Walker was therefore negligent in the manner in which it had carried out the sub-bailment to CN.

H. ASSESSING WHETHER A SUB-BAILEE HAS MET ITS STANDARD OF CARE IN A SUB-BAILMENT

1) Communications Between a Bailee and a Sub-bailee

In assessing whether a sub-bailee has met its applicable standard of care, much will depend on whether it acted on the proper authorities. The

62 *Punch*, above note 5 at para 21.

communications between the bailee and sub-bailee in a sub-bailment, or between the sub-bailee and the bailee immediately before it in a chain of bailments,[63] will always be a very relevant factor. For example, in *Punch*, had Savoy (head bailee) explicitly conveyed to Walker (sub-bailee) that it was authorized to carry on with the terms of the carriage in the manner it ultimately did — that is, without insuring the ring for its actual value — then Walker would probably have been exonerated from liability. It seems to be asking too much to expect a sub-bailee to confirm instructions received from a bailee, with whom it has privity of contract, directly with a bailor, even if such a party's existence is contemplated by the parties in their dealings. As a general rule, bailees should not expect, or receive, indemnity from sub-bailees where they have clearly conveyed the wrong, improper, or unauthorized instructions to the sub-bailee, who then dutifully carries them out.

Apart from proper authorities, certainly the sub-bailee is expected to avoid negligence and exercise reasonable care with respect to the bailed goods in its care, including in redelivering the goods to the bailee from whom it received them. Company policy and protocol of the bailee, as well as industry practice and what a prudent owner would have done in the circumstances, will always need to be considered. In *Punch*, it was acknowledged by CN in its evidence that the employee who attended at Walker's to pick up the jewellery had breached normal protocol and normal company procedure in accepting the jewellery for transport, given that its value had exceeded $300, and by completing the bill of lading form for the Walker employee (who said they did not have experience in such matters). As to the latter, the CN employee, consistent with the Walker explanation of industry practice for the transportation of jewellery in the jewellery trade, had attributed (only) a value of $100 to the ring, even though its actual value greatly exceeded this.[64] This was completely contrary to company policy, which required CN employees to advise customers of the need to set proper valuation on their goods to be transported.[65]

---

63 This party may be a bailee, or a sub-bailee of the goods, or even a further sub-bailee of the goods, depending on the number of subsequent bailments that have occurred since the start of the original or "predicate" bailment.

64 The Walker employee had also signed a contract of sub-bailment limiting liability per shipment to $50. That figure was less than the value attributed to the ring on the bill of lading, which was already a gross underrepresentation of the ring's true value: *Punch*, above note 5 at para 12.

65 *Ibid* at paras 5–6.

2) Ensuring Proper Insurance Cover on the Goods

Certainly, a failure by a sub-bailee to put appropriate insurance cover on goods where required during the course of the bailment, which, to be sure, will be in the minority of cases, can make it liable in damages to the bailor. In *Punch*, both Walker and CN grossly underinsured the plaintiff's goods or were careless in failing to put proper insurance cover on the goods in the event of loss. The fact that this stemmed, in some respects, from Savoy's failure to discuss the matter with Walker, or to require Walker's placing of insurance on the goods, was not a complete defence. This is because a bailee, whether a head or a subsequent bailee, must exercise (good) independent judgment during a bailment, when it is in exclusive possession of the bailor's goods and solely responsible for their safekeeping. A bailee should not be able to "piggy-back" on the negligent acts of a previous bailee arising before it in a chain of bailments, or to rely on a previous bailee's earlier questionable actions, to exonerate itself from liability, unless:

1) those earlier actions make it impossible for the subsequent bailee to carry out its duty of safekeeping once in possession of the goods;
2) the sub-standard practices employed by the present bailee leading to the loss have been expressly required and approved of by the previous bailee with whom it has privity of contract, in which case liability should be fixed against the previous bailee; and/or
3) the bailor (owner of the goods) itself has expressly approved of the lesser standard of care being employed by the latter bailee or can be said to have tacitly or implicitly agreed to it.

3) Industry Practice

Consistent with earlier discussion, adhering to industry practice will not always be enough to exonerate a sub-bailee from liability where that practice falls below what a prudent owner would have done in the circumstances or clearly fails to meet the needed minimum standard of care for the goods in the circumstances. In *Punch*, while it seemed to be accepted by the court that the jewellery industry of the time transported jewellery by mail with a value of $100 declared for insurance purposes, regardless of whether the valuables' true or actual value was much higher, Walker's failure to do better for the shipping of expensive jewellery put it, as well as CN and Savoy, in breach of their respective burdens of proof as bailees and sub-bailees. The appeal court was right to have refused to countenance such a practice, since clearly it was not one that could be said to be consistent with a bailee's heavy duty of care owed to a bailor in a bailment to take due care of the bailor's goods.

4) Exclusion Clauses

Exclusion clauses can insulate a sub-bailee for liability arising on a sub-bailment, including for fundamental breach of contract, but only where the plaintiff (bailor) has specific awareness of the limiting terms, either expressly or impliedly, such that the plaintiff can be considered to have consented to them.[66] The same rule would appear to apply to bailees as well, from whom sub-bailees receive the goods, who can also sue sub-bailees in bailment where goods in those bailees' possession are lost or damaged during the course of a bailment. In *Punch*, neither the plaintiff nor the defendant Savoy had consented to the limitation of liability clause in the contract of sub-bailment that had been entered into between Walker and CN. Indeed, neither party knew of the clause. Although Savoy knew that Walker had entered into a contract of carriage with CN, this knowledge was not enough for the exclusion clause to apply.

As for other considerations, the general law on exclusion clauses that apply to bailments applies to sub-bailments too, such that such conditions will be strictly interpreted. In *Punch*, the clause was found to be deficient, since it protected the sub-bailee CN from damages for losses flowing only from negligence, but not from theft (the likely culprit of the loss in the case), and was therefore underinclusive and could not insulate CN from liability coming from any of the relevant parties, including Walker and Savoy, both of whom the appeal court found to be entitled to indemnity from CN in relation to their liability found to be owed to the plaintiff (bailor). Similarly, in *Morris*,[67] the defendant sub-bailee was prevented from relying on the limiting terms in its contract with the bailee

---

66 There is English authority to the effect that, where a sub-bailment is for the very thing contracted for, rather than for an ancillary service, any protection of a limited liability clause is lost: see *Davies v Collins*, [1945] 1 All ER 247 (CA), cited at para 5 of *Governor and Co of Adventurers of England Trading into Hudson Bay v Canadian National Railway Co*, [1959] OJ No 191 (HCJ). However, in *Banks*, above note 19, this does not appear to have occurred, although the point was not explicitly addressed in the court's reasons for decision.

67 Above note 9 at 734 [cited to All ER].

as against the plaintiff (bailor), as they applied only to goods "belonging to customers" and not to "goods belonging to the customers of its customers," to losses occurring during the process of cleaning, or to the theft of goods by one of the defendant's own employees occurring before or after processing.

I. JOINT AND SEVERAL LIABILITY OF NEGLIGENT BAILEES AND SUB-BAILEES AND OTHER RELEVANT PARTIES

1) Apportionment of Liability Among Bailees and Sub-bailees

Consistent with the law regarding apportionment of liability among tortfeasors,[68] bailees can be found to be joint wrongdoers, where they all have engaged in negligent acts causing damage to or loss of bailed goods, such that one judgment can be entered against them all in favour of the plaintiff (bailor), on the basis that the bailor was injured by all of them acting together as one.[69] Such was the case in *Punch*, where the court entered a judgment against Savoy (a bailee), Walker (a sub-bailee), and CN (a sub-bailee) in the sum of $11,000, being the value of the ring, plus costs.[70]

2) Lack of Evidence Indicating (Exactly) When Bailed Goods Were Damaged or Lost Can Result in Joint and Several Liability of a Sub-bailee and a Previous Bailee of the Goods

In some cases, there will be a lack of evidence before the court indicating (exactly) when the sub-bailed goods were lost or damaged. This will not necessarily be a bar to a court's finding that a sub-bailee of the goods, together with another previous bailee of the goods, should be held jointly and severally responsible for the damage or losses caused to the bailor's goods:

---

68 See Margaret Helen Kerr, Laurence M Olivo, & JoAnn Kurtz, *Canadian Tort Law in a Nutshell*, 4th ed (Toronto: Carswell, 2014) at 111.

69 The distinct advantage of this is that, since the bailees are joint wrongdoers in a single legal proceeding and each are deemed to be responsible for the acts and injuries occasioned by all the others, the plaintiff (bailor) may attempt to collect on a judgment from any one of them. In other words, failure to collect on a judgment from one bailee does not forbid collection attempts being tried on the others, provided they were all sued in the bailment action.

70 *Punch*, above note 5 at paras 45–47.

1) where it is clear on the evidence that the injury to the bailor's goods occurred during a time when either the sub-bailee or other bailee (including a defendant insurer, pursuant to the terms of an insurance contract) was legally responsible for the welfare of the goods; and
2) where the loss at issue is clearly due to the negligence of the parties.

In these circumstances, it is possible for a court to make a judgment holding the defendants jointly and severally liable for the bailor's losses. In *Gulliver v Unifund Assurance Co*,[71] the plaintiff's vehicle was stolen from the vicinity of the plaintiff's residence and was subsequently found and retrieved by police after the plaintiff made a report of the theft to police. The vehicle was then delivered by the first defendant (bailee) insurance company[72] into the custody of the second defendant repair shop (sub-bailee) for certain repairs and servicing. Certain work and servicing were authorized by the insurer, with all work being completed by the second defendant on 26 May. The vehicle, however, remained on the repair shop's premises thereafter. On 11 June, the plaintiff removed the items of her insurance policy pertaining to the vehicle covering collision and vandalism. On 30 June, the plaintiff contacted the repair shop.[73] She was told that the vehicle had been repaired and was still on the premises awaiting pickup.[74] The plaintiff went to the defendant's premises the next day to pick up the vehicle, discovering that the vehicle had been vandalized and damaged beyond repair. The plaintiff, accordingly, refused to take delivery of the vehicle and reported the matter to her insurer, who attended at the premises of the repair shop on three separate dates subsequently, albeit without removing the vehicle from the lot. On each of those dates, the insurer noticed that additional parts were missing from the vehicle but, for reasons that were not made clear on the record, chose not to remove the vehicle from the lot. The vehicle was subsequently transported by the repair shop to the dump, without the plaintiff's knowledge or consent.[75]

---

71 [1985] NJ No 284 (Dist Ct) [*Gulliver*].

72 They had become involved after the plaintiff notified them of the theft of the vehicle: *ibid* at para 2.

73 *Ibid* at paras 2–12.

74 The defendant repair shop claimed that it had notified the insurer that the vehicle had been repaired and expected it to pick up the vehicle, which is why it claimed that it did not contact the plaintiff: *ibid* at para 14.

75 *Ibid* at paras 14–22.

Justice McCarthy of the Newfoundland District Court Judicial Centre of St John's found that the damage to the vehicle had occurred between 26 May, when the repairs had been completed, and 1 July, when the plaintiff had attended at the defendant's repair shop premises intending to pick up her vehicle. Under the contract of insurance, the learned judge found that the (first defendant) insurer was liable for any vandalism committed against the vehicle up until the date of 11 June. This was true, even though it was not in possession of the vehicle, pursuant to the terms of the insurance contract, which were in effect to that date. After this, the second defendant acted as a bailee for reward exclusively, and was liable for any breaches of the duty of reasonable care owed by it to the plaintiff during this period of time. Justice McCarthy found the defendant shop to have failed to negative negligence and to be liable as bailee. Indeed, one of its own witnesses (an employee) had admitted that, at some point in time, the defendant had stopped taking due care of the vehicle. While the shop had mentioned that the reason for this might have been that it had expected the insurer to pick up the vehicle from its lot once it notified the insurer that all remaining work on the vehicle was done, the learned judge *did not* find this argument sufficient to overcome the heavy burden placed on the repair shop.[76] However, since it was not clear whether the loss occurred before or after 11 June 2017, both defendants were found to be liable, jointly and severally, for the losses to the plaintiff's vehicle. Given the lack of records and the general indifference shown by the defendants in the case over the safety of the plaintiff's vehicle, and the importance of monitoring the vehicle to ensure its safekeeping, it is not surprising that neither were able to pinpoint when the losses occurred to avoid liability, or to shift liability completely to the other.[77] The importance of a

---

76 With respect, if the bailment of the vehicle to the shop was a bailment between the insurer and the shop, then clearly the terms of that bailment and the intention of the parties were relevant to determining whether the defendant shop had met its applicable duty of care under the law in the circumstances. The learned judge should have made a determination on whether a communication was made by the shop to the insurer to pick up the vehicle and on whether the insurer was under a legal duty to pick up the vehicle to avoid the bailment becoming gratuitous, involuntary, or even a licence, the latter legal relationships all imposing a significantly lesser duty of care on a bailee than would a bailment for reward.

77 *Gulliver*, above note 71 at paras 24–31. Under the *Contributory Negligence Act*, the defendants ending up sharing liability for the plaintiff's damages in the case on an equal basis: paras 32–33.

bailee's maintaining such records to avoid liability has been underlined elsewhere in this text.[78]

3) A Bailee's Right to Indemnity from Co-bailee(s) Who Are the Immediate Cause of the Bailor's Losses

While a bailee, or sub-bailee, may be found to be liable to a bailor in damages for its own negligence, or failure to take reasonable care of the goods in their exclusive possession at the material times, it may be entitled to partial or complete indemnity from a subsequent bailee who actually caused the bailor's losses or in whose possession the goods fell when they were lost or damaged. In *Punch*, that certainly was the case. There, CN lost the plaintiff's (bailor's) jewellery and offered no explanation for the loss, which was likely caused by theft by one of its own staff, and was ordered by the court to fully indemnify both Walker and Savoy for any damages they had to pay to the plaintiff, including the plaintiff's costs.[79] So a judgment in damages against a bailee does not mean that that bailee will not be entitled to seek contribution by way of indemnification from another bailee who had possession of the bailed goods when they met their demise.

In *Banks*,[80] after the plaintiff's jacket was lost while in the sub-bailee's possession, the defendant (sub-bailee) paid $500 to the defendant (head bailee) in accordance with the requirements of the contract that had been entered into between those parties before the plaintiff brought an action in bailment after she discovered that the item had been lost. The payout was equal to the value that had been attributed to the jacket by the plaintiff in her bailment contract with the defendant (head bailee).[81] In the bailment action that followed, the plaintiff's claim against the defendant sub-bailee was dropped and she proceeded to obtain a judgment in the

---

78 For an example of joint and several liability being fixed against a bailee and a sub-bailee due to a lack of records indicating that reasonable care had been exercised by them during their respective possessions of the bailor's goods, see *Webb*, above note 3.

79 Walker, however, was not entitled to its costs for defending the plaintiff's action against CN, because it had to bear some responsibility for undervaluing the goods at a $100 when turning them over to CN: *Punch*, above note 5 at para 46.

80 Above note 19.

81 While this value was considerably below the true value of the jacket, the court found that the plaintiff's undervaluing of the goods was likely done so that she should could save on the substantially higher storage fees that would have been required based on an accurate valuation of the jacket: *ibid* at para 9.

sum of $500 in damages against the sole defendant remaining, namely, the head bailee, who had failed to deliver up her garment to the plaintiff in breach of its duty of redelivery owed to her under the bailment contract between those parties.[82] The payment made by a sub-bailee to a head bailee in these circumstances should constitute a complete indemnity between those parties, where the payment itself represents the true value of the damages arising on the breach of the sub-bailment contract between bailee and sub-bailee, as defined in that contract, even if the payment is made before liability is fixed against the bailee by the bailor in the bailment action.

4) Sub-bailment May Terminate Bailee Duties Owed by a Head Bailee to a Bailor Under a Contract of Bailment

A sub-bailment may terminate the underlying bailment where the head bailee divests itself of possession of the goods permanently in favour of the sub-bailee, provided that:

1) the work or services to be provided under the contract of bailment have been performed completed fully and properly;
2) the contract of bailment does not contemplate redelivery of the goods by the bailee to the bailor personally, but instead delegates this duty to an independent third party over whom the bailee has no direct control and who may or may not be nominated by the bailor (in other words, the sub-bailee is not acting as an agent of the bailee, but completely independent of them);
3) the contract of bailment does not specify that possession is to remain in the bailee during the course of the sub-bailment;
4) the bailee has properly initiated the sub-bailment, including conveying all needed information to the sub-bailee, as required, and is not deviating from the authorities and instructions received from the bailor in order for the sub-bailee to be able to complete the subsequent bailment correctly, safely, and properly; and
5) the bailee *has not* been negligent in delivering up possession of the goods to the sub-bailee, including in selecting a sub-bailee where that party was not named by the bailor itself.

---

82 *Ibid* at paras 4, 5, and 14.

Where the above requirements are met, the bailee will be relieved of all legal obligations and duties owed to the bailor. Should damage or loss befall the goods, the bailor will have to look elsewhere, to the sub-bailee or others beyond this, to recover its losses. Interestingly, while a sub-bailment can terminate a contract of bailment and terminate all duties owed by a bailee to a bailor, the sub-bailee will owe a non-contractual duty to the bailor not to damage or lose its goods thereafter at common law. In *Scott Maritimes Pulp*,[83] the plaintiff (Scott) transferred a press roll from its pulp mill into the possession of the defendant (Goodrich) to have the roll recovered and made operational again. The roll was ultimately returned to the plaintiff by the defendant common carrier (Day), with whom the defendant had privity of contract. When the roll was removed from the trailer in which it had been housed by Day, the plaintiff found the roll to be damaged; the skid on which the roll was situated had been bent out of shape and the trailer itself was damaged. The roll was also found to have been housed with additional heavy freight. The plaintiff reported the damage to Goodrich and sought its recommendation, which was to have the roll reground to see if the defect would disappear. Ultimately, this was done by the plaintiff: the roll was sent out to an independent third party, but to no avail — the roll ultimately failed when in operation a short time later.[84]

As a result, an action by the plaintiff against the defendants followed. The court had to determine the relations between the various parties as well as the cause of the damage in sorting out the plaintiff's various claims put in tort, contract, and bailment. Not surprisingly, counsel for each of the defendants tried to shift legal responsibility for the plaintiff's losses to the other defendant. The evidence from the court below indicated, clearly, that the damage had been caused by the negligence of the defendant carrier and that Goodrich had repaired the roll properly and delivered it in the required good state of repair to Day for redelivery to Scott. Day acknowledged as much in its evidence. It was also established that no damage had been caused by the third party who performed the regrinding work for the plaintiff.[85]

Justice Cooper of the Nova Scotia Supreme Court Appeal Division, in tackling the bailment questions, applied most of the framework outlined above in concluding that the defendant Goodrich should be relieved of

83 Above note 10.

84 *Ibid* at paras 1–23.

85 *Ibid* at paras 21–25.

legal responsibility for the plaintiff's losses because its contract of bailment with the plaintiff had been properly discharged. Specifically, the court found the following:

1) The plaintiff's roll had been recovered properly by the defendant Goodrich; there was no more work or servicing left to be done by Goodrich and no breach of the bailment there.[86]
2) Goodrich had not been negligent in transferring possession of the roll into the hands of the defendant carrier, and that the damage done was due solely to the negligence of the carrier in transit, presumably in leaving the roll next to heavy freight in the trailer that could damage the roll.[87]
3) Goodrich had not selected the defendant carrier and could not be said to have been negligent in transferring possession to Day, in accordance with the contract of bailment.[88]
4) Goodrich had delegated redelivery of the goods not to one of its own employees or servants (which would not have divested it of possession of the roll until a proper delivery to the plaintiff was effected), but to an independent third party that was to redeliver the goods to the plaintiff directly itself in its own name and on its own behalf.[89]
5) The contract of bailment did not state or imply that legal possession was to remain in Goodrich after it transferred factual possession to the third-party defendant carrier.[90]

Accordingly, the bailment was at an end, and Goodrich owed no further duties to the plaintiff under the contract of bailment and could not be held liable in damages to the plaintiff for the damage done to its roll. Nor was Day entitled to any contribution or indemnity from Goodrich. Instead, Day, as sub-bailee, owed legal duties, albeit non-contractual ones, to the plaintiff (bailor) at the time of loss and had breached those duties to the plaintiff. Indeed, Day had failed to provide a satisfactory explanation for why the damage occurred, including why the roll had been packed and stored beside additional heavy freight in the trailer, where it was

86 *Ibid* at para 30.
87 *Ibid* at paras 23 and 30.
88 *Ibid* at para 34.
89 *Ibid* at para 26.
90 *Ibid* at para 34.

susceptible to being damaged[91] or why the trailer had a dent in it. In the result, Day was found liable to the plaintiff for its losses as bailee.[92] As a final point, it is submitted that the recommendation given by the defendant Goodrich to the plaintiff on how the damage done to the roll might be remediated — that the roll be sent out by the plaintiff to a third party for regrinding — was not enough to revive the bailment between the parties, since Goodrich did not retake possession or control of the roll.

J. CONCLUSION

A sub-bailment is necessarily a more complicated relationship than a mere bailment. It involves no less than three parties — namely, a bailor, a bailee, and a sub-bailee — who may all owe legal duties to each other. Having said that, there does not need to be privity of contract between bailor and sub-bailee for a sub-bailment to come into existence. Nonetheless, the sub-bailee must know of the existence of a bailor in order for a sub-bailee to owe legal duties and obligations, including a duty of safekeeping, to a bailor. While the bailor is required to have knowledge of the terms of a sub-bailment, including knowledge of any limiting terms, such knowledge can be constructive or actual. For example, where a bailee is given a *carte blanche* by a bailor to enter contracts of sub-bailment on any terms it so chooses, a bailor will generally be bound by such contracts regardless of their terms. Where a bailee acts unlawfully to make a sub-bailment, a sub-bailment may still exist where a bailor chooses not to repudiate it after it learns of the unauthorized bailment, instead choosing to ratify it. Where there are alternative contractual regimes available to the sub-bailee, containing different contractual terms as between the head bailment and the sub-bailment, the sub-bailee may elect which contract of bailment it wishes to rely on. As we have seen, a sub-bailee can take full advantage of the head contract between bailor and bailee where those terms are more favourable than the terms of the sub-bailment. While the conduct of bailees and sub-bailees must be adjudged contextually and will

---

91 *Ibid* at paras 23, 33–36, and 42–48.

92 Day was also confirmed to be a common carrier by the appeal court: *ibid* at para 36. As such, it owed the plaintiff a standard of perfection. Having been found to have carried out its contract of carriage negligently, Day also failed in its legal duties as a common carrier, and liability was fixable against it on this additional basis as well (although the court did not make such an explicit ruling in the case): *ibid* at para 46.

need to have regard for the communications and instructions conveyed by a bailee to a sub-bailee, and to consider the actions and omissions of previous bailees in a chain of bailments, a measure of good independent judgment will always need to be exercised by a sub-bailee over a bailor's goods in order for the sub-bailee to avoid liability to a bailor for failure to take due care of its goods.

Table of Cases

Index

About the Author

Robert H Tanha holds a BA (Hons) in law and society and political science from York University and earned an LLB from the University of Ottawa. He holds a bachelor degree in education and a graduate degree (MA) in Canadian politics, both from the University of Windsor. He is a barrister and solicitor in Ontario. He is currently a law instructor at Centennial College (The Business School—Progress Campus), and he also teaches law classes to students in the School of Continuing Education at George Brown College (St James Campus) both in Toronto, Ontario. In the past, he has taught law courses for Durham College, Seneca College, Sheridan College, and Algonquin College. He has acted as a university sessional lecturer as well, having taught law and law-related courses for the Faculty of Social Science and Humanities at Ontario Tech University (Oshawa) and for the Department of Sociology at the University of Toronto (Mississauga). He has other legal publications on the law of evidence and the law of personal property, appearing in the *Manitoba Law Journal* and *College Quarterly*, respectively.

FSC
www.fsc.org
MIX
Papier | Fördert gute Waldnutzung
FSC® C083411

Kolibri 360 GmbH
Ferdinand-Jühlke-Straße 7
99095 Erfurt, Deutschland
produktsicherheit@kolibri360.de